The COMPLETE IDIOT'S GUIDE TO Cooking Basics

by Ronnie Fein

alpha books

A Division of Macmillan Computer Publishing
A Prentice Hall Macmillan Company
201 W. 103rd Street, Indianapolis, IN 46290

To Ed, who once bought me herbs and spices. Even then he knew.

©1995 Alpha Books

International Standard Book Number: 1-56761-523-6
Library of Congress Catalog Card Number: 94-72431

97   96   95   8   7   6   5   4   3   2   1

Interpretation of the printing code: the rightmost number of the first series of numbers is the year of the book's printing; the rightmost number of the second series of numbers is the number of the book's printing. For example, a printing code of 95-1 shows that the first printing of the book occurred in 1995.

Printed in the United States of America

Publisher
Marie Butler-Knight

Product Manager
Thomas F. Godfrey III

Managing Editor
Elizabeth Keaffaber

Development Editors
Lisa Bucki
Seta Frantz

Technical Editors and Reviewers
Sarah Bush
Pat Keenan
Leslie Sussman

Production Editor
Phil Kitchel

Copy Editor
Audra Gable

Cover Designer
Karen Ruggles

Designer
Barbara Kordesh

Illustrator
Judd Winick

Indexer
Brad Herriman

Production Team
*Lissa Auciello, Angela Calvert, Dan Caparo, Brad Chinn, Kim Cofer,
Juli Cook, Jennifer Eberhardt, David Garratt, Erika Millen, Angel Perez,
Beth Rago, Bobbi Satterfield, Karen Walsh, Robert Wolf*

Contents at a Glance

Contents

Desserts

Beverages

Foreword

I learned to cook at my mother's knee. I was the eldest daughter in a family of eight children, and it was simply a matter of course that I pitch in and cook a meal or part of a meal with some regularity. Lucky for me, my mother enjoyed time in the kitchen and passed on her enthusiasm. Consequently, I was excited when my first apartment brought with it my first kitchen—and ever since I have preferred the kitchen to all other rooms, no matter where I have lived. However, despite my youthful confidence, I could have used Ronnie Fein's sure hand and practical advice back in those days when I was organizing and enjoying my first kitchen.

I can only imagine how delighted and *relieved* beginning cooks, as well as those who have already logged some kitchen hours, will feel when they read this book. Relieved because here, at last, is a book so packed with straightforward, sensible advice that even the most terrified novice will feel as though a trusted friend has walked into the room with the sole purpose of helping. From organizing kitchen countertops, cupboards, and drawers to success with your first dinner party, Ronnie is there. Her measured advice never wavers: be sensible, follow your own style, read the recipe several times, keep it simple, use good equipment, trust yourself, and plan ahead.

This advice is not doled out like cheese and stale crackers at a political fund-raiser. It is carefully and thoroughly presented. She discusses such details as where to keep the measuring spoons, store the nutmeg, and put the fish. She emphasizes such major points as the importance of good organization for good cooking, telling readers (among other things) to clean up as they go along, to measure accurately, and to put things back where they belong. As Ronnie explains, a kitchen can be sleek or cluttered, depending on the taste of the cook, but regardless of its appearance, the kitchen should be organized as a serious work center. This means you will be able to find the long-handled spatula, the baking sheet, or the balsamic vinegar when it's needed, and will have ample space to roll the pastry, chop the onions, and drain the pasta.

In her friendly manner, Ronnie teaches beginning cooks how to stock the kitchen and buy cookware, how to buy meat and vegetables, when to buy food in bulk and when not to, what tastes fine if bought frozen and what should only be purchased fresh. She includes extensive glossaries for meats, poultry, fish, dairy products, vegetables, fruits, and herbs and spices. In addition, there is a glossary of kitchen procedures in which Ronnie defines not only common cooking terms, but everything from *bind* and *coddle* to *stud* and *truss*.

More experienced cooks can benefit by brushing up on skills and picking up tips and kitchen wisdom generously served by the author. Or, such readers might just skip to the end of each chapter, where Ronnie summarizes the chapter's information in a handy section entitled "The Least You Need to Know." Just skimming these boxes is a refresher course in good kitchen sense.

One of the sections I most appreciated was the one on reading a recipe. Few cookbook authors dare broach this subject because (I suspect) it strikes too close to home. But with obvious regard for the intelligence of the reader, Ronnie explains her idea of a good recipe: "A good recipe tells all. A well-planned recipe lists all ingredients in the order they are used." As would any conscientious recipe writer, she urges readers to read the recipe at least once to determine its appeal, its level of difficulty, and its usefulness. Consider such things as, are all ingredients listed used in the method? Do you have a five-quart Dutch oven or the equivalent? She then suggests that the reader read the recipe at least one more time for familiarity. Excellent advice!

Page after page of helpful advice builds in a crescendo that leads to the recipes. The actual recipes in this book are simply written and tend to be easier than difficult. However, the author goes way beyond meatloaf and apple pie. The recipes are meant to inspire the beginner as well as the more adept cook to enter the kitchen with enthusiasm, tie on an apron, and *cook*! In other words, just because the book is directed toward the novice, the author never assumes the novice is not interested in eating well.

This is a book all parents will want to give grown children starting out on their own. However, it's not just for newlyweds and single people—it's for everyone who is the least bit doubtful about his or her cooking skills. With Ronnie Fein's assurance and helpful hand at every step of the way, an entire generation of beginning cooks will come to experience the sheer joy of time spent in the kitchen.

—Mary Goodbody

Mary Goodbody is the Senior Contributing Editor for *Chocolatier* magazine, author of *The Best of Chocolate*, and co-author of *Spring Evenings, Summer Afternoons*.

Introduction

People have been cooking food since Neanderthal man discovered fire hundreds of thousands of years ago. We humans have been at it for so long that too many people believe they are supposed to grow up just sort of *knowing* how to cook. Some feel like idiots if they don't.

But let's not confuse lack of intelligence with something else. You may not have lots of confidence and may feel intimidated about cooking. You may think you could never get a meal to come out right. You may already have classified yourself as a "gourmet wannabe" who's only a "make-it-from-a-mix moron." But no one who buys a book about cooking could possibly be an idiot. In fact, the people who buy cookbooks typically are students and teachers, tradespeople, and professional men and women who are capable at their jobs. They just feel they should be more competent in the kitchen.

This book was designed to let you be just that—competent in the kitchen. It will help you understand that cooking skills are something you can learn easily.

What You'll Learn in This Book

This book is divided into seven parts that take you through the cooking process, from your first look at the empty kitchen of your abode to the recipe masterpieces you will prepare in it. You will see that learning to cook means learning to organize your space and your time, as well as knowing how to shop and what to buy. It involves reading—of food labels and recipes. It includes a basic knowledge of cooking terms and some awareness of the appropriate tools you will use when you cook. With this step-by-step approach, you will build your confidence as well as your competence along the way. Here's what the seven parts cover:

Part 1, "Organizing Your Kitchen," mentally plants you in your empty kitchen and describes what you are likely to see. It focuses on the most convenient places to put the food and kitchen tools, and also gives tips on how to organize recipes.

Part 2, "You've Gotta Have Them: Kitchen Staples," talks about filling in the bare cupboards with the staple foods, pots and pans, and appliances you'll probably need and explains why you need these items.

Part 3, "Did Anyone Ever Give You a Shopping Lesson? (Or, How to Be a Confident Consumer)," begins by discussing your personal shopping style. Knowing how you shop will help you know how to shop. The chapters then turn to general buying decisions (such as whether to buy brand names or generic and stuff like that) and then to specifics. If you go to the bother of cooking and want your meals to taste terrific, you've got to know how to choose quality ingredients. This part will guide you through the picking process, give some information on how to use the ingredients (using round steak vs. sirloin steak, for example), and offer tips on how to store them.

Part 4, "Getting Ready to Cook," helps you make the transition from shopper to cook. It begins by explaining how to read a recipe so you will be fully prepared when you start cooking, and then focuses on how to tell whether or not a recipe is a good one. This section also tells you in detail how to measure and substitute ingredients, and gives you basic ideas about what various cooking terms mean. The "Compendium of the Top 100 Cooking Terms," a "super-glossary," does not merely define 100 of the most common cooking terms but, in appropriate cases, explains how they work or why they are important. This part also has a Compendium of Catchwords (a second "super-glossary") that explains food terms (so you'll know what words such as *al dente* mean) and equipment terms (so you'll know a bain-marie from a double-boiler). Finally, this part describes fundamental cooking methods so you can easily distinguish the difference between stir-frying and sautéing.

Part 5, "Now You're Cooking," helps you create your first dinner, covering not just the cooking aspect but getting all the different parts of the meal to come out on time and doing all the non-cooking tasks such as setting the table. If you've made a mistake, don't worry: there's a chapter here that will help you determine if it's fixable and how to fix it if it is. There's also a bit on beverages to serve with and after dinner. And if you feel like you're an accomplished cook at this point, it's time to invite company. There's a chapter here (complete with menus) that helps you plan a few simple get-togethers.

Part 6, "The Tools of Success," goes into more specific detail about cookware and appliances. If you don't have much in the way of pots, pans, and appliances or you want to replace older pieces, these chapters can help you choose the right equipment to help you cook better and save time.

Part 7, "Recipes," is simply that. The recipes (kitchen-tested, every one of them) cover everything from hors d'oeuvre to desserts. Most are easy, easy, *easy* to prepare—even though some may contain ingredients you may not have used before. (These are marked Easy.) There also are a few more involved recipes (marked Intermediate) for when you gain some confidence, and a few even more challenging ones (marked Challenging) for you to tackle when you are ready—which you will be. The recipes are marked to indicate difficulty level.

By the time you finish the book and have honed your skills preparing some of the recipes, you will find that you feel smarter and more sophisticated about food. It is simply a matter of learning something easily learnable, having the courage to test your abilities, and being a bit adventurous.

Extras

Besides all the explanation and advice, this book has lots of tidbits of useful or interesting information strewn here and there in sidebars throughout the chapters. The following icons set these tidbits apart:

Kitchen Clue
Kitchen Clues are hints that serve the purpose of making cooking more organized, more accurate, more fun, and more easily understandable.

Fein on Food

These boxes contain fascinating morsels of history and folklore about a particular food or ingredient. You don't need this information to be a good cook but it makes great dinner conversation.

NEVER...
do anything these sidebars warn you against while cooking.

Warnings help you avoid danger and costly mistakes.

Something Simple

The present simple, tasty, almost-recipes anybody can throw together.

Definition sidebars define cooking terms you may be unfamiliar with. Some of these words can also be found in the "super-glossary" sections.

Second Thoughts
These sidebars appear in the recipe section to tell you how to change the recipe a bit so you can wind up with two, three, or more recipes in one.

Acknowledgments

I would like to say thanks to the entire team of hard-working professionals at Alpha Books for their support and cooperation and for assigning this new project to me. But special mention must be made of the contributions of Tom Godfrey, whose willingness to listen and accept new ideas was most encouraging, and to Lisa Bucki, for her insightful and probing questions. Abundant thanks also go to my colleague Mary Goodbody, for her generous and gracious words—they are deeply appreciated. I am also most grateful for the thoughtful comments and suggestions of my colleague Sarah Bush. Finally, I would like to say thank you to my special friend Leslie Tse-Yung Sussman for her advice and her honesty.

Part 1
Organizing Your Kitchen

You've finally got a place of your own. But it's EMPTY! Even if you bought a bed to sleep in, a couch to sit on, and a TV to watch, the kitchen cupboards are BARE! The refrigerator might not be turned on. You haven't got a plate to put a sandwich on. How are you going to feed yourself?

Independence is terrific, but starting out can be a bit scary. Relax and read on. The next two chapters will introduce you to the logic of your kitchen. I'll show you where things belong and how to take advantage of counter space, cabinet space, and refrigerator space so you can be prepared to buy what you need. Ready? Let's begin.

Chapter 1

Staking Your Claim to Your Kitchen

In This Chapter

➤ Sizing up your kitchen to see where you want things

➤ The "outer space" of your kitchen and how you want it to look

➤ What goes on the countertops

➤ What doesn't go on the countertops

You've been in a kitchen before—but maybe not your *own* kitchen. Maybe you've moved, or redesigned your kitchen. Or maybe you simply want to change your cooking style, learn new ideas, and develop better culinary habits so you can be a better cook.

Here you are in this space that's all yours. Not Mom's. Not your former spouse's. This chapter explains how to size up your space so you can make it convenient and fun to cook in. You have complete control.

Taking Charge of Your Kitchen Space

Well, almost complete control. The refrigerator, oven, sink, cabinets, and such are already there, and you can't do anything to rearrange them. But the rest of the space is yours to reign over. If you arrange the space to suit yourself, you won't feel like you're trying to be someone else. If you fill the kitchen spaces to satisfy your lifestyle, you will *like* being in that room. You'll want to cook in it. What's more, you'll be a more confident cook because you'll be on your own turf, where you have made the decisions about where things go.

Asserting your authority in your own place doesn't mean you can't take advice from people who have lots of experience. It also doesn't mean you're married to a particular arrangement. If you find that you need to put the can opener somewhere else, move it. Changing doesn't imply failure; it suggests thoughtfulness.

Take a Good Look Around

When you first come into your kitchen, walk through it and take a good look around to get a feel for the size of the place. Look at the counter space to determine which will be the likely work area. The part nearest the sink is usually the most convenient, especially when you prepare vegetables or other foods that require quick and easy access to running water.

Open the drawers and cabinets. You'll see that some drawers are wider, some deeper than others. You may even find an unexpected drawer, like maybe the one under the oven. (Most likely it's the dirtiest, too.) Some cabinets will be too high to reach without using a step stool.

You probably will form an initial impression about what belongs where. But before you start putting things away, think about the kind of kitchen that makes you happy. Being content in your kitchen is the first step to good cooking.

Your Kitchen Style—The Homey Kitchen or the Stark Look

Because a kitchen has outer spaces and inner spaces to fill, one of the first particulars to think about is whether you are an outer space person or an inner space person. Do you like the kitchen to look like an operating room: stark, with no appliances, books, plants or other paraphernalia to distract you from what you're doing? Or are you the type of person who is happier in a kitchen with cute canisters, herb pots, and cooking magazines on the counter, artwork or craft items on the walls, and coffee mugs, potholders, and car keys displayed on hooks? Perhaps you're somewhere in between these two types.

Suit yourself, with this one caveat: leave plenty of room to work, so any items left out don't interfere with the task at hand or cause more work. For example, if you're preparing a

Kitchen Clue
If you're short on counterspace, you can store a toaster or toaster oven on a tray in the cabinet. The tray prevents the crumbs from being scattered about.

recipe that calls for orange juice and you spill some—it happens to everyone—the more stuff you have on the counter, the longer it will take to clean up.

What Goes in Outer Space

Whether you're a neat-freak or someone who likes a "busy-looking" kitchen and is comfortable with clutter, there are a few simple guidelines to follow when deciding what to keep on the countertop.

If you use an item with regularity, keep it out. Your coffee maker, for example. You can also keep out a dish rack and drain board if you don't have a dishwasher.

Items that would create too much dirt in storage or are too large or heavy to store and lift out should also be on the countertop. This category includes appliances such as toasters and toaster ovens (you don't want crumbs in your cabinet), stand mixers, standard size food processors, and the like. Speaking of big, if you're really lucky and someone wants to buy you a microwave oven, or if you've decided to spend some savings on a kitchen TV or radio, look for compact models. Obviously, these go on the countertop.

Kitchen Clue
Most people keep blenders on the counter simply out of habit. Food processors have eclipsed blenders for tackling most tedious kitchen tasks. Blenders are still superb as beverage mixers. But if you use one only occasionally for this purpose, why not store it?

In kitchens with minimal drawer space, you may need a tall, durable urn or jug on the countertop to hold long-handled tools such as whisks, wooden spoons, skimmers, spaghetti forks, and ladles. Plastic covered boxes or pretty baskets that hold small gadgets may be needed in kitchens with minimal drawer space.

Decorative items that are also practical (such as cute cookie jars, bread boxes, and canisters for flour, sugar, and so on) can go on the countertop. (However, foods that typically go in canisters can just as easily be stored in plastic containers and hidden in a cabinet or the refrigerator, depending on the item.)

Skimmers are long-handled tools that you use to remove unwanted pieces of food, soup scum, or fat from the surface of soup, stew, and so on.

Wooden knife holders keep blades sharper longer. Because of their size, they must be on the countertop. However, knives also will be fine if you keep them in a separate drawer that has a knife holder, or in a regular drawer (in which case you should cover the blades with plastic knife sheaths).

A knife block: The best way to keep your knives clean, sharp, and handy.

Some people like to keep a garbage can out. Some prefer to store the trash in the cabinet under the sink. This is a question of room and taste. In either case, line the garbage can with a plastic bag so clean-up will be minimal.

Those who can't function without a calendar or calendar book should keep one in plain sight on the counter. If you only look at it occasionally, stuff it in a drawer or cabinet.

Mountable Under-the-Counter Appliances and Other Outer Space Savers

If you don't have enough room or counter space for all your stuff, there is a solution to this problem. A number of manufacturers sell space-saving appliances, including coffee makers and toaster ovens, that you can mount under the cabinets. Another idea is to purchase racks or hanging devices for pots and pans. You can also buy wall hooks for items such as dishtowels, potholders, mugs, and so on.

What Doesn't Fly in Outer Space

Some items don't belong on the countertop. To protect yourself, your worldly goods, and your privacy, and to prevent messes and counter-clutter, you're better off keeping the following items somewhere else:

➤ Breakable items—jars and oil and vinegar cruets

➤ Food items—spices, ketchup, salt and pepper shakers

➤ Small items—measuring cups, pencils, toothpicks

➤ Paper items—napkins, coffee filters, paper towels

➤ Work papers, documents, the deed to your gold mine, your Last Will and Testament

A cabinet-mounted coffee maker.

The Least You Need to Know

➤ Keep items you use regularly on the countertop.

➤ Bulky, heavy, and dirt-catching items belong on the countertop.

➤ Don't keep food, tiny or breakable items, paper goods, or important documents on the countertop.

Cruets are containers that you use to store oil and vinegar for salads. Sometimes they look like bud vases, sometimes like wine bottles. They're usually glass or ceramic.

What To Do with All Your Stuff

In This Chapter

➤ Where to put food and non-food items

➤ How to capitalize on refrigerator space

➤ How to organize your recipes

Now that you've decided which items to keep on the counter, you have to figure out where to put everything else. Everything else means the food, the cookware you use to prepare the food, and the dishes and tableware you need to serve the food. This chapter helps you find the best places for these items so cooking will be hassle-free. You also get some suggestions about where to put your cleaning supplies, even though you may not want to think about the cleaning up part of cooking. And, oh yes, you've got to keep your recipes somewhere. What's the best place? You'll find that here, too.

Do You Have to Line Your Drawers and Cabinets?

When you first investigate your kitchen drawers and cabinets, you'll notice more than their size and location. If you've moved into someone's former space, you're likely to find dirt. Little crumbs in drawers. Sticky stuff in cabinets. Dried ketchup in the fridge. No one really needs to tell you to clean these before you fill them, right?

But do you have to do anything else? Some people line cabinets and/or drawers before storing things in them. There are pros and cons to this. Lined shelves and drawers are easier to keep clean. However, the process takes time, and invariably the edges of self-stick paper stick together and are hard to pull apart. Paper that's not self-stick isn't durable. Is it worth it to line shelves and drawers? It's up to you.

What Type of Drawers and Cabinets Are Best for What?

There's a logic to using your kitchen's inner spaces. Some of it is obvious. No one would put dish detergent in the high cabinet over the refrigerator. It's more convenient to keep the detergent under the sink, near where you'll use it. Those high places are best for the paella pans, french-onion soup crocks, and other wedding cookware gifts you never returned, as well as the electric juice extractor you were sure you needed until you found out how messy and expensive it was to use.

Wide drawers are better for items that usually go together: flatware, serving utensils, cooking utensils, and so on. Sometimes these drawers have dividers that separate spoons from forks and the like. Or you can buy flatware trays or drawer separators to serve this purpose. Deep drawers accommodate paper goods, plastic storage containers, dishtowels and aprons, and other stackable items; some are wide enough to fit pots and pans or bowls.

What to Do with All the Stuff That Isn't Food

You'll be a happier cook if you put things in places that are convenient to where and how you will use them. Bear this in mind: cooking, serving, and cleaning up go faster when dishes, glassware, cups and saucers, and such are stored near the sink or dishwasher. Flatware is best separated into categories—knives, forks, and so on. Pot holders and trivets must be within easy reach if a hot pot requires immediate attention, so you should place them near the stove or oven, either on a hook or in a nearby drawer. Pots and pans are handier if you put them in a large cabinet where you can stack them. Unless you are lucky enough to have a special cabinet for trays and cookie sheets, the pot cabinet is useful for these, and for cutting boards.

 You use a *trivet* to put hot pots and casseroles on, to protect your table. They can be made of metal, marble, ceramic, or thick fabric.

If you keep similar items together, you only need to go to one place to find them. For example, you might keep cake pans, pie pans, muffin pans, measuring cups, and perhaps even measuring spoons stored in a bowl or jar, on one cabinet shelf.

You'll find it saves time to store items that you work with on a regular basis—wooden spoons, vegetable peelers, spatulas, tongs and such—near your work area. Gadgets you use less frequently can go into drawers or cabinets further away. The honey stirrer, melon-baller, and butter curler that you got practically brand new from your mother can go in the drawer you rarely open.

It's a good idea to have a separate drawer for tools you may use in the kitchen that aren't actually cookware—screwdrivers, scissors, and twine, for example. This drawer might also be a good place for all those cords from electric appliances. Unless you have a separate drawer for low-use items such as corkscrews, cheese planes, and chopsticks, this is the place for them also. You know all those manuals that come with appliances? You can put them here, too.

If you are one of those people who can't live without a junk drawer, use the smallest possible drawer for stuff like the deck of cards you play solitaire with while waiting for the scones to brown, as well as labels, note pads, cake candles, pennies, your extra keys, the plastic-bag ties you removed from the plastic-bag carton, your recent sales receipts, and all the other little stuff that collects. You can just throw this stuff in, but you should know there are plastic drawer organizers in all sizes for the purpose of organizing these items. Clean your junk drawer every two to three months. You'll be amazed at how many pennies you'll find.

Most people find it convenient to store cleaning supplies and tools, such as steel wool pads and rubber gloves, under the sink. This also is a handy place for a dish rack and drain board, trash and garbage bags, and if you have room, a garbage pail lined with a plastic trash bag. You can mount shelves on the door of this cabinet to hold the soap and soap dish, sponge, or dish scrubber if you don't want to keep them at the sink.

> **Kitchen Clue**
> Potholders get dirty! Wash them occasionally with your regular laundry and you'll find they'll last longer and look better.

Put Things Back in the Same Place

Although it's important to be an individual and arrange your kitchen to suit your needs, you always should follow one important rule: Wherever you decide to store an item, put it back in the same place. The refrigerator has its place. The sink has its place. So should your wooden spoons and spaghetti fork. If you put things back where they belong, you'll never have to ask, "Where did I put that thing?"

You will surely remember where you keep the tools you use regularly, but you may not always recall where you put those rarely used items. Why rely on memory? Make a list of where you stored your stuff so if you forget where you put those snail shells you got as an engagement gift, all you have to do is look at the list.

By the way, make sure you put the *list* in a place you'll remember—a desk drawer or taped inside a cabinet. What's the use of a list if you can't find it?

> **Kitchen Clue**
> It's a good idea to keep a small fire extinguisher under the sink. In the event of a small fire, you might be able to control it quickly. Know exactly where it is and how to use it. Obviously, call the fire department if the fire is large or out of control.

Where to Put the Food

Storing groceries follows the same logic as storing non-food items; that is, store like items together. For instance, you could stock canned tomatoes, tomato paste, and pasta on one shelf, and all sweet items, such as sugar, jam, honey, and molasses, on another. It's handy to store salad dressing ingredients such as oil, vinegar, dried herbs, salt and pepper, and spices together and to store baking goods such as baking powder, baking soda, yeast, chocolate chips, and so on together.

Kitchen Clue
Dried herbs in cardboard boxes get stale quicker than bottled ones. Once you open a box of herbs, transfer the contents to a small bottle or plastic container. Label it and store it with the bottled herbs.

This may sound nutty, but it pays to keep dried herbs and spices in alphabetical order. Wait until you need the dried rosemary in a hurry. If it's always between the paprika and the sage, you don't have to move every bottle to find it. And as long as you're being so organized, why not separate the herbs and spices you use for cooking from the spices you use for baking? Cinnamon, nutmeg, and other spices used for baked goods belong with ingredients such as vanilla extract and baking chocolate.

How to Organize and Capitalize on Refrigerator Space

You will be happier and richer if you arrange your refrigerator shelves conveniently. Some of the drawers, sometimes called crispers, are specially humidified to keep certain produce moist and fresh, so use them for the fruits and vegetables that require moisture for storage. (Some refrigerators also have specially marked meat drawers, and some have basket drawers for produce that doesn't require moisture.)

Kitchen Clue
Your refrigerator won't smell like a restaurant dumpster if you keep an open box of baking soda in the back on one of the shelves. Change the box every six to eight weeks.

Everything that doesn't have a designated holder goes on a shelf. Foods that are piled on top of one another deteriorate faster. You also tend to forget about them, and they become hideous-looking mold experiments that you have to discard. If you keep the perishable and most-used foods unstacked and toward the front, they will stay fresher longer, and you are more likely to use them. That saves money. The door is the perfect place for storing ingredients with a long shelf life: jarred olives, ketchup, jelly, and so on.

You also can save money if you don't open the refrigerator door frequently and don't hold it open to take inventory while you decide what you want. Keeping the door open lets warm air in. This wastes energy and makes the food deteriorate faster. For the same reason, don't put extremely hot foods in the fridge. Let them cool down slightly first.

No More BIG BOX (Or, How to Organize Your Recipes)

If you think it's silly to spend time organizing recipes, consider this scenario: You have photographs of all your friends—childhood friends, high school friends, college friends, and married friends. You collect all these photos in a box and label it "Friends." After several years, the box is crammed with pictures, and it takes hours to find the baby photo of your friend Jim, which you want to have enlarged for his 30th birthday. If you had organized the photos in some logical way—"Baby pictures," or "Pictures of Jim," or even "Photos, 1974"—it would be easier to find the one you wanted.

It's the same with recipes. If you throw all your recipes into a BIG BOX, thirty years from now when you finally sort through them, you will find that recipe for Chocolate Decadence cake that you always wanted to make but didn't because you couldn't find the recipe. Only you can't make it because you have to watch your weight.

NEVER... use the the baking soda you put in the fridge to absorb odors for cookies, biscuits, or any other recipe. You don't want this stuff in your stomach.

Whether you are the type of person who files information as soon as you collect it, or the kind who procrastinates and lets papers pile up for awhile, there are several handy ways to organize recipes.

Discard Those Dumb Recipes

Before you begin to organize your recipes there is something you must do first: *Discard.*

Discard duplicate recipes, or recipes that are so similar they might as well be. You don't need four recipes for applesauce. If you have a good one, keep it. When you gain experience, you will know you can use brown sugar in place of white or add lemon peel, cinnamon, and raisins without a recipe telling you so.

Discard recipes that are so complicated you know you'll never cook them.

Discard recipes that are so simple you don't need a recipe. Do you really need instructions for an ice cream sundae?

Discard recipes that say "Continued on the next page" if you don't have the next page.

Just Say No to Some Popular Methods of Storing Recipes

There are several ways to organize recipes. Some that are popular don't work well, either because they are inefficient, time consuming, or perishable.

You'll be happier if you just say *No* to cute accordion files. These are better than the BIG BOX—but barely. There are separate sections, but the categories are too broad, and when one or two become overburdened, the flimsy cardboard compartment will tear. Besides, in order to find a recipe, you have to stick your hand into the compartment, lift out all the recipes, and finger through them to find the one you're looking for.

Say *No* to index cards/file boxes. These require you to rewrite recipes by hand on small pieces of cardboard (what a nuisance!) or clip only those recipes that will fit on the file card (how limiting!).

Say *No* to notebooks. These don't allow for expansion beyond the confines of the book, and you can't remove a page when preparing a recipe.

The Most Convenient Way to Store Recipes

Three methods work well for recipe organization. One easy-to-manage method is the loose-leaf binder, which allows for expansion. All you have to do is open the center ring and add paper. An added plus is that the pages lay flat, so it's easy to see the recipe when you are preparing food. You also can take out a single page if it seems more convenient. For this reason, it's a good idea to tape one recipe per page. If you have lots of recipes, you can divide them into categories by separating the sections with tabs that indicate food categories. Loose-leaf binders rarely become overburdened. If yours is filling up, start a second one just for desserts, ethnic specialities, or some other category that appeals to you.

Kitchen Clue
You might want to keep a running index of your recipes. Add the recipe title to your list each time you add a recipe file to your collection. Keep the list in a convenient place so it won't seem like so much trouble to take 15 seconds to write down the recipe name.

A cabinet and file folders work the same way as loose-leaf binders, but you place the recipes inside file folders instead of taping them onto loose-leaf pages. This is a handy system if you have a deep desk drawer in your kitchen or a filing cabinet somewhere in your house. As with loose-leaf binders, you separate foods into categories and file them alphabetically. It's smarter to break down categories somewhat; file chicken and turkey separately rather than as poultry, because file folders on general subjects can become overburdened and tear apart, like accordion files. Your file folder categories can become quite specific. You can divide them by event (picnics), holiday (the Super Bowl), ethnic or regional speciality (Cajun entrees or Caribbean food), ingredient (dishes with mustard), and so on.

Computer files work like cabinet files, only you have to type the recipes. If you want to go to this bother, arrange the recipes in separate files as you would for a loose-leaf binder or cabinet.

The Least You Need to Know

➤ Arrange cabinets and drawers so that most-used gadgets and utensils are near your work area, and infrequently used items are farther away.

➤ Don't put hot food in the fridge; don't stack food in the fridge; and try not to keep the door open too long.

➤ The best way to organize recipes is in a loose-leaf binder or file folders.

Part 2
You've Gotta Have Them: Kitchen Staples

Now that you've got a handle on how the kitchen works, it's time to focus on "filling in." By that we mean SHOP. That's no simple task. So, to make the matter a little less awesome, the next two chapters offer suggestions on what basics you need: staple foods as well as paper goods and (ugh) cleaning supplies, as well as cookware, appliances, and table items. I also offer a few ideas on what NOT to buy. Let's start "filling in."

JULIA CHILD AND THE FRUGAL GOURMET DEBATE OVER PAPRIKA.

Chapter 3

The Bare Essentials: Supermarket Staples

In This Chapter

➤ The essential grocery items (herbs, condiments, oils, and such)

➤ The necessary refrigerator items

➤ Freezer necessities

➤ Paper goods and cleaning supplies

By now you're familiar with your kitchen and have an idea where you want to store things. What's next? Shopping. For this you need three things: ample time, a wad of bills, and a list.

Before you even begin to think about cooking, you have to buy some basic ingredients for your house. We all know people who don't have anything but a beer and an orange in the fridge, or those take-out types who keep costly pre-packaged dinners in the fridge or freezer. But if you're going to be cooking for *real*, you have to stock up accordingly.

No matter what you cook, how often you cook, or how well you cook, some staple items are a must for every household. In this chapter, we will discuss the essential grocery items you need to cook properly.

Filling Those Bare Cupboards

What are the staples you need to fill your cupboards? Practically everyone you know will have a different list, but there's usually is a lot of overlap. If you really want to gain confidence in the kitchen and prepare meals you know are winners, start with the items mentioned next. They are broken into categories to avoid confusion.

The Whys and Wherefores of Herbs and Spices

Herbs and spices enhance food's aroma and offer variety by providing subtle or robust flavor. They also encourage creativity in cooking. Fresh herbs taste better than dried ones, but dried herbs suffice for many dishes. Experiment with different ones to discover which you enjoy.

Kitchen Clue
Have you noticed that the produce department frequently is the first aisle in a supermarket, and the frozen food section is never last? That means you have to move the produce in your cart so it isn't damaged by heavier items you choose later. And you have to skip the frozen foods and go back to them last, or the ice cream may melt!

Because dried herbs deteriorate after time, keep them in tightly closed bottles or plastic containers for best results. Buy herbs and spices in small quantities and store them in a cupboard that's not near the oven's heat. Except for salt, pepper, garlic or onion salt, and whole spices (such as nutmegs or whole allspice), discard herbs and spices after a year.

You needn't buy items such as apple pie spice, pumpkin pie spice, or poultry seasoning. These are blends of seasonings that limit your culinary creativity. For example, a typical blend of "pumpkin pie spice" includes cinnamon, nutmeg, ginger and allspice. But you may prefer pumpkin pie that has more nutmeg or contains cloves instead of allspice. Why not season the pie the way you like rather than use someone else's all-purpose mixture? The same applies for poultry seasoning, which typically contains thyme, marjoram, sage, rosemary, pepper, and nutmeg. If you season the chicken with herbs of your own choosing it will taste the way you want. Even better, if you change the seasoning each time you make chicken, rather than using the same old blend, your meals will be more interesting.

Fein on Food

Peppercorns were the only ingredient ever enticing enough to make men risk their lives or kings and queens risk their fortunes. If it weren't for peppercorns, there may never have been a famous Columbus, a European settlement in America, Thanksgiving with turkey and all the trimmings, and so on. Pepper is the spice that changed history. You've got to respect it. Treat peppercorns properly, and you will notice how their flavor brings vitality to food.

It's important to treat peppercorns properly. That means you should never buy the ground kind, whose flavor dissipates as soon as you open the bottle. Because you never need much pepper in a recipe anyway, take the time to grind it yourself with a peppermill.

A nutmeg grater. Just slide the nutmeg back and forth.

Shopping List: Essential Herbs and Spices

❑ basil

❑ bay leaf

❑ chili powder

❑ curry powder

❑ dill weed

❑ ground cinnamon

❑ ground red pepper

❑ ground cloves

❑ oregano

❑ paprika

❑ peppercorns

❑ powdered ginger

❑ powdered mustard

❑ rosemary

❑ salt

❑ thyme

❑ whole nutmegs

Herbs and spices both come from aromatic plants and are used to enhance the flavor of food. Herbs come from the plant's leaves and stems and can be used either fresh or in dried form. Spices generally come from the plant's seeds, roots, bark, and flower buds or berries.

The Essential Oils, Vinegars, and Condiments

Oils, vinegars, and condiments are used for salad dressings, marinades, and lots of other recipes. Oils are also used to help keep foods from sticking to pans and to add a rich quality to dishes. The word "fat" has taken on a sinister reputation in recent years. No one wants to have too much of it, but sometimes you need fats in recipes. Vegetable shortening, for example, makes pie crust flaky. It also is useful for greasing pans for baking cakes and cookies.

Olive oil is a must on the basic buy list. Not only is it considered one of the healthier oils, but it also is rich, full-bodied, and useful for all sorts of recipes. You can't use olive oil to deep fry foods, though, because its smoke point is too low.

NEVER...
keep dried marjoram more than three or four months; it loses flavor rapidly. Never buy dried parsley; it's flat and tasteless. Never buy ground nutmeg. It loses flavor in the jar before you even open it. You can keep whole nutmegs indefinitely, and a small nutmeg grater costs very little.

Because there are a gazillion varieties of olive oil, picking one can be confusing. First things first—just because it's expensive doesn't mean it's better. There are two main types of olive oil, *extra virgin* and *pure*. As a general rule, the more-costly extra virgin oil, which comes from the first pressing of the olive and has a more delicate flavor, is best for salads and subtle dishes. Pure olive oil is fine for hearty foods. Many cooking experts believe French olive oil tastes the best, but taste is personal. Over time, try several brands from several countries.

Vegetable oil usually means soybean oil, though manufacturers are reluctant to say so. Years ago everyone thought the word soybean would scare people off, and the prejudice stuck. Look at the label on the container of vegetable oil and see for yourself. There are other types of vegetable oil, too, all specifically labeled. They include canola, corn, peanut, safflower, and sunflower oils. You can use them interchangeably in recipes. However, they taste different, so sample all of them at some point to see which you like best. You can use vegetable oil for deep frying, pan frying, and stir-frying, as well as for salad dressing.

Red wine vinegar is another staple for salad dressing and marinades; white vinegar is needed to make certain dishes taste tangy. Balsamic vinegar is not essential but it's a worthy splurge, because it's the kind of ingredient that sets your recipe apart from someone else's. People know your salad tastes better, but they can't figure out why. Balsamic vinegar labels should say "from Modena."

Condiments enhance food's flavor. Whether you use them for salad dressing, barbecue sauce, or as a way to add some extra oomph to soups and casseroles, Dijon mustard and Worcestershire sauce are condiments you ought to have handy. Others are noted in the shopping list.

Shopping List: Oils, Vinegars, and Condiments

❑ balsamic vinegar	❑ red wine vinegar
❑ Dijon mustard	❑ shortening (small can)
❑ extra virgin olive oil	❑ soy sauce
❑ hot pepper sauce	❑ vegetable oil
❑ ketchup	❑ white vinegar
❑ mayonnaise	❑ Worcestershire sauce
❑ pure olive oil	

If You Want to Bake, You Need These

Baking items are a must if you plan to bake even a minimum amount of cookies, pies, and cakes. These include the obvious—flour and sugar—as well as things like unsweetened cocoa powder, used for baking and for making hot chocolate. Don't confuse this with presweetened hot-cocoa mixes, which make the kind of hot chocolate you get in the hospital or college cafeteria. (Try the recipe for hot chocolate in the "Beverages" recipe chapter.)

> **NEVER...** buy imitation vanilla extract. It seems cheaper, but isn't. Its flavor has no depth, and you need twice as much of it as pure extract. Even then, the recipe doesn't taste right.

Shopping List: Baking Staples

- ❏ baking powder
- ❏ baking soda
- ❏ brown sugar (light or dark)
- ❏ chocolate chips
- ❏ confectioner's sugar
- ❏ corn syrup (light or dark)
- ❏ flour, all-purpose
- ❏ granulated sugar
- ❏ honey
- ❏ unsweetened cocoa powder
- ❏ vanilla extract

The Miscellaneous Shopping Staples You Need

There are several miscellaneous staples you need. Notice that this shopping list does not include bouillon cubes. Lots of recipes call for bouillon cubes, but because these tiny nuggets can be loaded with salt and additives, you might consider substituting homemade or canned broth instead. You also could make your own bouillon cubes (there's a recipe in the "Soups" recipe chapter).

Another ingredient you don't have to buy is bread crumbs. Bread crumbs are relatively expensive, and you can easily make your own. Tear bread into pieces and whirl them in a food processor or blender. Or crush bread with a grater or rolling pin. For dry bread crumbs, toast crumbs in the oven at 350 degrees for a few minutes until they turn light brown. Store homemade bread crumbs in plastic bags in the freezer.

One item you should consider keeping on hand is sun-dried tomatoes. They aren't essential, but many contemporary recipes call for them. Sun-dried tomatoes have an intense, tangy tomato flavor that livens up a variety of dishes, particularly pasta. They come either packed in oil or in dry packages. The dry ones must be reconstituted in oil or hot water.

> **NEVER...** buy instant white rice; it has the taste and texture of styrofoam. Real rice is one of the easiest foods to prepare (see the "Grains and Vegetables" recipe chapter). Bottled salad dressing is another item you never should buy. It's salty, often fatty, and expensive. It may contain an assortment of frightful sounding additives. Vinaigrette dressing is a foundation recipe that every competent cook should know (there's one in the "Sauces" recipe chapter).

Never buy canned parmesan cheese. It doesn't taste fresh and can sour a recipe. Keep a chunk of fresh parmesan cheese (preferably Reggiano) in the fridge to grind as needed. Another never buy is "cooking wine." It doesn't taste like wine and can ruin a good recipe. The rule to using wine in cooking is this: if you wouldn't drink it, don't cook with it.

Shopping List: Miscellaneous Must-Haves

❏ brownie mix	❏ maple syrup
❏ canned tomatoes	❏ oatmeal
❏ canned tuna	❏ peanut butter
❏ chicken and beef broths	❏ popcorn kernels
❏ coffee	❏ raisins
❏ cold cereal	❏ rice
❏ crackers	❏ snacks
❏ dried white beans	❏ spaghetti
❏ jelly	❏ tea

Also suggested: sun-dried tomatoes, white wine, and if you can afford it, a bottle of brandy.

The Staples You Need for Your Fridge and Freezer

There are certain refrigerator staples that you'll need. Notice that the refrigerator items include onions, potatoes, and garlic. Most people will tell you not to store these items in the fridges, but you can safely keep them in the baskets or on the shelves—just not in the moisture drawers.

Shopping List: Cold Essentials

❏ apples	❏ lemons
❏ baking soda	❏ milk
❏ butter	❏ onions
❏ celery	❏ Parmesan-Reggiano cheese
❏ eggs	❏ parsley
❏ freezer pie shells	❏ plain yogurt
❏ frozen juice concentrate	❏ potatoes
❏ garlic cloves	❏ waffles
❏ ice cream or frozen yogurt	

Paper Products and Cleaning Supplies

There are several non-food items you'll need for your kitchen. This shopping list includes the paper and related supplies, and the cleaning supplies, you'll need.

Shopping List: Paper and Cleaning Items

- ❏ all-purpose spray
- ❏ aluminum foil
- ❏ baking soda
- ❏ Band-Aids
- ❏ cheesecloth
- ❏ coffee filters
- ❏ dish/pot scrubbing pads
- ❏ dishwasher detergent
- ❏ food storage bags
- ❏ glass spray
- ❏ liquid detergent
- ❏ matches
- ❏ napkins

- ❏ non-perfumed soap
- ❏ oven cleaner
- ❏ paper towels
- ❏ parchment paper
- ❏ plastic wrap
- ❏ rubber gloves
- ❏ sink cleanser
- ❏ small fire extinguisher
- ❏ sponges
- ❏ steel wool pads
- ❏ toothpicks
- ❏ trash bags
- ❏ waxed paper

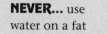

NEVER... use water on a fat fire. You can easily extinguish flames from burning fat by throwing baking soda on them. Therefore, you need another box of baking soda under the sink.

Kitchen Clue
Throw away sponges every two to three weeks or when they start to smell bad, whichever comes first. You can wash sponges with the laundry if you prefer.

The Least You Need to Know

➤ Buy whole peppercorns and nutmegs and grind them fresh into recipes.

➤ Use fresh parsley, regular (not instant) rice, fresh (not canned) parmesan cheese, and pure vanilla extract.

Chapter 4

The Bare Essentials Part Deux: Equipment Staples

In This Chapter:

➤ Pots and pans you need

➤ Must-have appliances

➤ Gadgets and miscellaneous kitchenware you've got to have

You may never need fancy cookware in a multitude of shapes and sizes, a pasta-making machine, or a device for pitting cherries, but you can't cook without pots and pans, mixing utensils, and stuff like that. An appliance or two that cuts kitchen time can come in handy, as can some interesting little gizmos such as a lemon juice squeezer (a terrific labor-saver). This chapter describes those cookware items, appliances, and gadgets that are fundamental for your kitchen.

Do You Need Expensive Cookware?

A hundred years ago, home cooks had a trusted cast iron skillet and cooked everything in it. Today there are so many types of cookware it's almost bewildering, even to experienced cooks. Part 6 of this book deals with types of cookware, what type is best for different kinds of cooking, and what to look for when buying pots and pans.

For now you need only remember this: buy the best cookware you can afford. That doesn't mean it has to be the most expensive stuff in the store, but it does mean you should buy for value, not merely price. You call upon cookware for years of service, so it's like an investment. Cheap cookware is flimsy, and it often has hot spots, which can result in unevenly cooked food—or ruined recipes. Cheap pots are also dangerous. They tend to wobble and warp, and their handles often fall off. In the end, if you wind up replacing them, you haven't saved any money.

If you are really strapped for money, buy fewer pieces and make do with what you have for awhile. It is better to buy one size of better cookware and save for the second size than to buy two pots or pans of poor quality.

People may think that the kind of pots and pans they buy doesn't matter, then when a recipe doesn't come out right, they think it's their fault and they aren't good enough to be "gourmet" cooks. Guess what? Sometimes it's the pots and pans, folks! You can tell the difference in as simple a recipe as French toast. See for yourself. Borrow two pans—a cheap one and a well-constructed one—and see which cooks more evenly and quickly, and gives the crispiest, best-looking French toast.

The Indispensable Pots and Pans

A beginner's kitchen should include pots and pans that will give you the most use with the least equipment.

Skillet generally refers to any type of frying pan. However, for buying purposes, it usually refers to a frying pan that has sloped sides and may or may not come with a lid. A *sauté pan* has a more specific meaning—this is a straight-sided pan that's deeper than a regular skillet and usually comes with a lid. You can sauté foods in either kind of pan, but the sauté pan holds more, so it's handier for dishes that have lots of sauce, vegetables or other ingredients.

➤ Two saucepans with covers: a 1 ¹/₂ to 2-quart and a 3-quart

➤ Two skillets/sauté pans/frying pans: a 7"–8" slope-sided pan, with or without a lid (it can be nonstick, especially if you use it to double as an omelet-pan) and a 10"–12" straight- or slope-sided pan with a lid

➤ An 8-quart soup/stock pot (can double as a pasta pot) with a lid

➤ A roasting pan

If you have some extra money and space, add one or more of the following items as you build your supply:

➤ A wok or stir-fry pan

➤ A double-boiler insert

➤ A 3-quart Dutch oven

➤ A 1-quart saucepan with cover

➤ An omelet pan

➤ A cast-iron skillet

➤ A 5-quart Dutch oven or deep, straight-sided sauté or braising pan with cover

➤ A griddle

➤ A teakettle

The Essential Appliances

Years ago there were no electric appliances. You don't need them today, either. You can brew coffee by pouring boiling water over coffee grinds and letting it drip through to a carafe. You can chop vegetables with a chef's knife and mix cookie dough by hand, so you don't have to buy a food processor or handmixer. But appliances save time and work. Part 6 deals with the most popular appliances found in housewares stores, how they can help you, and what features to look for. In the meantime, consider buying these basic appliances:

➤ An automatic drip coffeemaker

➤ A toaster oven

➤ A handmixer

➤ If you can afford one or if someone tells you they want to buy you a housegift, the next appliance on the list is a food processor.

You Can't Get Along Without These Gadgets

There are loads of gadgets, utensils, and other sorts of paraphernalia you need to equip your kitchen. You should know, however, that shopping for them could put a serious dent in your budget. You can collect them gradually over a long period of time, but eventually, you should fill your kitchen with the items discussed in the following sections.

Bakeware Basics

Here are some of the tools you need for baking:

➤ Measuring cups and spoons

➤ A glass measuring pitcher

➤ Three mixing bowls (different sizes)

➤ Two 9" cake pans

➤ An 8" or 9" square cake pan

➤ A 9" × 5" × 3" loaf pan

➤ A cake rack

➤ One 9" pie plate

➤ Two cookie sheets (one can be a jelly roll pan)

A *jelly roll pan* is a cookie sheet with a rim around it.

➤ A cake tester

➤ A rolling pin

➤ A pastry board—a wooden, marble, or granite slab on which you roll pastries

Cutting Tools

To chop, slice, or otherwise cut food, you need the following:

➤ A chef's knife

➤ A paring knife

➤ A serrated bread knife

➤ Steak knives

➤ A knife holder

➤ Poultry shears

➤ A cutting board

➤ Scissors

NEVER... use a knife as a screw driver, letter opener, or device to open packages. Not only can these actions ruin the blade, they can also maim you. Never put knives in the dishwasher. This loosens handles and dulls the edges of the blades.

Knives require careful maintenance. If they aren't sharp, they don't cut effectively and could cause injury because you tend to use more force. One way to keep knives sharp is to have them sharpened professionally. Cookware stores and butchers in your area may have special knife-sharpening sessions; however, these can be expensive. The knife sharpening devices that come with can openers are not effective and often warp blades. A special home knife sharpener is a good compromise. There are several electric and manual models available.

Different kinds of knives.

Mixing, Stirring, and Turning Tools You'll Need

You can't get along without implements to help you mix, stir, and turn food:

➤ Several wooden spoons

➤ A long-handled slotted spoon

➤ A medium size rubber spatula

➤ A small rubber spatula

➤ A rigid metal spatula

➤ A potato masher

➤ A whisk

➤ A two-pronged long metal fork

➤ Tongs

➤ A spaghetti fork

➤ A soup ladle

Odds and Ends: Kitchen Necessaries You Can't Forget

In addition to all the food preparation tools, there are some rather unglamorous items you have to buy and little odds and ends that you can't do without. An apron, for instance, can save you cleaning bills and distress, so it pays to get at least one and actually wear it when you cook. Here are some other necessaries:

➤ Plastic containers for storage

➤ Canisters (or large plastic containers)

➤ Four pot holders

➤ Four dishtowels

➤ Dish rack

➤ Drain board

➤ Salt and pepper shakers

➤ Garbage can

➤ Flatware tray (if there are no drawer dividers)

➤ Stepstool

➤ Microwaveable dishes (if you have a microwave oven)

➤ A soap dish for the sink

➤ You might also consider wall hooks and a paper towel holder

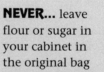

NEVER... leave flour or sugar in your cabinet in the original bag once the bag is opened. You should put the bag inside a Ziploc bag or, even better, in canisters or large, covered containers. There's a specific reason: an open bag is an invitation to wildlife.

The Handiest Gadgets

Finally, here are several gadgets that will make your life a whole lot easier:

➤ A vegetable peeler

➤ A manual can opener (for when there's a power outage)

➤ A bottle opener

➤ A meat thermometer

➤ A nutmeg grater

➤ A grater (flat or four-sided)

➤ A lemon juice squeezer

➤ A corkscrew

➤ A peppermill

➤ A funnel

➤ A kitchen timer (if you don't have one on the oven)

➤ A steamer insert for vegetables

➤ An ice cream scoop

➤ A bulb baster

➤ Two 1" brushes

➤ An 8" strainer

➤ A small strainer

➤ A salad spinner

A salad spinner. It's in to spin.

You Don't Need These Gadgets, But They Sure Would Help

If you have any money left, a few other non-essential gadgets come in handy in most kitchens. Consider splurging for these:

➤ A muffin pan

➤ A 9" × 13" cake pan

➤ A 10" tart pan with removable bottom

➤ A 6–8-cup soufflé dish

➤ A 9"–10" springform pan

➤ A small serrated knife for tomatoes

➤ A colander

➤ A skimmer

➤ Chopsticks

➤ Wooden skewers

➤ A meat mallet

➤ A cheeseplane

➤ A microwave leak tester

What You Need for Serving

Once you've bought the ingredients and cooked them, you need serving utensils and equipment with which to eat. You may have some odds and ends to use, but if you are just starting out or wish to restock, you'll need four each of the following:

➤ Dinner plates

➤ Salad or dessert plates

➤ Cups and saucers or mugs

➤ Cereal/soup bowls

➤ Tumblers

➤ Juice glasses

➤ All-purpose wine glasses

➤ Knives

➤ Forks

➤ Teaspoons and tablespoons

… two each of these items:

➤ Platters

➤ Vegetable serving bowls

➤ Serving spoons

➤ Serving forks

➤ Trivets

And finally…

➤ A salad bowl and servers

➤ A cream pitcher

➤ Sugar bowl

➤ A pitcher

Although they aren't absolutely necessary, a tablecloth (or two or four placemats), candlestick holders, and an ice bucket add a gracious touch.

The Least You Need to Know

➤ Buy the best pots and pans you can afford.

➤ Never put your good knives in the dishwasher.

➤ Wear an apron when you cook.

Part 3
Did Anyone Ever Give You a Shopping Lesson? (Or, How to Be a Confident Consumer)

You now have a list of the grocery staples and kitchen supplies you need, but the real nitty-gritty of daily meals means real food: meat, veggies, fruit, milk, and so on. For that, again, you have to SHOP.

Wait a second! You can't just go out and shop. Which is the most convenient place to go? Where can you get the best stuff for the best price? When you get there, how do you distinguish between cuts of meat or poultry parts so you won't waste time and money cooking them improperly? You may be curious about some curious-looking produce you've never tried, or unable to figure out how to choose even the most familiar lettuce or pears. You may want to know which kind of cheese or butter or coffee to buy, or how to select canned goods from among the dozens of brands facing you on the shelves.

In short, you want to be a smart shopper. Read on. The next several chapters will show you the way.

Chapter 5

Filling in the Spaces

In This Chapter

➤ Knowing your shopping style

➤ Where and when to shop

➤ Basic principles of buying: understanding value, reading labels, choosing fresh or packaged, brand name or generic

Have you forgotten that you have to eat? Well, you aren't going to make a meal out of flour and olive oil, or any of the other staple items on the shopping list. You have to buy real food. Meat and vegetables. Fish and fruit. Stuff you can cook for dinner.

You don't have to buy food items all at once. In fact, if you have the time, it's better if you don't shop for these *en masse*; buy them during the week on mini-shopping trips. That way foods that should be fresh will be. Besides, it will make the shopping trips for staples shorter. Before you go out and do the actual shopping though, it's a good idea to have some awareness of your shopping style.

What's a shopping style? It has to do with where, when, and how often you like to shop. Knowing your shopping style makes the job easier and more fun, so we will discuss that in this chapter. This chapter also talks about the best places and times to shop and how you can become a discerning buyer.

Developing Your Shopping Style

Just because you're not completely confident about cooking doesn't mean you don't know the difference between high- and low-quality ingredients or good food and bad. You may have noticed, for example, that items from a specialty store—fish from a fish store, for example, or tomatoes from a farm stand—taste better than the same items from a supermarket. If it makes a difference to you, then you won't mind making two stops: one for the fish or tomatoes, the other for everything else.

But you may not have specialty shops where you live, or the luxury of time it takes to make several stops. You may not wish to spend so much leisure time shopping for food. Think about how much time you want to devote to shopping.

Where to Shop

There are several types of food retailers. Before you shop the first time, check them out to see what they're like and to determine which ones will make your shopping experience a pleasant one, which ones give you the best value, and which ones give you a headache. In most areas, you will find one or more stores that fit each of these descriptions.

What You Can Expect at a Supermarket

Supermarkets are full-service grocery stores that stock food items, paper products, produce, and so on. They all have weekly specials posted in their windows. Some have a policy of discounting certain items only to people who clip store coupons from newspaper flyers. Some give a "double bonus"—that is, they double the discount on manufacturer's coupons. Some supermarkets have "club memberships," where practically anyone can be a member for no charge. Members use little plastic cards when they shop to get special bonus discounts.

Prices vary from supermarket to supermarket. It pays to read the flyers, use coupons, and check the windows to see which one is selling what for how much. Comparison shopping is good, but don't overdo it. If you have to drive for miles to find better prices for just a few items, it wastes time and gasoline money.

If you are shopping for one or two people, you must decide whether to buy large or small quantities. Individual servings and small quantities cost more. But if you buy "family" size packages and don't use up the item before it becomes stale (breakfast cereal, for instance), it wastes money. Undeniably, you can save money if you buy staple items that stay fresh (such as ketchup) in big packages or containers.

Store managers come up with all sorts of ways to tempt you to buy, which is why everyone will tell you not to go to the supermarket when you're hungry. But even if you just finished eating, it is difficult to resist the fragrance of fresh-baked goods or other tantalizing foods when you come into the store. To save money and calories, enjoy the smell but don't let your nose control your pocketbook. Be vigilant at the checkout counter, too—they keep the candy and gum there to tempt you while you're waiting in line. Instead of buying some, survey the magazines and newspapers. Without even buying a copy, you can find out which movie stars are getting divorced, which soap opera characters are romantically involved, which aliens have come from outer space, and where Elvis was last sighted.

Are Warehouse Clubs Worth Joining?

Warehouse clubs are mammoth-sized, no-frills places that usually aren't very attractive. They sell grocery items and paper goods, along with tires, office supplies, over-the-counter drugstore items, and hundreds of other products. Some also sell fresh produce, meats, and frozen foods. Prices are generally the lowest of all retailers for most items, but not for all items. Because you have to buy in bulk in these places, you may not save money if you don't use the product before it deteriorates. However, they're the ideal place to purchase staples. If you join (and there is a fee), remember that at warehouse clubs you have to bag your own groceries; so bring boxes and shopping bags.

Fun at Farmer's Markets, Farm Stands, and Green Grocers

Farmer's markets and farm stands are often the best places to buy produce. Because the food is locally grown, you know it's fresh. The prices are usually decent, too. In addition to these produce markets, you should consider shopping at a green grocer—a retailer who sells fruits and vegetables that may or may not be locally grown. Many have higher-quality produce than supermarkets, and they don't prepackage them (as many supermarkets do), so you can pick your own fruits and vegetables. Prices are usually higher at a green grocer, but in some cases it's worth it. You may not notice a difference between supermarket and produce-stand broccoli, celery, apples, or bananas, but when it comes to summer fruits (berries, tomatoes, and other delicate, fragrant items), the differences can be significant—and even a novice can tell.

Kitchen Clue
When you first start to cook, you may not realize that quality differences in produce can determine whether or not a recipe will be successful. For example, if you make gazpacho with hard, mealy, orange tomatoes, it won't be good. It's not your fault—it's the tomatoes. It's better to choose a different recipe than use an inferior ingredient.

Are Thrift Stores Worthwhile?

Thrift stores can provide huge savings opportunities. Cakes and baked goods that didn't come out perfectly, for example (perhaps the sugar glaze was thicker on one side or the other) taste just as good as the prettier ones. Bread that's a day or two old still has flavor. If there are thrift stores in your area, it might be worth your time to check into such savings.

When to Visit (and When to Avoid) the Neighborhood Convenience Store

A neighborhood convenience store, often lovingly called "the pirate" by the locals, is not the place for a major shopping excursion. Prices are high because these stores buy in small quantities. However, if it's convenient and you're in a hurry, or you only need a couple things, go for it.

Shopping Takes Time

Some people enjoy the shopping experience, and others are impatient shoppers. Whichever you are, be sure you allow enough time to shop wisely. The following tips suggest several ways you can cut down on shopping time and some of the frustrations that shopping brings:

➤ Make a shopping list. That way you will only be looking for the items you need.

➤ Organize cents-off coupons. Here are a few tried and true ways to do it: by type of item (bread/detergent/frozen foods), by alphabetical order of manufacturer, by the order in which the aisles of your favorite supermarket are laid out, or by expiration date. If you follow any logical procedure you will use, not lose, your coupons and will save money.

➤ Avoid shopping during the late morning and early afternoon, early evening hours, and on Saturdays when stores may be most crowded.

➤ Unless it's urgent, don't shop if the weatherman predicts a major snowstorm, hurricane, or other bad weather occurrence. That's when the stores become crammed with folks in a frenzy to buy everything in sight in case the world comes to an end.

➤ Count on the fact that sometimes people will take advantage. You know how it is: they'll go to the express line with more than the limit. Relax, and leave yourself enough time.

How Often to Shop

How often you shop depends primarily on the demands of your schedule. Your schedule may not have room for more than one shopping trip per week. But there's a dilemma here: If you want fresh fish, produce, poultry, or other perishable items, you have to buy them more often. Being a good cook means planning meals around fresh, available foods—not a particular recipe. Buying way ahead of time discourages innovation and creativity.

There are ways to alleviate this problem. One is to stock up on staples so you don't have to shop for these even once a month. Then make short frequent trips to the store for ingredients that demand freshness. Another is to freeze items that keep well in cold storage: chicken, meat, bread, and pastries, for example.

In addition, you should keep two shopping lists: one for staple items and one for ingredients for meals you'll prepare in the next few days. But don't wait for the staples to disappear completely before you put them on the list. On one of your major shopping trips you can buy enough staple items to last a long time. On your short but frequent trips, you can pick up the items you need for the next few days quickly, without having to make a major effort. Keep your shopping lists where you'll remember them so you don't wind up writing "apples, flour, peanut butter" on the back of a sweepstakes-entry envelope you might throw away.

Intro to Buying, Part I

Now that you've decided which store to go to and how often to go, what do you buy? Before we get to actual products, there are some factors you must consider.

Which Is Better—Brand Names or Generic Products?

Some generic foods taste as good as the famous brands, but you have to compare for yourself. The nutritional value is probably the same (you can tell by reading the label, which we'll discuss later), so if you like how the generic one tastes, buy it. It's probably cheaper. Generic paper products (paper towels and napkins) don't fare as well as food. They're cheaper, but are usually of poor quality, and if you have to use twice as many to be effective, you're not really saving.

Which Is Better—Fresh, Frozen, or Canned?

Most people agree that fresh food tastes better than frozen or canned food does. It's often a lot less expensive, too. So why buy frozen or canned green beans just because they are handy, when you can get fresh green beans so readily?

There are some exceptions to the fresh over frozen/canned rule. Frozen peas briefly steamed, frozen winter squash, and canned beets taste substantially like fresh food. Frozen chopped spinach is ideal for soup or quiche. Canned broth, tuna, beans, and tomatoes are so useful that they're kitchen staples. And of course, some frozen products, while not quite as good as fresh, are good enough and simply too convenient to pass up: waffles, juice concentrate, french fries, and pie shells.

Frozen entrees may be convenient, but they also have a lot of sodium and sometimes a lot of fat. If you learn to cook simple entrees that don't take much time, you will wind up with a tastier meal with less salt and fat—and you'll pay less too. You also won't feel fatigue the next day from all the salt you consumed.

Which Is Better—Convenience Foods or the "From Scratch" Kind

Some people can't tell the difference between a cake from a mix and one baked from scratch; and some like them equally. Some people even prefer package-mix brownies to the homemade kind. These convenience items are fine, unless buying them means you'll never make a real attempt at baking. Other convenience items just don't cut it—"instant" hot cereal and meat/macaroni-type casserole dishes, to name two. Preparing these is not cooking, it's just mixing ingredients so you can fill your stomach.

Expiration Dates Are Important

Expiration dates tell you when certain products cease to be fresh. Never buy a product whose expiration date has passed. Look for expiration dates on perishables such as dairy products, breads, meats, and eggs. Some products, such as cold cereals, have a date stamped on them indicating that they are better if eaten before that time. These products can taste stale after the given date.

What's on That Label?

Labels tell you more than who manufactured the product: they also contain important information that is worthy of your attention. For example, the label lists ingredients in the order of quantity, which gives you an idea of how the product will taste. By comparing brands of jam, for example, you will see that some list fruit first, and some list corn syrup first. The first product will taste more fruity; the second one will be sweeter. Labels also give nutritional content *per serving*. You can tell how much sodium and fat you will be ingesting per serving, for example. Labels also tell you to refrigerate after opening if necessary, and some even have recipes.

Nutrition Facts		
Serving Size ¾ cup (30g)		
Amount Per Serving		
Calories 120 • Calories from Fat 20		
		% Daily Value*
Total Fat 2g		3%
Saturated Fat 0g		0%
Cholesterol 0mg		0%
Sodium 140mg		6%
Potassium 20mg		1%
Total Carbohydrate 26g		9%
Sugars 12g		
Protein 1g		
Vitamin A 25%	•	Vitamin C 25%
Calcium 2%	•	Iron 25%
Vitamin D 10%	•	Thiamin 25%
Riboflavin 25%	•	Niacin 25%
Vitamin B$_6$ 25%	•	Folic Acid 25%
Not a significant source of dietary fiber.		
*Percent Daily Values are based on a 2,000 calorie diet.		

A typical nutrition label. You see 'em everywhere now.

Reading labels is especially important for people who have allergies and food sensitivities or are trying to avoid certain ingredients in their diets. If you are sensitive to gluten, for example, and can't eat products that contain modified food starch, the label can be extremely helpful. Unfortunately, some labels give only general references to some ingredients. They may say "spices and flavorings added" without listing the specific spices and flavorings, so people with sensitivities to specific additives will find no help here. Some of the more common ingredients you may see on a label are listed by type in the table below.

Kitchen Clue
If you want to avoid sugar in your diet you'll have to look beyond the obvious on the label. Sucrose, glucose, fructose, dextrose, and lactose are all forms of sugar, as are corn syrup, maple syrup, and molasses.

Common Ingredients and Their Uses

Ingredients	Use
Sodium benzoate, sorbic acid, sodium nitrate, sodium nitrite, sulfur dioxide, potassium sorbate, calcium proprionate	Preservatives
Monosodium glutamate	Flavor enhancer
Carob bean gum, modified food starch, guar gum, xanthan gum, gum arabic	Thickening agents
Lecithin, mono- and diglycerides, polysorbate 60, polysorbate 80	Increases shelf life
BHA, BHT, ascorbic acid	Antioxidants
Dextrose, fructose, glucose	Sweeteners

Comparing Cost and Value

Don't be fooled by low price. Certain foods have a funny way of seeming to cost less, when they really cost more. For example, "ground beef," which has a high percentage of fat, is less expensive per pound than "ground round." However, if you make a hamburger, meatloaf, or chili with ground beef, you will notice how much it shrinks when you cook off the fat. You pay more for the ground round, but get more meat and less fat.

Past-its-prime produce also is inexpensive, but you must look it over carefully. If the produce is still in good condition, it's a bargain. If it's soft and has brown spots, any price is too high.

Certain foods cost less because they entail some work. For example, whole broiling chickens are cheaper than cut-up broiler parts. You can save money if you divide the bird yourself.

The Least You Need to Know

➤ Compare generic and brand name products and buy the generic one if it tastes just as good. It's probably cheaper.

➤ Fresh food is usually preferable to canned or frozen. However, certain canned or frozen items—tuna and pie shells, for example—are as good as fresh ones and too convenient to pass up.

➤ Never buy food whose expiration date has passed.

Chapter 6

The Meat Market

In This Chapter

➤ What you need to know about beef, veal, pork, and lamb

➤ All about chicken and turkey

➤ A guide to seafood

➤ Simple starter recipes that aren't really recipes

Now that you have an idea of what kind of shopper you are, and where and how often you might shop, it's time to go to the store with your shopping list. For most people, that list includes meats, poultry, or seafood. Although many people have cut down on meat in recent years, it's still a major source of protein—and enjoyment—in our diets. Choosing good meat will help you cook better because you won't have to worry about covering up flavor with chemical "enhancers" or masking food with heavy sauces.

By learning about different varieties and how to use them, you can quickly become an expert (well, almost). This chapter describes the more common types of meats, poultry, and seafood you're likely to see in stores, and tells you how to select them and prepare them for storage. We've also included a few simple starter recipes that are so easy you really can't call them recipes.

Please! Gimme More Than Meatloaf!

Even beginning cooks and kitchen "idiots" don't have to be content with meatloaf all the time. Sometimes you want something more glamorous, more enticing, more modern—or maybe just less *boring*.

The first thing you should know is that cooking meat can be incredibly easy, and it doesn't have to be expensive. You do have to find appropriate recipes and understand the ingredients, and you have to be willing to experiment and try new foods (and different ways of preparing old foods). You may have to rethink old, treasured recipes, too. If you've tried to cook your family favorites and failed, there's something you should know: Meat, particularly pork, is a lot leaner today than it used to be. That means you might have to adjust old recipes by changing cooking times and temperatures or by adding liquids to prevent the dish from being dry.

A Mini-Manual on Meat

In the United States, meat typically means beef, veal, pork, and lamb. There are several grades for these meats, but most of what you will find in the stores is *choice. Prime* meats are usually reserved for speciality shops and restaurants. The difference has to do with the marbling of fat within the flesh (prime has more, which makes the meat juicier) and sometimes with age (prime is aged longer where appropriate).

If you shop for meat in a supermarket rather than a butcher shop, you'll find that various portions are already pre-cut and packaged in shrink wrap. Sometimes the market also has a special meat counter where you can get prime meats (the pre-packaged kind is usually choice) as well as more unusual or expensive meats such as sweetbreads, venison, game birds, crown roasts and so on. On the other hand, there are markets where the "butcher counter" meat and pre-packaged stuff is exactly the same—the manager is simply accommodating the styles of two types of customer, one who likes to quickly pick up a package, one who enjoys the process of selecting meat and having it cut or packaged individually. When in doubt, ask the butcher or manager what the differences are in the market you shop in.

Kitchen Clue
Just because you don't buy meat at a butcher doesn't mean you can't get the cut and size you want. In supermarkets and warehouse clubs that have in-house butchers, though most of the meat is sold in packages, you can ask the butcher for a particular cut, a smaller piece, a thicker steak, or whatever you want. Don't hesitate to assert yourself.

The different cuts of meat break down into two general categories. Tender meat comes from the least-worked parts of the animal. Tougher, more muscular meat comes from the more exercised sections. You usually cook tender meat by dry heat methods such as grilling, broiling, pan frying, stir-frying, baking, and roasting. Tougher portions require slow, moist heat methods of cooking, such as stewing and braising, which allow them to soften and absorb moisture.

It's important to check expiration dates and store your purchases in the coldest part of the refrigerator. If you're going to use the meat the same day you buy it, you can leave it in the original package. Otherwise, remove the meat from its wrapper, put it on a plate and cover it with plastic wrap. If you want to freeze meat, remove it from its wrapper and cover it with plastic wrap and then freezer wrap. Label and date the item, and use the oldest package first. You'd be surprised how all the packages start to look the same; you really don't remember which package contains what or when you bought it.

To prevent food poisoning, always wash your hands before handling food—especially meat, poultry, and fish. If you use a cutting board, scrub the board and your hands with hot water and soap. Defrost meat in the refrigerator or by microwave, not on the countertop. Bacteria grow wildly at room temperature.

The Bottom Line on Beef

Cuts of beef can be confusing. Tender portions include these steaks: *rib, delmonico, club, porterhouse, T-bone, sirloin, shell, New York strip*, and *filet mignon*. You grill, broil, pan-fry, or stir-fry these. It also includes these portions for roasting: *rib, top round, top sirloin*, and *tenderloin*. Tougher portions include *brisket, chuck, shoulder, cross-rib, rump, bottom round*, and *plate*. Use these for stew, and pot roasting and braising.

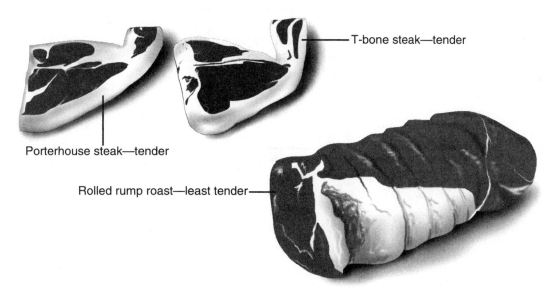

T-bone steak—tender

Porterhouse steak—tender

Rolled rump roast—least tender

You usually cook tender meat with dry heat and tough meat with moist heat, but there are exceptions. You can grill a flank steak even though it's fibrous, stir-fry skirt steak even though it's muscular, and roast an eye round beef even though it isn't tender. That's because there are ways to make meat tender besides making it into pot roast or stew. For example, you can marinate the meat for "London broil" (cut from the shoulder, bottom round, and so on). You can cut gashes in the meat, as butchers do for flank steak, or you can pound it with a meat mallet, as you do minute steaks. Tenderized meat can then be cooked using dry heat methods.

If a recipe tells you to *marinate* food, that means to let the food rest for a while in a mixture, usually an acidic liquid, that will make the food more tender and/or flavorful.

Grinding is another way to make meat tender. That's why ground beef is soft no matter which portion the meat comes from. Ground beef varieties have varying amounts of fat. Some stores will give the fat percentage on the package. Others sell ground meat by name. *Sirloin* has less fat and fewer white flecks than ground round. *Ground round* has less fat and fewer white flecks than *ground chuck*. There is all-purpose *ground beef*, too, which is the fattiest of all. We all know it's better to avoid fat in our diet, but if you want to make a tasty, juicy hamburger, you have to use a moderate fat variety such as round or chuck (or a mixture of the two) because you cook burgers by dry heat. On the other hand, if you want to make chili con carne, which has a moist sauce, you can use the drier ground sirloin. Generally, ground beef has too much fat to be serviceable for any dish.

Whatever cut of beef you buy, always look for meat that's bright red, with tiny flecks of fat in the flesh and a small amount of fat around the edges. Pass up meat that has dark spots or discolored brownish streaks. Torn packages are another no-no.

You can keep larger cuts of meat, such as roasts, in the refrigerator for 3–4 days or in the freezer for 6–9 months. Steaks are fine for 2–3 days in the fridge (3 days if marinated) or 6 months in the freezer. Store kebabs and stew meat no longer than 2 days in the refrigerator or 3 months in the freezer. Ground beef must be used within 24 hours of purchase. However, you can freeze it for up to 3 months.

Beef Summary Chart

Cut of Beef	Texture	Best Way to Cook	How to Store	When Is It Done?
Steaks (t-bone, rib, delmonico, club, porterhouse, sirloin, shell, New York strip, filet mignon, minute)	Tender	Grill, broil, pan-fry, stir-fry	2-3 days R 6 mos. F	
Skirt Steak	Tough	Grill, stir-fry, braise	2-3 days R 6 mos. F	
Roasts (rib, top round, top sirloin, tenderloin)	Tender	Roast	3-4 days R 6-9 mos. F	120-130 (rare) 135-140 (medium) 140+ (well done)

Cut of Beef	Texture	Best Way to Cook	How to Store	When Is It Done?
Brisket, Chuck, Shoulder, Cross-Rib, Rump, Bottom Round, Plate, Eye Round ("roasts")	Tough	Stew, braise	3-4 days R 6-9 mos. F	
London Broil	Tough	Grill/broil (marinate first)	2-3 days R 6 mos. F	
Flank Steak	Tough	Grill/broil (marinate or score first)	2-3 days R 6 mos. F	
Kebabs	Tender	Grill/broil	2 days R 3 mos. F	
Stew Meat	Tough	Stew	2 days R 3 mos. F	
Ground Beef	Tender	Most cooking methods	1 day R 3 mos. F	

R = Refrigerator   F = Freezer

What You Need to Know About Veal

Veal is the delicately flavored meat of young calves. It lacks fat and can dry out easily if you don't cook it properly. You have to baste even the tender portions.

If you see packages that say "milk fed" veal, that means the meat is from animals that weren't weaned and never ate grass. Milk fed is prize veal—pale, tender, and mildly flavored. It also is expensive.

All veal should be a light pinkish-cream color. If it has a deep, reddish hue, it is too old (somewhere between veal and beef). This dark, in-between meat lacks the delicacy of veal and the richness of beef. Why bother with it?

NEVER... use commercial meat tenderizers. They change the taste and texture of the meat. Besides, they're chemicals. Do you really want to *eat* that stuff?

The most tender veal portions include the *loin* and *rib*. You broil, grill, or pan fry them as chops, or you roast them as larger pieces. *Boneless shoulder* is more tender than the corresponding portion in beef, and although you can roast it, you have to baste this cut often. Tougher veal sections include the *shank*, which should be braised (as in the famous *osso buco*) and the *leg* (round and rump), which should be braised or roasted. The best veal *cutlets* are carved from the leg and pounded to tenderness. You pan-fry or grill these.

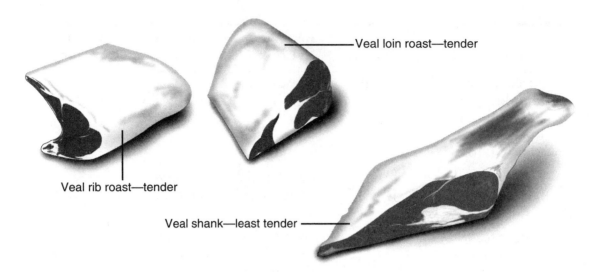

Veal loin roast—tender

Veal rib roast—tender

Veal shank—least tender

Large veal roasts and chops can last up to 3 days in the refrigerator; cutlets can be refrigerated 2 days; stew meat and ground veal should be eaten with 24 hours of purchase. All cuts do fine in the freezer for up to 6 months, except ground veal, which should be frozen no longer than 2 months.

Veal Summary Chart

Cut of Veal	Texture	Best Way to Cook	How to Store	When Is It Done?
Chops (loin, rib)	Tender	Broil, grill, pan-fry	2 days R 6 mos. F	
Roasts (loin, rib)	Tender	Roast	3 days R 6 mos. F	165
Shoulder	Tough	Roast, braise, stew	3 days R 6 mos. F	165
Shank	Tough	Braise	2-3 days R 6 mos. F	165
Whole Leg	Tough	Roast, braise	3 days R 6 mos. F	165
Cutlets	Tender	Pan-fry, grill	2 days R 6 mos. F	
Stew	Tough	Stew	1 day R 6 mos. F	
Ground Veal	Tender	Most cooking methods	1 day R 2 mos. F	

R = Refrigerator   F = Freezer

This Little Piggy—The Story on Pork

Pork has gone on a huge diet in recent years. Pigs are slimmer, and their meat is leaner. That's great for your health, but it creates cooking problems. Less fat means the meat can dry out easily. Since pork must be cooked well-done to kill off possible parasites that cause trichinosis, dryness is even more of a problem. But too many people overcook pork. What they don't realize is that well-done doesn't mean *parched*. As long as the meat reaches 150–160 degrees, it's safe to eat. Use a meat thermometer to check (put it in the thickest part of the roast), but also look carefully at the juices when you carve the meat. The juices must be clear and yellow, not reddish. Pork has lots of benefits. The meat is rich and sweet. It contains plenty of vitamin B1, and it adds variety to the diet.

Fein on Food

Pigs are funny looking, but beauty aside, these wobbly, bristly creatures with short stubby legs are among the most generous animals on earth. Every part of the animal is edible or otherwise useful—the meat for food, the skin for leather, and even the bristles for brushes. It's no wonder that pork has been a mainstay of civilization for centuries and is the most widely eaten meat in the world. Pigs are prolific too: Some say that all the pigs in America are the descendants of the thirteen hogs originally brought by the explorer DeSoto.

Pork should have a pale, pinkish-cream color, though shoulder sections may be slightly darker than the rib or loin. Look for meat that's marbled or "grainy" looking.

Most pork portions are tender enough for baking, broiling, roasting, and other dry heat methods, but since the meat is so lean, it's a good idea to cook pork slowly and at moderate temperatures so the middle cooks through before the outside is parched. Basting is recommended.

Loin and *rib* chops can be grilled, broiled, or pan fried. Double-thick ones can be roasted. Those portions are sometimes packaged as whole pieces (such as *pork loin roast* or *crown roast* made up of two rib-loin portions tied together in a circle) suitable for roasting. *Spareribs* and *sausages* are good grilled, broiled, or baked. You can parboil spareribs and sausages for 10 minutes or so before you cook them to add moisture and decrease cooking time. *Country-style ribs*, which are carved from the bottom of the loin, are more tender than regular spareribs and do well baked or grilled. *Fresh ham*, or leg of pork, is a large piece and comes both as a whole ham or as shank or butt portions. Either cut is suitable for roasting or braising. *Picnic roasts* (from the arm) and *Boston Butt* (shoulder portion) also may be roasted or braised. The most tender part of the pig is the *tenderloin*. You can roast it, grill it, pan-fry it, stir-fry it, and even carve it into cutlets.

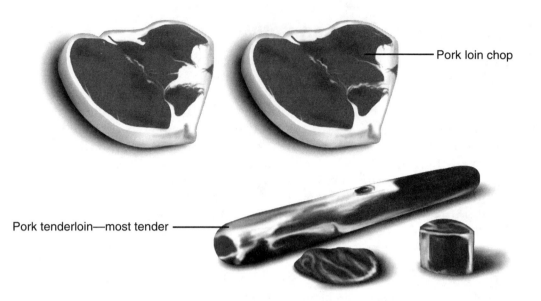

Pork loin chop

Pork tenderloin—most tender

You can keep large cuts of pork in the refrigerator up to 3 days; chops, sausage and spareribs keep 2 days; and ground pork keeps 24 hours. Freezer time for roasts is up to 6 months; chops and sausage 3 months; ground pork, bacon, and hot dogs, 1–2 months.

When you *parboil* food, you cook it partially in boiling water before cooking it completely by some other method.

Ham is cured leg of pork. People first began preparing meat this way in the days before refrigeration, when salt curing kept meat fresh and safe. Although salt-curing is no longer necessary, people still eat ham because they like the taste. You can buy whole or half hams. Most of the ones offered in the supermarkets are fully cooked and need only to be seasoned and heated through (about 10 minutes per pound)—but read the label to be sure. The tastiest hams are the ones with the bone still intact. A *picnic ham* is smoked pork shoulder (also called Boston Butt) and tastes like ham, although there is more fat and, therefore, more waste. You can also buy fully cooked ham steaks that are good for grilling, baking, and broiling.

Refrigerate ham in its original wrapper. You can keep a whole ham approximately 2 weeks, a half a ham one week, and ham slices up to 3 days. Canned ham lasts about one year if unopened. Long-term freezing is not recommended for ham because the flesh becomes watery. If you must freeze ham, do so for no longer than one month.

Pork Summary Chart

Cut of Pork	Texture	Best Way to Cook	How to Store	When Is It Done?
Chops (loin, rib)	Tender	Grill, broil, pan-fry	2 days R 3 mos. F	
Roasts (loin, rib, crown)	Tender	Roast	3 days R 6 mos. F	150-160
Spareribs	Tender	Grill, broil, bake	2 days R 3 mos. F	
Sausages	Tender	Grill, broil, bake	2 days R 3 mos. F	
Country Ribs	Tender	Grill, broil, bake	2 days R 3 mos. F	
Fresh Ham (shank, butt or whole)	Tender	Roast, braise	3 days R 6 mos. F	150-160
Picnic Roast, Boston Butt	Tender	Roast, braise	3 days R 6 mos. F	150-160
Tenderloin	Tender	Roast, grill, pan-fry, stir-fry	3 days R 6 mos. F	
Ground Pork	Tender	Most cooking methods	1 day R 1-2 mos. F	
Cured Ham (whole, fully cooked)	Tender	Roast	2 weeks R 1 mo. F	125-130
Cured Ham (half, fully cooked)	Tender	Roast	1 week R 1 mo. F	125-130
Ham Steak	Tender	Grill, broil, bake	3 days R	

R = Refrigerator   F = Freezer

Lessons on Lamb

Lambs are benevolent, like pigs. The meat is used for food, the milk for cheese and other dairy products, the wool for clothing. Like pigs, lambs were among the first animals to be domesticated. Today, lambs are butchered when they are young, before they develop the strong taste that once characterized this meat.

The meat is mild-flavored but the fat can be gamy, so you should cut away as much of it as possible, leaving just a thin film to provide succulence. Light, rosy-hued meat is younger and more delicately flavored than deep red meat. There's no real significance to the words "spring lamb" anymore. Years ago, lambs were raised through the winter to be slaughtered in time for spring holiday dinners among Christians, Jews, and Muslims. Now we can get young lamb anytime.

Even the so-called tough sections of lamb are tender enough for dry heat cooking, with the exception of *shoulder roast, shanks*, and *neck meat*. These are better braised or stewed. *Spareribs* and *lamb breast* are inexpensive cuts you can roast or braise (sometimes the butcher puts a "pocket" in the breast between the bone and meat, which you can fill with stuffing). The most expensive and most tender cuts are *loin* and *rib chops*, which you broil, grill, or pan fry (or roast if they are extra thick). Loin and rib also can be made into a *crown roast. Shoulder chops* contain more fat than rib and loin chops, but you cook them the same way. The most familiar cut, *leg of lamb* is a large roasting portion sold either whole or in sections. A *butterflied leg of lamb* is boneless and flattened slightly so you can cook it easily on an outdoor barbecue grill (or an indoor broiler).

Something Simple

There's no need to be timid about your cooking abilities. This recipe for broiled lamb chops is so easy you can handle it right now, before you even get to the "real" recipes. Place loin or rib lamb chops (about $1^1/_2$" thick) in a broiler pan and sprinkle them on both sides with salt or garlic salt and black pepper. If you want to make a grand effort, add a pinch or two of rosemary (fresh or dried). Preheat the broiler and broil the chops about 3-5 minutes per side, depending on whether you like them rare, medium, or well done.

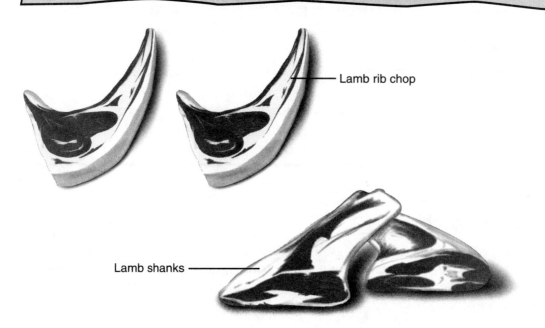

Lamb rib chop

Lamb shanks

Too many people eat lamb well-done, when it tends to be dry. It's tastiest and most succulent if you serve it medium or rare (120°–140° on a meat thermometer).

Large lamb portions keep well in the refrigerator 3–4 days and in the freezer 8–9 months. Chops, shanks, stew, and kebabs can be refrigerated 2–3 days, frozen 4–6 months. Ground lamb stays fresh in the refrigerator for 24 hours after purchase (1–2 months in the freezer).

Lamb Summary Chart

Cut of Lamb	Texture	Best Way to Cook	How to Store	When Is It Done?
Roast (loin, rib)	Tender	Roast	3-4 days R 8-9 mos. F	120-135 (rare) 135-140 (medium) 145+ (well done)
Chops (loin, rib, shoulder)	Tender	Broil, grill, pan-fry	2-3 days R 4-6 mos. F	
Leg	Tender	Roast, grill	3-4 days R 8-9 mos. F	
Shoulder, Shanks, Neck	Tough	Braise, stew	2-3 days R 4-6 mos. F	
Breast, Spareribs	Tender	Roast, braise	2-3 days R 4-6 mos. F	
Kebabs	Tender	Grill, broil	2-3 days R 4-6 mos. F	
Stew	Tough	Stew	2-3 days R 4-6 mos. F	
Ground Lamb	Tender	Most cooking methods	1 day R 2 mos. F	

R = Refrigerator   F = Freezer

A Primer on Poultry

Everyone loves a winner, and lately the big winner for dinner has been poultry, especially chicken and turkey. These barnyard birds have diet- and health-conscious folks to thank for their newly acquired culinary status. The meat provides high-quality protein with few calories, and is low in fat and cholesterol—especially if you don't eat the skin.

All poultry is extremely perishable. Don't stop off to see a movie if you just went shopping and bought some. Take it home and put it in the fridge. You can leave it in its original wrapper if you will be using it within 24 hours. Otherwise, you should rewrap the bird in plastic wrap (or put it on a plate and cover it with plastic wrap).

There's nothing glamorous about cleaning poultry, but you've gotta do it. Rinse the bird (or parts) under cold running water. Rinse the inside cavity too and remove excess fat. If you see any pinfeathers, take them out with a paring knife or tweezers. You can remove hairs by singeing them with a match.

When rinsing the whole chicken or turkey (and sometimes other poultry as well), you might find a surprise inside: packaged giblets. There have been more than a few cooks who didn't rinse the inside of the bird, cooked it, and to their embarrassment, came across plastic-packed giblets while carving the chicken or turkey at the dinner table. You can cook the giblets along with the poultry or use them for stock, gravy, or stuffing.

Poultry-Handling Guidelines

Salmonella is a serious problem associated with poultry, so you have to be extremely cautious about how you handle the meat. Not only do you have to wash your hands before you touch the poultry, you also have to wash afterwards, so you don't spread possible bacteria to other foods. If you use a cutting board, knife, or other utensil with poultry, be sure to wash these implements carefully in lots of hot, sudsy water (plastic, acrylic, and lucite boards can go in the dishwasher).

If you want to defrost poultry, you can let it thaw in the refrigerator or in several changes of cold water—never let it defrost on the countertop (bacteria multiply rapidly at room temperature). You can defrost birds by microwave, but if you do, be sure you cook the meat immediately after it has thawed.

You never cook poultry partially. If there is bacteria in the uncooked portions, it will flourish and affect the whole dish. Be sure you cook poultry completely to eliminate all possible bacteria. That means the thigh meat should register 180 degrees on a meat thermometer (or the breast 170–175 degrees).

Finally, don't stuff poultry until just before you want to roast it. The warmth and moisture of the stuffing also encourages bacterial growth.

Chicken, the Champion

Of all poultry, chicken is champion in the kitchen. In addition to its nutritive value, cooks love chicken because it is among the world's most versatile foods. It pairs well with almost any herb, spice, or condiment. It lends itself to every cooking method. Cooking chicken means you never have a boring meal.

The color of a chicken's skin is irrelevant to cooking. What matters is how fresh the chicken is and what condition it's in. Look for chickens with moist skin. Don't choose any that look like they've been in a barnyard fight and have bruises and blemishes. Avoid chickens with a lot of visible pinfeathers and long hairs. If the seller didn't take care enough to make his wares look good, how well could the bird have been treated? Look inside the package—if there's lots of runny red liquid, it's a sign the bird has been frozen and defrosted.

Chicken parts are even more perishable than whole birds. You can keep whole chickens in the refrigerator 2–3 days, but you can only keep the parts 1–2 days. Whole chicken or parts freeze well, double wrapped, for up to 8 months. Defrosting chicken in the refrigerator takes 3–4 hours per pound defrosting time. You can defrost whole poultry by immersing it, wrapped in plastic wrap, in cold water. You can speed up the defrosting process by changing the water occasionally.

Broiler-fryers are the most common type of chicken you are likely to see in the market; they generally weigh from 2 ½–4 pounds and serve three to four people. They may be cut up into separate parts or sold as wholes. Whole or cut-up broiler-fryers do best when you grill, broil, pan fry, deep fry, or poach them. Some people roast these small birds, but they can be dry when cooked that way. True *roasters* are larger birds, which weigh approximately 4 ½–8 pounds and serve six people. *Stewing hens* are older, tougher chickens that require slow cooking in moisture to soften the flesh and bring out flavor. Stewing hens are excellent for making soup and stock, and you can use the cooked meat for salad. *Capons* are castrated male chickens whose meat is extraordinarily tender and sweet. Capons are large enough to serve approximately eight people and make an impressive roast. At the other end of the scale are *Rock Cornish Hens*, which are tiny chickens that weigh about a pound. Two of these hens, which you can roast, grill, or pan fry, will serve three people.

Boneless, skinless chicken *breasts* are the Oscar winners of the poultry department, and for good reason. Few foods perform as well so consistently. The meat is lean and low-calorie, and versatile enough to combine with all sorts of flavorings. You can cook them by almost any method, though they're best when grilled, sautéed, poached, or stir-fried. Chicken breasts also cook quickly enough to satisfy even the busiest people, and few other foods are as easy to prepare.

Let's Talk Turkey

Turkey always used to be considered a feast bird, suitable for Thanksgiving and Christmas. Now you can buy small turkeys and turkey parts for everyday dinners. There are fresh and frozen turkeys, plain and self-basting ones. Fresh turkey is infinitely tastier than frozen, and its texture is more tender. Self-basting turkeys are a waste of money and calories, and they taste artificial. You pay extra for vegetable oil or broth that's injected into the meat, when you could just as easily baste the bird with some non-fat liquid such as orange juice or wine. Or you could furnish your own fresh basting oil or chicken stock.

To figure out how much turkey you need, consider the weight: one pound per person (including the bone) is about right. As for stuffing, the general rule is to use half as many cups of stuffing as weight of the bird—five cups of stuffing for a 10-lb. bird, for instance. But don't forget, you shouldn't stuff the bird until just before you roast it. You can refrigerate a turkey for about one week, or freeze turkey or parts for up to 8 months.

Fein on Food

If Benjamin Franklin had had his way, the turkey—not the bald eagle—would have been America's symbol. Franklin believed the eagle was of "bad moral character," while the turkey was "a much more respectable bird." Elsewhere in the Americas, turkey also ranked high. In the Yucatan, before Europeans colonized the continent, turkey was considered so special that only the aristocracy and members of the priesthood were allowed to eat it. Likewise, Montezuma, emperor of the Aztecs, served turkey at court functions.

Poultry Summary Chart

Type	Weight	Best Way to Cook	How to Store	When Is It Done?
Broiler/fryer chicken	2½-4 lbs.	Grill, broil, pan-fry, deep-fry, poach	2-3 days R (whole) 1-2 days R (parts) 8 mos. F	
Roaster chicken	4½-8 lbs.	Roast, poach	2-3 days R 8 mos. F	180
Hen chicken	4+ lbs.	Stew, poach	2-3 days R 8 mos. F	
Capon	6-9 lbs.	Roast	2-3 days R 8 mos. F	180
Rock Cornish Hen	1+ lbs.	Roast, grill, pan-fry	2-3 days R 8 mos. F	180
Boneless breasts (chicken)	12-16 oz.	Most cooking methods	1-2 days R 2-3 mos. F	
Turkey	7+ lbs.	Roast	1 week R 8 mos. F	180

R = Refrigerator   F = Freezer

The Subject Is Seafood

The first rule of fish is this: It isn't rectangular and it doesn't come in a box. That is to say, fresh fish is unequivocally better than frozen. Lots of people who grew up on the frozen stuff, which is tasteless and watery, say they hate fish and only eat it because it's healthy. Shellfish also is infinitely better when fresh, though some varieties freeze well.

The second rule of fish is that fish shouldn't smell like fish. If that sounds like an oxymoron, here's an explanation: If fish smells like seaweed (or anything else that's sat on the beach too long), don't buy it. Fresh fish—*really* fresh fish—has no odor. Neither does shellfish, except for scallops (which have a distinctive, almost sweet, ocean scent) and mussels (which often have a salty aroma).

Going Fishing

Fish has so much to offer that you just can't overlook it. Not only is it a healthy and nutritious food, it also is quick and easy to cook. And there are so many varieties with different flavors, textures, and even colors, that it provides endless culinary possibilities.

There are dozens of varieties of fish for sale, but they fall into two general types: *lean* and *oily*. Lean fish have a mild, delicate flavor and firm, light-colored flesh. Because they are lean, their flesh can dry out easily, so these varieties are best when cooked with additional fats or liquids. You can poach, steam, deep fry, pan fry, bake, or broil them. The more common types include *flounder, sole, snapper, halibut, cod, grouper,* and *haddock.*

Oily fish are richer, with a more intense flavor, and they tend to have darker flesh. These varieties do best when they are grilled, broiled, and baked. Familiar varieties include *salmon, swordfish, mackerel, bluefish, catfish, tuna, monkfish,* and *trout.*

Oily fish don't usually fare well when poached or fried. The flesh is just too rich. But there are notable exceptions. Poached salmon, for example, is moist and tender and perfect for company. Fried catfish is succulent, juicy, and satisfyingly crispy. It makes a terrific casual meal or first course, and if you cut the fish into bite-size pieces, it's suitable for hors d'oeuvre. And pan-fried trout is a classic—light, delicate, and satisfying.

Before you buy fish, be sure it is odor-free, and check the skin, which should be tight, and the scales, which should shimmer. The eyes of whole fish should be clear and shiny. Fillets must look moist and lay flat; if the ends curl up like potato chips, the filet is past its prime. When you buy fish, figure 6–8 oz. of fillet per person, 8 oz. of fish steak per person, or 12 oz. of whole fish per person.

You must cook fish the day you buy it or, at worst, the day after. Fish is highly perishable. Freezing can make fish watery, but if you want fish at the ready, freeze it by double-wrapping it. Keep it in the freezer no longer than one month.

Old-fashioned cookbooks instructed readers to cook fish until it flakes. Frankly, by that point the flesh is so dried out it tastes like rubber bands. Fish should be "just cooked" to the point that the thickest flesh is opaque and no longer adheres to the bone, but doesn't disintegrate. You should be able to part the flesh with a fork. A simple guideline to follow is this: measure the fish at its thickest point and cook it at a rate of about 9–10 minutes per inch of thickness.

Some Info on Shellfish

Shellfish is even more perishable than fish and must be eaten within 24 hours of purchase. It is advisable to keep shellfish in the coldest part of the refrigerator, preferably with ice packs surrounding it. Freezing is not recommended except for king crab legs, lobster tail, and shrimp. Place these in double plastic bags and keep them frozen no longer than 2 months.

A number of sea items qualify as shellfish, and they are treated differently for culinary purposes. The most common ones are *shrimp, soft-shelled crab, king crab, lobster, clams, oysters, scallops,* and *mussels.* You can cook shrimp by almost any cooking method. However, you have to first remove the shell and the gritty vein on the outer curve of the back. To do this, pierce the curve with a paring knife to reveal the vein, and then scoop it out. (See Chapter 13 for an illustration.)

You have to buy crab *live* from a reliable fish merchant to assure yourself it's fresh. The merchant will kill the crab and remove inedible portions. You can grill, pan-fry, stir-fry, or deep-fry soft shelled crabs and eat them in their entirety, shell and all. King crab legs (often sold frozen) should be poached or steamed. You can also buy fresh crab meat to make crabcakes and salad. (You can freeze the meat for about one month.)

There are two types of lobster. Maine lobster has huge, meaty claws. Spiny lobster (lobster "tail," often sold frozen) has no claw meat. Except for frozen tail, lobster should be alive and thriving when you buy it. You can tell how vigorous a lobster is if you pick it up and the tail flaps back and forth like Flipper. You can poach, steam, grill, broil, bake, and stir-fry lobster.

People eat many types of clams and oysters raw, on the half-shell. When you buy clams or oysters to eat this way, be sure the shells are tightly closed before you have the merchant open them. You can grill clams and oysters, too— but you have to buy them unshucked. There are some outstanding recipes for baked, stuffed clams and oysters. You can steam any type of clam, though the tastiest steamed clams are the special "steamers" with soft shells. In any case, if you steam or grill clams, discard any that don't open.

> ### Something Simple
>
> Want something heavenly to eat that's also incredibly easy? Scrub some unshucked oysters (you could also use clams) and place them on a preheated grill. Let them sit on top of the heat until the shells pop open (in a few minutes). Discard any oysters whose shells haven't opened with the others. Serve the oysters with melted butter. Everyone will think you're an angel.

Fein on Food

An old wives' tale warned against eating oysters in any month that didn't have an "R" in it, as if by some magic, oysters that were okay on April 30th would suddenly become poisonous May 1st. No one pays attention to that anymore. It is true that oysters are the fattest and most succulent in cold months (those with "R"), but with quick transport, oysters from cold waters can be shipped anywhere, anytime, and you can get good oysters in June or December.

Mussels are bivalves with bluish-black shells. Make sure the shells are tightly closed and clean them thoroughly with a scrub brush. You can steam or grill mussels.

Fish Summary Chart

Type of Fish	Best Way to Cook It
Lean: flounder, halibut, snapper, sole, cod, grouper, haddock	Poach, steam, deep-fry, pan-fry, broil, grill, bake
Oily: swordfish, mackerel, bluefish, tuna, monkfish	Broil, grill, bake
Salmon	Poach, broil, grill, bake
Catfish	Pan-fry, broil, grill
Trout	Pan-fry, bake, broil, grill
Shrimp	Most cooking methods
Soft-shell crabs	Broil, grill, pan-fry, deep-fry, stir-fry
King Crab	Poach, steam
Lobster	Poach, steam, broil, grill, bake, stir-fry
Clams, Oysters	Eat raw, grill, steam, bake
Mussels	Steam, grill

The Least You Need to Know

➤ Tender meats are usually cooked by dry heat methods, while tougher cuts require long, slow, moist heat methods.

➤ Wash your hands before and after handling meat, poultry, and seafood, and scrub any cutting boards and utensils you use.

Chapter 7

You Only Think You Hate Vegetables

In This Chapter

➤ All about vegetables

➤ Salad stuff

➤ All the other little items you see in the produce section

➤ Simple starter recipes that aren't really recipes

Once you have what you want in the way of meat, poultry, or fish, you need something to serve on the side. That often means vegetables and salad. This chapter discusses vegetable produce in three categories, because we tend to serve them that way: side dish vegetables, salad stuff, and the miscellaneous items (such as garlic and onions) that you use to enhance other foods (though some of these, such as mushrooms, also are eaten as side dishes). We've also included a few simple recipes that are so easy you really can't call them recipes.

A General Overview of Vegetables

You may not have tried or even heard of some of the vegetables mentioned in this chapter. You may have passed them in the produce section and wondered what they were and how they tasted. This is your opportunity. When you know a little about these ingredients, perhaps you'll be more willing to try them and learn more about what you like or don't like. You may be surprised to find flavors you never knew could be so enticing. You also may find that this is a simple way to expand your cooking skills without getting involved with complicated recipes.

Many vegetables and salad items are available all year, but some are seasonal. It is better to buy these in season when they taste their freshest; you may be able to purchase locally grown varieties. Always look for fresh-looking, unwithered leaves and stems. Avoid vegetables with obvious bruises and the over-aged, woody look of fossils—giant broccoli stems with brown ends, for instance.

Kitchen Clue
Most experts will tell you that potatoes, onions, and garlic should be kept in a cool, dark place— not the refrigerator. If you lack space, you can keep them in the basket (not moisture drawers) in your refrigerator. Do not store them in plastic bags (you may use paper bags or towels) because they may perish more quickly. Potatoes taste slightly more sugary and less starchy when kept under refrigeration.

If you can, buy vegetables that are loose, rather than pre-packaged. That way you can see and feel the entire item to be sure it's fresh. It's also best to buy loose salad greens rather than the cut-up pre-packaged kind. Not only can you select items based on freshness that way, you also can choose your own quantities and your own "mix"—more arugula, for example, or no chicory—and you can be sure that every leaf is cleaned properly. *However*—sometimes you're too tired, too rushed or too whatever to bother preparing fresh salad, and those packaged salads sure come in handy. Take advantage on those occasions; just be sure the greens look fresh, crisp, and moist.

Many people choose organically grown vegetables to avoid what they consider to be health risks posed by products grown in commercially fertilized soil or sprayed with chemical pesticides. This is a personal choice. There is no readily apparent difference in flavor between regular and organically grown produce.

You have to use your common sense about storing vegetables. You also have to use your eyes and nose. Refrigeration guidelines are given below, but don't feel married to the numbers. Go by appearance and smell, not by the actual time the vegetable has been in the refrigerator, and discard or keep the vegetables accordingly.

For optimum storage, keep fresh vegetables and greens in the refrigerator in special plastic vegetable bags (available in supermarkets in the same place as the other plastic storage bags). These bags are ideally suited to the job. The tiny vents help maintain the perfect balance of air and moisture needed to keep the produce fresh.

Speaking of storing vegetables, if you're one of those lucky people with a garden and a green thumb, you might find yourself with a bounty of produce at the end of a season. You can only store your harvest for so long in the fridge— then what should you do with the leftovers? There are lots of options, depending on the vegetable.

Of course, some people freeze vegetables, but frozen veggies never taste quite right (and neither does frozen vegetable soup) because they become watery, with a mushy texture. If you can't think of anything else to do with the bounty, why not give it away? Neighbors, friends, soup kitchens, and homeless shelters would be grateful.

Side Dish Vegetables

The word vegetable sometimes makes people grimace. But people who think they hate vegetables probably just ate them overcooked all their lives. Old-fashioned recipes from days gone by recommended cooking vegetables until they were mush. Today we know better. We have learned to cook vegetables to tenderness but to keep them as crunchy as possible. Although some vegetables, such as spinach and other leafy greens, wilt, even they don't have to suffer from too much time over the heat.

Shorter cooking time does not only benefit vegetables' flavor and texture. It also means healthier eating because fewer nutrients are lost.

With so many varieties of vegetables, it's impossible to give one rule to determine when vegetables are done. But here are two important things to keep in mind: Cut vegetables to a uniform size so they cook evenly, and cook them for the shortest time possible, so they become tender but still keep their nutrients and vibrant color. The "Vegetables" recipe section gives specific cooking times for several vegetables.

Tomatoes, particularly plum tomatoes, make terrific sauce (you can make a big batch of sauce but freeze the sauce in small containers to have some ready for pasta). You can prepare chutney, chow-chow, or other relishes with bell peppers, corn, zucchini, carrots, and beans. Cabbage can become sauerkraut or coleslaw. You can make a big pot of vegetable soup or stew.

The following sections describe common side dish vegetables. For most of them, you can count on the vegetables serving three to four people per pound. In cases where this estimate does not hold true, we will indicate the serving quantity under the specific heading.

Artichokes

This unusual-looking vegetable is best in fall and spring. Look for tight, closed leaves and an even-colored surface. If the leaves have sharp points, snip the tops with scissors before you cook the artichokes. Note, however, that cut surfaces turn color quickly, so rub them with the cut side of a halved lemon to prevent discoloration. Artichokes keep 4–5 days. One artichoke serves one person.

> **Kitchen Clue**
> Use a stainless steel or enamel pot with stuff like artichokes and asparagus because they "react" chemically with other metals (such as aluminum). That is, they discolor and take on an off-taste.

Something Simple

People will think you're a genius if you serve artichokes. They look difficult to prepare, but they really aren't. Cut 1" from the stems of four large artichokes, put the artichokes in a stainless steel or enamel pot just big enough to hold them, and cover them with water. Add half a lemon. Bring the water to a boil, cover the pan, lower the heat, and cook for about 35 minutes. (When they are done, the stem feels tender when pierced with the tip of a sharp knife.) Remove the artichokes with tongs, holding them with the leaves pointing downward to drain the water. Serve them hot with melted butter or oil and vinegar, or cold with mustard or mayonnaise. That's all there is to it.

Asparagus

These regal-looking spears taste best in the spring. You decide whether you like the fat ones (you must peel these) or skinny ones (which you needn't peel). Some people cook asparagus in a special pot that keeps the tips above the water, because the tips cook more quickly. But you can use a stainless steel or enamel frying pan with a cover. If you buy asparagus with stems and tips of about equal width, you won't have a problem. Look for firm, straight spears with tightly closed tips. The stems should not be withered and should have no more than 2"–3" of purple-white at the bottom (which you cut off). Asparagus will last up to 5 days if you wrap the bottoms in moist paper towels.

Avocados

Avocado is a fruit that we eat as a vegetable. The flavor and texture is rich and buttery. There are two types: large, shiny, and light-green-skinned (*Fuerte*) or small, dark, and pebbly-skinned (*Haas*). The Haas has a more intense flavor. Store avocados on the counter top until they're ripe; that is, when the surface "gives," or yields to slight finger pressure. After that, store them in the refrigerator, where they keep about a week.

Beans

Both green and yellow "snap" beans should be firm, slender, and crisp, and should have no bulging bumps beneath the pod. Remove the ends before you cook them. Beans keep well in a plastic bag for as many as 4–5 days. *Fava* ("broad") beans are thicker and wider. You only use the mature bean inside the pod. Three pounds of favas serve four people.

Beets

This dark red root vegetable is the sweetest one in the larder, with about 10% sugar, which is the reason most people like it. Small beets are the sweetest. Look for those with smooth skins. Because beet flesh is claret red, this vegetable makes a stunning side dish. In addition, the leaves are delicious. You cook them the same way you would spinach. Beets keep up to 4 weeks, but the leaves perish after 3–4 days.

Belgian Endive

Endive are small, oval-shaped heads that are best in late fall and winter. Look for pale, compact leaves. To use as a side dish, you need 1 or 2 endive per person. You also can use endive raw in salad or as crudites. They last approximately 3–4 days when kept in a plastic bag.

Crudite means "raw thing" and refers to raw (or briefly cooked) cut up vegetables that people serve as hors d'oeuvres.

Belgian endive.

Broccoli

Broccoli is more versatile than most people think. Too many people don't use the stem and only buy florets; however, if you peel the stem, it is the tastiest and crunchiest part. Two large spears will serve four people. Look for tight, dark green florets and moist-looking stems. Broccoli in a plastic bag will last approximately 5 days.

Broccoli Rabe

This vegetable looks a little like broccoli but the stems are thinner and there are more leaves. It is a bitter but tasty vegetable that keeps 4–5 days. Be sure the stems look moist, as if they will snap.

Brussels Sprouts

Brussels sprouts are miniature cabbages that are best in the fall, winter, and early spring. Look for compact heads. The tiny ones are the sweetest. Some stores sell brussels sprouts in cartons; some sell them loose or on the stem. Brussels sprouts keep 4–5 days.

Cabbage

All varieties of cabbage are available year-round, except for Savoy, which you can get only in the fall and spring. Look for compact heads that feel heavy for their size. Cabbages keep approximately 2 weeks.

Carrots

This yellow root vegetable has almost as much sugar as beets, which is why these also are among the more favored vegetables. Slender carrots are sweeter than fat ones, and those with the leaves still on top taste better than packaged ones. Carrots should be firm and stiff. Avoid those that are split. Carrots keep for weeks, and you can use those that soften for soup and stew.

Cauliflower

Cauliflower usually is sold as a whole white head (there are also green and purple varieties), though some stores sell florets only. Look for heads that are evenly white and, if possible, those that still have green leaves clinging at the bottom. These leaves are edible and quite tasty. Cauliflower keeps approximately 5 days, and one head serves four to six people.

Celery

Celery is hardy enough to last up to 2 weeks in the fridge. Look for stalks that are stiff and crisp. Color is irrelevant; one variety, called Pascal, is darker green than most. Use the leaves of celery to flavor soups or as a garnish. If you peel celery, it is less stringy and easier to digest. Use a vegetable peeler and start at the smaller end of the stalk.

Corn

Corn is America's favorite summer vegetable. The sooner you cook the ears after you buy them, the better; over time natural sugars turn to starch. The kernels can be white, yellow, or mixed. Peel the husk back and look for medium-size, even kernels. Overly large kernels will taste woody; teeny ones will not have flavor. The husks should feel moist and be tightly wrapped around the corn, and the silk should be golden brown. Remove the husk just before you cook the corn. For serving, figure 1–2 ears per person.

NEVER... buy ears of corn whose husks have been removed, even though it means more work for you. Removing the husks accelerates the speed at which the corn's sugar turns to starch, and greatly affects flavor and texture.

Fein on Food

Everyone knows that our third president, Thomas Jefferson, was a genius. Along with some of his other credentials (such as writing the Declaration of Independence and founding the University of Virginia), he also offered some sage advice about corn. He recommended that a person rush an ear of corn to a pot of boiling water as soon as he or she picks the ear, before the sweet sap in the stem stops flowing in the plant from which it comes. The best cooks still follow this advice.

Eggplants

Western eggplants have either dark purple or creamy white skin. Smaller Asian eggplants are light purple with white streaks. In either case, look for skin that is shiny and firm. Eggplants last about one week. Although a medium-size Western eggplant will serve four, you need 1–2 Asian eggplants per person. Because Western eggplants can be bitter, some cooks salt the flesh for 30 minutes and then dry it with paper towelling before cooking the vegetable.

Fein on Food

People once thought eggplants were deadly. Others claimed eggplants caused insanity and called them "mad apples."

Fennel

This bulbous vegetable is called anise in some markets. It has feathery leaves in the center and is best in the late fall and winter. Fennel has a faint licorice-like flavor. The crunchy texture makes it ideal when used raw for salad or crudites, but it becomes delightfully tender when cooked. In addition, the leaves make a pretty garnish. Look for compact, even-colored bulbs. One bulb serves two people. Keep fennel for no more than 4–5 days.

Kohlrabi

Kohlrabi is a roundish, light green fall-winter vegetable that has a crunch like broccoli. Look for evenly colored, moist-looking skin. Larger bulbs need peeling. You need 2–3 small bulbs per person. They keep one week.

Kohlrabi.

Leafy Greens

Leafy greens have large leaves that range from mild (*chard* and *beet greens*) to hearty (*kale, collards,* and *spinach*) to bitter or spicy (*mustard, dandelion, escarole,* and *turnip greens*) to sour (*sorrel*). All are fragile, lasting only a few days in the fridge, but are worthy and add variety to the diet. Leafy greens should look moist and not wilted.

Greens are classically overcooked but, as with all vegetables, if you treat them right, they'll treat your palate right. Cook them just until they soften.

Spinach is always available. Some of the others are winter items only. Leafy vegetables also wilt considerably and lose volume. You need approximately 2 pounds for four people.

Kitchen Clue
Leafy vegetables can be quite sandy. Wash them thoroughly, a few times, or you will wind up crunching down on gritty sand.

Okra

Okra is a summer vegetable in most parts of the country. The long, slender pods should be crisp-looking and bright green. Okra becomes sticky when it is cooked. The pods keep 3–4 days.

Okra.

Parsnips

Parsnips look like cream-colored carrots, but you can't eat them raw. They are available in fall and winter and keep 1–2 weeks. Look for firm, straight parsnips that aren't cracked.

Peas

English (or "common") *peas* are available only in the summer, which is why so many cooks use the frozen kind. Only the seed, found inside the pod, is edible. *Snow peas*, available all year, have flat pods with teeny seeds inside. *Sugar snap peas* are short, plump, and dark green with small seeds. Snow peas and sugar snaps are entirely edible, pods and all. All should look crisp and vibrantly green. Peas keep 2-3 days; after that, English peas taste too starchy and pod peas wither.

Potatoes

Potatoes are among the more popular vegetables. New varieties come and go, but there are always the same basic types: waxy and starchy. You use different potatoes for different purposes. In general, the round waxy kind (such as *red bliss*) are best for salad; the starchy oval ones (such as *Idaho russets*) are best for baking and french fries; the large round all-purpose ones (such as *Maine* or *Long Island*) are best for mashed potatoes. Potatoes keep for weeks, even in the refrigerator. (Use the basket or shelves, not moisture drawers. Do not put potatoes in plastic bags.) Avoid buying potatoes that have "eyes" or that look "wet."

> ### Fein on Food
>
> Europeans discovered potatoes quite by accident. Driven by a lust for gold, the 16th century Spanish conquistadors set out to find El Dorado, land of plenty. What they found were plenty of potatoes among the Inca tribes of Peru. The conquistadors brought potatoes back to Europe but no one would eat them. Most people thought the vegetable was poisonous. It took centuries for this renowned kitchen staple to gain complete acceptance.

Squash

There are several types of squash. *Zucchinis* and *crooknecks* are available in summer; *acorn, hubbard, butternut, pumpkin,* and other hard-shelled varieties are marketed in fall and winter. Thin-skinned summer squashes are entirely edible; however, you only eat the flesh of winter squash. Summer squash last 3–4 days, but winter squash keeps for several months. One pound of winter squash will serve two people. One interesting variety of fall squash is spaghetti squash. When you cook it, its flesh becomes stringy like spaghetti. All squash should look firm and unbruised.

Sweet Potatoes and Yams

These two vegetables are the same in the United States. What stores sell as yams are actually dark orange-fleshed sweet potatoes, which are moister, sweeter, and more flavorful than the pale-yellow fleshed ones. Sweet potatoes last only about 10 days. Look for firm, evenly shaped potatoes with tight skin.

Turnips and Rutabagas

These are fall and winter vegetables. Turnips should have tight-looking, thin skin (cream and purple). Rutabagas, which have a waxy coating and must be peeled, sometimes are called sweet turnips or "swedes." Turnips last up to 3 weeks, but rutabagas are hardier, and will keep up to 5 weeks. You can cook turnips or slice them into salad to add a zesty flavor.

Something Simple

Turnips have a bad reputation. One mention of this potent vegetable conjures up images of malodorous meals at a Dickensian orphanage. Turnips aren't easy to love, but once you learn how to temper and take advantage of their unique flavor, you'll wonder what the fuss was all about. Here's something simple: mix equal amounts of cooked, pureed rutabagas with mashed potatoes, carrots, applesauce, or winter squash. Season with salt and freshly grated nutmeg and serve.

Salad Stuff

John Evelyn, a 17th century writer, once said that a good salad should be composed like music, with each ingredient a component part and not one of them overwhelming the other. It is good advice. If you want to prepare salad for dinner or as a side dish, make the parts interesting and harmonious. That means you should buy different types of greens and ingredients. You've probably heard of arugula and radicchio, and maybe you've even tried them in a restaurant. Why not have them at home? Your meals will be more interesting if you branch out from the standby iceberg lettuce that most beginners use.

Experiment with various types of greens. Some are crunchy, some soft, some bland, some hearty. You will learn which varieties you like. Some salad greens are expensive. But you need only a handful to perk up the flavor and provide texture or color. In addition to greens, you may want to use other items, such as cucumbers and tomatoes.

Whatever greens you use, do yourself a favor and get a salad spinner. In all but the rarest cases, greens need washing just before you use them. And washed greens need drying or they won't absorb the dressing properly. If you wash greens before storing them, be sure to dry them thoroughly.

If you go to the bother of buying and preparing salad, don't mess it up with bottled salad dressing. Try your hand at vinaigrette dressing. It's incredibly easy and there are lots of variations. There are several recipes in the "Sauces" part of the recipe section. Always dress a salad just before you serve it, otherwise you'll wind up with a soggy mess.

Kitchen Clue
Don't cut lettuce. Instead, tear it into bite-sized pieces with your hands.

Always look for fresh, evenly colored salad greens that don't look wilted. Keep the greens in a plastic bag (preferably a special vegetable bag) in the refrigerator. Fragile varieties such as arugula, mache, and watercress will last up to 3 days. Hardier greens and lettuces will keep up to 5 days.

Arugula

Also called "rocket," this green with dark leaves has a pungent, peppery flavor that adds pizzazz to salad. Use just one bunch in a large salad, or half in a small one.

Arugula.

Cucumbers

There are three varieties of cucumbers, including the familiar dark green variety. You can peel it if you want but it isn't necessary, even if the cucumber has a thin "waxy" coating. Common cucumbers have lots of seeds. The "English," or burpless, type has no seeds. Kirbys are used for pickling but can be used for salad, too. All cucumbers should be firm and evenly colored. They keep 6–8 days.

Lettuce

There are four basic types of lettuce:

➤ *Iceberg* is a "crisphead" and, as the name implies, the leaves are crisp. Food snobs hate iceberg lettuce because it is so common, but iceberg has value—it adds a pleasant crunchy texture to salad. Look for those heads that are compact and heavy for their size, with no "rust" at the stem.

➤ *Butterhead* lettuces, such as Bibb, Boston, and limestone, have soft, loose leaves that provide a rich, buttery texture and mild flavor.

➤ *Romaine* lettuce has an elongated head and dark leaves that give salads a hearty taste. Always pass up the giant romaines; leaves that are overly large can be bitter and tough.

➤ *Looseleaf* lettuces, such as oak leaf, are wonderful for the color and delicate flavor they offer.

Kitchen Clue
One way to quickly remove the core from an iceberg lettuce is to hold it with both hands and strike the core straight down on the countertop. The leaves break apart easily then.

Something Simple

Need an easy, snazzy salad to impress company? Wash and dry some Bibb lettuce leaves, put them on a plate, and top them with wedges of camembert cheese. Let the salad sit out of the fridge for an hour or more so the cheese oozes onto the lettuce. Just before you serve the salad, drizzle some mildly flavored vinaigrette over it.

Mache

Mache is also known as "lamb's lettuce." It has a mild, vaguely nutty flavor. The soft leaves go well with stronger greens such as arugula and radicchio. It's expensive, so use it sparingly—just a bit adds color, texture, and variety to the salad bowl.

Mache.

Radicchio

This salad item looks like small purplish cabbages. It is slightly bitter, has crisp leaves, and provides super color for salad. One small head of radicchio may suffice for two salads. Just a few torn leaves invigorate lettuce and other greens. In addition, radicchio goes beyond the salad bowl: you also can grill it.

Radish

The most familiar radishes are red, but Japanese *daikon* is white. Radishes give salads a crunchy texture and a peppery zing. Red radishes are useful for garnishing dishes, too. Wash radishes and remove the hairy piece at the tip. In addition, you need to peel the daikon variety. Radishes keep for a week or so.

Scallions

Scallions are also called "green onions." The stalks should be straight with a moist-looking white bulb at the bottom. Remove the roots, but use the green part of the stalk to add vivid color and a delicate oniony flavor to salad. Scallions last 7–8 days.

Tomatoes

You always can find tomatoes in the market, but nothing beats a vine-ripened summer tomato. To pick the best one, smell it. If it doesn't smell like a garden, keep sniffing until you find one that does. Summer tomatoes may not be the most beautiful; often the tops are deeply ridged or have small cracks or other blemishes. Good tomatoes should be firm, not mushy, and richly red. If they're partly green, keep them near a sunny window to ripen.

During seasons other than summer, you may have a problem buying good tomatoes. The hard orange ones that come in a box are so awful it is better to do without. Imported tomatoes are prohibitively expensive and don't always measure up. Here again, go by fragrance and texture. Plum tomatoes are useful for salad, and they also are the best varieties for homemade tomato sauce (because they're fleshy and are drier than other varieties). Cherry tomatoes are ideal for tossed salads. Tomatoes last 3–5 days.

Something Simple

Need an easy salad? Try one of these. Slice tomatoes, sprinkle with a few tablespoons of chopped purple onion, and drizzle with thyme-seasoned vinaigrette. Or, slice tomatoes, slice fresh mozzarella cheese, and cover with basil-flavored vinaigrette. Or, try slicing tomatoes and sweet onions (such as Vidalias), sprinkle with some type of crumbled blue-veined cheese, and cloak it with mustard-scented vinaigrette.

Watercress

Watercress is sold in bunches. The small green leaves have a spicy flavor that adds variety to salad. However, you also can sauté watercress and serve it as a vegetable, or use it as a stuffing in pita pocket or tea sandwiches.

All Those Other Little Produce Items

Believe it or not, there are still more items in the produce department that are worth considering. Lots of modern recipes call for chili peppers and wild mushrooms. Learn about them, and don't feel like they're only for "gourmets." The following are some common produce items you might have occasion to use.

Garlic

Garlic is a bulb covered with a thin papery sheath. Beneath the skin are individual "cloves" that you use in recipes. (These cloves are *not* the same as spice cloves used for seasoning hams and baked goods.) When buying garlic, choose fat ones. Alternatively, you can buy chopped garlic in oil in a jar, but it loses its fragrance and flavor in about a week, so this may be a waste of money if you don't use the garlic in that time. Whole garlic lasts a few weeks, even in the fridge.

Garlic *smells*. It gets on your hands and you smell it in your hair, your clothes—everywhere. There are a few things you can do: First, wear disposable gloves when you work with garlic. Second, peel the garlic by placing a clove on a flat surface and banging it with the side of a large knife. Don't kill it, but use gentle force. The paper will come away from the clove, and you can easily remove the paper and lift the clove with a utensil.

Ginger

Ginger is a knobby rhizome with thin brown skin. Buy only a small piece and make sure it has tight skin and no wrinkles. You have to peel ginger. Inside is fragrant yellowish flesh that might have some "hairs," depending on the plant's maturity. Ginger is super for marinades, stir-fries, steamed fish, and vinaigrette dressing. It doesn't taste anything like powdered ginger, and the two are not interchangeable. Ginger lasts 2 weeks or so.

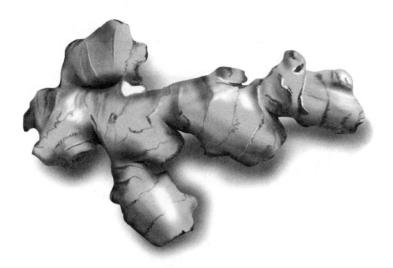

A ginger root.

Herbs

Fresh herbs are a must for people learning how to cook. If you know how to use herbs, you can do almost anything you want—you'll be a kitchen genius in a flash. Herbs make food interesting and delicious. They also add variety to foods—change an herb and you change the whole dish. Fresh herbs are significantly tastier than dried ones, and are preferred in recipes that you cook quickly (grilled chicken breasts, for example) because dried herbs take too long to soften and impart flavor. Herbs last from 4–8 days in a plastic bag, depending on the variety.

Some of the more common herbs are listed below with some suggestions for their use with other foods. But don't let that stop you from trying these herbs with other ingredients.

Herb	Use with...
Basil	Tomatoes, fish, pasta, chicken, pesto sauce
Chives	Potatoes and cheese dishes
Cilantro (also "Chinese parsley")	Asian, Latin American, and Spanish dishes, Shrimp, fish, soup, tomatoes
Dill	Chicken, fish, cucumbers
Marjoram	Eggplant, tomatoes, beans, potatoes, lamb, pork, chicken, grilled and roasted meats

continues

continued

Herb	Use with...
Mint	Cucumbers, beverages, yogurt dressings, lamb marinades
Oregano	Tomato and potato dishes, eggplant, shrimp, lamb, pork, chicken, grilled meats
Parsley	Almost any savory food you can imagine (the flat type is more pungent than the curly)
Rosemary	Eggplant, beans, beets, shrimp, poultry, lamb, rabbit, veal, pork
Savory	Eggs, summer squash, beans and other legumes, veal, pork, chicken, fish
Tarragon	Chicken, fish, and shellfish
Thyme	Tomatoes, potatoes, rice, pasta, chicken, duck, pork, fish, shellfish

Horseradish

This root is an ugly thing that looks like a tree limb with dark brown, muddy-looking skin. You have to peel it, and usually grate it or chop it in a food processor, before you put it to use as a condiment. Mixed with ketchup, it becomes cocktail sauce; mixed with sour cream or yogurt, it becomes a sauce for beef and poached fish. It keeps for over a week. Keep grated leftovers buried beneath vinegar in a covered container.

Leeks

Leeks are at their best in fall and winter. They look like fat scallions. Though onion-like, they are less potent. Leeks can be very dirty, so wash them carefully—especially between the layers. They are useful for stock and as a flavoring agent, but they also are a delicious side dish when braised. Leeks keep 7–10 days.

Lemongrass

Also called "citronella" or "citronella grass," this looks like a stiff scallion. It has fibrous outer husks that you have to peel away. The flesh has a delicate lemony taste and is super as a flavoring for fish, shellfish, chicken, and pasta. Stalks keep 3 weeks.

Lemongrass.

Mushrooms

White button mushrooms are familiar enough, but the new kids on the block are "wild" mushrooms you may see as an ingredient in contemporary recipes. Wild mushrooms can make a huge difference in a recipe because their flavor is intense. They can be expensive though, so use just a few and mix them with white mushrooms if you want to enhance flavor without spending a bundle of money. Here's a list of some of the more common ones:

➤ *Chanterelles* have a small ivory cap and hearty, meaty flavor.

➤ *Oyster* mushrooms usually come in clusters.

➤ *Shiitakes* have dark brown large, flat caps—Shiitake stems are inedible.

➤ *Portobellos* are enormous mushrooms that some people eat like steak. You can brush the caps with olive oil, sprinkle them with herbs, and grill them.

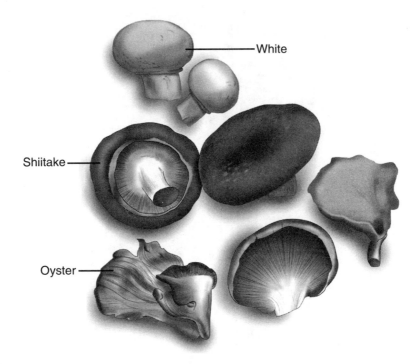

Different kinds of mushrooms.

Mushrooms perish quickly and you must use them within 3–4 days. Most people advise that you clean mushroom caps with a special brush or moist paper towel. If they're really dirty, rinse them quickly in cold running water, cap side up, so no water will get into the gills underneath the cap.

Onions

Onions are among the more useful ingredients in the kitchen. Look for crisp-looking onions that have no green sprouts. Onions last 4–5 weeks in the refrigerator basket. Don't put them in the crisper or moisture drawers. There are several varieties for different purposes:

➤ The familiar yellow ones that may come in a net bag are all-purpose.

➤ Sweet onions (Vidalias, Walla-Wallas, Mauis) are great when raw.

➤ Spanish onions make wonderful onion rings.

➤ Bermuda onions are best on hamburgers.

➤ Purple onions are suitable for salad.

Fein on Food

No one need shed any tears for onions. They are among the world's worthiest vegetables, revered through the ages. Ancient Egyptians thought the layers symbolized eternity. Ancient Chinese prescribed the vegetable for high blood pressure. In the first known labor strike in history, the slaves who built Pharaoh's pyramids refused to work until they got their daily ration of onions. In addition, onions sustained the armies of Alexander the Great and General Ulysses S. Grant. Not a bad record.

Peppers

This category includes *bell peppers* and *chili peppers*. Bell peppers have made a fashion statement in recent times and come in lovely shades of green, yellow, orange, red, and purple. The green ones are the cheapest; red ones the sweetest. Whatever the color, choose those that feel heavy for their size. Look for tight, glossy skin without wrinkles. They will last about 7–8 days.

Bell peppers are among the more useful produce. You can cut them into salad or slice them for crudites. You can roast them and serve them as a first course or for an antipasto (see the "Vegetable" chapter in the recipe section), or you can sauté them and use them as a side dish vegetable. Always remove the stem, seeds, and interior pith of peppers before you serve them.

Hot peppers are smaller than bells. You don't eat them as food, but use them to give foods a hot and spicy liveliness. Some variety or other of varying degrees of hotness is available throughout the year. More common varieties include the long *Anaheim* (with bright green skin), the *jalapeno* (a short stubby pepper with dark green skin), the *poblano* (with a tapering end and deep green skin), and the *serrano* (a medium-size chili pepper with pointy ends).

Always wear rubber or disposable gloves when handling hot peppers, and wash your hands several times when you're finished. Chemicals in the seeds can irritate the skin. Also, be sure not to touch your skin, tongue, or eyes after working with hot peppers—and don't clean your contact lenses and put them back in your eyes.

Fein on Food

Pepper, as in bell or chili pepper, is a culinary misnomer. The plant's pungency fooled Columbus and his men when they first tasted it on one of their trips to the New World. (Or did it?) The men reasoned that because these fruits of the vine were hot, they must be related to the prize peppercorns (*piper nigrum*) that the explorers originally set out to find. In those days the word pepper guaranteed acceptance and shiploads of money. Maybe Columbus wasn't fooled; maybe he was. In any event, fresh peppers (really *capsicums*) were an immediate success in Europe.

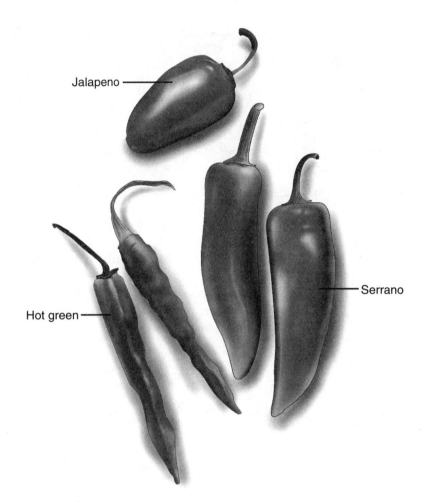

Jalapeno

Serrano

Hot green

Different kinds of peppers.

Shallots

These look like a cross between onions and garlic. They are mild and are used to season foods in recipes in which onions would be too strong. Look for large shallots that have tight, crispy-looking skin with no sprouts. They keep several weeks.

The Least You Need to Know

➤ Where appropriate, buy vegetables in season.

➤ Look for firm, fresh-looking vegetables that aren't withered or wrinkled. Some vegetables, such as tomatoes, also should smell fragrant.

➤ You can keep potatoes, onions, and garlic in the refrigerator.

Chapter 8

Getting the Skinny on Fruit

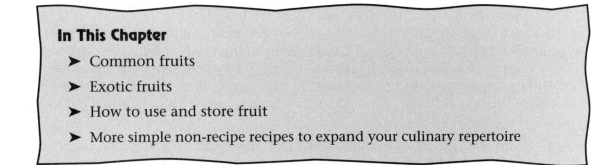

In This Chapter

➤ Common fruits

➤ Exotic fruits

➤ How to use and store fruit

➤ More simple non-recipe recipes to expand your culinary repertoire

After you finish choosing vegetables for dinner, you still have a lot left to consider in the produce department—oodles of fresh fruit. Years ago, consumers had to be content with limited varieties. Today, there is a treasure of fruit to be had for the asking. You can get almost any kind of fruit anytime these days, thanks to rapid transit. Want a peach in December? You can have it. Want a carambola? You may not even know what one is, let alone what to do with it, but you may see one in your local market. In this chapter, you learn about the fruit you're likely to see, how to make selections, how to tell if fruit is ripe, and how to store it. And I'll even include a few simple starter recipes.

A General Overview of Fruit

It may seem terrific to have any kind of fruit anytime, but all this availability does have some drawbacks. Sure, it may seem splendid to feast on strawberries when it's freezing outside, but out-of-season fruits (much more than out-of-season vegetables) often don't taste good. They usually have a mealy texture,

Kitchen Clue
Cold fruit doesn't taste good and often hurts your teeth. Take fruit out of the fridge about 15 minutes before you serve it.

too. And the price is typically outrageous because of built-in transportation costs.

The best guideline for fruit is this: buy it in season, when it has the richest, fullest flavor and the proper texture, and also when it's cheapest. Some fruit is available all year, but some is available only for part of the year, as indicated in the upcoming sections describing specific fruits. If possible, buy locally grown fruit that hasn't been conditioned for transportation. If you can, buy fruit at a store where you can choose your own, instead of one that prewraps it.

Of course, you can buy fruit in season, freeze it, and enjoy it out of season, but don't expect it to taste or feel like fresh fruit. It's also a bother to freeze fruit (except for berries, as you'll see in the paragraph below on "berries"). Besides, part of a fruit's magic is knowing that the enjoyment is fleeting. Enjoy fruit in season, pass up out-of-season and frozen stuff, and eagerly anticipate next year's harvest.

Buying organic fruit is a personal choice about whether you wish to avoid produce grown in commercially fertilized soil or sprayed with pesticide. It tastes just like regular fruit.

Depending on the type of fruit, there are several ways to tell if fruit is ripe; these are discussed later in this chapter. In general though, soft-fleshed fruit such as peaches should "give," that is, yield slightly, when you press them with your finger. You probably already know not to buy fruit with soft spots and bruises. Unless you want to eat the fruit right away, buy it slightly underripe and let it ripen at home on the counter. You can put fruit in a brown paper bag to make it ripen faster.

Once fruit is ripe, store it in the refrigerator (with the exception of bananas, which you should store on the counter). You can store fruit loose or in plastic bags—preferably vegetable storage bags. In the upcoming sections, you find guidelines for how long you can store individual fruits but, as with vegetables, use your eyes, nose, and common sense to decide if fruit is bad. Keep fruit longer than indicated if it still seems fresh; discard it if it does not. Some fruits are useful for cooking when past their prime eating time—overripe bananas make great banana bread, for instance.

Fruit is sweet, juicy, and likable. It's hard to believe it's so *good* for you! There's no cholesterol and no fat in most fruit, so it's filling without being fattening. And fruit has a lot going for it: You can use fruit to make simple desserts that replace fatty, fattening cakes and pies. First, however, you have to understand what different fruits have to offer and how you can use them to your advantage. Try some of the more unusual varieties as well as the old familiar ones.

Apples

The apple is a basic year-round fruit, though the freshest crop is in the fall, when you can buy apples that haven't been in storage. Look for fruit that is unbruised and appears crisp. The best baking apples are *York Imperial, Rome Beauty,* and *Cortland.* Good pie apples include *Granny Smith, Rhode Island Greening, Golden Delicious, Newtown Pippin, Northern Spy, Stayman,* and *Idared.* For applesauce you can use pie apples plus *McIntosh, Macoun, Jonathan, Winesap,* or *Gravenstein.* Apples keep for weeks. Cut apples darken on exposure to air, so sprinkle or brush the cut flesh with lemon juice.

Something Simple

Almost everyone loves applesauce from the time they eat it as babies. Here is the simplest recipe for applesauce you can find: wash and cut up 8 apples and put them—seeds, core, and all—in a deep saucepan with a $1/2$ cup of sugar and $1/2$ teaspoon of ground cinnamon. Add a tablespoon of lemon juice if you wish. Cover the pan and cook the apples over low heat, stirring them occasionally, until they are soft. Then press the ingredients through a strainer.

Apricots

This small, bright-orange fruit is at its peak in summer. Apricots should "give" but not feel soft, and the ones with the most flavor have a pleasant floral fragrance. Avoid the hard green ones. Store ripe fruit 4–5 days. Dried apricots, like all dried fruit, keep best in a plastic bag in the refrigerator moisture drawer.

Bananas

This is another year-round fruit, and it is best when it's bright yellow with no brown spots. There are red varieties too, which are shorter and sweeter than the yellows. They too are best when unspotted. Bananas sweeten and the skin becomes darker with age. Brown spots don't mean the fruit is bad, but if the banana is completely dark, use it for baking breads and cakes. Don't store bananas in the refrigerator; it changes the texture.

Berries

Except for cranberries, berries are spring and summer fruit. Look for plump fruit that glistens but doesn't look wet. If the berries are packed in cartons, lift the carton to see if there are fruit stains. If there are, it means the fruit on the bottom is crushed. Buy another box. Avoid berries with mold. Berries are fragile and perishable. Put them in the refrigerator and eat them within a day or so. Rinse them quickly just before you eat them. To freeze berries, put them, unrinsed, in a single layer on a jelly roll pan. When they're frozen solid, transfer them to a double plastic bag for long-term storage.

Raspberries may be available through the late fall. Strawberries are available in the early spring and throughout the summer. The tastiest ones are the small ones, even though the big ones may look better. Don't buy strawberries with lots of white near the stem. Remove the stem after you rinse the fruit, otherwise the berries may get mushy.

Fein on Food

Strawberries are one of the most popular fruits in the world and have been for some time. Over 400 years ago, an English physician named William Butler said, "doubtless God could have made a better berry, but… God never did." King Henry VIII planted strawberries in his garden, and Cardinal Wolsey (who, when played by Orson Welles in the movie *A Man for All Seasons*, looked like he knew how to eat) was the first to think of serving strawberries with cream. Strawberries were so highly regarded that the leaves were used to symbolize the rank of duke.

You usually have to buy cranberries in bags, and they are available only from September through December. Cranberries should be firm and evenly colored. You can keep them in the bag for a month in the refrigerator or for a year in the freezer. You needn't thaw them for recipes. At the end of the season, cranberries get cheaper. Buy a couple bags and put them in your freezer so you can have homemade cranberry sauce in the spring or summer. You'd be surprised how this can lift your spirits and make meals less boring.

Carambolas

This unusual, golden-yellow exotic fruit has deep brown-edged ridges. When you slice it, the pieces look like stars—it's sometimes called "star fruit." It is available from August through late winter. The entire fruit is edible. You can slice it and eat it raw (you need not peel it), though it makes a terrific salad ingredient and a great-looking garnish. Carambolas have a tart, plum-like flavor and are crispy. Buy the ones that look shiny and moist. They last up to two weeks in the fridge.

Cherries

Cherries are at their best in late spring and summer. Look for firm, plump, evenly colored fruit. Sweet cherries are darker than sour, bright red ones. Keep cherries about 4 days.

Citrus Fruits

Most citrus fruits are available for most of the year, but grapefruit and tangerines are best in the winter. Citrus fruits are hardy and keep several weeks. You can store citrus fruit loose instead of using a plastic bag.

You don't eat lemons or limes as fruit, but they are extremely useful for cooking. The best ones have thin, smooth skins. Thicker skinned lemons with bumpy ends have less juice than the others. In addition to the juice, the skins of the lemon and lime (also called the "peel," "rind," or "zest") are also used in recipes.

Look for well-rounded grapefruit with tight, smooth skin. Pink grapefruit are sweeter than yellow varieties.

There are two basic types of oranges: those for eating and those for juicing. Navel oranges, without seeds, are good to eat. Juice oranges are thin skinned and have lots of seeds. An orange's skin should be smooth, and a spot of green here and there on the surface is okay.

Tangerines have loose, dark orange skin. They are more fragile than oranges and last up to two weeks. Tangelos are a cross of tangerines and grapefruit. They are juicier and more tart than tangerines.

Figs

Figs are fragile fruit that come to market in late summer and fall. There are green and purple varieties, all of which are tender with abundant seeds inside. You eat the entire fruit—skin, seeds and all, fresh or cooked. Figs deteriorate quickly, so you must eat them within a day or so of purchase.

Something Simple

If you're looking for a quick, glamorous first course for dinner, buy some prosciutto ham and wrap a piece around a fresh fig (or, if it's big, half a fig). That's all there is to it. Want a glamorous brunch dish? Boil 2 cups of water with a 1/2 cup of sugar and a slice of lemon. Add some fresh figs, remove the pan from the heat, add 1/2 teaspoon of vanilla extract if you'd like, and let the fruit cool. Serve the figs plain or with cream.

Grapes

Green, red, purple, and black grapes are available all year. Look for thick, firm stems that are moist looking and not withered. The fruit should be plump and firm. Grapes keep several days.

Kiwi Fruit

You would never guess that inside this small, unassuming oval fruit with the fuzzy brown skin is flesh that is bright green, like a gemstone emerald. Its taste is a treasure, too, like a cross between a melon and a raspberry. Look for fruit with "give." Kiwi fruit are available year-round. You can keep them approximately 10 days. You can't eat the peel, so peel the fruit or slice it in half and scoop the flesh out.

> **Fein on Food**
>
> Kiwis became popular in the 1980s, though they were first imported from New Zealand in the 1950s. They were called "Chinese gooseberries" then, but didn't catch on because of the name. At that time, anything that smacked of communist leanings was bound to be a loser.

Mangoes

This tropical fruit is best in late spring. There are two types, oval and kidney shaped, in a variety of colors: red, orange, and yellow. The surface should "give." Green, hard mangoes don't ripen well. Mangoes are juicy and have a spicy flavor. You use them for cooking and eating. They often are difficult to peel, but the taste is worth the effort.

To peel a mango, score the skin with a sharp paring knife into wide, long strips. Pierce the skin near the top and pull back each strip between the knife and your finger. Then cut the flesh into slices down to the pit and scrape each slice from the pit with your knife.

Melons

Melons are summer fruit. Their flesh contains a high percentage of water so, with few exceptions, you cannot cook with them. Melons do not sweeten as they soften, they just get juicier. Whole cantaloupes and honeydews should "give" when you press at the ends. Another way to tell ripe melons is to knock on the surface. If you hear a hollow sound, the fruit is fine. Melons keep 4–5 days. Cut melons last about 3 days.

Cantaloupes are small and round with a netted surface and smooth orange flesh. The best ones have a fragrance you can smell when you lift the fruit. *Honeydews* are large, green-fleshed, and juicy. *Watermelons* are large, either oval or round, and have dark green skin or green and white striped skin. The flesh usually is red, though there are some yellow varieties. Unless you are feeding an army, it is sensible to buy cut watermelon. Look for rich, uniformly red, moist-looking flesh and dark black seeds.

Less familiar but sweet and tasty are *Casaba* melons, which are round, with ridged yellow skin and creamy flesh; and *Cranshaw* melons, which are large and quite aromatic, with mottled skin and spicy flavored, pale orange flesh.

Papayas

This tropical fruit looks like a tall, fat pear that starts out green and turns yellow when ripe. It tastes similar to melon but is hardier and lasts 7–10 days. Buy papayas with "give."

Peaches and Nectarines

These summer fruits are similar, and for culinary purposes are interchangeable. There is only one way to tell which ones are really good: you have to smell them. Only the ones with the flowery fragrance will ever taste like they are supposed to. Color is irrelevant to ripeness or flavor. Nectarines are sturdier than peaches and last a few days longer (about 7–8 days) in the refrigerator. Peaches will keep 5–6 days. You must peel peaches for cooking, but not nectarines (peach skins are tougher).

Fein on Food

During the Dark Ages, when Western Civilization was at its lowest point, art, literature, and gastronomy flourished in China. The cultural elite looked forward to a special banquet known as the "Feast of Peaches." All sorts of epicurean delights were served, but the *raison d'être* of the dinner was the peaches, which were said to come from trees that bore fruit only once every several thousand years.

Pears

Everyone asks why pears in the store are always hard as rocks. The reason is that pears, unlike most fruit (which benefits from tree-ripening) are harvested and sent to market before they're ripe—when they're rock-hard. Growers have found that pears that ripen after they're harvested and kept at room temperature for several days taste better and have a better texture than partially or fully tree-ripened fruit. Strange but true. Keep pears out on the counter for several days and they will become buttery-tender. Be careful though—pears bruise easily. The place where you accidentally hit them will be a soft spot, like a black and blue mark. You'll know when they're ripe, because they "give" and have a sweet floral scent.

There are several varieties of pears, most of which are available during the fall and winter. You have to taste each to see which you like. All pears are fine for eating out of hand, except the Seckel, which is hard and grainy and is usually used for preserves. The best pears for baking and pies are Comice, Bosc, and Anjou. Ripe pears will keep 4–5 days.

Something Simple

Here's a special dessert that takes almost no time at all to prepare. Peel some pears, cut them in half lengthwise, and remove their cores. Brush the cut surfaces with lemon juice. Fill the hollows with sweetened cream cheese or, better yet, mascarpone cheese. Sprinkle the cheese with chopped toasted nuts (especially hazelnuts or almonds), and serve.

Pineapples

This tropical fruit comes from Hawaii or Central America. Though all pineapples are high in sugar, the Hawaiian ones are sweeter. They should have a floral smell, but if the scent is overwhelmingly fragrant it can mean overripe fruit. The center leaves of the stalk should come out easily, and the bottom should be tender but not overly soft. Pineapples keep 4–5 days.

Plums

Plums are summer and fall fruit, depending on the variety. They should be firm and plump with tight looking skins. Green and yellow varieties are harder than the red varieties. You can keep them about a week. Though most people eat them out of hand, plums are perfect for poaching, baking, and in pies. They keep about 5 days.

Rhubarb

This is a spring and summer vegetable that we eat as a fruit. Because it is so acidic, rhubarb requires bountiful amounts of sugar. The stalks resemble celery and are either slim and light pinkish-green (hothouse rhubarb) or thick and dark red (field rhubarb). You can't eat rhubarb raw.

Because of its acidic nature, rhubarb is a terrific side dish for rich meats and poultry such as duck, turkey, and pork. It used to be called "pieplant" because it is such a tasty pie ingredient, especially when combined with strawberries. Most rhubarb is sold without the leaves because the leaves are poisonous, and you should never eat them.

> **Something Simple**
>
> Need another easier-than-you-can-believe recipe? Cut $1^1/_2$ pounds of rhubarb into $^1/_2$"-thick slices and put it in a stainless steel or enamel pan with $^3/_4$ cup sugar and 2 tablespoons of water or orange juice. Cover the pan and cook the mixture over moderate heat for 10 minutes. Remove the cover and cook another 5–6 minutes, stirring the ingredients occasionally. Chill well before serving.

The Least You Need to Know

➤ Buy fruit in season.

➤ Soft-fleshed fruits should "give" to indicate ripeness, although certain varieties (such as nectarines, peaches, apricots, melons, and pineapple) also should smell fragrant when ripe.

➤ Keep underripe fruit on the countertop until it ripens (or in a paper bag for faster ripening). Then store it in the refrigerator, except for bananas.

Chapter 9

A Trip to the Dairy Barn and Down the Grocery Aisles

In This Chapter

➤ Essential dairy products

➤ Buying eggs

➤ Selecting and storing canned goods and packages

➤ Buying coffee and tea

➤ A few simple non-recipes

Everyone knows how to buy a quart of milk, right? And you probably also know how to buy butter or margarine and ice cream. You don't need lessons on this stuff. But some details are worth repeating. Besides, there's always some little tidbit of information, even about everyday groceries, that can help you be a better and more confident cook. Sometimes the small, seemingly insignificant detail—for example, most good cooks recommend sweet, unsalted butter for recipes—makes a world of difference.

This chapter goes over these everyday items, offering buying and storing suggestions. You'll also uncover some crumbs of information here and there that might come in handy when you start to cook and serve meals.

Discussing Dairy Products

Dairy products include milk—usually cow's milk (sheep, goat and buffalo milks are used for certain cheeses and yogurt)—and all foods based on milk: butter, cheese, cream, ice cream, and yogurt.

While margarine, tofu, and eggs are technically not dairy products, they are classified as dairy for purposes of organization.

Butter

In the United States, butter comes in either one pound blocks or four quarter-pound sticks. There are 8 tablespoons in each stick and each stick equals a half cup. That means a pound of butter is 32 tablespoons, or 2 cups. *Whipped butter* has air whipped into it, giving it terrific spreadability. Use it for toast or to fry an egg if you want, but don't expect it to work as a substitute for stick butter in recipes. The two don't measure up the same way.

There are two types of butter: *sweet* and *lightly salted*. However, the word "sweet" is a misnomer: there's no sugar or any other sweetener in it. It means it's made from sweet cream and is simply plain butter, without salt. Sweet butter has a more delicate flavor than the salted kind, and for that reason it is the butter of choice for recipes. Most recipes assume you're using sweet butter. Therefore, if you use salted butter you should cut down the amount of salt the recipe calls for. Sweet butter usually costs a few cents more per pound than salted. Butter lasts for up to two weeks in the refrigerator and up to a year in the freezer.

Margarine

In many cases, margarine (which is solidified vegetable fat) serves as a substitute for butter. You can use it to sauté or in cakes and pies, for example. In addition, margarine is softer than butter, so it spreads more easily. However, it isn't as rich as butter and is, therefore, unsuitable for butter-based sauces such as Hollandaise or *beurre blanc*.

Margarine is derived from various oils—corn, canola, soybean, and so on. And even among various brands of margarine there are many differences in the ingredients (some have more water, for example), which affect flavor, texture, and cooking qualities. Ultimately, what you choose depends on your taste buds.

What Are All Those Cheeses?

Cheese is a cook's good friend. You can serve certain varieties for hors d'oeuvre and other varieties for dessert, so when you first learn to cook, you can count on cheese for those parts of the meal you don't want to fuss with while you concentrate on the entree. Come to think of it, experienced cooks rely on cheese for the same reasons.

Something Simple

Is this a joke? Cheese for dessert? No, it isn't a joke. Stilton cheese and juicy comice pears is a classic duo. So is sharp cheddar cheese with crisp apples or Brie cheese with grapes. Soft ripened cheeses, semisoft cheeses, and blue-veined cheeses are the smartest choices for dessert, paired with grapes, peaches, pears, apples, apricots, or oranges. There are three advantages to serving fruit and cheese for dessert: You don't have to fuss; it's delicious; and everyone will think you are sophisticated and intelligent. You may accompany the cheese and fruit with a dessert wine such as Port, Sauterne, or Zinfandel, and with nuts.

There are so many kinds of cheese—and new ones coming to market every day—that it's difficult to decide what to buy. Some cheeses are mild, some assertive. There are sheep's milk, goat's milk, cow's milk cheeses, and so on. Some smell so intense you should make sure you're with good friends before you open the package. No cheese should have a rancid odor though—even the most robust one should smell fresh, not stale. Don't buy rank-smelling cheese, and if any of your stored cheese starts to smell foul, throw it out.

The assertive, even, shall we say, *odoriferous* cheeses, are among the tastiest and most interesting though, and if you haven't given them a chance, consider them as you expand your culinary repertoire. In the following lists, we group some of the more commonly available cheeses by type. If you wanted to serve a cheeseboard with cocktails, you would pick from among different categories, not two in the same category. For example, you might serve these cheeses together: Brie, Port Salut, and Cheddar; or Pont L'Eveque, Gouda, and Fourme D'Ambert; or Chevre, Jarlsberg, and Saga. Most importantly, try out a number of kinds, and experiment to find your favorites.

➤ Moist white cheeses such as *cottage cheese, cream cheese,* and *ricotta* are mild. They perish quickly, so check the dates on the packages. Keep these cheeses in covered containers and use them within 7–8 days. Use them to eat on crackers, make spreads, or cook recipes such as cheesecake and lasagna.

➤ Soft cheeses such as *Brie, Camembert, Boursin, Boursault,* and *Pont L'Eveque* are useful for both hors d'oeuvre or dessert. Keep them in plastic wrap, changing the wrap every other day, for about 2 weeks.

➤ Semisoft cheeses such as *Muenster, Gouda, Monterey Jack, Havarti,* and *Port Salut* are suitable with cocktails. They also melt well, so they are terrific for grilled cheese and macaroni and cheese. If you change the wrap every few days, these cheeses will last for 2–3 weeks.

➤ Firm cheeses such as *Cheddar, Edam, Fontina, Jarlsberg,* and *Emmanthaler* are perfect at either end of the meal, and you can cook with them because they melt beautifully. If you change the plastic wrap every few days, these will last over a month. If you see any mold, cut it away, but don't throw away the cheese. You can still use it for cooking—even those portions that have cracked or hardened.

➤ Hard cheeses such as *Parmesan* and *Romano* should be firm, but not dry and cracked. They store beautifully for months if you wrap them in plastic wrap and change the wrap every few days. Most accomplished cooks regard these cheeses as staples and would never use the pre-grated canned varieties. The best Parmesan cheese is called *Parmesan-Reggiano*. You can use young, still-pliable Parmesan and Romano cheeses for dessert, but their primary purpose is for cooking. Grate Parmesan or Romano cheese just before you use it for a more intense flavor. Ungrated cheese lasts longer, too.

➤ Blue-veined cheeses such as *Stilton, Blue, Roquefort, Gorgonzola, Saga,* and *Fourme D'Ambert* have varying textures that range from creamy to hard. You can serve any of them for hors d'oeuvre or dessert. They also are super when you crumble them into salad. Wrap them well and change the plastic wrap every few days. These cheeses last over a month.

➤ *Goat* (Chevre) *cheese* is tangy and aromatic and comes in an assortment of shapes and sizes. Some are creamy, some firm, some plain, others covered with ash or herbs. Goat cheese is useful for hors d'oeuvre or dessert, and it is outstanding as a first course at dinner or crumbled into a green salad. Change the plastic wrap every other day and it will last up to 2 weeks.

Something Simple

Here's an easy "almost" recipe for a first course at dinner: cut some goat cheese into small rounds about $1/2$" thick, put them on a plate, and sprinkle each one with a teaspoon of olive oil. Grind some fresh black pepper over them, and sprinkle with a small amount of freshly minced rosemary, thyme, savory, or chives.

➤ Sheep's milk cheeses such as *Feta,* are tangy, sharp, and sometimes salty. You can use them in casseroles or salads. Change the plastic wrap every few days, and sheep's cheese will last up to 3 weeks.

NEVER... serve cheese cold. One of the most important rules of the cheese road is to keep cheese refrigerated but not serve it cold (except for cottage cheese, cream cheese, and ricotta, which aren't typical hors d'oeuvre and dessert cheeses). Let cheese stand at room temperature for at least an hour before you plan to serve it.

➤ *Fresh mozzarella* has become a fashionable table and salad cheese over the past few years. There also is Buffalo Mozzarella, which is tangier than the cow's milk kind. Fresh mozzarella is delicate and spongy, tasting somewhat like solidified milk. It deteriorates quickly, lasting only a few days in the fridge. Keep it immersed in cold water and covered with plastic wrap. (You also could use an air-tight covered container.) Change the water every day.

➤ *Packaged mozzarella* just doesn't cut it for out of hand eating because it is too rubbery. However, it is absolutely fine for cooking. It lasts much longer than fresh mozzarella, and you can freeze it, too, for up to 6 months. For refrigerator storage, change the plastic wrap every few days. It lasts about 2 weeks.

Understanding Categories of Cream

Cream spoils quickly, though there's less chance of spoilage with "ultrapasteurized" cream. Check the date carefully and buy the one with the latest date if you have a choice. Heavy cream (36 percent milkfat) is especially perishable. Before you beat it to make whipped cream, pour a drop on your finger and taste it. If it's spoiled, you'll know.

Cream is useful for several purposes, one of which is to enrich sauces and soups. Just a generation ago, people used more cream than they do today, when we are looking to cut dietary fat. That doesn't mean you have to throw out all your old favorite recipes; most of them can be adapted by using lighter creams such as half and half. The dish won't be as rich, but still can be delicious.

When cream is marked *ultrapasteurized*, it means the cream has been heated briefly to extremely high temperatures that destroy bacteria. This greatly increases shelf life (though it inhibits the cream's whipping qualities).

You can't use light cream (18–30 percent milkfat) or half and half (10–18 percent) for whipped cream, but you needn't use heavy cream. Medium ("whipping") cream (30–36 percent) whips well, too, though heavy cream holds its shape better. Cream lasts from 7–10 days. Make sure the container is closed as tightly as possible.

Sour cream also has gone on a diet. There's the standard kind (18 percent fat), but also low-fat and non-fat varieties. They differ in taste and texture, but for most purposes can be used interchangeably in recipes. Sour cream lasts over 2 weeks.

Creme Fraiche is a tangy cultured cream similar to sour cream or yogurt. You can use it as a dessert topping or to enrich soups and sauces. You can buy creme fraiche in some supermarkets and specialty stores. Or—make your own (see the sauces section in the recipes).

America's Favorite Dessert—Ice Cream

Ice cream and other frozen desserts, such as sherbet, frozen yogurt, and so on, should be the last items you buy when you shop. They defrost quickly and become crystallized more easily the longer they are out of the freezer. These items lose a lot in taste and texture after 3–4 weeks, when they become gummy. Eat them in a hurry (as if you have to be told).

Making the Most of Milk

Milk is available as whole milk (which has about 3.5 percent fat), low fat (2 percent, 1 percent, and $1/2$ percent), and skim (less than $1/2$ percent). You can use them interchangeably in most recipes with a less rich result for lower fat varieties. Acidophilus milk has added bacterial cultures that help people maintain bacterial balance in their digestive tracts. It frequently is recommended for those who are taking antibiotics and for those who are lactose-intolerant.

Buttermilk also has bacterial cultures added, but while acidophilus milk tastes like regular milk, buttermilk has a tart flavor. It is available in low fat or skim varieties. Buttermilk is underutilized in American kitchens. Yet it is one of the handiest items to have, especially if you like to bake. It helps assure that pie crusts, biscuits and scones will be flaky, quickbreads will be tender and crumbly, and pancakes will be rich and fluffy. You can use buttermilk to replace cream in many soups and sauces. The dish will taste tangier. Buttermilk also is a terrific thirst quencher on torrid days. You can drink it straight or process it with some fresh fruit. It lasts over 2 weeks in the refrigerator.

Yogurt

Yogurt is considered a snack food, but you also can cook with the most common varieties (plain, coffee, lemon, and vanilla, for example). It is a perfect substitute for more fatty sour cream in many traditional recipes for dips and sauces. It also is an outstanding ingredient for thirst-quenching beverages and is ideal for baking, giving baked goods much the same qualities as buttermilk does. Yogurt lasts over 2 weeks.

Tofu

Tofu is made from soybeans and sometimes is called bean curd. Tofu looks and feels like cheese. It has a smooth, moist, satiny texture. There are firm and soft varieties, and fresh and packaged varieties. You have to keep the fresh kind in water (change it every day) and eat it within 4–5 days. The packaged kind lasts longer until you open it, but you have to finish it within 2–3 days (with a fresh change of water every day). Tofu is bland and absorbs other flavors well, so it is especially good for soups, stews, stir fries, or other sauced dishes.

Eggs

Eggs have had some hard times lately. Because they're loaded with cholesterol, people are trying to figure out how not to use them. On the other hand, eggs are one of nature's perfect foods, with plenty of high-quality protein and vitamin A. They also are one of the kitchen's most useful staples—not just for eating alone, but in all sorts of recipes: custards and quiches, cakes and breads, cookies and meringue, and more. Most recipes assume that you are using "large" eggs. Egg size depends on the weight of a *dozen* eggs. Large eggs are a minimum of 24 ounces per dozen; jumbo eggs are 30 ounces per dozen. Therefore, you can't substitute one for the other without doing some arithmetic.

Because eggs are a source of salmonella, a type of food poisoning, be sure to cook eggs thoroughly and do not use raw eggs for recipes. Wash your hands carefully before and after handling eggs.

The color of an egg's shell (white or brown) makes no difference in taste or cooking. People in certain parts of the country simply prefer one color to the other. The grade of egg makes a difference though. Gradings are based how thick the white is and how firm and rounded the yolk is. When you crack open an egg and the white is thick and gloppy, that's good. If it runs out in a thin stream like a leaky faucet, it isn't. Eggs become more runny as they age. You can use a runny raw egg for cooking, but it won't taste terrific for breakfast. Never use an egg that is cracked or that smells foul or is spotted with blood when you crack it open.

While many refrigerators have special egg-holding spots, it is better to keep eggs in the carton. They stay fresher that way. Eggs last about a month. If you separate egg parts for cooking, you can store the yolks for 2–3 days in a covered container; the whites will keep for a week. You also can freeze the whites (one white fits neatly into a typical ice cube freezer section).

Kitchen Clue
When using eggs in a recipe, crack them one at a time into a cup, and add each to the other ingredients singly. That way, if one egg is spoiled, you can throw it away.

Fein on Food

It's the age-old question: which came first, the chicken or the egg? Well, according to the Bible used by Christians and Jews, the answer is... the chicken. Genesis I:20–22 says, "...Let birds fly above the earth across the firmament of the heavens. So God created... every living creature that moves... and every winged bird according to its kind."

About Canned, Jarred, and Packaged Goods

Choosing canned foods is simple. Other than deciding whether you prefer brand name or generic products, the only guidelines have to do with what you shouldn't do. Don't buy cans that bulge, that are dented or rusted, that don't have labels, or that leak. Also, don't buy cans whose labels have been taped back on. Discard cans in your cabinet that bulge, that spray out loud with a hissing sound when you open them, or whose contents smell bad. All of these are indications of spoilage and poor maintenance. Don't store leftovers in their cans either. Food deteriorates more rapidly in the can and takes on a metallic taste.

Jellies and preserves in jars keep indefinitely on the shelf and, when opened, in the refrigerator. Sometimes preserves become crystallized in the fridge, but they're still useful—just cut away the sugary stuff. Mayonnaise, worcestershire sauce, ketchup, mustard, and similar jarred ingredients also keep indefinitely on the shelf; once you open them, store them in the refrigerator. Food items that come in jars (vegetables, for example) last a couple of days in the refrigerator once they're opened. Salsas last a while longer. You can store these items in the jars with their covers tightly closed.

Many packaged goods such as crackers have "sell by" dates. These foods taste better before those dates but aren't spoiled after that time. Grainy packaged items such as cookies, crackers, and cereals will keep fresher and crisper if you transfer them to air-tight plastic containers. Keep chips in their bags, but close the bags tightly.

Unless the container says otherwise, you can keep all unopened canned, jarred, and packaged items in cabinets. That includes peanut butter, instant coffee, chocolate chips, rice, sugar, flour, dried beans, oil, vinegar, and the like. Most last indefinitely, though flour can taste stale after 9–10 months.

How About Coffee?

If you're not finicky about coffee, the only decision you have to make is which brand to buy. That's a matter of taste. Just be sure you buy the right grind for your coffeemaker—automatic drip coffeemakers use drip grind, percolators use perk grind, and so on. You can store unused coffee in the can with the plastic cover on. For a fresher taste, keep the can in the refrigerator—or freezer, if you use less than a pound per week.

Coffee lovers may want to buy whole beans instead of pre-canned coffee. (There's more about this in the chapter on beverages.) Keep extra beans in the refrigerator or, even better, in the freezer. There are several types of whole bean coffee, from all parts of the world and with a multitude of flavors. You can grind your own beans or have them ground for you in the store.

Tea

Stores offer a huge variety of commercial teas in individual tea bags. Tea bags contain blends of different types of tea. You can buy herbal teas and flavored teas in bags too. Tea lovers who are more particular can buy selected teas and tea blends (all available in tea bags) that have richer flavor than the commercial blends. Well-known tea blends of this type include English or Irish Breakfast Tea and Earl Gray. Single teas of this type include Darjeeling, Oolung, Keemun, and Ceylon. Loose tea also is available. (There's more on brewing tea in the chapter on beverages.) Store tea in an airtight container in a dark place for maximum freshness and flavor.

The Least You Need to Know

➤ Fresh eggs have thick whites and rounded yolks. Older eggs are thin and runny, but may be used for cooking recipes. Discard any eggs whose shells are cracked or that smell foul or contain blood spots when you crack them.

➤ Don't buy or use food in cans that bulge, are rusted, dented, or leaky, or don't have labels attached.

➤ Keep coffee or coffee beans in the refrigerator or freezer.

Part 4
Getting Ready to Cook

You must be shopped out by now. Your drawers and cabinets are filled with gadgets and goodies. Now the fun begins—you're ready to cook.

Or are you? You can't just cook, you've got to know how. Do you know how to choose a good recipe? To carry out recipe instructions? To measure ingredients? If a recipe tells you to "fold in" whipped cream, will you know what to do? Is folding whipped cream anything like folding laundry? If the recipe tells you to sauté chicken, will you know what that means and what to sauté the chicken in?

If you're not sure about cooking "how-to's," keep reading. In the next few chapters, I will show you how to read and follow a recipe so it works for you. I will explain how to measure ingredients and how you can substitute one ingredient for another. And I will explain the various cooking terms and cooking methods you'll need to know to be a confident and competent cook.

Organizing Your Game Plan

In This Chapter

➤ Reading a recipe

➤ Choosing and using a good recipe

➤ Planning your cooking strategy

➤ Planning how to serve the meal

Now that you know how to sniff out a ripe peach, tell the difference between a frying chicken and a roaster, and recognize lemongrass when you see it, you're on the way to becoming a virtuoso cook. All you have to do is learn some fundamental cooking techniques. Of course you can read cookbooks and gain bits of culinary wisdom from good cooks, but the best way to master the techniques is to get in the kitchen and start cooking. You will learn from practice and, yes, from your mistakes. Since it's almost time for you to actually cook a meal, this chapter tells you how to go about choosing recipes, organizing the meal preparations, and serving the meal you prepare.

A Good Meal Begins with a Good Recipe

Some people, even beginners, are instinctive cooks. They know without reading a recipe that if they add some chopped parsley and a few squirts of lemon juice to steamed white rice, it will taste pretty good. But most people, especially people who feel unsure in the kitchen, need recipes. So recipes are important before you begin to cook. As you practice cooking, you'll see how and why good recipes work—and bad ones don't.

You can approach cooking with recipes in two ways. The first way is to discover a recipe for a dish that sounds good. The second is to think about what you want to eat and then find a recipe for it. Either way, there is one basic rule you should follow once you have the recipe in front of you: Read, read, read! Reading is the Enlightenment; not reading is the Dark Ages.

Reading means *careful* reading, of course. Misreading is one of the biggest pitfalls of cooking, and it's often the reason people consider themselves bad cooks when they really aren't.

How to Read a Recipe

A well-written recipe lists the ingredients in the order they're used. It usually states the quantity to the left and the ingredient to the right, as shown here:

"8 apples"

Sometimes the ingredient is more specifically described. For example, because apple pie is made with a different kind of apple than applesauce is, an apple pie recipe may say:

"8 Granny Smith apples" or "8 pie apples"

In addition, sometimes there is an instruction directly before or after the named ingredient:

"8 Granny Smith apples, peeled, cored, and sliced"

or

"8 peeled, cored, and sliced Granny Smith apples."

That gives you precise instructions without going into lengthy detail in the instruction section. Once you know how to peel, core, and slice an apple, you'll be grateful for this shortcut; you won't have to read it every time.

A very helpful recipe gives alternative amounts, like this:

"8 Granny Smith apples, peeled, cored and sliced (about 3 lbs. or 8–9 cups)"

Or like this:

"8 cups of peeled, sliced apples; about 8 apples or 3 lbs."

Then you know precisely how many apples to buy. Once you make this recipe a few times, if you see another apple recipe, you'll know that a certain number of apples of that size weighs an approximate amount and equals a certain number of cups of sliced fruit.

Judgment Calls

Some recipes call for a cook's judgment. A "pinch of salt" or "salt to taste" are ones that seem to annoy many people. Recipe writers do this for two reasons.

100

First, they do it to let you know that when they say "pinch" they mean for you to use a teeny amount but that exactness isn't critical. If you have small fingers, your pinch will be a bit different than that of a person who has large hands. The point is, it doesn't matter, and you shouldn't feel imprisoned by minutiae. No one would actually want to bother counting precise grains of salt, would they?

The second reason is that people's tastes are different, especially when it comes to seasoning. When a recipe says "salt to taste," you should taste the dish, add the seasoning, and taste the dish again. This helps you focus on how much of the ingredient you like, and it encourages you to trust your taste buds, not someone else's.

There are other kinds of judgment calls in a recipe; some recipes give "options." A recipe for blueberry muffins, for example, may say:

"1 tsp. freshly grated orange peel, optional"

That lets you know that you can vary the taste and texture of the dish by using the optional ingredient, but that the recipe doesn't depend on it.

Other recipes give "choices." For example, a recipe for sautéed chicken may call for the following:

"1/2 cup white wine or chicken stock"

or

"1 tsp. fresh thyme or rosemary leaves"

That means the recipe works whether you use wine or stock, or thyme or rosemary, and you can decide which you like better, or use the one you have on hand. If you have both ingredients, try it one way one time, and the other way the next time. You'll soon realize that you can improvise in other recipes too—even the ones that don't offer alternatives. Next time you see a recipe for sautéed chicken that calls for stock, you'll know that you can probably use white wine.

> ### Fein on Food
>
> Old-time recipes require lots of judgment calls. In fact, the person who gave the recipe usually assumed that anyone preparing the recipe would know how to cook. Look in antique cookbooks, especially community cookbooks and those from charitable organizations. Look at your grandmother's spiral recipe notebook. Some recipes say things like "Bake as usual," or "Cook in a hot oven until done." Hmmmm. Still, these recipes can be treasures. To salvage such a recipe, find a similar recipe to see how the dish is prepared. Then you'll know what "bake as usual" means. A "hot oven" means 400 degrees or above, a "moderate oven" 350 degrees, and a "slow oven" 300 degrees or less. Knowing when it's "done" depends on the recipe and is discussed in Chapter 16.

What Else You See in a Recipe

Recipe instructions usually follow the list of ingredients. The instructions will tell you at what temperature to cook the dish and how long it will take until the dish is done. The instructions may also tell you how many people the recipe will serve (or sometimes this information comes at the beginning of the recipe, right after the title). Informative recipes specify any special pans or utensils you might need. Some recipes tell you how long it will probably take you to prepare and/or cook the food, and some provide nutritional information.

How Can You Tell If a Recipe Is a Good One?

A good recipe is like a map to buried treasure. Both give logical and concise clues, and when you figure them out, you get something really valuable in the end. So, in the first place, look for the logic—that is, be sure the ingredients are listed in the order they're used. Why would a writer list 2 TB. chopped chives first when the chives are added as a garnish at the end? Ingredients listed out of sequence are distracting; you can't follow the recipe because you're too busy looking through a confusing list. The recipe may, in fact, work; but if it's confusing, you're more apt to forget a step or an ingredient, and it won't come out right.

To find out if the ingredients are listed in order, you have to read the instructions. When you do, you will notice if an ingredient has been omitted from the recipe by mistake (for example, if the recipe says, "mix the sugar and the egg yolks together," but there are no eggs listed). Sometimes this happens on purpose if you ask for a recipe from someone who really doesn't want to give it to you. If it does happen, by mistake or on purpose, the recipe is useless. A good recipe tells all.

Speaking of telling all, a good recipe should also be descriptive. When it says "cook until thick," it should tell you *how* thick. Thick enough to coat the back of a spoon? As thick as ketchup?

Good recipes should describe time elements in two ways when appropriate, such as, "Cook for about 10 minutes OR until the sauce thickens enough to coat the back of a spoon." Suppose you cooked the sauce for "about" 10 minutes, and it was still as thin as consommé? Or as thick as jellied cranberry sauce? Your stovetop may cook more quickly. The ingredients you used may be colder or warmer than the writer's. Cooking times are approximate; it's important to know what the dish should look like.

Descriptions also should cover pan size where applicable. For example, a cake recipe ought to tell you the size cake pan to use. If the cake is supposed to be baked in two 8" cake pans and you use one 8" square pan—well, you can guess what happens. And if you use two 10" cake pans for the same amount of batter, you're going to have flapjacks instead of layer cake.

Sometimes giving sizes isn't absolutely necessary. For example, if you have to beat eggs and sugar, and the recipe doesn't say "beat eggs and sugar in a

102

medium bowl," the recipe will be fine no matter what size bowl you use. Common sense is important here. You know you can use a small bowl to beat one egg but will need a large pot to fit apples for applesauce.

Kitchen Clue
Recipes have to be descriptive and concise. For example, a writer won't describe "stir-fry" in every stir-fry recipe. The recipe assumes you know what that means. Those who don't will have to learn about stir-frying before they prepare the recipe. Chapter 15 covers basic cooking techniques.

A good recipe should also tell how many people it will serve. Most of the time quantities are averages. Some people eat more, some less. After awhile, you'll know if one broiler-fryer chicken is enough for your family, or if you always have a piece of chicken left over for lunch.

Good recipes don't contain obvious errors, so use some common sense. You know a recipe can't possibly work if it calls for $\frac{1}{4}$ cup of baking soda when every other recipe for that calls for $\frac{1}{4}$ teaspoon. A recipe that calls for teeny amounts of certain ingredients can't possibly be right either. A pinch of salt or an $\frac{1}{8}$ teaspoon nutmeg is okay, but $\frac{1}{4}$ teaspoon ketchup? How can $\frac{1}{4}$ teaspoon ketchup possibly make a difference in a dish? If you aren't sure about something, look at a similar recipe in another cookbook. You'll soon know.

Another thing to look for are reasonable combinations. Innovative recipes are fine but they have to make sense. Jalapeño Pepper Chocolate Cake and Dijon Mustard Vanilla Ice Cream don't.

Finally, good recipes should encourage you to use fresh foods. Recipes that tell you to take a can of this and a jar of that and mix it all up with some frozen stuff are just ways to put together food that will fill your stomach. They don't teach you how to cook or eat well.

What You Get from Reading a Recipe

Your first reading of a recipe tells you if the recipe is good. The second time you read it for familiarity. If you're more familiar with what to do, you'll be less intimidated and less likely to make mistakes. As you read, picture what you will be doing. If you feel like a fool, then feel like a fool and laugh at yourself. It's better than feeling frustrated if the recipe doesn't come out right.

Reading the recipe first also lets you know what ingredients to buy (make a written list) and what pans and utensils you will need (make note of them and get them out before you begin to cook). You will get some idea of the amount of preparation time.

Visions of Math Monsters: Doubling and Dividing Recipes

Many recipes can be doubled or divided but there are a few things you should bear in mind. First, you'll have to do some math. If a recipe for pancakes calls for 2 cups of flour and you want to make $\frac{1}{3}$ of a recipe, you have to take $\frac{1}{3}$ of 2, which equals $\frac{2}{3}$ cup. That one's easy.

But suppose your recipe called for ¹/₃ cup of shortening and you were making ¹/₂ a recipe. Then you would have to figure out ¹/₂ of ¹/₃. You would have to go to an equivalency chart (there's one in Chapter 11) to find out that ¹/₃ cup is the same as 5 ¹/₃ tablespoons and that there are 3 teaspoons in each table-spoon. Then calculate that half of 5 ¹/₃ tablespoons (5 tablespoons plus 1 tea-spoon) would be 2 tablespoons plus 2 ¹/₂ teaspoons.

Although ingredients for baked goods require mathematical accuracy, not every recipe that you double or divide has to be so precise. Take soups, for example. If you're making chicken soup and want to put some in your freezer, but you only have 6 carrots instead of the requisite 8, use what you have. You also will find that when you double a recipe that calls for onions, garlic, or other similar items to be sautéed in oil first (as in tomato sauce, for example), you won't need as much oil. So if you're doubling a recipe that calls for 2 table-spoons of oil, 1 garlic clove, and 1 onion, you can use 3 tablespoons of oil, 2 garlic cloves, and 2 onions.

First Timer? Follow the Recipe!

It's always a good idea for a cook who isn't confident to follow a recipe precisely the first time. That way you know what the goal is, although it still may taste different than you expected. Suppose you get a recipe from a friend because you liked the way a particular dish tasted. Even if your friend gave you the exact recipe and wrote it well, it may not taste the same. That's because dishes change depending on which brands you use, how fresh ingredients are, how you mea-sure your ingredients (there's more on this in Chapter 11), your oven's heat, the weather, and many other factors. As you gain experience and learn more about ingredients, you can substitute ingredients in recipes to suit yourself.

You Need a Cooking Strategy

Once you read and familiarize yourself with the recipe, it's time to plan the meal. If you feel tremendously insecure about your ability, stick to one recipe for a main dish and fill in for the time being with take-out or just a salad on the side. If you are feeling more confident and want to prepare an entire main course, choose your recipes carefully.

Pick recipes that are easy, or have just one that's more difficult. If you've made an entire dinner before, prepare familiar items and try one new recipe. Pick recipes that suit your kitchen; if you have only one oven, you can't make two items that must be baked at the same time at different temperatures (roast chicken at 350 degrees and baked potatoes at 400 degrees, for example). Select one oven recipe and one for the stovetop or vegetable steamer (roast chicken and sautéed rosemary potatoes, for example).

Setting the Table

Planning the meal involves more than just cooking. You have to eat somewhere. Sure, you can eat with your food on your lap while you watch TV—whole families do it. (That's how "TV dinners" began back in the Fifties. When you're staring at the screen with glazed eyes, it doesn't matter *what* you eat.) But conviviality and conversation are more pleasant, and more likely to happen if you sit around a table. Even if you're by yourself, eating at the table makes dinner more appealing. Therefore, you have to set the table.

If it's a family dinner, you may or may not want to use placemats or a tablecloth, depending on the type of tabletop you have. However, if you're having company for dinner, placemats or a tablecloth look more gracious. Set the plate in front of each diner with the napkin to the left of the plate. In general, you put forks on the left, on top of or to the right of the napkin. The napkin always has the folds facing left. In general, knives and spoons go to the right of the plate with the knife blade pointed in toward the plate.

A simple family-dinner table setting.

What Are All These Forks and Knives For, and Where Do I Put Them?

If your dinner calls for more than one of the same kind of utensil (a salad fork and a dinner fork, for example), place them next to each other in the order in which they will be used, from outside in. So the salad fork goes to the left of the dinner fork if you serve the salad first. There are two exceptions: a coffee or teaspoon goes to the right of the knife, and a shrimp cocktail fork goes to the right of the knife.

Here's how to set the table if you're serving a salad, a main course, and then cake and coffee.

If you get really fancy someday and have a more formal dinner with several courses, you'll need to use additional flatware pieces. In this case, items such as dessert spoons and forks go above the dinner plate. You lay these pieces horizontally. The spoon goes right above the plate with its handle facing right, and the fork goes above the spoon with its handle facing left. You do it this way because if you put any more pieces on the side of the plate, the table will look cluttered and your guests may not know which utensil is used for what.

Sterling silver and silverplate tend to tarnish even in their cloth bags. If you plan to use silverware, look at it the week before your dinner. You may need to give it a quick or not so quick polish.

Dessert Forks? Fruit Plates? Are You Kidding?

Just because you serve a multi-course meal doesn't mean you have to own a utensil of every size and shape. If you don't have dessert forks and spoons, you can reuse the sizes you do have, whether your dinner is casual or more formal. After you clear the table of salad forks, you can quickly wash them to use later for dessert, or you can use your dinner forks. Likewise, a soup spoon can double as a dessert spoon.

If you don't have all the plate sizes you think you need, you can double up on these too. Serve fruit or cake on a salad plate or even a dinner plate, if that's all you have—just garnish the sides with some berries so your dessert won't look lost.

You Only Have Odd, Assorted Plates? Not to Worry.

When plates match and you have all sorts of lovely silverware to go with them, the table looks elegant. But dinner is a total experience, not just a matter of whether or not you have the right stuff. Feel free to mix and match plates, with this caveat: use those that are similar in feeling and texture. If you have odds and ends, for example, use those that are rustic-looking together, use those that are more delicate together, and so on.

Speaking of plates, if it won't make you feel stressed, you may want to serve dinner on warmed (or chilled) plates. To do this, heat the oven to 140 degrees and then turn it off. Remove the plates from the set table and put them in the oven for a few minutes. (To chill plates, put them in the freezer for a couple of minutes.) Then return the plates to the table, or fill the plates and serve the food "plated." Some people warm plates by running them under hot water, but then you have to dry the dishes too, so it's more of a bother. Some dishwashers have plate-warming cycles. Honestly though, most people don't warm plates. No one expects your meals to be restaurant-hot.

What to Do with Those Extra Plates

Suppose you do have extra size plates. If you want to use them for a multi-course meal, the general rule is this: "eat to the left, drink to the right." The extra plates (salad, bread and butter) or salad bowls go to the left of the dinner plate above the fork. If the salad plate is too large to fit there, put it next to the fork with its top level with the fork's top.

Glassware goes to the right above the knife. If you are serving both wine and water, the water glass goes above the knife, and the wine glass goes to the right of it. For a two-wine dinner, put the white wine glass next to the water glass and the red wine next to it. Or, you can form a triangle of the glassware by placing the water and white wine glasses next to each other and the smaller red wine glass between and below them.

The water goblet goes above the knife, and the wine glass goes next to the goblet.

The Big Bonus: Flowers and Candles and Stuff Like That

Even a casual dinner is more appealing if you decorate the table. Flowers are always appropriate, but buy them a day ahead so they are in full bloom at your dinner. Try to buy flowers that go with your dinnerware, tablecloth, or placemats. You can save money by taking your own vase to the florist instead of paying for the one he or she provides.

You can decorate your table without flowers, however. Specialty items such as dried corn, Christmas ornaments, or tiny American flags all make attractive centerpieces or place setting decorations for seasonal dinners, and you can use them over and over again. Fresh herbs in tiny pots with ribbons around them will do for a spring dinner. You can also arrange fruit attractively, make puffs out of ribbons, or use knick knacks, tree branches, and the like on your table.

And don't forget candles. They add a decorative touch, and candlelight gives a meal more charisma. Be sure to put candles on your shopping list when you buy ingredients for the meal. It is one of the items many people forget.

Napkin Folds and Nightmares

If you know how to make fancy napkin folds for cloth napkins, you can make your dinner more stylish. But folding napkins can give some people nightmares. If you think you're all thumbs and can't make your dinner napkins look like some gorgeous origami creation, here are a few simple tricks you can do with cloth napkins:

➤ Buy napkin rings. Ringed napkins go in the center of the dinner plate.

➤ You can make simple "napkin rings" by tying satin ribbons into bows around each napkin.

➤ Pick up an unfolded napkin in the center and stuff it into a wine glass.

➤ Place a tiny flower within the folded napkin, so it sticks out on top.

➤ Use fancy cloth or paper napkins with borders or patterns. These are attractive enough to use flat.

Help! I Can't Make a Tomato Rose!

Meals are much more delicious and much more enjoyable when the food is presented attractively and not just thrown on a plate. But no one expects you to be a food designer who can "paint plates" the way they do in upscale restaurants, or make roses out of tomato skins or swans out of daikon radishes. Even if you are artistic and can make extraordinary-looking stuff out of food, the object of dinner is the food. If the garnish is too fancy, it will be intimidating. Here are a few tips to keep in mind when garnishing food:

➤ Use fresh herbs. The old standby, a sprig of rich green parsley, is never wrong—and it's cheap. But consider a sprig of rosemary, some dark, fuzzy sage leaves, or a cluster of shiny basil leaves instead.

A *carambola* is an exotic ridged fruit. When you cut the fruit crosswise, the slices look like stars.

➤ Use any small, fresh-looking, colorful food, such as berries, grapes, cherry tomatoes, or green olives placed here and there on the plate. Other colorful foods that make good garnishes include bell peppers cut into strips or crosswise into "circles," lemon wedges, chopped chives, carrot or orange slices, scallions, and red radishes.

➤ Prepared foods make terrific garnishes: cranberry sauce or mango chutney inside a mushroom cap, for example.

➤ Unusual-looking foods such as carambola are great garnishes too. Arrange the star-shaped slices on the side of the plate.

➤ Make sure the garnishes are edible. You don't want guests putting plastic, paper, or other non-digestible items in their mouths.

➤ Edible flowers make gorgeous garnishes. They're expensive but you only need a few to make a good impression.

➤ Keep the garnishes simple.

Yes! You Can Make a Tomato Rose!

If you want to get a little fancier, you can learn to make some easy sculpted garnishes, including tomato roses, strawberry fans, scored and sliced zucchini, or cucumber and lemon rounds.

To make strawberry fans, hold each berry in the fingers of one hand with the hull (stem) side down and the point side up. With a sharp paring knife, slice thin, parallel slices down from the point to the stem, but do not cut through the stem. Gently fan the slices to show some of the cut side of each slice.

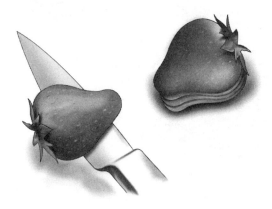

Turn strawberries into fans.

To create scored and sliced vegetables (for zucchini, cucumber, and lemons), use a citrus peeler, small paring knife, or vegetable peeler to remove narrow strips of the peel down the entire length of the vegetable or fruit. Then cut the vegetable or fruit crosswise into slices.

Even the simplest scored and sliced vegetable rounds make gorgeous garnishes.

To make tomato roses, with a sharp paring knife, cut the tomato's thin skin in a continuous, long strip, starting from the top of the tomato. The width of the strip should be between 1/2" and 1". Loosely roll the strip with the skin surface out and shape it into a flower. You can use the rest of the tomato of course, so don't throw it away.

You can make a tomato rose!

The Least You Need to Know

➤ Read a recipe *before you start cooking* to familiarize yourself with the ingredients as well as the techniques.

➤ Use your own judgment in recipes that say "use a pinch," "season to taste," "use this OR that," or "ingredient, optional."

➤ You can double or divide most recipes easily.

➤ Flowers, candlelight, and other decorative eye catchers make a meal more inviting.

➤ Garnishes add appeal to the meal, but avoid over-garnishing and be sure all garnishes are edible.

Chapter 11

Do I Really Need to Measure?

In This Chapter

➤ Why you have to measure

➤ How to measure dry and liquid ingredients

➤ What a "pinch" and a "dash" mean

➤ Measurement equivalents for foods (how many garlic cloves make 1/2 teaspoon chopped garlic and stuff like that)

➤ Measure for measure: how many teaspoons in a tablespoon, tablespoons in a cup, and so on

➤ A few more simple "non-recipe" recipes

Once you choose the recipes and plan your cooking strategy, it's time to don your apron, get out the ingredients and pots and pans, and start cooking. The recipes you will be using most likely instruct you to measure certain ingredients. That means you must get out some measuring tools too.

Is it really necessary to go to the bother of measuring? If so, how do you measure and with what? That's what you'll read about in this chapter. There are some foods you can't measure when you buy them. For example, your recipe may call for 1 tsp. of freshly grated lemon peel or 1 TB. of chopped shallots. How many lemons and shallots do you buy? You'll find some tips about that in this chapter, too.

Why Bother with Measuring?

Experienced cooks seem pretty blasé about measuring ingredients. To see what I mean, watch a cooking show on TV. One famous chef or another tells you to pour in a tablespoon or two of wine and then proceeds to add half a bottle. The audience laughs. You laugh. Then you wonder whether you should use a tablespoon or two, or a half bottle.

NEVER... skip the measuring steps when you bake, even as you become more experienced. Recipes for most baked goods are precise formulas that will not work if you don't measure the ingredients properly.

Cooking experts don't have to measure precisely for several reasons. First, they're on TV to entertain you, not merely to teach you about cooking; the antics make the show more fun. Second, because you never get to taste what they are preparing, you don't know whether they have overwhelmed the recipe with wine. Most important though, experienced cooks have developed a "feel" for precise measurements. They can pour salt into their hands and know what a half teaspoon looks like, or chop an onion and know it equals about a half cup. And they know something else too. They know when it isn't necessary to measure precisely—even when the recipe says so.

As you become more expert, you too will develop a feel for measurement. You will understand when it is important to measure and when it is not. Until then, however, measure. Measuring is important because it ensures that the recipe will work with consistent results.

What You Measure With

There are several types of measuring devices for the kitchen. Dry and solid ingredients such as flour and shortening are measured in handled cups. They come in plastic or metal in sets of $1/4$-, $1/3$-, $1/2$- and 1-cup measures. (Some sets include $2/3$-cup or $1/8$-cup cups.) There also are larger 2-cup size cups.

These handled cups are for measuring dry ingredients.

112

Liquid ingredients are measured in a pitcher-like cup with a spout. Those made of clear glass that have measurement marks on the side are the easiest to use.

Measuring cups for liquids are like pitchers; they have spouts for pouring.

When you have to measure ingredients in quantities smaller than ¹/₄ cup, you use measuring spoons. These are also either plastic or metal and most come in sets of ¹/₈-, ¹/₄-, ¹/₂-, and 1-teaspoon sizes plus a 1-tablespoon size. Some sets include a 1¹/₂-tablespoon spoon.

Use these special measuring spoons—not your tablewear—to measure small quantities of ingredients.

Something Simple

Need some fabulously easy recipes for terrific things you can do to add flavor to food? Here are some easy and easy-to-measure suggestions:

➤ To make cinnamon sugar, mix 1 cup sugar with 1 TB. cinnamon.

➤ For vanilla sugar, split open a 4" piece of vanilla bean and press it into 1 cup sugar (let the sugar stand 3–4 days before you use it). You can rinse the vanilla bean and reuse it.

> ➤ To make "Java Sugar" for use on toast or in cakes, pies, and so on, mix 1 cup sugar with 2 tsp. cinnamon, $1/2$ tsp. nutmeg, $1/2$ tsp. powdered ginger, $1/8$ tsp. allspice, and $1/8$ tsp. ground cloves.
>
> ➤ For vanilla brandy, split open a 4" piece of vanilla bean and put it into 1 cup brandy (let it steep two weeks before you use the brandy). You can use the vanilla bean again to poach fruit or make custard.

Kitchen scales measure ingredients by weight instead of by volume. In the United States, most recipes list ingredients by volume, but kitchen scales come in handy for those times when they do not. Recipes that call for pasta, for instance, frequently ask for that ingredient in ounces or pounds.

How to Measure Ingredients

One reason recipes often don't come out right is that the person who prepared the dish didn't measure ingredients properly. Not measuring properly and wondering why your cake fell is like not reading the instructions for your VCR and wondering why it didn't record the movie. You have to follow the rules if you want the cake (or the movie). Follow these guidelines for measuring, and never again ruin a recipe because of measurement mistakes (but good luck learning how to program your VCR):

NEVER... use your tableware to measure ingredients. The teaspoons and cups you use to drink tea or coffee are not equivalent to measuring cups and spoons.

Kitchen Clue Butter, margarine, and certain brands of shortening are available in sticks that are marked with tablespoon/cup measuring guidelines on the wrapper. If you buy these, use those guidelines instead of packing the ingredient into a measuring cup.

➤ Measure dry ingredients over a plate or aluminum foil so you can catch the excess and put it back in the container.

➤ Spoon flour and similar ingredients into the measuring cup. Do not scoop the ingredient using the cup itself.

➤ Add enough of the ingredient to come above the rim of the cup, then level it off with the straight edge of a knife.

➤ Never shake, pat, or pack down dry ingredients. This gives an imprecise measurement. There is one exception: always pack brown sugar.

➤ To measure salt and other dry ingredients used in small quantities, use measuring spoons and follow the same procedure as for flour. However, to measure baking soda or baking powder, you may scoop the spoon into the tin or box, and then level it off using the package lid.

➤ Measure fats such as shortening at room temperature, when they are easier to pack into the cup.

➤ To measure fats accurately, pack them down in the cup to get rid of air pockets that could cause mismeasurement. Add enough to come above the rim, and then level it off with the straight edge of a knife.

➤ When you measure liquid ingredients, don't raise the cup to eye level to see if the measurement is accurate. Leave the cup on the counter where you know it will be level, and lower yourself to see the cup at eye level.

➤ Measure small quantities of liquids (1 tsp., for example) over a bowl so excess amounts will not go into your recipe.

➤ To save washing and drying in the middle of a recipe, have two sets of measuring spoons handy—one for wet ingredients and one for dry ones.

Kitchen Clue
Certain sticky ingredients such as honey and peanut butter are messy to measure. If you spray the measuring tool with vegetable spray, or oil it lightly with vegetable oil, you will find it easier and less messy to measure the honey or peanut butter. In addition, the utensil is easier to clean.

Do I Measure or Sift Flour First?

One of the most confusing questions in cooking is when to measure flour for a recipe that calls for sifted flour. Do you measure before you sift or after? Here's a simple rule to follow: see whether the word *sifted* or *flour* comes first. If a recipe calls for 2 cups of flour, sifted, you measure the flour first, and then sift it. However, if the recipe calls for 2 cups of sifted flour, the recipe writer has qualified the kind of flour to be used: sifted flour. That means you sift the flour before you measure it. To use the recipes in this cookbook, measure the flour before you sift it.

Those Annoying Pinches and Dashes

Why would a recipe ask for a "pinch" or "dash" of something? The answer is that even a tiny amount of that ingredient makes a difference to taste or texture. "Pinch" usually refers to measurements of solid ingredients such as salt or cinnamon and means less than $1/8$ teaspoon. "Dash" is a measurement for liquids and means about 2–3 drops. You also may see a measurement of "handful." Old cookbooks used this so-called measurement for lots of ingredients including flour for bread. Today you only see that term occasionally, and it's usually in reference to fresh herbs. It means use several loose leaves (for example, 12–15 basil leaves) that you can cluster in your hand easily.

Equivalent Measurements

Sometimes a recipe asks for measurements by weight but you want to measure it by volume. For example, although the recipe calls for 8 ounces of milk, you'll probably want to measure it in cups. How many cups is that?

Sometimes a recipe lists an ingredient by volume, but you want to cut the recipe in half and the math is not so simple. If the original recipe calls for $^3/_4$ cup of milk, you need $^3/_8$ cup. How do you measure that with standard measuring cups and spoons?

Recipes that use liquor may ask you to add a "jigger" of some alcoholic beverage. What's a jigger? The following tables will help you convert these kinds of measurements to make measuring easier and more convenient.

Common Volume Measurement Equivalents (for Dry Ingredients)

$^1/_2$ TB.	=	$1^1/_2$ tsp.
1 TB.	=	3 tsp.
$1^1/_2$ TB.	=	1 TB. plus $1^1/_2$ tsp.
$1^1/_2$ TB.	=	$4^1/_2$ tsp.
2 TB.	=	$^1/_8$ cup
4 TB.	=	$^1/_4$ cup
$5^1/_3$ TB.	=	$^1/_3$ cup
$5^1/_3$ TB.	=	5 TB. plus 1 tsp.
$^1/_3$ cup	=	5 TB. plus 1 tsp.
6 TB.	=	$^3/_8$ cup
$^3/_8$ cup	=	$^1/_4$ cup plus 2 TB.
8 TB.	=	$^1/_2$ cup
$^5/_8$ cup	=	$^1/_2$ cup plus 2 TB.
$^2/_3$ cup	=	10 TB. plus 2 tsp.
12 TB.	=	$^3/_4$ cup
$^7/_8$ cup	=	1 cup less 2 TB.
16 TB.	=	1 cup
2 cups	=	1 pint
2 pints	=	1 quart
4 cups	=	1 quart
4 quarts	=	1 gallon

Common Measurement Equivalents for Liquid

2 TB.	=	1 oz. ($^1/_8$ cup)
$^1/_4$ cup	=	2 oz. (4 TB.)

Common Measurement Equivalents for Liquid		
1/3 cup	=	2–2/3 oz. (5 1/3 TB.)
1/2 cup	=	4 oz. (8 TB.)
1 cup	=	8 oz. (16 TB.)
2 cups	=	16 oz. (1 pint; 1 lb.)
4 cups	=	32 oz. (1 quart; 2 lbs.)

Liquor Measurement Equivalents		
1 pony	=	1 oz. (2 TB.)
1 jigger	=	1 1/2 oz. (3 TB.)
1 fifth	=	1/5 gallon (750 milliliters; 4/5 quart; approx. 3 cups plus 3 TB.)

How Many Lemons Make 1 Teaspoon of Grated Peel (and Things of That Nature)

When you first start to cook, you will not know how many ounces of cheese to buy to get the 2 cups of grated cheese you need for your recipe. As with measuring salt and pouring wine into a recipe, after a while, you will get a "feel" for these ingredients, too. In the meantime, you can use the following tables, which provide approximate equivalents for some of the more common food items you may use in your recipes. Bear in mind, though, that these are approximations only. For example, although a shallot usually provides 1 tablespoon of chopped shallot, a larger shallot gives you more, a smaller one gives you less, and so on. There is no way to measure these items precisely, but there also is no need to. Use your common sense here. If a recipe tells you to add 1 tablespoon of chopped shallot, you can chop one average size shallot and not measure it precisely.

Food Measurement Approximate Equivalents: Dry Ingredients		
Breadcrumbs, fresh: 1 cup	=	2 oz.; 2 slices white bread
Chocolate		
1 oz. baking	=	1 square; 4 TB. grated
6 oz. chocolate chips	=	1 cup
Cocoa, 1 lb.	=	4 cups
Coconut, flaked, 3 1/2 oz.	=	1 1/3 cups

continues

continued

Food Measurement Approximate Equivalents: Dry Ingredients

Flour, unsifted white, all-purpose, 1 lb. (bleached or unbleached)	=	$3^1/_2$–4 cups
cake flour, 1 lb.	=	$4^1/_2$ cups
whole wheat, 1 lb. (coarse grain)	=	$4^1/_2$ cups
Nuts		
almonds, 4 oz. slivere	=	1 cup
almonds, 1 lb. shelled	=	3 cups
almonds, ground, 8 oz	=	$1^1/_3$ cups
peanuts, 1 lb. shelled	=	3 cups
pecans, 1 lb. shelled	=	4 cups
pistachios, 1 lb. shelled	=	$3^2/_3$ cups
walnuts, 1 lb. shelled, broken	=	3 cups
Oatmeal, 1 lb.	=	$5^1/_3$ cups, uncooked
Rice, 8 oz.	=	1 cup raw, white
Shortening, 8 oz.	=	1 cup
1 lb. 4 oz.	=	3 sticks
Sugar		
white, 1 lb	=	2 cups
brown, packed, 1 lb.	=	$2^1/_4$ cups
Unflavored gelatin, $^1/_4$ oz. package	=	1 TB.
White navy beans, 1 lb.	=	2 cups

Equivalents: Fruits and Vegetables

Apples, 1 lb.	=	3 medium, 3 cups sliced
Bananas, 1 lb.	=	3 medium, $1^1/_4$ cups mashed
Bell pepper, 1 large	=	1 cup coarsely chopped
Cabbage, 1 medium	=	$4^1/_2$ cups shredded

Equivalents: Fruits and Vegetables

Carrots, 1 lb.	=	3 cups shredded
Celery, 2 large stalks	=	1 cup chopped
Garlic, 1 medium clove	=	$1/2$ tsp. minced
Lemon, 1 medium	=	3–4 TB. juice, 2–3 tsp. grated peel
Lime, 1 medium	=	2 TB. juice, 1–2 tsp. grated peel
Mushrooms, white, $1/2$ lb.	=	$2^1/2$ to 3 cups sliced
Onion, 1 lb.	=	3 cups chopped
Onion, 1 medium	=	$3/4$ cup chopped
Oranges, 1 medium	=	6–8 oz. juice ($3/4$ to 1 cup); 2 TB. grated peel
Peaches, 1 lb.	=	4 medium
Potatoes, 1 lb.	=	3 medium; $3^1/2$ cups sliced; 2 cups cooked, mashed
Raisins, seedless, 1 lb.	=	$2^3/4$ cups
Strawberries, 1 pint box	=	2 cups sliced
Tomatoes, 1 lb.	=	3–4 medium; $1^1/2$ cups peeled, seeded, chopped

Food Measurement Equivalents: Dairy, Eggs, Meat

Butter

1 lb.	=	4 sticks
1 stick	=	$1/2$ cup; 8 TB.
1 oz.	=	2 TB.
1 lb. whipped	=	3 cups

Cheese

8 oz.	=	2 cups grated (firm and hard cheeses)
4 oz.	=	1 cup crumbled (blue-veined)
8 oz. cottage cheese	=	1 cup
1 oz. cream cheese	=	2 TB.

continues

119

continued

Food Measurement Equivalents: Dairy, Eggs, Meat		
Cream		
$\frac{1}{2}$ pint heavy or whipping	=	1 cup; 2 cups whipped
1 cup heavy or whipping	=	2 cups whipped
Eggs		
large, 1 cup	=	4–6 whole eggs
large, 1 cup	=	8–10 whites
large, 1 cup	=	12–14 yolks
1 large white	=	2 TB.
1 large yolk	=	$1\frac{1}{4}$ TB.
Ground meat, 1 lb.	=	2 cups

Food Measurement Equivalents: Liquids		
Sweetened Condensed milk		
14 or 15 oz.	=	$1\frac{1}{4}$–$1\frac{1}{3}$ cups
Evaporated milk, 12 oz.	=	$1\frac{1}{2}$ cups
Corn syrup, 16 oz.	=	2 cups
Honey, 16 oz.	=	$1\frac{1}{3}$ cups
Maple syrup, 16 oz.	=	2 cups
Vegetable oil, 16 oz.	=	2 cups
Water, 16 oz.	=	2 cups

The Least You Need to Know

➤ Measuring is important to ensure accuracy and consistency.

➤ Do not use your flatware spoons and coffee cups as measuring tools; use the ones specifically designed for measuring ingredients.

➤ To measure flour and similar dry ingredients, spoon the ingredient into a measuring cup to a point above the rim. Do not shake, pat, or pack down the ingredient. Level off the ingredient with the flat edge of a knife.

➤ When you measure sticky ingredients such as honey or peanut butter, spray the measuring tool with vegetable spray, or oil it lightly with vegetable oil first to prevent sticking.

➤ Refer to the tables in this chapter for measurement equivalents.

Chapter 12

Can I Use Something Else Instead?

In This Chapter

➤ When it's okay to substitute and when it's not

➤ What happens when you substitute

➤ Substituting ingredients in baked goods

➤ Substituting dairy, produce, and miscellaneous ingredients

➤ Substituting pans

In the last chapter, you learned that it's important to measure ingredients accurately to ensure consistent recipe results. For the same reason, it's equally important that you use the ingredients the recipe calls for. That way, you know not only that the recipe will come out as expected, but that it will taste about the same each time you make it.

However, suppose you run out of an ingredient and don't have time to shop, or you are cooking at 1:00 a.m. and the stores aren't open. Can you substitute ingredients? What do you do if someone is allergic to a particular ingredient? And do you have to throw out an entire recipe as worthless just because you didn't like one particular ingredient? This chapter tells you how to substitute and explains when it's okay to substitute and when it isn't.

The Whys and Wherefores of Substituting

Substitutions have to make sense. Obviously, no one would substitute sugar for flour, or orange juice for mustard, but not all substitution issues are that clear-cut. The most important factor you need to consider before you substitute one ingredient for another is the function of the ingredient in the recipe.

The First Time, Follow the Recipe

When you are at the stove ready to cook, you face a moment of truth. Either you are the kind of person who likes detailed instructions that you can follow with precision, or you are one of those people who never reads instructions. Because cooking should be enjoyable, you should never feel bound to arbitrary rules—no matter what type of person you are. On the other hand, you need some discipline. It's good to follow recipes until you understand the nature of the ingredients and some basic cooking methods. Following a recipe means using the ingredients called for as well as proceeding in the order given.

As you gain confidence, you can start to substitute in small ways: substitute olive oil for some of a sautéed recipe's butter, for example. Use basil instead of oregano in the potato salad, or add wild mushrooms to the chowder. Improvisation unlocks the mystery of cooking. Use your head, and use your senses. Taste the food. Smell it. Watch it. Begin to rely on your own palate and your own judgment.

When It Is Okay to Substitute

Some recipes invite innovation and creativity because any of several ingredients could perform the same function. In such recipes, follow this guideline: you can substitute one ingredient for another if it does not change the intrinsic nature of the dish. Some examples are soups, rice pilafs, and vinaigrette dressing. If you are making vegetable soup and have no broccoli, for example, you can use green beans or some other vegetable instead. You could add peas and corn if you prefer chunkier soup. Regardless, it's still vegetable soup. You could add meats or vegetables to rice pilaf; it's still pilaf. Lots of changes are possible when you're making vinaigrette dressing. You can use almost any vegetable oil you like, season it with any herb, and switch from vinegar to lemon juice, and the dressing is still a vinaigrette.

Kitchen Clue
You don't need to use allergies as an excuse to spark creativity. When any number of ingredients will work in a recipe, try to substitute for the original item. For example, change the pecan pie recipe in the Desserts section of this book to cashew nut pie and see how different and delicious it is.

If someone is allergic to or otherwise intolerant of an ingredient, you must make substitutions. The guideline here is the same: if the new ingredient serves a similar purpose to the original one, go ahead and substitute. If a person is allergic to legumes, for example, use corn oil instead of soybean oil to sauté fish or prepare salad dressing. Use chopped almonds in the quickbread if someone cannot eat walnuts.

When It Is Not Okay to Substitute

When an ingredient serves a unique function in a dish and the recipe would not work without it, there is no substitute. For example, a soufflé will not rise without beaten egg whites. You cannot prepare yeast bread without yeast, pie crust without some sort of fat, and so on.

What Happens When You Substitute

When you substitute ingredients that are more or less interchangeable in recipes, you may end up "inventing" a new recipe. On the other hand, when you substitute ingredients that are less similar, you should understand that the recipe may change significantly in any number of ways, including texture, density, taste, or intensity of flavor. Suppose you were making muffins and the recipe called for applesauce. Because the applesauce provides moisture, you couldn't use peanut butter instead; it doesn't have the same moisturizing quality. However, you could substitute canned pumpkin or any other fruit puree without changing anything except the flavor.

NEVER... substitute artificial sweeteners for the sugar in a recipe; the measurements are not the same. Use artificial sweeteners in accordance with manufacturer's directions.

A change of flavor is just one type of change. Consider the more significant changes possible when you substitute sweeteners. They all serve the same sweetening function, but some have more powerful sweetening capabilities than others. They also have different weights and textures. For example, if you want to substitute a liquid sweetener such as honey for some sugar in a cake recipe, you will consequently have to adjust the amount of dry ingredients to account for the added moisture. The cake made with honey will also have a heavier, denser texture than one made with sugar.

How to Substitute Ingredients

Most recipes for cakes and pastries are precise formulas and will not come out unless you follow them to the letter. However, even with these precise recipes you can sometimes use substitutes if you know how to do it. For example, you can substitute buttermilk for milk in biscuits if you also add baking soda (about $1/2$ tsp. for each cup of buttermilk).

When you want to make specific substitutions in recipes, refer to the following tables to make wise decisions.

Kitchen Clue
When you substitute honey for one cup of sugar in a recipe, use only $3/4$ cup of honey and add a pinch of baking soda (unless the recipe also calls for an acidic ingredient such as buttermilk, yogurt, or sour cream) and reduce the liquid in the recipe by $1/4$ cup. When substituting molasses, use 1–1 $1/4$ cups to replace each cup of sugar, add $1/2$ tsp. baking soda for each cup of molasses, and reduce the liquid in the recipe by 5 TB. Never substitute more than half a recipe's solid sugar with a liquid one.

123

Substitutions in Baked Goods

1 tsp. double-acting baking powder	=	$1/4$ tsp. baking soda plus $1/2$ tsp. cream of tartar
	=	$1/4$ tsp. baking soda plus $1/2$ cup buttermilk or plain yogurt
	=	$1/4$ tsp. baking soda plus $1/4$ cup molasses
	=	$1^1/2$ tsp. phosphate or tartrate baking powder
4 extra large eggs	=	5 large eggs
	=	6 medium eggs
1 cup sifted cake flour	=	$7/8$ cup (one cup minus 2 TB.) sifted all-purpose flour
1 cup all-purpose flour (bleached or unbleached)	=	1 cup plus 2 TB. cake flour
1 cup white all-purpose flour	=	1 cup fine whole wheat flour
	=	1 cup plus 2 TB. coarse whole wheat flour
1 cup white sugar	=	1 cup brown sugar, packed
	=	1 cup superfine sugar
	=	$1^3/4$ cup confectioner's sugar
	=	$3/4$ cup honey, reduce liquid by $1/4$ cup
	=	$3/4$ cup maple syrup, reduce liquid by $1/4$ cup
	=	$1^1/4$ cups molasses, reduce liquid by 5 TB.
1 cup brown sugar	=	1 cup white sugar plus $1^1/2$ TB. molasses
$1/2$ cup honey	=	$1/2$ cup maple syrup
	=	$3/4$ cup molasses
1 pkg. dry yeast	=	1 cake compressed yeast
	=	2 tsp. dry yeast
1 1" piece vanilla	=	1 tsp. pure vanilla extract bean

1 square (1 oz.) unsweetened chocolate	=	3 TB. unsweetened cocoa plus 1 TB. solid fat (butter, margarine, shortening)
1 square (1 oz.)	=	3 TB. unsweetened cocoa plus 1 TB. solid semisweet chocolate fat plus 3 TB. sugar
¹/₄-oz. envelope unflavored gelatin	=	1 TB. gelatin (enough to gel 2 cups liquid)

Dairy Substitutions

1 cup butter	=	1 cup margarine
	=	⁷/₈ cup solid fat (such as lard or shortening)
1 cup buttermilk	=	1 cup plain yogurt or sour milk
	=	1 cup minus 1 TB. warm milk plus 1 TB. vinegar or lemon juice (let mixture stand 5 minutes)
3 TB. clarified butter	=	3 TB. vegetable oil
	=	2 TB. vegetable oil plus 1 TB. butter
1 cup heavy cream	=	³/₄ cup whole milk plus ¹/₃ cup melted butter.
1 cup half-and-half	=	¹/₂ cup light cream or medium cream plus ¹/₂ cup whole milk
	=	1 cup whole milk plus 5 tsp. melted butter
1 cup sour cream	=	1 cup plain yogurt
1 cup whole milk	=	¹/₂ cup unsweetened evaporated milk plus ¹/₂ cup water
	=	1 cup reconstituted non-fat dry milk plus 1 TB. melted butter
	=	1 cup minus 1 TB. skim milk plus 1 TB. heavy cream
1 cup skim milk	=	¹/₂ cup evaporated skim milk plus ¹/₂ cup water

Clarified butter is melted butter with the milk solids and sediment removed so that only the butter fat remains.

Kitchen Clue

The general rule in substituting herbs is about 1 TB. fresh to 1 tsp. dried, some dried herbs are more assertive than fresh. Use a minimum amount of herbs, and add seasonings to taste.

Fruit and Vegetable Substitutions

1 TB. fresh herbs	=	1 tsp. dried
1 tsp. fresh lemon juice	=	$^1/_2$ tsp. bottled lemon extract
1 tsp. freshly grated orange or lemon peel	=	1 tsp. dried (bottled) orange or lemon peel

Miscellaneous Substitutions

1 TB. prepared mustard	=	1 tsp. dry, powdered mustard plus water
1 TB. flour to thicken sauce	=	$1^1/_2$ tsp. cornstarch
	=	$1^1/_2$ tsp. potato starch
	=	$1^1/_2$ tsp. arrowroot
	=	$2^1/_2$ tsp. quick tapioca
1 cup tomato juice for cooking	=	$^1/_2$ cup tomato sauce plus $^1/_2$ cup water
1 cup ketchup	=	$^1/_2$ cup tomato sauce, $1^1/_2$ TB. sugar, 2 tsp. vinegar
1 cup seasoned bread crumbs	=	1 cup plain bread crumbs plus 1 TB. freshly grated parmesan cheese, 2 tsp. mixed dried herbs, $^1/_4$ tsp. salt, $^1/_4$ tsp. black pepper, and $^1/_8$ tsp. garlic powder

How to Substitute Pans

If you don't have the right pan size, should you just chuck the recipe, or can you substitute? The answer is: "It depends." As with ingredients, you should always use the size pan the recipe calls for. However, you don't have to go out and buy an endless assortment of pans. When you haven't the exact one, try to use a pan with similar capacity, size, and depth. To measure capacity or volume, count the number of cups of water it takes to fill the pan. Measure size and depth with a ruler.

When you substitute pans, bear in mind that you may have to alter cooking times and temperatures. For example, although you can bake the same cake in an 8" square cake pan or a 9"×5"×3" loaf pan, because the loaf pan is deeper, you must bake it longer. Likewise, the same amount of batter that fits into the 8" square pan also will make 12 muffins. But because each muffin is so much smaller, baking time will be much shorter. If the pan you use is much deeper than the one the recipe calls for, lower the oven temperature by 25 degrees. The following table gives approximate substitution possibilities for pans.

Pan Equivalents

Muffin pans	= $^1/_2$ cup (approx.)
8$^1/_2$"×4$^1/_2$"×2$^1/_2$" loaf pan	= 6 cups
7"×11"×2" brownie pan	= 6 cups
8" square cake pan, 1$^1/_2$" deep	= 6 cups
8" square cake pan, 2" deep	= 8 cups
9" round cake pan, 2" deep	= 8 cups
9"×5"×3" loaf pan	= 8 cups
9"×13"×2" rectangular cake pan	= 12 cups
10" springform or bundt pan	= 12 cups

The Least You Need to Know

➤ To obtain consistent results, use the ingredients called for in a recipe.

➤ You can substitute ingredients that do not serve a unique function in a dish.

➤ Ingredient substitutions will change the taste and/or texture of a dish.

➤ If you must substitute pan sizes, try to use pans of similar capacity, size, and depth.

Chapter 13

A Compendium of the Top 100 Cooking Terms

In This Chapter

➤ A super-glossary that defines and describes the things you do to foods before you cook them,

➤ While you cook them,

➤ And after you cook them

Now that you know how to shop for ingredients, choose a recipe, and measure properly, and you understand when and how to substitute ingredients, you are nearly ready to cook. As you look through the recipe you have chosen, you may notice a direction or a cooking term that is unfamiliar. Often a recipe will ask you to do something to the food before you cook it or as you are cooking it. For example, before you roast a chicken, the recipe may tell you to "truss" the bird. How do you do that? A recipe for cake may ask you to "beat" or "whisk" the batter. What's the difference? Sometimes the recipe directs you to do something after you cook the food, such as "adjust" the seasonings. Do you know what that means? In this chapter, not only will you find definitions for the 100 most common cooking direction terms, but you will also learn (where appropriate) why a particular technique is important and how you can master the technique.

Adjust   To change the seasonings in a cooked dish by adding salt, pepper, herbs, lemon juice, and so on, after you have tasted the dish and determined that it needs more flavoring.

Bake Blind   To bake an unfilled pie shell partially or completely. For example, to make a custard tart that requires further baking, you use a partially cooked shell to prevent the crust from becoming soggy after you add the custard. You use a fully cooked shell to make mousse, pudding, and fully cooked custard pies. To bake blind, follow these steps so the crust won't shrink:

1. Place the dough into the pie tin, flute the edge, and prick the surface with the tines of a fork.

2. Place aluminum foil or parchment paper over the dough.

3. Put pie weights (special bean-shaped aluminum or ceramic pellets available in cookware stores) or dry beans on top (about 2 cups).

4. Bake the shell in a preheated 400 degree oven for 10–12 minutes.

5. Remove the weights or beans and foil and return the shell to the oven to complete baking.

Kitchen Clue
If you use beans to bake blind, do not reuse the beans. They will be too hard. However, you could save them and use them over and over for pie crusts.

Bard   To cover meat with a thin layer of fat before roasting it. Cooks bard lean meats such as veal to keep the flesh moist. The fat gradually renders into the meat as the meat cooks, so there is no need to moisten manually at regular intervals (as you do when you baste). Bacon is a handy barding fat; however, you must blanch it for a couple of minutes to get rid of its excess salt.

Baste   To brush or pour a liquid on top of food at regular intervals as it cooks. The basting fluids keep the food moist and add flavor and color. You might baste with pan roasting fluids, water, stock, wine, beer, juice, or melted fat, depending on the recipe. A special tool called a bulb baster makes basting easy, but you also can baste with a spoon or a pastry brush. Most recipes for roasted meats and poultry will tell you to stop basting for the last half hour of cooking so the surface remains crispy.

Beat   To mix ingredients quickly and vigorously so they become smooth, light, creamy, and well aerated. You can beat with any number of tools, including forks, spoons, rotary egg beaters, hand mixers, electric mixers, and whisks. The most effective way to beat foods by hand is to firmly grip the beating tool and use your wrist and forearm in a circular motion.

Sometimes you will see more specific beating instructions that tell you to "beat until stiff but not dry." Whatever does that mean? It's used in reference to egg whites to describe the point at which they have the most volume and are the most stable. If you beat egg whites beyond this point, it will be more difficult to incorporate them into the recipe. Here are a few pointers to help you use and separate eggs and to beat the whites properly:

➤ Separate yolks from whites when the eggs are cold.

➤ To crack the egg most effectively, tap the center lightly on the edge of the bowl.

➤ Once the egg is halved, look at it and smell it. If it is discolored or has an odor, discard it.

➤ Pour the egg into an egg separator. If you don't have an egg separator, wash your hands immediately before cracking the egg. Pour the egg into your hands, hold the yolk in your palm, and let the whites flow through your fingers into a bowl.

➤ Remove any tiny specks of yolk from the whites with a spoon or paper towel. This is important because yolk contains fat, and even the tiniest particle of fat prevents whites from reaching their greatest volume.

➤ It's best to beat egg whites in a copper, stainless steel, glass, or ceramic bowl. Do not use aluminum because it discolors the egg whites. Do not use plastic, if possible, because it retains fats (even if you wash it thoroughly), and you won't get maximum volume.

➤ The best tool for beating egg whites is a whisk or an electric mixer with a whisk attachment. Hand mixers with beaters that do not have center posts also are suitable.

➤ Beat egg whites just before you use them, or they will deflate.

➤ For best results (the most volume), beat egg whites when they are at room temperature (separate eggs 45 minutes before you beat them for optimum results).

Egg whites tip over softly when you beat them to soft peaks.

➤ Don't add cream of tartar, salt, or sugar until the whites are "foamy" lookingEgg whites tip over softly when you beat them to soft peaks.

➤ If you use an electric mixer, start beating egg whites at a slow speed, and then increase speed gradually.

➤ *Soft peaks* means the whites tip over softly when you lift the beater from the beaten egg whites

➤ *Stiff peaks* means the whites tip over a tiny bit on top when you lift the beater from the beaten egg whites. Do not beat stiff egg whites past the point where they look moist.

Egg whites tip over only a tiny bit on top when you beat them to stiff peaks.

There also are special tricks to achieve the most tender and voluminous "whipped cream." Here are some easy guidelines:

➤ Be sure the cream, bowl, and beaters are thoroughly chilled.

➤ Do not use your copper egg white bowl for whipped cream (or any other ingredient that contains fat).

➤ The best tool for beating cream is a whisk or an electric mixer whisk attachment. Hand mixers with beaters that do not have center posts also are suitable.

➤ Both heavy cream and whipping cream are suitable for whipped cream. Whipped cream made with heavy cream keeps its shape better.

➤ Start beating cream at a slow speed, and then increase speed gradually.

➤ Add sugar gradually after the cream has thickened slightly.

Kitchen Clue
Use a copper bowl to get the greatest volume and most stable foam from beaten egg whites. However, if you use a copper bowl, do not add cream of tartar. Use cream of tartar for stability when beating egg whites in stainless steel, glass, or ceramic bowls. If you don't have cream of tartar, use a small amount of salt or sugar to help stabilize the foam.

➤ Beat the cream only until the mixture stands in soft peaks. Do not let the mixture curdle by beating it too long.

➤ If you want to make whipped cream (with whipping cream, not heavy cream) early in the day, dissolve 2 TB. non-fat dry milk to each cup of cream to help stabilize it.

Bind To add an ingredient that holds other ingredients together. For example, in classic tuna salad, you bind the tuna fish, celery, and hard cooked eggs with mayonnaise.

Blanch To plunge food briefly into boiling water. You might do this to set a vegetable's color, to remove the strong flavor of an ingredient such as bacon or onion, to help remove an ingredient's skin or peel (tomatoes and nuts, for example), or to prepare foods for freezing.

Blend To mix foods thoroughly until they are smooth, but in a less vigorous way than beating. Blending also refers to processing foods in a blender.

Bone To remove the bones, sinew, and gristle from meat, poultry, game, and fish.

Bread To coat foods with a dry ingredient such as bread crumbs, cracker crumbs, corn meal, or flour. You do this to add flavor and a crunchy texture, and to protect a food's surface from intense heat. Fried foods are breaded so they don't scorch in the hot fat. To assure that the breading will stay in place, follow these simple tips:

➤ Coat the food in beaten egg or egg white first to help the breading ingredient adhere better.

➤ For thicker breading, you can dredge the food in flour first, and then coat it with egg and the breading ingredient.

➤ Let breaded foods rest for at least 20 minutes before you cook them. This helps the breading ingredient adhere better.

Brown To cook foods quickly over moderately high heat so that they turn a rich golden brown color. Browning foods does more than provide color though. It also helps seal in natural juices. You can brown foods by frying them in hot fat, cooking them on a grill or broiler, or roasting them in a hot oven. To brown foods properly, be sure the surface is dry. Also be sure not to crowd the ingredients in the cooking vessel; that decreases heat, and foods will not brown if the temperature is too low.

Bruise To crush an aromatic ingredient slightly to release its flavor and aroma. You generally bruise such foods as garlic, ginger, peppercorns, and cardamom pods.

Brush With To use a pastry brush to apply an ingredient (such as melted jelly) to another ingredient (such as a fully baked tart shell).

133

Butterfly   To halve food (usually meat, poultry, or shellfish) horizontally without cutting all the way through, so that the food opens like a book or a butterfly's wings.

Caramelize   To heat sugar or sugar plus water slowly so the mixture turns a rich caramel brown. Or, to sprinkle food with sugar and brown it quickly under the broiler.

Carve   To slice meat or poultry into serving-size pieces. Before you carve a roast of any kind, let it stand for 15 minutes to ensure juiciness and give the meat or bird time to finish cooking.

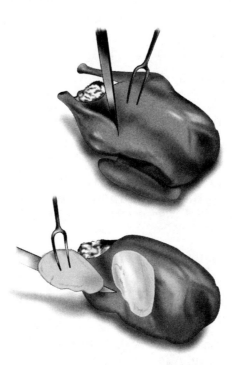

To make carving a chicken or turkey easier, begin by separating the legs and wings; then slice the meat.

Chill   To refrigerate foods or put them in a bowl filled with ice until they are cold.

Chop   To cut food into pieces, either small (finely chopped; minced) or large (coarsely chopped). When you chop foods, be sure to keep your fingers away from the blade. Put the food on a cutting board and hold it down with one hand, with your knuckles out and fingertips curved in; that way your knuckles serve as a guide for the knife blade. You won't cut yourself as long as you keep the blade edge lower than your knuckles. Hold the knife in your other hand with a firm grip around the handle, and cut the food straight down or with a forward motion, depending on the type of cut you want.

When you chop ingredients, use your knuckle as a knife guide so you won't cut yourself.

Clarify   To clear a liquid of solid particles. You clarify stock by adding egg whites and/or shells and heating the liquid gently. The sediment adheres to the solidified egg whites and can be removed easily. You clarify butter by melting it, and then pouring off the liquid yellow oil, which leaves the milky white solids in the pan.

Coat   To cover food completely with an ingredient or food such as flour, sauce, and so on. When a recipe tells you to cook a sauce until it is thick enough to "coat a spoon" that means the sauce will leave a film on the back of the spoon. When you wipe the spoon with a finger, it leaves a finger mark.

Coddle   To cook food in simmering water for a very short time. This technique is used primarily to warm foods.

Cool   To remove food from a heat source and let it stand until it comes to room temperature (or at least until it is no longer hot). It isn't a good idea to put hot food in the refrigerator to cool it.

Cream   To mix two or more ingredients until they are smooth, soft, and well blended. It is a good idea to remove butter from the refrigerator shortly before you cream it so that it softens a bit.

Kitchen Clue
To prevent bacteria from growing when you cool foods at room temperature, cool them as quickly as possible. For example, put a saucepan of hot food into a bowl of ice.

Crimp   To decorate the edges of a pie crust by pinching the top and bottom crusts together with your fingers.

Cut In   To incorporate solid fats such as shortening or butter into flour or another dry ingredient so that the fat becomes tiny flour-coated particles that resemble coarse crumbs. You can cut in with your fingers, or using two knives or a pastry blender. It is easier to cut in fats that are cold.

Deglaze   To loosen the natural juices and particles of coagulated foods that have accumulated at the bottom of the pan during cooking and formed a "glaze." To remove the glaze, you must add liquid to dissolve the particles. When you add the liquid (it can be wine, water, stock, juice, and so on), you stir and scrape up the bits at the bottom of the pan often using a whisk or a wooden spoon. You can use the deglazing liquid as a sauce (for a finer sauce, strain the liquid first), or you can boil the liquid until it is reduced to a syrupy texture and use the syrup in a more elaborate sauce.

Degrease   To remove the fat from food. Fat rises to the top of food, making it easier to scoop the fat out. To remove the fat from hot stock, soup, or sauce, you can use a special fat separator, but a spoon will do the job just as well. Alternatively, you can drop paper towels gently into the food, and the fat will cling to the paper towel when you lift it out.

If you have time, the best way to degrease is to chill the liquid. The fat hardens at the top, and you can scoop it easily. To remove fat from a casserole or roasting pan that contains bulky solid food, tilt the pan so the juices are in one corner. The fat comes to the top as with stock, and you can scoop it using the same methods. Always degrease foods before you deglaze the pan.

Deseed   To remove the inedible or fibrous seeds of fruits and vegetables. This can be done in several ways:

➤ Crush soft berries such as raspberries and strain them through a sieve.

➤ Slice the cap off bell peppers and pull out the seed cluster.

➤ Cut a cucumber in half lengthwise and scoop the seeds with a spoon.

➤ Cut open apples, pears, etc. and carve out the core and seeds together with a spoon or melon-baller.

Devein   To remove the vein from shrimp. To do this, hold the shrimp curved-side-up with one hand, and slit the curve open with a small paring knife using the other hand. You will see a gritty-looking black vein that you can pull out with the paring knife.

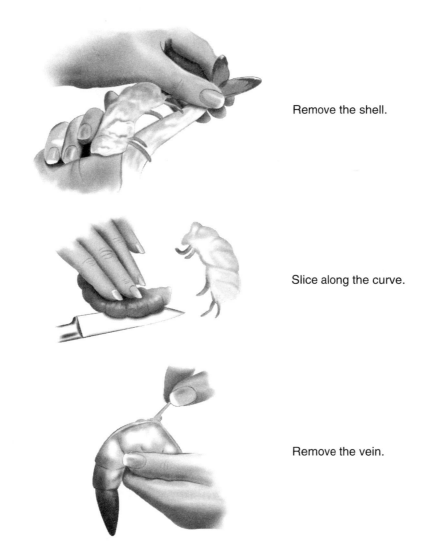

Remove the shell.

Slice along the curve.

Remove the vein.

Here's how you devein a shrimp.

Dice   To cut food into tiny cubes approximately $^1/_8$" to $^1/_4$" in size. To dice, first you slice the food, and then you cut those slices into julienne strips (see *julienne*). Turn the strips a quarter turn and cut down into cubes.

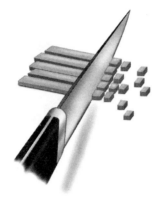

Cutting food into tiny dice cubes.

Dilute   To make a food weaker by adding water or another liquid.

Dot   To scatter the top of a dish with tiny bits of food, typically butter.

Drain   To strain food through a colander or strainer to remove liquid. You drain spaghetti, for example. It also means to pour out the fat from a cooking pan.

Dredge   To coat food lightly with a dry ingredient such as flour, bread crumbs, or sugar. This is similar to coating foods; however, after you dredge foods, you shake them to get rid of any excess dry ingredient.

Dress   To put a sauce or dressing on food. The word usually is used with salad.

Drizzle   To sprinkle drops of liquid lightly over food.

Dust   To sprinkle a small amount of dry ingredient lightly over food.

Eviscerate   To remove the entrails from an animal in preparation for cooking.

Fillet   To remove the bones from fish, meat, or poultry. This is similar to boning.

Flambee   A dramatic procedure by which you flame foods with brandy or another alcoholic beverage. It can create a spectacular effect at the dining room table, but the process is more than visual. When you flambee foods, you also add flavor. To do it properly, warm the liquid to be flambeed or it won't catch fire. Never pour the liquid to be flambeed near an open fire; the flames can escape into the bottle and cause it to explode. Move the pan away from the heat source before you set a match to it.

Flute   To make a decorative edge on pie or another pastry, usually by making a scallop pattern.

Fold   To incorporate one ingredient into another using a gentle, lifting motion, preferably with a rubber spatula. To fold, cut down into the middle of the mixture to the bottom of the bowl, scrape the bottom of the bowl, and lift up the spatula, bringing some of the mixture up with it. Repeat this until the mixture is uniform in color and texture. You may find this process easier if you turn the bowl with one hand as you use the spatula with the other.

You usually fold to incorporate a fragile or delicate ingredient into a heavier one to retain a light, fluffy, aerated texture. If you beat, stir, or mix the ingredient instead of folding it, the mixture would deflate. Folding also is used to incorporate berries, nuts, and other solids into batter for muffins and cakes. This avoids overworking the ingredients, which would activate too much gluten in the batter and cause the pastry to be tough and rubbery.

Garnish To decorate food to enhance visual appeal. For tips on garnishing, see Chapter 10.

Glaze To coat food to give it a glossy sheen and enhanced flavor. You can glaze meats, fish, cakes, and candies. Hot meats, fish, and vegetables are usually glazed with a liquid such as stock or juice that has been boiled down to a syrupy consistency. Cold foods are usually glazed with aspic (gelled stock). Cakes are usually glazed with icing.

Grate To cut ingredients into small particles using a food processor or a hand grater, which has tiny, sharp holes for cutting.

Grease To coat a pan with fat to keep foods from sticking.

Grind To make food into tiny particles using a food processor, food grinder, blender, or mortar and pestle.

Hull To remove the stem of strawberries by hand or with a special implement called a huller.

Husk To remove the outside leaves from ears of corn.

Julienne To slice food into thin shreds or strips. To do this, first slice the food, and then place the slices on a board, overlapping each other. Cut down on the slices to make match stick-like pieces about $1/8$" wide.

Julienne strips are thin match stick-like shreds.

Knead   To manipulate food either mechanically or by hand in a pressing-stretching-folding routine. You do this to develop flour gluten when you are preparing bread or to make fondant tender and shiny when you are making candy. When you knead bread by hand, do it on a lightly floured board until the dough is smooth and elastic.

Line   To cover a pan or cookie sheet with paper to prevent foods from sticking.

Macerate   To place fruits or vegetables in a liquid so they can absorb flavor and soften in texture. You macerate fruits in liqueur, fruit juice, or sugar syrup. This is similar to marinating.

Marinate   To place food (usually meats but sometimes vegetables) in a liquid so it will become tender and more flavorful. Marinades typically are composed of an acidic ingredient such as wine vinegar, yogurt, or lemon juice plus seasonings and vegetable oil, but sometimes marinades are simple blends of spices. To prevent food poisoning, be sure to marinate foods either in the refrigerator or for only a short time out of the refrigerator. Do not reuse marinades that you have used for meat, poultry, or fish.

Mince   To chop food into very small pieces (the same as "finely chopped"). The best way to mince foods is to chop them (see *chop*), and then hold the tip of the large knife down with one hand and bring the blade and wider end of the knife up and down quickly on the ingredients using the other hand. Gather the ingredients and repeat the process until you achieve the desired texture.

This is what minced food looks like.

Mix   To blend ingredients with a stirring motion using a spoon or fork.

Mull   To steep hot tea, wine, or cider with spices or other flavor enhancers.

Parboil   To partially cook food in boiling water before completely cooking it by some other process. Parboiling is a lengthier process than blanching is.

Pare   To remove the skin from fruits and vegetables (the same as peeling). Use a paring knife or vegetable peeler.

Patch   To repair tiny cracks in dough by pressing two pieces of dough together or using a strip of leftover dough and sealing it between the two cracked pieces. Patching is preferable to rerolling dough since rerolling toughens the pastry.

Pipe   To force a smooth, stiff, soft mixture through a pastry tube in order to decorate other foods or a plate.

Pit   To remove the seeds, stone, or pit from fruits such as cherries or olives.

Plump   To soak food (such as raisins or dried fruit) to make it soft and tender.

Pound   To flatten food, especially meat, to make it thinner and more tender. To flatten chicken breasts or other meat, place the meat between two layers of waxed or parchment paper. Bear down on the meat with a meat mallet, cleaver, or wide bottomed pot until the meat is as thin as you want it.

Preheat   To set the oven to a desired temperature so it is hot enough to receive food. It isn't usually necessary to preheat the oven when you are cooking casseroles and other moisture laden foods. However, you always should preheat an oven when you are making roasts and baked goods, so you get a crispy or properly browned surface and when you are reheating fried foods, so they won't be greasy.

Prick   To pierce food so it won't explode, rise, expand, or shrink unnecessarily as it cooks. Use the tines of a fork to prick pie dough; use the tip of a sharp knife to prick a potato for baking.

Proof   To test yeast to see whether it is still potent. To do this, dissolve the yeast in a small amount of warm water and add a pinch of sugar. Mix and wait 5–10 minutes. If bubbles appear around the edges of the bowl and the top of the mixture becomes foamy, the yeast is okay.

Punch Down   To hit dough with your hand to deflate it so it becomes more tender and evenly grained.

Puree   To blend food until it becomes completely smooth and uniform. You can puree food through a strainer or in a food mill, blender, or food processor.

Reconstitute   To rehydrate dried food (such as dried mushrooms or sun-dried tomatoes) by soaking it in water or another liquid.

Reduce   To boil a liquid to reduce its volume and intensify its flavor. The resulting thicker liquid is called a "reduction" and is the basis of many classic and nouvelle cuisine sauces.

Refresh   To place hot vegetables under cold running water or plunge them into a pan of ice cold water in order to stop the vegetable from cooking further, to set its color, and to retain its crisp texture.

Render   To melt fat to reduce the solid fat to liquid. Always render fat over low heat to avoid sputtering.

Rice   To force food through a strainer or special "ricer" to mash it. This is similar to pureeing, but a riced mixture may not be as smooth as a puree.

Scald   To heat liquids to just below the boiling point, when small bubbles appear around the edges of the pan. Or, to plunge food into boiling water for a short time (as for blanching) or pour boiling water over food.

Scallop   To make a decorative edge around a pie crust (see also *flute*). It also means to cook foods in a creamy sauce.

Score   To cut narrow gashes into the surface of meat or fish to help tenderize the flesh. Scoring also helps the meat or fish retain its shape as it cooks.

Scramble   To mix eggs with a fork or spoon while they cook so that curd shapes form.

Sear   To brown foods over high heat to seal in juices and create a rich color. You can sear foods in a hot pan, broiler, grill, or oven.

Season   To add flavor to food by adding salt, pepper, herbs, or spices.

Shell   To remove edible seeds from their fibrous, inedible pods, as with peas and lima beans, or to remove shrimp from its hard outer covering.

Shred   To cut food into long, slender pieces using a knife or special shredding blade in a food processor. Shreds are similar to julienne strips.

Shuck   To remove the flesh of mollusks such as clams and oysters from their shells.

Sift   To remove the lumps and lighten the texture of certain ingredients, especially flour, by forcing it through a sieve or strainer. There are special tools made specifically for sifting flour, but any old strainer will do and is cheaper and easier to use and clean.

Simmer   To cook food at temperatures just below boiling. When food is simmering, bubbles appear around the edges of the pan. Most often you will boil foods first, and then lower the heat so that the food stays at a steady temperature just below a boil.

Slice   To cut food into evenly shaped pieces. To slice ingredients, hold the knife the same way you do to chop, but cut across with a forward motion as you cut down on the food.

Skim   To remove the scum that rises to the surface of a liquid such as soup or stock.

Snip   To cut food, typically fresh herbs, into small pieces with a scissors.

Steep   To pour boiling water or another liquid over dry ingredients, typically tea leaves, and let the mixture stand in order to infuse flavor and color into the liquid.

Stir   To combine ingredients with a spoon using a circular motion.

Strain   To separate solids from liquids through a strainer or fine sieve.

Stud To insert spices, herbs, or other flavorings into the surface of food. The most common example of this is clove-studded baked Virginia ham.

Stuff To fill a cavity with food or a mixture of ingredients. You can stuff the inside cavity of a chicken, turkey, or other fowl, the circle of a crown roast or acorn squash, the center of a bundt cake, and so on. Never stuff poultry until just before you put it in the oven to roast.

Temper To prepare a cool ingredient before adding it to a hot one to prevent curdling. Sometimes, for example, a recipe tells you to add eggs to a hot sauce. If you add the eggs without tempering them, the mixture will curdle. To temper the eggs, you add a small amount of the hot sauce to them, beating constantly. When you have added enough for the egg to feel warm, you can add the egg/sauce mixture to the rest of the hot sauce and continue cooking. Never let the egg mixture come to a boil or it will curdle.

Toast To brown food by the indirect heat of an oven (as you do when you toast nuts) or by the direct heat of a broiler (as when you toast bread or brown foods under the broiler).

Toss To mix ingredients quickly and gently with a lifting motion using two utensils such as a salad fork and spoon. Salad and pasta are typically tossed.

Truss To tie the wings and legs of poultry close to the body so it will keep its shape during roasting. Sometimes people truss stuffed poultry to help keep the stuffing inside the bird's cavity.

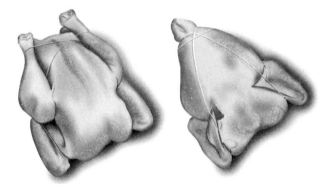

Trussing poultry helps a bird keep its shape during roasting.

Unmold To turn food out from a container or mold onto a serving plate. Foods that are unmolded include gelatin salads, custards, and cakes. Lots of people have a fear of unmolding. Here are some tips to help you do it successfully:

➤ Grease the pan lightly with vegetable oil or spray before adding the food.

➤ When you are ready to unmold the food, dip the mold to its rim in hot water for 5–8 seconds or until you see the edges loosen slightly from the sides.

➤ Place a serving plate upside down over the top of the mold, turn the mold and plate over, and shake the mold, and the filling should slide out.

➤ If your dish doesn't slide out, try the dipping process again for 3–4 seconds, or run the tip of a small knife around the edge where the food meets the side of the mold.

Whip   To beat, except that when you whip you always use a beater or whisk (when it may be called whisking) but never a fork. When you whip, you mix ingredients quickly and vigorously to incorporate air, increase volume, and lighten the mixture.

Work In   To incorporate one ingredient into another ingredient using your hands or tools. For example, when making pie dough, you work the fat into the flour.

Chapter 14

IT **SAID**, "AL DENTE ..."

A Compendium of Catchwords Used in Recipes

In This Chapter

➤ A super-glossary that describes food terms found in recipes

➤ A super-glossary that describes unfamiliar cooking equipment terms found in recipes

Even though you understand recipe directions and are acquainted with cooking procedures, as you read your recipe, you may come across some food terms that are unfamiliar to you. The recipe may tell you to cook the pasta "al dente," for example. It may name an ingredient or type of food you don't know, such as "duxelles" or "Sole Meuniere." Or the recipe may refer to special types of equipment you never heard of or don't know very much about, such as a "bain-marie" or "whisk." This chapter describes some of the more important food and equipment terms you are likely to find as you begin your adventure into good cooking.

Al Dente and Other Terms You Need to Know

You may be familiar with a few of the following food terms, but even the most experienced cooks have no idea what some of these things mean. Is it important to understand all of them? You may never make an aspic nor use a liaison to thicken a sauce. But a good cook ought to know about them anyway. It makes you more knowledgeable and that knowledge helps you understand what you are doing as you cook. At the very least, knowing food terms makes you sound smart at parties.

Acidulated Water   Because certain fruits and vegetables turn brown when they are cut open and exposed to air (apples and artichokes, for example), a recipe may tell you to place the food in acidulated water. This is simply a mixture of water and some acidic ingredient such as lemon juice or vinegar, usually in the proportion of 1–2 TB. acid to 3–4 cups water.

Al Dente   An Italian term that translates to "in the tooth" and refers to the way the texture of cooked pasta and vegetables feels in your mouth. Foods prepared al dente should offer resistance: tender yet still-crunchy vegetables, pasta that is vaguely chewy.

Aperitif   A before-dinner drink (such as vermouth, dry white wine, or champagne) that stimulates the appetite.

Aspic   A savory jelly made from meat, fish, poultry, or vegetable stock. This can be a plain aspic that you cut into shapes to serve as a garnish for food, a molded salad containing meat and vegetables, or a glossy coating for cold food.

Au Gratin   A dish topped with cheese, bread crumbs, and butter that is baked in a shallow dish known as an au gratin pan and browned briefly under the broiler. Also known as just plain "gratin."

Au Jus   Meat served with natural cooking juices.

Au Lait   Any food made with milk, although the term usually refers to coffee with milk: cafe au lait.

Beurre Manie   A creamed mixture of equal parts flour and butter used to thicken sauces and soups at the end of their cooking time.

Bouquet Garni   A bundle of fresh and/or dried herbs and spices used to flavor stock, soup, stews, and braised dishes. The herbs and spices are tied in cheesecloth and are removed before you serve the dish. The most common bouquet garni ingredients are bay leaf, thyme, peppercorns, parsley, and sometimes celery tops.

Brochette   Skewered meat, poultry, fish, and/or vegetables that are usually grilled. This is the same as a kebab.

Canapé   A small cut of bread topped with savory foods such as smoked salmon or herb-flavored butter and served as hors d'oeuvre.

Chutney   A highly seasoned sweet and spicy relish made of fruits and vegetables that is served as a condiment with meats.

Cobbler   A deep dish fruit pie with a top crust only. The crust can be made of standard pie dough or biscuit dough. When the pie is fully baked, the crust is broken up and pressed gently into the filling so that it looks "cobbled." Sometimes cobbler is made with discs of dough or blobs of biscuit instead of a single crust, in which case it looks cobbled even before it's baked.

Condiment   A condiment is a sauce or relish used to enhance food. The most well known condiments are ketchup, mustard, Worcestershire sauce, salsas, and hot pepper sauce.

Court Bouillon   A liquid mixture of water, wine, vegetables, herbs, and spices used for poaching fish.

Crudites   Assorted, cut up raw or blanched vegetables, usually accompanied by a dip; one of the most popular hors d'oeuvre in America. You can place the dip in a bowl, but for more dramatic effect, put it inside a hollowed, crusty round bread, bell peppers, or cabbage head.

Creme Fraiche   A tart-tasting dairy product that has the texture of sour cream or plain yogurt. It is used plain on top of berries but also is a fabulous enrichment for many sauces. You can buy creme fraiche in specialty stores, but it is easy to make at home. See the recipe section.

Curdle   The result of heating an egg-based mixture too quickly or over too high a temperature, which causes the egg particles to coagulate and separate from the other ingredients. This is a word that is unpleasant; something has gone wrong when a recipe curdles.

Duxelles   A classic mixture of minced mushrooms and shallots sautéed with butter. It is used in many sauces and as a stuffing for such diverse foods as stuffed mushrooms and ravioli.

Egg Wash   A mixture of whole egg, yolk only, or white only, mixed with a small amount of water to brush onto something. It is used to give a shiny glaze to bread (brushed onto the dough before baking the bread), to patch two pieces of pastry together, to help seeds adhere to dough, or to serve as a "film" that prevents an unbaked pie shell from becoming soggy when some moist filling is added.

Filo Pastry   Also known as phyllo pastry, a tissue-thin dough used primarily in Greek and Middle Eastern cooking, especially to make Baklava and Spanakopitas.

Fines Herbes   A mixture of any combination of fresh or dried herbs used to season foods. Unlike a bouquet garni, which is placed inside cheesecloth and is later removed, the fines herbes are scattered into the recipe.

Liaison   Any mixture used to thicken sauce, stew, or soup. A beurre manie is a type of liaison.

Lukewarm   Something that is at body temperature. Recipes often say to heat or cool something to lukewarm.

Marinade   A mixture (usually a seasoned acid-based liquid, though it can be a dry mixture) used to enhance flavor and/or tenderize the texture of food.

Meringue   A mixture of stiffly beaten egg whites and sugar. Some meringues are soft, as in Lemon Meringue Pie. Some are firm and crispy, such as Meringue Pie Shells. Soft meringues usually contain less sugar than firm ones do. It is difficult to make meringue on a humid day, because the whipped mixture tends to soften and "weep."

Meuniere   A classic sauce made with butter, lemon juice, and parsley.

Mirepoix   A mixture of chopped vegetables used to flavor stocks, braised foods, and sauces. They may be removed from the dish (by straining them off) before the food is finished. However, mirepoix ingredients often are pureed with pan juices and cooking fluids to thicken and enrich a sauce, which means you don't have to use flour or some other starch as a thickener. The most common mirepoix ingredients are carrots, onions, and celery.

Mousse   A French word that means "frothy" and refers to a light, ethereal, spongy-textured dish that can be sweet or savory, cold or hot. Mousses are made of pureed food such as meat or fruit, or melted chocolate, which are folded with whipped cream and/or beaten egg whites. Sometimes gelatin is added as a stabilizer.

Paillard   A boneless chicken breast that has been pounded thin. Sometimes it is called a supreme or cutlet. Though the word technically refers to chicken, sometimes it refers to any meat (veal, pork, and so on).

Pilaf   A dish containing rice that is sautéed before being cooked with liquid. Any number of seasonings or textural ingredients, from chopped shrimp to raisins to mushrooms to almonds, may be included in a pilaf. The Spanish dish Paella is an elaborate pilaf that may contain seafood, poultry, and meats.

Roux   A mixture of fat (usually butter) and flour cooked together before adding a liquid to make a sauce. It is the basis of dozens of sauces from classic white sauce (roux plus milk or cream) to veloute (roux plus stock) to mornay (white sauce plus cheese). Old fashioned macaroni and cheese begins with a roux-based cheddar cheese sauce.

A classic roux contains equal amounts of fat and flour; you vary the texture of the sauce by using different quantities of liquid. For example, a medium-thick white sauce (also known as *béchamel*) is made with 2 TB. fat, 2 TB. flour, and 1 to $1^1/_4$ cups of milk. To make a thicker sauce (for a soufflé, for example), you would use 3 TB. fat, 3 TB. flour, and 1 to $1^1/_4$ cups of milk. However, if you want to cut down on dietary fat, you can increase the flour by as much as 3 TB. without adding more fat. So a thick sauce for croquettes could be made with 2 TB. fat, 5 TB. flour, and 1 to $1^1/_4$ cups milk.

To make a roux, you melt the fat in a small, heavy saucepan over low heat. (Do not use an aluminum pan because it imparts a metallic taste.) Then you add the flour and incorporate it into the fat with a whisk. Continue to cook and whisk the ingredients constantly for at least two minutes over low heat. This assures that your sauce won't have an unpleasantly "starchy" taste. A "white roux" is the most common type and is ready after two minutes of cooking for use in classic white sauce and all its variations. There is something called "blond roux" also. This is slightly darker (cooked a minute or so longer) and is useful for ivory to light amber colored sauces. A "brown roux" is just that: roux cooked over low heat for even a few minutes longer so it becomes golden brown. A brown roux goes into brown sauces.

Scallop   A type of seafood (sea scallop, bay scallop), or a thin slice of meat. Also known as a cutlet.

148

Smoke Point The point at which fat breaks down, starts to smoke, and gives off an odor. Different fats have different smoke points. To stir-fry or cook by any other method that requires high heat, you need a fat that has a high smoke point: peanut, canola, corn, soybean, safflower, and sunflower oils all are fine. Olive oil has a lower smoke point than these and is not appropriate for high heat cooking. Butter has a low smoke point. It burns easily as temperatures get higher. Clarified butter has a higher smoke point than regular butter. Sometimes a recipe will tell you to use clarified butter or plain butter plus vegetable oil. This is because the butter provides flavor and a rich color, and the vegetable oil withstands the heat, giving the mixture about the same smoke point as clarified butter.

Stock Sometimes called broth, the long-simmering poaching liquid from cooked meat, poultry, fish, or vegetables. The solids are strained from the liquid when cooking is complete. Stock is used to make soup and sauce.

Truffles High-priced types of fungus, these are difficult to find, are hunted down by specially trained pigs or dogs, and are highly prized because they are rare and have an astonishingly rich, earthy flavor and tantalizing aroma. Truffles are used mostly in patés and pasta dishes, but also are used to garnish food. (Chocolate and other candy truffles are confections shaped to resemble fungus truffles.)

Vegetable Cooking Spray This is vegetable oil (plus other ingredients such as alcohol and lecithin) in an aerosol can. You spray it onto pans to prevent food from sticking. A sprayed pan has fewer calories and less fat than one greased with shortening.

Zest The outermost layer of the skin of a citrus fruit. It does NOT include the white pith, only the thin, colored part. You can grate zest off the pith with a hand grater or with a special "zesting tool."

A Bain-Marie and Other Equipment Terms You Ought to Know

Most of the time you will know about the pots, pans, and equipment your recipe mentions. But sometimes you see an odd item mentioned in a recipe or notice something in a store and you don't know what it is. Do you know what a citrus reamer does, for example? A bain-marie? The following are some of the more useful equipment items you should know about.

Bain-Marie Literally "Marie's Bath," a hot-water bath used to provide even heat and a moist environment for foods. You use a bain-marie to cook foods steadily and slowly or to keep them warm, either in the oven or on the stovetop. To make a bain-marie, place a dish containing food inside of a larger vessel containing simmering water (or fill the larger vessel with water after you put the dish inside). The larger vessel may be a roasting pan or cake pan (for the oven) or a large saucepan (for the stovetop). You usually use a bain-marie to cook delicate items that crack or curdle easily, such as custards, cheesecake, and egg-based dishes.

A bain-marie is useful when you cook foods such as cheesecake or custard that crack or curdle easily.

Bulb Baster   A two-part device used to baste food. It has a long, tapering tube made of metal or plastic and a rubber bulb at the wider end. To baste, you place the tube in the basting liquid and squeeze the bulb, which sucks the liquid into the tube. Then you aim the tube at the food to be basted and release the bulb. The liquid flows out of the tube onto the food.

This bulb baster has a metal tube; some have a plastic tube.

Cake Tester   A long, wiry rod with a loop handle on top. You insert it into the center of a cake to see if the cake is done. The cake is done if the rod comes out dry (with no batter clinging to it). This is an invaluable tool.

Chafing Dish   A sauté pan that sits inside another pan containing water (similar to a double boiler in concept). The water is heated with canned fuel that sits beneath the pan. Most often, chafing dishes are used to keep foods warm for buffet service at parties; therefore, many are decorative or fancy. Although these dishes can be used as cooking devices, because the heat is indirect, cooking can be slow.

Charlotte Mold   A tinned-steel container that has gently flared sides and is used to hold charlottes (a type of pudding) and just about any other molded food.

Cheesecloth   A gauzy cotton cloth used to wrap foods such as bouquet garni or whole fish and hold them together during cooking. Food wrapped in cheesecloth is easier to remove from the cooking vessel.

Double boiler   A two-part pot in which one pan sits inside another. The lower pan holds water; the upper pan holds food. The water in the lower pan cooks the food, yet protects it from intense, direct heat. Double boilers come in handy for delicate foods and those that would burn too easily over direct heat, such as chocolate, custard, or egg-based dishes. You can buy a double boiler, but it is easy to make your own by placing a bowl over the rim of a saucepan.

Dutch Oven   A large, heavy casserole dish or short-handled pan used for braising and other slow, moist-heat cooking methods. You can use it in the oven or on the stovetop.

Gratin Dish   A shallow, heatproof pan or casserole dish in which you brown foods by putting them briefly beneath the broiler. You can also serve directly from these pans.

Jelly Roll Pan   A cookie sheet with a rim around it. You can use it for classic jelly rolls, for baking cookies, for toasting nuts, bread crumbs, or other "loose" ingredients, or for reheating foods.

Non-Reactive Pan   A pan made of materials that won't react with acidic ingredients such as vinegar, wine, lemon juice, or tomatoes. Non-reactive pans include those made of stainless steel, ceramic, glass, enamel, or anodized aluminum. Regular aluminum or copper are not non-reactive.

Nutmeg Grater   A small metal grater with one curved side fitted with sharp cutting holes and one flat side; it tapers at one end. To grate nutmegs, you rub them against the sharp side and the gratings fall through the middle and out the narrow end. There also are nutmeg mills that look exactly like pepper mills.

Pastry Blender   A tool used to cut fat into flour. It is made of curved, rigid metal wires that are held together with a thick handle.

Pie Weights   Pie weights are ceramic or aluminum bean-shaped pellets used for baking blind so pie crusts won't shrink.

Skillet   A general name for a frying pan. There are many types of skillets, including sauté pans, braising pans, and omelet pans. When a recipe does not indicate otherwise, you may use any all-purpose skillet.

Skimmer   A utensil used to skim fat, scum, or solids from food. A skimmer has a long handle with a disk-shaped end. The disk is perforated metal with either large holes (for removing solids) or mesh-like holes (for straining scum and fat).

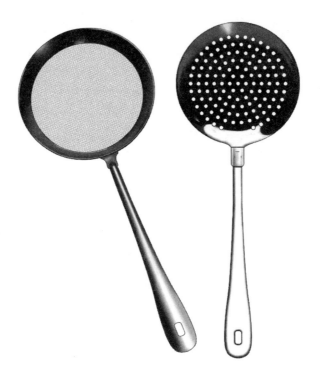

Skimmers help you get rid of fat and scum from stock, soup, and stew.

Soufflé Dish A deep, straight-sided casserole dish. The straight sides allow soufflés to rise properly. These dishes are useful for other types of recipes too, including savory casseroles and puddings, as well as cold mousses.

Springform Pan A two-part pan with detachable sides that clamp onto a base and can be removed easily by opening the clamp. It is used primarily for cakes that stick, such as cheesecake, or molded cakes and confections, such as chocolate mousse-lady finger cake.

Whisk A wire whip used to beat foods and incorporate air into them. The wires are made of stainless steel, and the handles are stainless steel or wood. Whisks come in many shapes and sizes for different purposes. A balloon whisk is large and wide with flexible wires and is used when you want to incorporate as much air as possible (to beat egg whites and whipped cream, for example). Smaller, more tapered whisks with rigid wires are better for thick batters that don't require much aeration. Those with flexible wires are useful for light batters, marinades, and fragile foods.

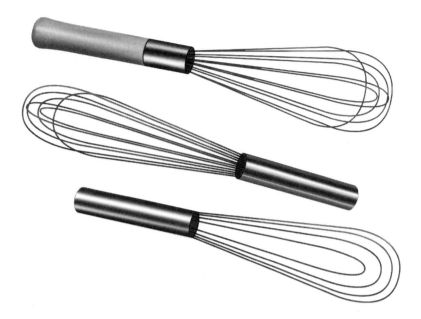

Whisks come in different shapes and sizes to serve different purposes.

Wok   A round-bottomed pan once used exclusively in Asian cooking, that is now useful for stir-fries and other dishes cooked quickly over high heat. The rounded sides ensure quick, even heating and cooking with a minimum of fat and help keep the food in the pan (instead of falling onto the stovetop).

Zester   A small cutting device used to remove the outermost layer of citrus fruit.

This tiny tool can remove the zest of citrus fruit in a flash.

Chapter 15

Method Acting: How You Cook Food

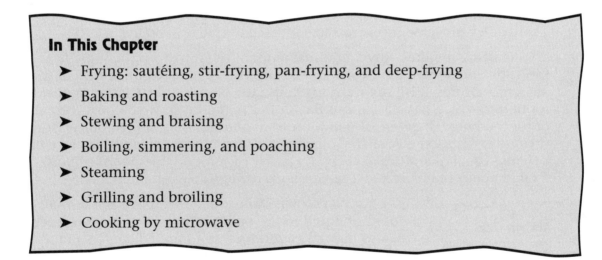

In This Chapter

➤ Frying: sautéing, stir-frying, pan-frying, and deep-frying

➤ Baking and roasting

➤ Stewing and braising

➤ Boiling, simmering, and poaching

➤ Steaming

➤ Grilling and broiling

➤ Cooking by microwave

Your apron is on, your recipe is out, and your hands are clean. You are about to cook. You know how to chop the garlic and follow other recipe instructions, and you know what it means to cook an ingredient *al dente*. You know what a springform pan is.

All of these directions and terms lead to the actual cooking of your food. But you don't just cook the food any old way. You roast some foods and stir-fry others. Which ingredients do you poach, and which do you grill? Just as a method actor must understand a role for a film, you must understand the role an ingredient plays in a dish and use the appropriate technique to cook it to advantage. This chapter explains the basic cooking methods and gives tips on how to use those methods successfully.

Frying

There are several methods that use the technique of frying. All frying methods involve cooking food in hot fat. Most of the differences among these sub-methods have to do with the kind of food you cook, the amount and temperature of the fat, and the type of pan you use.

Sautéing

When you sauté foods, you cook them quickly in a small amount of fat over moderate heat. You can use a specially designed shallow pan with straight sides, but any open skillet will do. Because the cooking time is relatively brief, only tender cuts of meat, small types of poultry, and water-rich vegetables such as mushrooms and spinach are suitable. You may sauté firm-textured vegetables if you parboil them as well. Foods good for sautéing include broiler-fryer chickens, beef steaks (such as strip or sirloin), veal, pork and lamb chops and cutlets, fish fillets, shrimp and scallops, and vegetables (such as bell peppers, mushrooms, spinach, onions, and zucchini).

There is no adequate translation of the French term "sauter," which means "to jump." The food doesn't jump, nor do you. The bottom line is that you have to keep the food moving in the pan so it won't stick, scorch, or dry out. Shake the pan. Shake the food. Turn the pieces often (except for delicate fish fillets). These quick movements characterize the technique of sautéing.

Sautéing requires only a minimal amount of fat to keep the ingredients from sticking to the pan. However, because you have to keep the heat at moderate temperatures, it is important to choose the fat carefully. Classic sautés call for butter, which has a luxurious flavor. But butter burns if you heat it too high or for too long. Therefore, if you want to use butter, use clarified butter or mix the butter with some vegetable oil, which doesn't burn as readily. To mix the two, use equal quantities of each: if a recipe calls for 4 tablespoons of butter, use 2 tablespoons of butter and 2 tablespoons of vegetable oil.

After you brown sautéed food, you can add a small amount of liquid to the pan. The liquid becomes a sauce. You also may add additional solid ingredients to a sauté, adding mushrooms to sautéed fish, for example.

Follow these tips for successful sautéing:

➤ Bring food to room temperature so it browns quickly and stays juicy.

➤ Make sure the food is dry, or it won't brown properly.

➤ You can sprinkle delicate foods such as chicken, fish, and veal with flour before sautéing them to prevent scorching, add color, and thicken the sauce.

Kitchen Clue
Spattering grease is a potential problem when you're frying. Make sure the food to be fried is dry and that the frying pan has some depth so grease bubbles hit the sides. If a grease spatter burns your skin, put ice on the burn immediately.

➤ Use a pan that conducts heat well.

➤ Make sure the pan is big enough to allow space between the pieces of food. If the pan is crowded, the food will steam rather than fry, and it won't be browned and crispy.

➤ If you only have a small pan, sauté the food in batches.

➤ Use uniform size pieces that cook evenly.

➤ Drain excess fat from the pan before you add the liquid.

➤ If the ingredient is fully cooked and you want a thicker sauce, remove the ingredient before you reduce the pan fluids, otherwise it will become over-cooked. If the ingredient isn't fully cooked when you add the liquid, cover the pan to finish the cooking.

Kitchen Clue

Sautés are among the most versa-tile recipes. You can vary almost any dish by changing the meat (veal cutlets to chicken cutlets, for example), changing the liquid (stock to wine, for example), or changing or adding embel-lishments (changing onions to leeks, for example, or adding shrimp or sausage to a dish of sautéed chicken).

Stir-Frying

As the name implies, you stir as you fry, moving the food very quickly. This method is similar to sautéing, except you use higher heat and you cut the food into bite-size pieces so you "toss" rather than turn or shake them. Like sautés, you must use ingredients that cook quickly and can withstand high tempera-tures. The best foods to stir-fry are tender cuts of meat such as sirloin beef, marinated meats, boneless chicken, firm-fleshed fish and shellfood, water-rich vegetables, parboiled vegetables, or vegetables that you can steam in the pan fluids when you finish stir-frying.

A wok has rounded sides that help radiate heat quickly and evenly.

While you can use any type of skillet to stir-fry, the handiest pan is a wok. A *wok* is a rounded pan of Asian origin; the rounded shape helps radiate heat quickly and evenly up the sides of the pan. That means the food cooks more

Kitchen Clue
You can stir-fry fibrous vegetables but they need special attention. In addition to parboiling or steaming them prior to or at the end of stir-frying, you should peel them. Broccoli is a particular stir-fry favorite. To peel broccoli stems, cut off about a half inch of flesh at the bottom, and then peel the topmost layer of skin back with a paring knife to the top of the stem where it meets the florets. Peeled stems are delightfully tender.

evenly. The pieces benefit from the heat at the side in addition to that at the bottom of the pan. Therefore, you can use even less fat than you need with a wide-bottomed skillet.

Since you stir-fry at high heat, you have to use a cooking fat with a high smoke point, that is, one that will not burn and become smoky at high temperatures. Butter is unsuitable. Olive oil is okay only when you will stir-fry an ingredient such as spinach that cooks exceptionally quickly. The best choices are blandly flavored vegetable oils such as peanut, soybean, corn, canola, safflower, and sunflower oils.

As with sautés, sometimes stir-fries include both meats and vegetables. You usually cook the meats first so the vegetables don't soften too much while you wait for the meat.

Follow these tips for successful stir-frying:

➤ Get out all your ingredients and tools before you cook. That includes any thickening mixtures such as cornstarch and water.

➤ Organize the ingredients into separate containers so it will be easy for you to add them to the pan quickly.

➤ Be sure to cut the ingredients about the same size so the pieces cook evenly.

➤ Preheat the wok or other pan. It should be very hot before you add any ingredient.

➤ Add a minimal amount of oil to the pan. If you use a wok, swirl the pan to coat the sides with a film of oil.

➤ For better flavor, always stir-fry seasoning ingredients such as garlic and ginger before you add other ingredients.

Pan-Frying and Deep-Frying

These two similar methods involve cooking food over moderately high heat until it is cooked through and the inside is juicy while the surface is crunchy and golden brown. You can use any type of skillet to pan-fry since you need only about 1" of cooking fat (though a straight-sided sauté pan is recommended). When you deep-fry, you immerse the food completely in the fat, so you need a deep pan or a specially designed deep-fryer. Most foods that are pan-fried can also be deep-fried and vice-versa.

Pan- and deep-fried foods are cooked for moderate amounts of time so you have to protect them from the intense heat. One way to do that is to coat them. The most delicate, quick-to-cook foods, such as flat fish fillets and thinly sliced vegetables, need only a light coating of flour or bread crumbs. Thicker pieces,

158

such as boneless chicken breasts, do better when you coat them with batter or with beaten egg or egg white plus flour or bread crumbs. Soft-centered foods, such as croquettes, need additional protection: coat them with flour first, then beaten egg, and then bread or cracker crumbs. Starchy foods such as potatoes and doughnuts need no coating.

Another way to protect fried foods is to "double-fry" them. To double-fry, fry the food for a short time to brown the surface, and then remove it from the fat for a minute or so to cool down the outside and let the heat penetrate the inside. When the food has cooled slightly, return it to the fat to finish cooking. This is the ideal way to fry chicken parts. When you double-fry food you need only give it a flour coating.

The temperature at which you pan-fry or deep-fry food depends on what you are cooking. The larger the food, the lower the temperature. For deep-frying, you can use a special thermometer that tells you the temperature of the fat; an electric deep-fryer has a built-in thermostat. Otherwise you can use the "bread-cube test." Drop a small piece of bread into hot fat. If it sizzles slowly (gentle bubbles around the edge), the fat is about 350 degrees. If it bubbles briskly and the bread browns quickly, the fat is about 365 to 375 degrees. If the fat is above 375 degrees, you will see a haze begin to form on the surface of the fat; above 400 degrees, the fat will start to smoke. Obviously, it is important to choose a fat with a high smoke point. Butter, margarine, and olive oil don't qualify. Use vegetable shortening or peanut, soybean, corn, canola, safflower, or sunflower oils.

Follow these tips for successful pan-frying and deep-frying:

➤ Cut foods into uniform pieces so they cook evenly.

➤ Do not fry extremely large pieces such as a half chicken.

➤ Do not add too many pieces of food to the fat at one time. This lowers the temperature too much.

➤ Fry food in batches and let the fat return to its proper temperature between batches.

➤ Never add wet ingredients to hot fat.

➤ Coatings stick to fried foods better if you coat the foods at least 15 minutes prior to frying time.

➤ You can reuse frying fats about three times. Strain the fat and store it in the refrigerator. Before you use it again, add about $1/3$ of its volume of fresh fat.

➤ Remove fried foods with a skimmer, slotted spoon, basket, or tongs. Drain the food on paper toweling.

Kitchen Clue
Grease-free frying has nothing to do with which brand or type of shortening or vegetable oil you use. It has to do with the temperature of the fat. Frying fat must be hot enough to seal the surface quickly so the fat will not be absorbed during cooking. Keep the fat at the proper temperature throughout the cooking process, and you will have grease-free, crunchy food.

Use tongs to remove fried foods from cooking fat.

Baking and Roasting

Baking and roasting are almost exactly the same: you cook the food in an enclosed oven with dry currents of hot air. There is no apparent reason why one is called baking and the other is called roasting. The distinction seems to be that you roast meat and poultry. But what about baked ham? It really makes no difference.

Roasting

Roasting usually involves cooking large pieces of meat, which means you have to cook the food in a large pan. However, the pan's sides have to be low enough to allow air to circulate freely around the food. It is best to put a roast in the pan fat side up so that as the fat renders in the heat, it bastes the meat. It also is a good idea to use a rack that raises the roast out of the rendered fat. If you are roasting foods that are exceptionally lean, you can bard them (cover them with a thin layer of fat such as bacon) or baste them frequently to keep them moist.

Just because a meat is labeled a roast doesn't mean you should roast it. Only tender cuts of meat such as rib or top round can withstand dry heat. Chuck "roast," shoulder "roast," and other fibrous "roasts" cut from the more exercised parts of the animal need moist heat cooking methods to soften them. You may roast tougher cuts if you marinate them first. All poultry except for older stewing hens are suitable for roasting. You also may roast cut up chunky vegetables.

The best way to roast meat is to cook it first at a high temperature for a brief time, and then cook it to completion at more modest temperatures. This helps give the surface a deep, rich color and keep juicy fluids inside.

Follow these tips for successful roasting:

➤ Bring the meat to room temperature before you roast it.

➤ Make sure you preheat the oven.

➤ Make sure the pan is slightly larger than the roast. If it is too small, rendered fat will drip onto the oven. If it is too large, rendered fat will burn in the pan.

➤ Never cover a roast with a foil "tent." This steams the meat.

➤ Let a roast stand for 15 minutes before you carve it. This gives it time to finish cooking and lets the meat reabsorb juices that keep the meat moist.

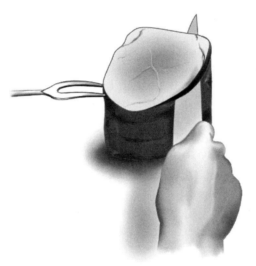

To carve a boneless roast, place it on a meat board and hold the meat with a large fork. Slice down for a small roast; stand a large roast on its end and slice across.

Baking

You bake foods such as cakes, pies, cookies, and other pastries, as well as soufflés, casseroles, small portions of meat, and fish. These foods generally are smaller than roasted foods, so you cook them in smaller pans, baking sheets, casserole dishes, muffin pans, or pie pans. However, as in roasting, it's important that air be able to circulate freely for food to cook evenly, so you should not crowd the oven with too many pans. If you have to use two oven shelves, try to alternate them one to the left, one to the right.

Follow these tips for successful baking:

➤ Make sure you preheat the oven. This is especially important for cakes, pies, pastries, and cookies.

➤ Bake cakes on the center shelf, except for angel food cakes, which go on the lower shelf.

➤ Don't open the oven door during baking unless basting is necessary.

➤ Keeping your oven clean helps foods cook more evenly.

Stewing and Braising

Stewing and braising are methods for cooking sinewy, fibrous cuts of meat such as chuck, shoulder, bottom round, rump, brisket, and shank; older poultry such as stewing hens; and hardy vegetables such as celery and endive. They both are processes of moist heat cooking by which you cook foods slowly in a covered pan for a long period of time. Tough foods cook to tenderness with these methods. Meat sinew melts into rich, glossy gravy, and even though you use the so-called "inferior" cuts of meat, most people like stewed and braised foods because of their satiny sauces.

There are some technical differences between a dish that's stewed and one that's braised. Textbook definitions say that braised foods are large and that you have to brown them before adding liquid. Food is braised in a minimum amount of liquid (about $1/2$" of fluid), and a *mirepoix*, or mixture of diced vegetables, frequently is added to a braised dish. A stew usually has smaller pieces of food that may or may not be browned first, and calls for a large quantity of liquid (enough to cover the food).

But you may see recipes for braised foods to which you are told to add a lot of liquid. Likewise, some stew recipes tell you to brown the meat first, and so on. The point is that you cook these foods more or less the same way. Sometimes these methods are called "pot roasting," which isn't roasting at all, and sometimes foods cooked by these methods are called fricassees.

The best type of pan for stewing or braising is an enamel pan, which heats slowly but retains heat well, giving the food evenly balanced heat. In lieu of enamel pans, you can use any deep, heat-proof casserole dish, a braising pan (a deep, long-handled skillet), or a Dutch oven.

Stews and braises are the ideal dishes to cook ahead. Their flavors mature as they stand, so they are even better a day or so after you cook them. In addition, when you chill a stew or braised dish, pan fat rises to the top and you can scoop it easily. You also can freeze stewed and braised foods for future use.

Follow these tips for successful braising and stewing:

➤ Dry the food before you stew or braise it.

➤ If you brown the meat, cook it in batches so there is enough room in the pan for the food to brown properly.

➤ If you brown the food, you may cook it in its own fat or add a film of vegetable oil to the pan to prevent sticking. Drain excess fat before you add other ingredients.

➤ You may cook a stew or braised dish on a stovetop at low-moderate heat or in the oven at 325–350 degrees.

➤ Do not let the stewing or braising liquid boil. Keep it at a simmer or the food will be tough and rubbery.

➤ Cook stews and braises for a long time; that's what it takes for them to become tender.

Boiling, Simmering, and Poaching

Boiling, simmering, and poaching are similar processes: all involve cooking foods by immersing them in hot liquids. To boil is to cook food in water at a temperature of 212 degrees, when water bubbles rise rapidly to the surface of the liquid. Foods are rarely boiled; even hardboiled eggs (properly called hard-cooked eggs) aren't really boiled. That's because most foods fall apart if you cook them in rapidly boiling water. The only foods you actually boil are pasta products and vegetables that cook quickly (green sugar snap peas and spinach, for example). Cooking these vegetables rapidly in boiling water preserves their nutrients and sets their color. When you boil vegetables, don't cover the pan.

To simmer food is to cook it at temperatures just below a boil. The bubbles form around the edges of the pan and rise slowly to the surface. Most so-called boiled foods (potatoes, eggs, and meat) should be cooked at a simmer. You may or may not cover the pan, depending on the ingredient being cooked.

Poaching is more of an art form than the other two methods are, but it follows the same principles. When you poach food, you have to keep the liquid just below a simmer, so the food cooks more slowly. Cooking time is longer for poaching than it is for boiling or simmering, and during the cooking process, an exchange of flavor takes place between the poaching fluids and the food being poached. Both benefit, because the food absorbs lovely flavor, and you can use the poaching liquid to make sauce, stew, or soup.

Poaching is ideal for delicate fruits and also for fibrous fruits and vegetables that take a long time to cook. You also can poach fish and shellfood, eggs, meat (such as corned beef and short ribs), chicken breasts, and small whole chickens.

There are two ways to poach foods. The first is to immerse the food in the near-simmering liquid. This is the best way to poach small foods such as fruits and eggs. You also can poach food by covering it with cold liquid and bringing the liquid to a near-simmer. This is the best way to poach larger foods such as whole fish and chickens.

You can use any deep pan for boiling, simmering, or poaching. Although there are special long vessels for poaching fish, you can create your own fish poacher using your roasting pan. Most foods are poached in water; however, you also can use wine, stock, or court bouillon. You can keep the liquid plain or season it with herbs, spices, and vegetables (such as onion and celery tops) for meats and fish, or with orange peel, lemon slices, or vanilla beans for fruits.

Court bouillon is a blend of water, wine or vinegar, and seasonings. You use a court bouillon to poach fish and shellfish.

Follow these tips for successful poaching:

➤ Don't let the liquid come to a boil or the food will toughen or disintegrate.

➤ Let poached fruit cool in its cooking liquid.

Steaming

Steaming means to cook food by the heat of moist steam. Food is placed on a rack above the steaming liquid, and the steam rises to cook the food above it. This cooking method has become extremely popular in America because it is quick and easy, uses little or no fat, and preserves a food's nutrients well. It is an ideal method for cooking fish, chicken and chicken breasts, shellfood, and vegetables. Steamed foods have a lovely, delicate flavor and a moist, succulent, and tender texture.

 Be extremely careful when you use an electric steamer; these handy appliances build up a lot of steam. Lift the cover quickly and keep your hands and face as far away as possible to prevent the steam from hitting your skin.

You can use any of several utensils for steaming. You can use a saucepan with a steamer insert set inside, concoct a steamer by setting a colander or strainer above water in a saucepan, or use Asian bamboo steamer baskets that stack on top of woks. Of recent vintage are electric steamers that make the whole process of steaming a cinch.

Most often you steam foods over water. However, for added flavor, you could use stock, wine, or juice in whole or in part, or you could add herbs, spices, and vegetables to the water to enhance flavor. If you use an electric steamer, be sure to follow the manufacturer's instructions regarding steaming fluids.

Follow these tips for successful steaming:

➤ Don't crowd the steamer. Steam must be able to circulate freely around the food.

➤ Don't let the liquid touch the food.

➤ Keep boiling water nearby when you steam. If you have to replenish your steamer with water, you must use boiling water.

Grilling and Broiling

Grilling and broiling are substantially the same and refer to food that's cooked over (or under) high, intense dry heat one side at a time. You control the cooking not by adjusting the temperature but by raising or lowering the cooking rack from the heat source. When foods are grilled or broiled, the high heat sears and browns the surface and keeps the natural juices in the food. Grill larger pieces of food about 6" from the heat; grill thinner foods about 4" from the heat. An oven broiler is not as hot as an outdoor grill, so it's better to broil foods about 3–4" from the heat.

Only tender meats that can withstand high, intense heat and quick cooking should be grilled, but never cook a piece of meat more than 2" thick by this method. Your best bets for grilling or broiling are beef steaks, veal, pork and lamb chops, cutlets, broiler-fryer chickens, and shellfish such as lobster or soft-shelled crabs. You also can grill or broil marinated meats and water-rich or tender vegetables such as onion, eggplant, zucchini, leeks, and bell peppers. Grilling time depends on the type and thickness of the food.

Fein on Food

Historians suspect that the world's first barbecue came about when lightning struck deep within a forest and set trees and wildlife aflame. Human survivors fed on charred flesh and realized that cooked, smoky-tasting meat tasted okay. That was over a million years ago. There is evidence that prehistoric people cooked their food on a grid over a fire. Europeans lost touch with grilling until Columbus came back from one of his journeys to the Americas and brought news of a "barbacoa" (later Anglicized to barbecue) on which the Carib Indians grilled foods. The cult of barbecue has been growing ever since. About 50 years ago when the GI Bill made it possible for lots of folks to move to the suburbs, the backyard patio brought back the barbecue in a big way. Today, even city dwellers grill outdoors on small hibachis on their terraces.

Follow these tips for successful grilling and broiling:

➤ Brush grill grids or broiler racks with vegetable oil to prevent sticking.

➤ Preheat the broiler; let the coals on an outdoor grill turn to white ash before you cook.

➤ Before you grill or broil, bring foods to room temperature.

➤ Use tongs to turn the food so natural juices won't escape.

➤ When you broil in an electric oven, leave the oven door slightly ajar.

➤ For additional grill flavor, you can add flavor chips such as mesquite or hickory chips to the coals.

Microwaving

Judging by the number of microwave ovens sold each year, microwave cooking has millions of advocates in America. It is a clean, fast cooking method that keeps a kitchen cool and is remarkably convenient. In a microwave oven, foods are cooked by high frequency radio waves. What matters with this method is time, not temperature.

Microwaving is an ideal method for cooking plain vegetables because the vegetables retain nutrients and keep their crunchiness and color. It also is useful for cooking fish and chicken breasts, both of which stay remarkably tender and juicy when cooked this way. Melting chocolate by microwave is a cinch, and there is much less chance the chocolate will scorch than with other methods. Microwave ovens are handiest for thawing frozen food and reheating foods such as casseroles.

How long you cook foods in the microwave depends on the oven. There are tremendous differences among microwave ovens. Wattages are different. Some microwave ovens have carousels to rotate the food; others do not. Some are small; some are large. Your best bet is to pay attention to the manufacturer's instructions about time until you get used to your oven. The biggest problem for beginners is overcooking and scorching foods. It's easy to do that in a microwave oven until you get used to the timing.

Not all foods cook faster in a microwave oven. Dried grains and rice, for example, take as long to cook this way as they do on the stovetop.

Because you cannot brown foods in a microwave oven, this cooking method is not suitable as a substitute for roasting, grilling, sautéing, and so on. You cannot achieve the crispy texture of "fried food" in a microwave oven either. Many people are disappointed when they try to use a favorite old recipe and adapt it to microwave cooking. Microwave cooked foods have a distinct texture that is unlike that of foods cooked by conventional means. It is a matter of getting used to it.

Follow these tips for successful microwaving:

➤ Always use microwave-safe dishes, such as glass, ceramic, or paper. Never use metal plates, trays, utensils, or even aluminum foil in a microwave oven.

➤ Never put food on the oven floor; always use a dish or paper towel.

➤ Never turn on the microwave oven if there is no food in it.

➤ Rotate foods if the microwave oven has no carousel.

➤ Remove foods with a potholder. Dishes can be very hot.

➤ Microwave ovens with higher wattage cook foods faster.

➤ Increase cooking time as you increase the amount of food you microwave.

➤ Remove microwave foods when they are slightly underdone. They continue to cook for a few moments after you remove them from the oven.

➤ If you cover foods to be microwaved with plastic wrap, pierce the wrap with a couple of holes to allow steam to escape.

➤ Do not microwave whole eggs, foods to be deep fried or reheated after being deep fried, large turkeys, whole grains, or rice.

The Least You Need to Know

➤ Successful frying depends on careful control of the heat. Keep the cooking fat hot, and foods won't be greasy.

➤ Cut stir-fried foods into like-size pieces so they cook evenly. Prepare and organize all stir-fry foods and tools before you begin to cook.

➤ Always preheat the oven before you put in a roast or food to be baked; preheat the broiler or grill for broiled or grilled foods.

➤ Don't let braised or stewed foods boil, or they will be tough and rubbery. These foods depend on long, slow cooking for tenderness and taste.

➤ Don't boil eggs in their shells; cook them at a simmer, just below the boiling point.

➤ If you put too much food in a steamer, the steam won't circulate around the ingredients properly.

➤ Always use microwave-safe dishes in a microwave oven; never use metal plates, trays, utensils, or aluminum foil.

Part 5
Now You're Cooking

Can you believe it? You're finally ready to cook! The next few chapters will help you fix your first dinner. Because when you serve the food you'll want all the parts (entree and side dishes) to be ready at the same time, I'll make some suggestions on how to do that. I'll also offer advice on when to do everything else (like set the table). If you make a mistake, I'll show you how to correct it, if possible.

After you've cooked a few dinners, you might be ready to take the plunge and invite company over so you can show off your culinary skills. There's one chapter in this part—complete with menus—that goes over three types of get-togethers, and another chapter that tells you all about beverages.

Let's begin to cook for real.

Chapter 16

Timing Is Everything: Creating Your First Masterpiece

In This Chapter

➤ Making everything come out at the same time

➤ How far ahead you can cook it

➤ Freezables

➤ Knowing when a dish is done

➤ When to do everything else besides the cooking

The reason you're cooking is so you can serve a meal. That means you have to consider details other than the food itself. You have to get the meal, not just a particular dish, to "come out." This chapter deals with the details and the "whens" of cooking: timing the foods so they all come out at the same time. It means knowing which foods you can cook ahead, when you should do all the other meal-related tasks (such as setting the table), knowing when foods are "done," and so on. The more you master the details, the more confident you will be. The best cooks are the confident ones.

Are You Kidding Me? Re-Read the Recipe?

Before you start to cook you need to read the recipe again. The first reading helped determine if the recipe was good. The second reading enabled you to make a shopping list, figure out what equipment you need, and familiarize yourself with the procedure. Reading again now helps you get non-cooking, secondary chores out of the way. Do you have to grease a pan? Do it before you mix the ingredients. Do you have to preheat the oven? Do it before you begin to cook.

As you re-read your recipe, you can begin to prepare the ingredients: chop the onions, bring a pot of water to boil, and stuff like that. You also can take out the proper pots, pans, and utensils. If you're cooking ears of corn, you'll need tongs to lift the ears out of the water, for example. If you re-read the recipe, you'll know enough to have tongs ready so you don't have to go searching for them at the last minute and maybe overcook the corn.

When you re-read, you should also consider what you'll do with the food when you're finished cooking it. What will you do with the contents of the pan? (Do you need a platter? A bowl?) How will you remove the food from the pan? (A spatula or a large spoon?) Get these details out of the way before you begin to cook.

One of the most important reasons for re-reading the recipe is to help you prepare a timetable of what you have to do and when you have to do it.

Is This a Railroad Station or a Kitchen?

If you were meeting a friend at a train station and both of your trains were scheduled to arrive at 7:03, you'd be upset if either one of them was an hour late. The same holds true for recipes: when you're making several different dishes for dinner, you want them to come out at the same time. So you've got to prepare a schedule of arrival times to make sure they do.

Arrival times take everything into consideration, not just cooking time. Suppose you decide to prepare roast chicken, cooked rice, and stir-fried spinach. A roasted chicken should stand about 15 minutes after you remove it from the oven (to keep it juicy). In addition, it will take you about 5 minutes to carve the bird and put it on a platter. Therefore, if the roasting time is 2 hours, resting time is 15 minutes, and carving time is 5 minutes, the arrival time is 2 hours and 20 minutes after you begin. Because rice takes about 20 minutes to cook and needs 10 minutes of standing time, it's arrival time is 30 minutes after you begin it. So you begin to cook the rice 1 hour and 50 minutes after you put the chicken in the oven. Then factor in the time for the third recipe so that you can have all three dishes ready within minutes of each other.

Kitchen Clue

Timing is everything. Help yourself out and use a kitchen timer. There may be a working timer on your oven, or you might have a separate timer (some of which can be set for up to three different times). If necessary, use both timers if the two different sounds will help you remember what it is you're timing.

Early in your culinary adventures, you'll find it easier to choose at least one recipe that you can prepare ahead and reheat or serve cool or at room temperature. Whatever recipes you choose, write the timetable on paper and use it as a cooking guide.

Like train schedules, recipe arrival times aren't always precise. And even when they are, it can be nerve-wracking trying to get the dishes to the table on time, present them attractively, and be sure they're hot. A few tricks of the trade can help. Preheat the serving dishes; warm dishes help keep the food warm. You can rinse them with hot water or place them for a brief time in the oven before you put the food in them. In addition, some dishwashers have plate-warming cycles. Take advantage. You can also pop the filled serving platters and bowls into the turned-off oven while you finish up the last item.

What You Can Cook Ahead

Instead of getting yourself into a frenzy about arrival times and schedules, you can make some foods ahead of time. You can completely cook many dishes ahead of time (moisture-laden casseroles or chili con carne, for example). Soups, stews, pot roasts, and braised foods taste even better when they're reheated, so these are ideal to prepare ahead. Likewise, you can partially cook some foods ahead of time, up to the point at which you would place them in an oven (macaroni and cheese, for example).

You can cook many deep-fried foods (such as fried chicken or fritters) ahead of time, too. Although these lose something in texture, for the sake of convenience you can make them ahead and reheat them by placing them on a rack on a cookie sheet and putting them in a preheated 400 degree oven.

Certain foods are breeding grounds for bacteria and should never be cooked partially. Chicken, turkey, and other poultry fall into this category. Don't ever partially cook poultry.

What You Can't Cook Ahead

There are some foods you simply can't cook ahead of time. These include dishes in which texture is critical. For example, many steamed and stir-fried vegetables are supposed to be crunchy. If you make them ahead of time they become soggy. Canapés on little rounds of bread are supposed to be firm. If you make them more than two hours ahead of time, the bread will be too damp. Salad greens are supposed to be crispy. If you dress the salad more than 10 minutes before you serve it, you'll have soggy salad. Foods that rise to the occasion, such as soufflés, also can't be cooked ahead. They fall fast after you take them out of the oven.

What You Can Prepare a Little Ahead

Even if you can't cook a dish ahead of time, you can prepare the separate parts that constitute the whole dish, just up to the point of actually putting it together. You can wash and cut all the vegetables, garlic, onions, and other seasonings for steamed and stir-fried vegetables and set them aside. You can prepare salad greens and dressing and keep them aside separately. You can prepare the canapé breads and the toppings and keep them separate until 2 hours or so before serving time. You can prepare the pasta for sauced pasta dishes, rice for fried rice dishes, and so on.

While it's all right to prepare the separate parts of a dish ahead of time, you've got to use some common sense about how far ahead. For example, you can chop many sturdy vegetables (such as broccoli, cauliflower, carrots, and green beans) the day before you need them. But more delicate vegetables (such as zucchini, snow peas, and mushrooms) will lose freshness more quickly, so chop them the same day you'll be cooking them (early in the day is fine). Onions and garlic also lose their zip if you chop them too early. Wait until the morning of the day you're cooking (and cover them tightly with several layers of plastic wrap to keep the onion/garlic odor from spreading).

To keep salad greens fresh, don't prepare them before the morning of the day you'll be using them. However, you can prepare vinaigrette dressing for salad two or three days ahead, with this caveat: if you use fresh herbs for your vinaigrette, add these to the dressing just before you pour it onto the salad. You can cut bread for canapés the day before you cook (keep the pieces in plastic bags), but you can prepare many toppings for canapés (flavored butters and smoked trout spread, for example) as much as two days ahead. It's okay to prepare pasta the morning of the day you'll sauce it. Rice is easy; you can cook it a whole day ahead.

You surely are not going to want to carve a radish swan or swirl tomato skins into a rose at the last minute. Get your garnishes (whatever they are) cut, carved, and cleaned early in the day as you prepare the ingredients for the recipe, and set them aside, labeled for each dish.

What You Can Freeze

Some foods you can cook ahead and freeze. Foods ideal for freezing include tomato sauce, stew, pot roast, many soups, cooked casseroles, meat and poultry pies, quiches, crepes, cookies, fruit pies, cakes, and breads.

You can't store food in the freezer forever, of course. Tomato sauce is good for about 6 months, as are fruit pies and cookies. Other freezables can lose taste and texture if kept for more than 3–4 months. Be sure to let foods cool before you wrap them for freezing. Wrap the food in plastic wrap and then freezer paper, or put it in air-tight plastic containers. Don't forget to label and date each item.

It's not a good idea to defrost most foods (particularly meats) on the countertop because of the risk of food poisoning. Though it takes a lot of time, the best place to defrost most food is in your refrigerator. (Don't forget to put a plate beneath it to catch the drippings.)

You can plunge large items (such as a roasting chicken in its wrapper) into cold water to speed up the defrosting process; change the water occasionally. Smaller items defrost within 24 hours, but a roast may take up to 2 days, and a large turkey may take as many as 2 ¹/₂ days to defrost. You also can defrost by microwave, but you have to cook those items as soon as you defrost them. You can defrost breads, cakes, and cookies on the countertop.

What You Can't Freeze

Some foods don't hold up well in the freezer. Sorry, but you can forget freezing such things as cooked pasta (as opposed to pasta casseroles such as lasagna); lettuce and salad greens; cooked potatoes; foods made with cream cheese, mayonnaise, vinaigrette dressing, or gelatin; egg-based dishes; grilled foods; delicate, lightly sautéed foods; meringue; and whipped cream. If you have cake with cream cheese frosting or whipped cream on it, go ahead and freeze it, but don't expect it to be as smashing as it was when it was fresh.

Going Together

You'll find that if you prepare as much of the dish as possible beforehand, you won't be as rushed and stressed when you actually have to cook. Here's another tip: if you are preparing two recipes with the same ingredient (onions, for example), chop them at the same time. Keep all the ingredients for one recipe together, either on one large platter or in small separate bowls or plates. Cover the platter and/or bowls with plastic wrap until you are ready to use the ingredients, and then add them one by one or together as the recipe states. If you are preparing several recipes with some of the same ingredients, it's a good idea to label all the bowls. That way you'll know which bowl of onions is for which recipe.

When Do You Set the Table?

You can set the table for a company dinner early in the day. Some people worry that dust will fall on the plates and glasses. If this is a real concern for you, turn the plates and glasses over until just before your company comes.

Put everything out: the candlestick holders and candles, the bread basket, serving utensils, platters, and so on. That way you will be sure you have everything you need and won't have to think about where you hid the ceramic pitcher you got as a housewarming gift. (Before you call your guests into the dining room for dinner, fill the pitcher with ice and water.) If you forgot to buy candles, you'll know early enough to do something about it. If you will be serving cocktails and hors d'oeuvre, don't forget to get out the cocktail napkins, corkscrew, and such.

Kitchen Clue
Cooking a meal gives you a sense of accomplishment and lots of memories. Keep a journal of your important dinners so you can reminisce about them. Journals have other advantages too: you know what you served so you don't duplicate a meal for the same people, and you know which recipes you liked (or didn't) so you can prepare them for others (or throw them away).

How Do You Know When a Dish Is Done?

Even though a good recipe will tell you how long to cook the dish until it's done, that time is only an approximation. Even that approximation may be within a time range. For example, a recipe may say "bake the pie 45–55 minutes." Always check for doneness at the minimum time given (in this case, after 45 minutes).

Kitchen Clue
Want to save even more time? As you're preparing food, clean up as you go. That way there isn't a big mess when you finish the recipe. And take advantage of certain old tricks of the trade, such as lining a roasting pan with aluminum foil to keep the pan cleaner, or soaking crusty pots overnight so you don't have to scrub.

There are various ways to tell when food is done after the given amount of time. You can tell some things by sight, some by taste, some by feel. However, for some foods you must have special tools to test for doneness.

As a general rule, a cake or quickbread is done when you can see that the sides are starting to pull away from the pan. If you touch the top gently, the cake will feel spongy and "bounce" back a bit when you lift your finger. Alternatively, you can use a cake tester, long wooden skewer, or toothpick. Insert one of these into the center of the cake, and if it comes out "clean" (with no liquid batter on it), the cake is done.

When pasta is done, it will be tender, but still somewhat "resilient," not hard (remove a piece from the water and test by biting into it); rice will be soft, and all the water in the pan will be gone. All fully cooked vegetables should be vibrantly colored: jewel-green peas, fire-colored carrots. If they're drab, you've overcooked them, so watch out next time. Thick vegetables such as broccoli and carrots are done when they are still firm and resilient but are tender enough for you to pierce them with the tip of a sharp knife. Vegetables such as sugar snap and snow peas should be crunchy but tender; taste one to know if the batch is done. Soft vegetables such as kale or spinach are done when they have just wilted and are soft but not mushy.

Pork and poultry are done when you prick the thickest part (the center of the roast, the poultry thigh) with the tines of a fork or the tip of a sharp knife and the juices run clear. A meat thermometer can be very helpful here. There are two types of meat thermometers: "instant-read" thermometers (which you insert into the meat briefly to check the temperature at a given moment) and the more traditional kind that you leave in the meat throughout the cooking process. Either is fine, so the choice is yours. Whichever you choose, insert the thermometer into the thickest part of the roast and make sure it doesn't touch a bone. The thickest part of a turkey or roasting chicken is either the center of the thigh or the breast. Insert the thermometer deep into the flesh at an angle (from the lower part of the thigh upward, or in the breast, from the neck toward the back).

The following table indicates internal temperatures to which various cuts of meat and poultry must be heated. You may disagree with the term *rare*. Technically, rare is 120 degrees, but some people like their meat rarer, or *bleu*. You will learn to satisfy your own particular requirements after you have worked with a meat thermometer for awhile. Remember that meat continues to cook for a short time after you take it out of the oven. That means you should remove the food slightly before it reaches the temperature you want.

Temperatures for Fully-Cooked Meats

Type of Meat	Rare	Medium	Well-Done
Beef	120–130	135–140	140+
Veal	N/A	140–145	165
Pork	N/A	N/A	150–160
Lamb	120–135	135–145	145+
Poultry	N/A	N/A	170–175 (breast) 180 (thigh)

Fish is done when the flesh has softened and is opaque; you should be able to put a fork completely through the flesh. Casseroles are done when their tops are golden brown or the top layer of cheese is bubbly, lightly browned, and obviously hot.

Pancakes should be turned when the batter on the top starts to bubble. The pancakes are done shortly thereafter, when the second side has browned. You have to lift the pancake slightly with a rigid spatula to see the underside.

Pies are done when the top crust is golden brown. Most cookies are done when the edges are browned and crispy. If you make homemade whipped cream you know it's done when it stands in soft mounds and there appears to be no liquid left in the bowl. Whipped egg whites are done when they stand in stiff peaks but still look glossy. Here's a trick to tell whether egg whites are completely whipped: start to turn the bowl over. If the egg whites don't move as you move the bowl (they don't even fall out when you turn the bowl completely over), they are done. If they swish back and forth, you need to beat them a bit more.

The Least You Need to Know

➤ Plan ahead (you can even write out a time chart) so that several different dishes will be ready at the same time.

➤ You can cook casseroles, stews, soups, quiches, pot roasts, filled crepes, fried foods, and braised foods ahead of time.

➤ Certain foods such as stir-fries, many cooked vegetables, dressed salad, and other foods that are intended to be crispy cannot be cooked ahead, but you can prepare the component parts in advance.

➤ Set the table, make garnishes, and do other non-cooking tasks early in the day.

So You've Made a Mistake?

In This Chapter

➤ Common mistakes and how to avoid them

➤ What to do when mistakes happen

During the days when Louis XIV ruled France and gastronomy was considered one of the highest art forms, a man named Vatel, chef to the Prince de Conde, committed suicide because he made a culinary mistake. (The fish he ordered for dinner didn't arrive on time.) I don't recommend such severe measures, but you can bet there will be lots of times when you'll make cooking mistakes and you'll at least want to kick yourself.

Remember, even the best cooks make mistakes. The heat may have been too high. The phone rang and distracted you. You forgot a step. Forgive yourself. Many mistakes can be remedied. This chapter discusses mistakes that you can correct and those you cannot correct. It also deals with the most common mistakes people make in cooking, and tells you how to avoid making them.

Mistakes with Different Types of Foods

Some cooking mistakes are disasters: you have to throw out the dish or the ingredient you are working with. But not every food disaster is total. The following sections outline some of the more common mistakes people make and tell whether or not you can salvage the food—and if so, how.

Mistakes with Fruits and Vegetables

If you see vegetables beginning to discolor because you cooked them too long, quickly scatter a pinch of baking soda into the cooking water. However, if the vegetables are already overcooked and dull-looking, puree them (add some butter and seasonings), and serve them as is or use the puree to create soup or to thicken gravy or soup. If a baked potato has burst, you can salvage the parts that haven't scattered over the oven and prepare the potato flesh as mashed potatoes.

If you find that peeled fruit has begun to turn brown, you can cut off the film of flesh with a vegetable peeler and rub the fruit with the cut side of a lemon or put it in acidulated water to prevent further browning. Browned fruit is fine as-is for pies, cobblers, and the like; fruit darkens as it bakes anyway—especially when coupled with richly colored spices such as cinnamon. You can prevent guacamole from discoloring by storing it with the avocado pit stuck in the center until serving time.

Mistakes with Meat, Poultry, and Fish

Pot roasted, stewed, and braised meat can be tough for several reasons, but it's often because you haven't cooked the meat long enough or over low heat. Give the meat more time. If possible, add an acidic ingredient such as tomatoes or wine to help tenderize the meat. If you have no more time, slice the meat exceptionally thin and let it sit in the pan juices for 10–15 minutes.

If a roast beef, chicken, or turkey is not browning well, it probably is because your roasting pan is too deep. Put the roast in a shallower pan. If you overcook meat, you can no longer serve it rare, but you don't have to throw it out either. Make hash, chili, pot pie, or some other type of casserole dish. If the meat is not cooked well enough, give it more time. If dinner guests are waiting, that may mean cutting the meat into serving portions and putting the portions back in to cook. Fish that's dried out and overcooked can still be okay if you make a rich sauce to cloak it with or if you mash the fish for fishcakes.

Mistakes with Dairy Products

You can't use overbrowned butter in recipes that call for delicate butter sauces. However, some of the best-tasting recipes have been created out of overbrowned butter. If the recipe is for a dish that can stand a creative touch (soup, for example), use the browned butter. If you cook cheese and it becomes rubbery, your heat was probably too high; try cutting the mass into chunks and processing the pieces in a food processor or blender for 10–15 seconds. If you have over-whipped whipped cream, don't throw the ingredients out. Keep whipping the cream until the solids and liquids separate completely. Discard the liquid and knead the solid matter to extract as much liquid as you can. The result is sweet butter.

Mistakes with Soup

If a soup tastes too salty, there are several things you can do. If there is time, add more liquid and let the soup cook more. If you have no time or the soup cannot stand to be thinned, add sugar or brown sugar, beginning with ¹/₄ tsp. Although the sugar will not eliminate the salt, it will cover the salty taste. Or, you could add a peeled, sliced, raw potato and let the soup cook 10 minutes (the potato will absorb some of the salt). Remove the potato and discard it before serving the soup. Always add the minimum amount of salt to soup as you cook it, and taste for seasoning after the soup has cooked awhile.

For soup that's too thin, there are several remedies. You can cook the soup longer so it reduces. You could add a liaison, such as buerre manie or cornstarch and water mixed to a smooth paste, or you could add raw rice or pasta and simmer the soup, covered, until the rice or pasta is fully cooked. If you don't have time for that, you could stir in leftover pureed vegetables, mashed potatoes, or cooked rice.

A *liaison* is any kind of mixture that you use to thicken a sauce, soup, or stew. A *buerre manie*, a particular type of liaison, is made by mixing equal parts of butter and flour until the mixture is smooth.

If you made stock and it looks cloudy, add crumbled egg shells or a couple of lightly beaten egg whites, let the stock simmer 2–3 minutes, and then lift out the shells or poached egg whites and strain the stock.

Mistakes with Bread, Dough, Pasta, and Pastry Products

There are several reasons why yeast dough doesn't rise, the most common being because the yeast is too old. It is important to proof yeast (see Chapter 13) before you use it for bread and other pastries. Sometimes the dough doesn't rise because the place you have set it to rest is not warm enough. The best place to let yeast dough rise is in a warm oven. To warm the oven before you put yeast dough in to rise, turn the oven on to 450 degrees for two minutes, and then turn the oven off; the oven is now ready for the dough. Don't open the door while the yeast is rising. Another way to make the oven warm is to put a pan of very hot water beneath the bowl of dough.

If a cake doesn't rise, the baking powder you used might be too old. Throw the cake out. However, if the cake does rise but then falls, you may be able to salvage it. Cut it into small pieces, cover it with ice cream, whipped cream, and/or fudge sauce, and call it pudding. If you see (through the oven window) that a cake is rising lopsided in the pan, gently open the oven door and turn the pan halfway around for the remainder of the baking time.

Overbaked cookies can be turned into tasty crumbs for pie crusts. Let them cool, then crumble and process them in a food processor or blender or crush them under a rolling pin.

If cream puffs come out limp, it is because there is too much moisture inside them. Slit a cap off the puff and scoop the soggy insides. Return the puff with its cap to the oven to reheat for a minute or so at 400 degrees.

If your pasta sticks to itself, plunge it into near-boiling water for a few seconds and gently separate it with a spaghetti fork, chopsticks, or a wooden spoon. Or, set it in a colander and let very hot water run over the pasta as you separate it.

Mistakes with Chocolate

One of the most common cooking mistakes is letting chocolate stiffen to a dull-looking, hard-as-a-rock mass. The main reason chocolate "seizes" is that water or steam droplets fall on it as it cooks. Here's what to do if your chocolate seizes: for each ounce of chocolate, add one tsp. shortening—NOT butter—to the pan and melt the chocolate again slowly over low heat.

To prevent chocolate from seizing the next time, here are some tips for how to melt chocolate:

➤ Chop the chocolate into small pieces so they melt faster.

➤ Melt the chocolate in the top part of a double boiler. Be sure the top pan fits snugly into the bottom one so steam cannot escape from the lower pan. (If you use a makeshift double boiler, be sure the bowl fits snugly in the lower pan.)

A good way to prevent melted chocolate from stiffening into a hard mass is to use a double boiler.

182

➤ Heat the water in the bottom pan over low heat, but do not let the water boil. The water in the lower pan should be at a near-simmer, about 200 degrees.

➤ If you prefer, you can melt chocolate in the microwave oven. Follow the manufacturer's instructions.

➤ If you burn chocolate, throw it out. It will have a burnt flavor.

Mistakes with Rice

If rice is undercooked, all you have to do is sprinkle 2–3 TB. of water over it, cover the pan, and continue to cook it another few minutes. If rice is over-cooked, some of it will stick to the bottom of the pan. You can use the unstuck portions the way you planned, but you will have less of it, of course. Here's what to do with the crusty part at the bottom of the pan: lift it out with a rigid spatula and deep fry it in hot oil for 2–3 minutes or until it is crispy. Serve the crisped rice as a bed for stir-fried vegetables.

Kitchen Clue
While it isn't difficult to cook rice (see the recipe in the "Pastas, Rice, and Grains" recipe section), you can buy special electric rice cookers that make the process foolproof. Or, you can make rice in an electric vegetable steamer if you have one.

If rice is burned at the bottom, the taste often permeates the entire pot of rice. Taste the unburnt portions. If they taste burnt, try adding a chunk of rye bread to the pan, covering it, and letting the rice stand for 5 minutes. Taste the rice again. If it still tastes burnt, you'll have to throw it out. (Sorry.)

Mistakes with Gravy

If you have a knack for making lumpy gravy, here's what to do: beat the lumpy gravy with a whisk or hand mixer with a vigor that shows you're angry at it. That should straighten the gravy out. Otherwise, put the gravy in a blender or food processor and process it until it is smooth. You also could strain the gravy through a fine sieve.

If your gravy is too salty, slice a potato into it and let it cook 8–10 minutes. If the gravy is too thin, let it cook longer, or bind it with one of the following mixtures (per cup of gravy) and cook and stir the gravy another minute or so:

➤ 1 tsp. cornstarch dissolved in 1 TB. water

➤ 1 TB. flour dissolved in 2 TB. water

➤ 1 TB. beurre manie

Mistakes with Meringues

Meringues can *weep* (become watery), *bead* (have amber colored droplets on them), or be too soft or sticky. This often happens in humid weather because sugar absorbs moisture from the air. It also can happen because you didn't

183

dissolve the sugar properly. When you make a meringue, you must add the sugar gradually so the egg whites can dissolve the granules properly. When a meringue weeps, beads, or becomes soft, there is nothing you can do about it. It still tastes okay, it just doesn't have the best texture. Next time wait for a dry day or add the sugar more gradually.

When Something Burns

You can save some burned foods, but often, as with chocolate, you have to throw them out. The decision here is: how does it taste? For example, if you burn a cake layer, you often can slice the burnt part off. Taste a crumb from the unburnt part, and if it tastes okay, use the cake. If you heat $^3/_4$ cup of water with one TB. of brandy for 2–3 minutes and then brush this on the bottom cake layer, it will taste even better.

Burnt vegetables usually are gone for good. However, if you catch the vegetables just before they burn, you can try to correct the error by plunging the bottom of the pan quickly into some very cold water. You also could try cutting away the burnt parts, putting the rest over very low heat in a new pan, and covering the pan with a damp kitchen towel for a few minutes (the towel may absorb some of the burnt odor).

When Something Curdles

Foods curdle for several reasons, such as when you cook products that contain eggs at too high a temperature or when you mix an acidic ingredient with milk or cream. To prevent foods that contain eggs from curdling, make sure you cook them over low heat or in the top part of a double boiler set over near-simmering (*not* boiling) water. Before you add eggs or egg yolks to a hot sauce, *temper* them (prepare the eggs by gradually adding about a half cup of the hot sauce to them before you put the eggs in the pan). Stir the ingredients in the pan constantly so all portions of the food reach the heat. If possible, add a small amount of flour to the recipe since recipes containing flour will not curdle.

However, if you already have made the mistake of letting the mixture curdle, try one of these remedies:

➤ Remove the pan from the heat and plunge the bottom into ice water. Obviously, when you cook a sauce that could curdle, it helps to prepare a large bowl of ice water on the side, just in case.

➤ Beat the sauce vigorously with a whisk or hand mixer. If that doesn't work, add an ice cube to the sauce and beat it in.

➤ Add one TB. of sauce to one TB. cream or milk and mix until creamy. Then gradually add more curdled sauce and beat it into the creamed mixture until all the curdled sauce has been incorporated.

➤ Make a new sauce and gradually whisk or beat in the curdled sauce a tablespoon at a time.

184

In cases where you must mix an acidic ingredient (such as lemon juice or wine) with milk or cream, be sure to cook the ingredients over low heat, add the second ingredient gradually, and whisk or beat the ingredients vigorously.

Miscellaneous Mistakes

There are oodles of other cooking mistakes. Here are some tips to avoid common errors:

➤ If you are making a recipe that contains gelatin and the gelatin becomes too firm before you add another ingredient, set the gelatin over a bowl of very hot water. It will soften.

➤ If your cheesecake cracks, sift some confectioner's sugar on top of the cooled cake.

> When you *flambée* food, you flame it with brandy or another alcoholic beverage.

➤ If the brandy for a flambéed dish won't ignite, warm it separately in a pan, or raise the heat of the pan if you already poured it into other ingredients.

The Least You Need to Know

➤ To reduce the salty taste in oversalted dishes, add a small amount of sugar to cover the taste or a sliced raw potato to absorb some of the salt.

➤ Burnt chocolate must be discarded. Many burnt foods also cannot be saved. Taste the food first, and if the entire dish tastes burnt, throw it away.

➤ To salvage "seized" chocolate, melt each ounce of it with a tsp. of shortening.

➤ Always temper eggs before adding them to a sauce by mixing a small amount of the hot sauce to the eggs first.

Chapter 18

So You Thought You Were Done? What About Beverages?

In This Chapter

➤ A bit about cocktails

➤ A brief wine primer

➤ Some info on bottled water

➤ Making coffee and tea

You already know that preparing a meal means more than making the food. Whether you are eating alone, serving dinner to your mate or family, or having company, part of the plan involves setting the table, garnishing the food, and so on. It may also mean serving a beverage. Not everyone drinks a cocktail before dinner or wine with dinner; not everyone drinks coffee or tea after dinner. However, this chapter will help you when you want to serve these beverages. We will talk about how to serve cocktails and wine and how to prepare coffee and tea.

Serving Cocktails

Cocktails are not the popular predinner drinks they were once. These days most people pass up the old-fashioned, heavy, sweet, mixed alcoholic beverages in favor of white wine or even bottled water before a company dinner, or nothing at all if it's an everyday dinner. Still, many people enjoy a predinner cocktail to stimulate their appetite. Certain classic cocktails, such as Martinis, Margaritas, and Bloody Marys, continue to be favorites. Other people prefer a straight alcoholic beverage such as Scotch or Bourbon "on the rocks" or mixed with "soda" (club soda) or ginger ale. If you plan a cocktail time, consider these pointers:

➤ Serve cocktails with a nibble of food that will moderate the effects of the alcohol. Predinner food and drink should stimulate, not satisfy, the appetite, so the rule is to serve a little of each.

➤ Have an ice bucket filled with ice and tongs handy for serving the ice.

➤ You need different size glasses depending on the drinks: short glasses for drinks "on the rocks" and taller or stemmed glasses for mixed drinks.

➤ Be sure to have ginger ale, tonic water, club soda or seltzer, and orange or tomato juices on hand for mixed drinks, as well as sliced lemon or lime and olives or cocktail onions as garnishes for certain drinks.

➤ Chill the beverage glasses if you have room in your fridge.

How to Choose and Serve Wine

There's an old adage that says, "The more you learn, the less you know." On one hand, people today are more knowledgeable than ever about wine. On the other hand, they are more intimidated about choosing wine because they may know a little something, but not enough. Some experts will advise you to stick to the classic rule: white wine with fish and chicken, red wine with meat and cheese. Others tell you not to pay any attention to those rules. Therefore, it can be very confusing. The following sections give you some guidelines for choosing and serving wine with dinner.

"White Wine with Fish, Red Wine with Meat," and All That

While the rules regarding which wines to serve with foods may have relaxed, beginners will still feel more comfortable starting with classic combinations. In general, you can serve dry white wine with fish, chicken, and veal, and you can serve red wine with beef, pork, lamb, and rich poultry such as duck. Rose wine goes with fish and chicken also, as well as with cold summer foods and baked

 A *dry* wine is one that is not sweet.

ham. Blush wines are most appropriate as an aperitif, though some people enjoy them with veal and chicken. Sweet white wines are suitable for dessert.

When in doubt, you can always serve champagne. While it is a favorite aperitif, champagne is a delightful choice to continue throughout the meal.

Which White Wine? Which Red Wine?

Saying that white or red wines go with particular foods is only the first step. When you go into the wine store, you will see so many different types of wine that you soon will realize exactly how much is involved in your choice. Here's a tip: befriend a wine merchant. He or she will not laugh at you because you don't know about wine. A smart businessperson will teach you about wine to keep you as a happy customer. Ask questions.

It's smart to visit a wine store to ask questions even if you usually buy wine in a grocery store or warehouse outlet. Most wine stores carry popular brand name wines at competitive prices. They usually don't carry (or at least don't feature) expensive vintage wines, so you don't have to be intimidated going in. And it may actually be worth an extra dollar, if that turns out to be the case, to buy wine this way because of the education you'll get.

What you communicate to the wine merchant is important. It isn't enough to say you are planning to serve chicken. Describe the recipe, list the seasonings, and describe the sauce. Is the dish heavy? Light? Mild? Rich wines go with rich foods, delicate wines with delicate foods, and so on. The best rule is to speak up so your wine merchant can help you pair the proper wine with the dish. Make a note of which wine you buy and what you serve it with. That's the best way to gain experience.

If you don't want to shop in a wine and liquor store, your next best bet in getting a wine education is to buy a book (there are many) that explains which wines are dry, which fruity, which spicy, and so on, so you can get a better handle on which one to buy with your dinner.

Keep this easy tip in mind: if you cook with wine, serve the same wine (or at least a similar type of wine from the same area) with the dish. For example, if you prepare Coq Au Vin with burgundy wine, serve a burgundy wine with it.

When Not to Serve Wine

Sometimes it is inappropriate to serve wine. Foods that are highly spiced or acidic overwhelm wine, so don't serve wine with foods such as Cajun-style blackened meats, salad, or antipasto. You usually don't serve wine with soup either (although Sherry or Madeira wines are swell with onion soup). In addition, egg dishes and wine don't couple well. With these foods, ice water is appropriate.

When You Serve More Than One Wine

If you wish to serve more than one wine at a meal, the general rule to follow is to serve a white wine before a red one, a dry wine before a sweet one, a light wine before a full-bodied (less delicate) one, and a young wine before a more mature one. It is important to progress to heavier, more complex flavors. If you serve the heavier or more complex wine first, it would overwhelm the one to come.

NEVER...
serve red wine in the same glass as the white wine you served with a previous course. Likewise, never serve two different whites or two different reds from the same glass.

How to Keep and Serve Wine

Once you have made your wine selection, bring it home and store it in a cool, dark, dry place. Lay it down horizontally so the cork will continue to soak. Once a bottle of wine is open, you can store leftovers about one week. Put the cork back or use a special gadget that keeps wine bottles capped.

When you *decant* wine, you pour it from its bottle into another container, such as a special wine decanter. This hastens the breathing process and makes wine more mellow tasting.

Champagne, sparkling wines, and white and rose wines are always served chilled. That doesn't mean so ice-cold that your teeth hurt; if the wine is too cold, you won't be able to taste it. Red wines are served at room temperature. Ask the wine merchant if the red wine you have chosen must be decanted first. If so, decant the wine (or at least open the cork to let the wine breathe) some time before you serve it.

Some Info on Bottled Water

Bottled water has become extremely popular in recent years. Varieties include:

➤ Mineral water, which has a higher mineral content than most tap water.

➤ Spring water, which comes up to the surface from underground sources.

➤ Sparkling water, which is carbonated water. It may be naturally or artificially carbonated.

➤ Seltzer and club soda, which are artificially carbonated waters. (The old guideline here was that seltzer contained no salt, and club soda did. This distinction may or may not apply anymore. Read the individual brand label to find out for yourself.)

About Coffee

Drinking coffee has almost become a national pastime in recent years. Not only are more people drinking more coffee, they are more particular about it than they ever were. If you serve coffee, it pays to know how to prepare a good brew.

Fein on Food

According to conventional wisdom, coffee was discovered centuries ago by accident in the Ethiopian village of Kaffa. A herd of goats began to dance around shortly after nibbling on some wild coffee beans. A monk who happened to be passing by saw the whole thing and munched on some of the beans too. Then he spent time experimenting with the beans until he realized how good the stuff tasted when steeped in hot water. The first canned coffee was produced in 1878 by Chase and Sanborn.

Help! Buying Coffee Is Almost As Confusing As Buying Wine!

It is really easy to go into a supermarket and choose a can of coffee; perhaps you just buy the same brand you always saw around the house. But these days supermarkets and specialty coffee shops tempt you with fresh beans, and the fragrance can be tantalizing enough to make you rethink buying canned coffee. Although there's nothing wrong with canned coffee, coffee lovers find that freshly ground beans have more flavor.

There are only two types of coffee beans: *robusta* and *arabica. Coffea robusta* beans are grown at lower elevations. They are the type used for most canned coffee, although canned coffee may also include some arabica beans. *Arabica* beans are grown at higher elevations and are more flavorful; most speciality coffees are arabica beans. Because the best tasting beans are grown at higher elevations, some packages boast that the product is "mountain grown." Flavor differences have to do with the type of beans and also with the soil and climate where the coffee grows. Decaffeinated coffee is either type of bean from which the caffeine is removed.

When you buy fresh beans, you can have them ground for you at the store. If you are really particular though, you should grind the beans yourself at home just before you make the coffee. Just-ground beans make the most flavorful, most aromatic coffee. There are several types of coffee grinding equipment available; see Chapter 21 for a brief discussion of these. You can grind beans in some food processors or blenders (see manufacturer's instructions). But many coffee grinders are quite inexpensive and are preferable because they are designed for this specific purpose. Besides, coffee oils can leave an odor on blades (and the odor, however pleasant, can invade other food you process).

From the two basic types of coffee (arabica and robusta) come dozens of varieties. Some familiar names are Mocha, which is a light roasted coffee, Columbian, which has a full-bodied flavor, and French roast, which comes from a dark, hearty-flavored bean. If you use speciality coffees, you'll have to try several to see which kind you like.

The best place to store coffee is in the refrigerator or freezer, depending on how often you use it. Whole beans last up to 4 weeks in the fridge before they begin to lose flavor and up to 6 months in the freezer. Freshly ground coffee can stay fresh for up to 10 days in the fridge and 2 months in the freezer. Unopened canned coffee is fine for about a year. After you open it, it keeps 10 days in the fridge or 2 months in the freezer.

There are several grinds of coffee. Drip coffee is a moderately fine grind for drip and automatic (electric) drip coffee makers. You also can use drip coffee for "pressed" coffee made in a plunger coffee pot. Perk is a coarse grind for percolator pots. And espresso grind (very fine) is for espresso coffee and cappuccino (espresso coffee with frothed milk).

How to Make Good Coffee

To make good coffee you have to brew ground beans with near-boiling water slowly enough to extract the most flavor from the beans, but quickly enough to prevent the coffee from becoming bitter. There's an art to it. Some people like percolator pots; some like plunger pots; some like drip pots. All of these make good coffee. Regardless of which method you use and which type or variety of coffee you use, follow these guidelines for brewing tasty coffee:

NEVER... pass coffee through the grinds a second time or let coffee water boil.

➤ The freshest beans make the best tasting coffee.

➤ If you buy pre-ground coffee or have it ground, be sure to buy the proper grind for your coffee maker. If you grind your own beans, be sure you grind them to the proper texture.

➤ Use 2 TB. coffee for each 6 oz. of water. If you like your coffee stronger, use more the next time.

➤ To brew small quantities of coffee in an automatic drip pot, use a smaller machine or one with a switch for brewing small quantities; otherwise, the coffee will be weak and lack flavor.

➤ Always begin with cold, fresh water. The best coffees are made with water that is 190–200 degrees.

➤ Remove wet grounds from the coffee maker as soon as the coffee is brewed.

➤ Use brewed coffee quickly. Coffee deteriorates after about 45 minutes.

➤ Make new coffee instead of reheating old coffee.

➤ Be sure to keep your coffee pot clean. Residual coffee oils become rancid and leave a bitter taste.

➤ To make iced coffee, double the strength of the grinds to water. You can freeze leftover coffee in ice cube trays to use for chilling iced coffee.

Teatime

Tea also has become more popular in recent years, and as with coffee, there are lots of decisions to make. It's no longer just a matter of grabbing the most familiar box of tea bags.

Fein on Food

The biggest tea party in American history took place near tea time (actually 6:00 p.m.) on December 16, 1773, when groups of anti-British citizens of Massachusetts dumped 90,000 pounds of tea into Boston Harbor as a protest against newly imposed taxes. After the famous Boston Tea Party, patriotic Americans gave up drinking tea. Now, hundreds of years later, tea finally is gaining popularity in the United States.

You can buy tea in bags or loose. You can buy commercial teas, made from tea leaves blended for consistent flavor by various manufacturers, or you can buy specialty teas. While true tea comes from the leaves of a plant called *camellia sinensis*, there are several other tea-like beverages that we buy and prepare as tea today. For example, you can brew herbs or other leaves, seeds, roots, and barks with hot water to make such "teas" as chamomile and rose hip.

Flavor differences among specialty teas have to do with the soil and climate where the tea plant grows and with how the leaves are processed. There are three main varieties of true tea. *Black teas* come from tea leaves that are allowed to ferment (oxidize) and darken in the sun. They produce deeply colored, full-bodied teas such as Darjeeling, Ceylon, Assam, and Keemun. Earl Gray is a blend of several types of black tea plus citrus flavoring. English Breakfast Tea generally consists of blends of Keemun, and Irish Breakfast Tea usually combines Assam and Ceylon teas. *Oolong tea* (the kind you get in Chinese restaurants) comes from semi-fermented tea leaves. These teas are hearty and flavorful and are medium amber in color. *Green tea* leaves are not fermented. They are steamed soon after harvesting to prevent oxidation and are always pale in color and delicate in flavor.

Spice teas are any of these varieties to which spices have been added. The words "pekoe" and "orange pekoe" have to do with the size of the tea leaves. Commercial bags of tea labeled with these words are blends of small, cut-up tea leaves.

Teas of all types should be stored at room temperature in airtight containers, preferably dark tins that are kept out of the sunlight. They will stay fresh for up to one year.

How to Make Good Tea

You have a greater variety of flavor if you use specialty teas, and you can control strength better if you use loose tea instead of bagged tea. However, you can make good tea with tea bags or loose tea, commercial blends or speciality tea. Whatever you decide, you can count on these tips for brewing tasty tea:

➤ Always begin with cold, fresh water. Be sure the water comes to a full boil or the tea's full flavor will not be extracted.

➤ Prewarm your teapot by filling it up halfway with hot water, swirling it, and pouring out the contents. An earthenware, porcelain, or glass pot works well (although the best tea is brewed in a silver teapot). Aluminum pots discolor tea.

➤ Use 1 rounded teaspoon of loose tea for each 6 oz. of water (2 bags per 3 cups of water). If you like your tea stronger, use more tea, but do not let the brew steep longer than the recommended time.

➤ Pour the boiling water over loose tea leaves and let them steep 3–5 minutes. Pour the tea into cups through a small tea strainer.

➤ Let tea bags steep 2–3 minutes. You can then remove the bags and pour the tea into cups or leave the tea bags inside the pot and add more boiling water.

➤ To make iced tea, double the strength of tea leaves to water and let the brew cool. To make iced tea immediately from hot tea, triple the strength.

➤ Serve tea with sugar, lemon, or milk.

The Least You Need to Know

➤ Serve some edibles with cocktails to moderate the effects of alcohol.

➤ The old rule of white wine with fish and chicken, red wine with meat and cheese still applies in a general way, but other considerations include serving light wines with light foods, rich wines with rich foods, and so on.

➤ To help you pair the right food and wine, discuss the dinner you're serving (in detail) with a wine merchant.

➤ Fresh ground beans make the best tasting coffee. Use the proper coffee grind for your coffee pot.

➤ Loose specialty teas make the best tasting tea. Make sure you use boiling water, and let the tea steep for a few minutes before you pour it.

Chapter 19

Inviting Company: A Menu and Planning Guide

In This Chapter

➤ How to plan a cocktail party, with menus

➤ How to plan a small dinner party, with menus

➤ How to plan a casual cookout, with menus

By now you can be confident about your cooking skills. You can shop and chop, grill and garnish. Why not show off your newly acquired skills by inviting company? In this chapter, I will talk about three simple ways to entertain. Once you get the hang of cooking for company, you'll see how rewarding it can be to serve at home and relax with family or friends or to be a competent host or hostess to business associates.

Your First Cocktail Party

Cocktail parties are a good introduction to entertaining. These parties typically are short (about 2 hours) and can take place in one room. The food you serve can be easy and simple and, for the most part, prepared ahead of time. Because you only serve hors d'oeuvre, a cocktail party can be easier on your wallet too.

In addition to the food and drinks, you need lots of other items for a cocktail party, including a bottle opener, corkscrew, jigger for measuring, pitcher, stirrers, cocktail strainer, knife and cutting board, and ice bucket and tongs. You'll need glasses (two per person), cocktail napkins (approximately 3–4 per person), and mixers such as club soda, tonic water, and ginger ale. And don't forget lemons, limes, green olives, and cocktail onions.

Choosing the Liquor for a Cocktail Party

Most people today do not drink creamy, heavy, or overly sweet cocktails. But you will be serving alcoholic drinks at a cocktail party, so it's smart to keep vodka, scotch, blended whiskey, bourbon, rum, and gin on hand. (A particular type of alcohol may be more popular in one part of the country than another.)

Kitchen Clue
A blender can be very helpful at a cocktail party, but it isn't essential.

You'll need Vermouth for martinis and tequila for margaritas, and you will need white and red wines (approximately two bottles of white for every bottle of red) for those people who do not drink hard liquor. Keep some beer handy, and don't forget soda and juice for people who pre-fer not to drink alcoholic beverages at all. As a general rule, you can figure that each person will drink one alcoholic beverage per hour. One bottle of wine will serve 2–3 people.

Choosing the Food for a Cocktail Party

For your first cocktail party the key is this: keep it simple. Serve pre-prepared finger-foods that don't require plates and utensils. Make sure the foods aren't messy, so they are easy to eat, and don't make foods that require cutting or need more than 2–3 bites. It also is a good idea to offer both hot and cold edible tidbits in a variety of colors and textures. If you don't want to make all the hors d'oeuvre, you can supplement homemade morsels with upscale store-bought items. In this case, choose foods that are obviously store-bought (herb-coated French salami and mini-mozzarella cheese rounds) so everyone will know you cooked the rest.

It will make life easier if you set out some of the food (crudites and dip or cold canapés, for example) on platters or in bowls here and there in the room and pass the other hors d'oeuvre. In general, you'll find that each person will eat about 8–12 hors d'oeuvre during a 2-hour party.

Sometimes you will want special friends or relatives to stay past cocktail party time. If you do, have some more substantial food ready: a casserole or salad, depending on the weather. Party "post-mortems" with good friends can be fun, but you may feel exhausted, so an oven-ready dish or a salad is perfect.

Cocktail Party Etiquette

It takes more than food and drink for a party to be a success. Here are a few tips that can make an evening at your home seem special to your guests:

➤ Be sure your invitation is clear that yours is a cocktail party, not a dinner party. Setting beginning and ending times and writing "hors d'oeuvre and cocktails" is one way to handle this.

➤ Arrange trays of food strategically in the room so guests will spread out.

➤ Don't invite all the people to whom you owe social obligations. It's too much work. If you invite more than 18 people, consider getting serving help.

➤ Decorate the pass-around platters to make them attractive. You don't have to fuss: use edible flowers, a sprig of basil, slices of lemon, and so on.

➤ Have some music playing in the background.

➤ Buy lots of ice.

➤ Provide some non-alcoholic beverages.

➤ Make sure you put out coasters so people don't place wet drinking glasses on your furniture.

NEVER... let any guest drink and drive. Everyone knows this but it can't be said enough.

Menu Suggestions for Cocktail Parties

If you're planning your first cocktail party and are unsure what to serve, consider the following menu suggestions for simple hors d'oeuvre combinations. You can find all the suggested recipes in Part 7 of this book. Prepare approximately 8–12 tidbits per person for a two-hour party.

Menu I: Crudites with Radish Dip, Royal and Not So Royal Potatoes, Wrapped Shrimp, Kielbasa En Croute, Bruschetta

Menu II: Guacamole (with corn chips), Ham and Asparagus Rolls, Smoked Trout Spread Canapés, Stuffed Mushrooms, Kielbasa En Croute

Menu III: Goat Cheese and Sun-Dried Tomato Tidbits, Roasted Garlic (with crackers or pita bread), Bruschetta, Wrapped Shrimp, Chutney Cheese Dip (with crackers, toast, bread, or crudites)

If you don't mind using serving plates, you can supplement these menus with Corn and Barley Salad, Roasted Red Peppers, or plain, boiled shrimp and cocktail sauce. If you are having some friends stay after the party, consider such items as Gillian's Ziti Casserole, Macaroni and Cheese, Chili Con Carne, Tuna and White Bean Salad, or Chicken Provencale.

Your First Dinner Party

You will remember your first dinner party forever. You will remember who you invited and what you served. A first dinner party is an accomplishment, and you deserve applause. Of course you will be nervous; but if you have mastered some cooking skills and equipped yourself with a few good recipes, you can be confident that it will turn out wonderfully.

The first rule of the road when planning a dinner party is this: expect the unexpected. Someone may cancel, the roast may take longer than you thought it would, and so on. That means leave yourself enough time for possible pitfalls. Even if you are a last-minute person who works well under stress, give yourself extra time before a dinner party—enough time to relax before your guests come.

Small dinner parties of 6–8 are large enough to make the evening lively, yet cozy enough to exchange real conversation. You can easily adapt most recipes to serve this number of people.

A few days before the dinner, make a list of what you need to do. Plan your menu, but be flexible and market-sensitive. If the pears you wanted to serve look awful, you might have to switch the dessert. Shop for staples the week before, and pick up everything else (including ice, flowers, and wine) the day before. Get out your tablecloth, flatware, serving platters, and utensils, as well as dessert plates, cups and saucers, and a coffeepot. Prepare a cooking schedule as suggested in Chapter 16.

In addition to all the cooking-related things you have to do, remember these tips for successful dinner parties:

➤ Make sure you have enough chairs.

➤ Put out clean towels in the bathroom.

➤ Prepare your clothes the day before.

➤ If you are preparing the dinner with someone else, decide beforehand what each of you is responsible for.

➤ Get wood for the fireplace if that is appropriate.

Some Menu Suggestions for Dinner Parties

If you're planning your first dinner party and are unsure what to serve, consider the following dinner party menus. The majority of the menu items can be prepared ahead of time, leaving you stress-free for your guests. You will find most of the recipes in Part 7; however, the first (and easiest) menu contains "non-recipe" recipes called "something simple" that are scattered throughout Chapters 6–9. Most guests will eat 4–6 cocktail tidbits before dinner.

Menu I:

Hors d'oeuvre: Figs Wrapped with Prosciutto, Crudites with Radish Dip, Roasted Garlic (with crackers or pita bread)

First Course: Cooked Artichokes

Main Course: Broiled Lamb Chops, Baked Potato, Applesauce or Cooked Rhubarb

Dessert: Fruit and Cheese

(The recipes for Radish Dip, Roasted Garlic, and Baked Potatoes are in the recipe sections; the others are in the text.)

Menu II:

Hors d'oeuvre: Goat Cheese and Sun-Dried Tomato Tidbits, Ham and Asparagus Rolls, Kielbasa En Croute

First Course: Shrimp Cocktail

Main Course: Lemon-Oregano Roasted Chicken, Mashed Potatoes or Cooked Rice; Sautéed Dill-Scented Carrots

Dessert: Apple Brown Betty

Menu III:

Hors d'oeuvre: Bruschetta, Wrapped Shrimp, Royal and Not So Royal Potatoes

First Course: Asparagus with Shallot-Mustard Dressing

Main Course: Roast Beef, Baked or Baked Stuffed Potatoes, Low-Fat Creamed Spinach

Dessert: Fresh Fruit with Almond Cheese Dip or Kentucky Bourbon Pecan Pie

Kitchen Clue
Some of these menus will take more time and effort than others. Remember, you don't have to make every item suggested. Supplement with store-bought foods until you feel confident you can do it all.

Menu IV:

Hors d'oeuvre: Smoked Trout Spread Canapés, Stuffed Mushrooms, Crudites with Radish Dip

First Course: Hot Leek and Potato Soup

Main Course: Roast Loin of Pork, Sautéed Rosemary Potatoes, Wilted Kale

Dessert: Brownies with Ice Cream

Menu V:

Hors d'oeuvre: Roasted Garlic, Guacamole, Stuffed Mushrooms

First Course: Tomato Soup with Rice

Main Course: Broiled Salmon with Mustard and Tarragon, Cooked Rice or Wild Rice, Broccoli with Garlic and Lemon

Dessert: Cocoa Fudge Cake or Irish Cream Parfait

Menu VI:

Hors d'oeuvre: Chutney Cheese Dip (with crackers, toast, bread, or crudites), Smoked Trout Spread Canapés, Wrapped Shrimp

First Course: Lemon Scented Angel Hair Pasta with Prosciutto Ham and Thyme or Green Salad with Vinaigrette Dressing

Main Course: Broiled Butterflied Leg of Lamb or Roast Rack of Lamb, Cooked Rice or Rice Pilaf with Mushrooms, Baked Acorn Squash

Dessert: Chocolate Mousse or Fruit and Cheese

Menu VII (meatless):

Hors d'oeuvre: Goat Cheese and Sun-Dried Tomato Tidbits, Roasted Garlic (with crackers or pita bread), Not So Royal Potatoes (with chives)

First Course: Bruschetta

Main Course: Green Salad with Vinaigrette Dressing, Pasta with Peas and Wild Mushrooms

Dessert: Coffee Apricot Parfaits or Dipped Strawberries

Thanksgiving Menu:

Hors d'oeuvre: Crudites and Dip

First Course: Asparagus with Shallot-Mustard Dressing or green salad with Vinaigrette Dressing

Main Course: Roast Turkey; Gravy; Sweet Potato Casserole; Egg Noodle Stuffing; Low-Fat Creamed Spinach; Cranberry Sauce

Dessert: Pumpkin Ice Cream Pie

Casual Entertaining at a Cookout

A cookout is probably the easiest way to cook for company. You don't have to have a porch or patio; a city terrace can accommodate a small grill (assuming this is okay with the fire department and/or building code). People love the smell of barbecue. The pre-heating coals emit a tempting aroma that make people glad they're at your house to eat.

Flavor chips are fuel nuggets that give intense flavor to barbecued foods. You can buy them in bags in supermarkets and specialty cookware stores. Varieties include mesquite, applewood, and hickory.

Cookouts are casual, so tell your guests to dress accordingly. Use casual plates and utensils and stack them near the table. Guests can bring their own plates, napkins, and such.

You can pre-cook some foods to be grilled, such as spareribs. You can make slowly cooked foods such as turkey by the indirect heat of a barbecue. There also are many items you can cook extremely quickly on a grill (hamburgers, grilled steaks, and marinated chicken cutlets, for example). When you plan a cookout, it is a good idea to serve salads or other types of pre-prepared dishes on the side.

Besides the food items, you need charcoal briquettes for a cookout. Because foods cook better over very hot coals, be sure to preheat the grill, and make sure the coals are ashen white before you barbecue the food. You can enhance the flavor of barbecued foods by adding some flavor chips to the fire. Follow these additional tips for successful cookouts:

➤ Wear an apron to protect your clothes.

➤ Bring food to be barbecued to room temperature before you put it on the grill.

➤ Grease the grill to prevent food from sticking, or use foods that have been marinated.

➤ Remove excess fat from foods to be barbecued.

➤ Turn the food with tongs.

➤ Keep your grill clean; the food will taste better.

➤ Have extra napkins on hand. Grilled foods can be messy, especially if they are the kind you eat with your hands.

Some Menu Suggestions for Cookouts

When planning a cookout, consider these simple cookout menus. All the recipes can be found in Part 7, Recipes.

Menu I:

Grilled Marinated Chicken Breasts, French Potato Salad, Green Salad with Vinaigrette Dressing or Sliced Tomatoes with Dressing (see the "Something Simple" in Chapter 7), Blueberry Crumb Pie, Spiced Apple Iced Tea

Menu II:

Grilled Steak or Broiled Butterflied Leg of Lamb, Potato Salad with Lemon-Oregano Dressing, Spicy Tomato Salad, Fresh Fruit with Almond Cheese Dip

Menu III:

Grilled Swordfish, Corn and Barley Salad, Green Salad with Vinaigrette Dressing, Apple Pie, Spiced Apple Iced Tea

Menu IV:

Southern Style Barbecued Chicken, Rice and Pea Salad, Sliced Tomatoes with Dressing or Spicy Tomato Salad, Lemon Bars, and Sherbet.

Menu V:

Grilled Hamburgers, Baked Beans, Buttermilk Herb Slaw, plain sliced tomatoes and Bermuda onions, Brownies and Ice Cream, Lemonade.

The Least You Need to Know

➤ Offer easy-to-eat, 1–2 bite finger-foods with cocktails.

➤ Buy lots of ice and have non-alcoholic beverage choices at a cocktail party.

➤ Plan a dinner party with enough time to prepare for unexpected occurrences.

➤ Make sure you grease the grill and preheat it and bring the food to room temperature before you barbecue.

Part 6
The Tools of Success

Sure, cavemen got by cooking in rustic clay and earthenware vessels. Great-grandma only had cast iron pots. You don't need fancy pots and pans, appliances, gadgets and all that stuff to make food taste good. But they sure make life easy. And you'll make fewer mistakes when you use cookware designed for a particular type of cooking. You also will be more successful because the right cookware helps make the job easier.

Speaking of easier, it's much, much easier to chop foods in a food processor, mix cake batter with an electric mixer, and so on, than to do those jobs by hand. Modern cookware and appliances cut down on the boring, time-consuming, and tedious kitchen tasks we no longer have time for. They help us finish faster and do a better job. To find out about the advantages and disadvantages of particular cookware and the benefits of certain popular appliances, read on. That's what the next two chapters are all about.

Chapter 20

A Simple Guide to Pots and Pans

In This Chapter

➤ Buying in sets or buying individual pots and pans

➤ What pots and pans are made of

➤ Which cookware is best for what

➤ What to look for before buying

Once you learn to cook you probably will become pickier about the pots and pans you are using. Whether you stocked your kitchen with hand-me-downs or new wares, sooner or later you will take a closer look at them to see if they suit your cooking needs. Maybe you determine that you need a particular size pan you don't already own. Maybe you want to replace the odds and ends you've been using with some decent cookware. Or maybe you hate the stuff you have and you simply want to replace some or all of it. What do you buy? How do you go about buying? That's what this chapter is all about.

You Could Buy a Television for What These Pots and Pans Cost

Market-sensitive manufacturers try to lessen the sting of high prices by offering package deals of multi-piece sets at lower prices. Because the savings can be substantial, sets are worth considering. However, if the set has pieces you don't really need, you might be paying for something that has little value for you. For example, you may invest lots of money on an expensive set of anodized aluminum or stainless steel cookware that comes with an 8-quart stock or spaghetti pot. However, you can get away with a stock or spaghetti pot that's much less expensive. Likewise, butter warmers, meat racks, and tea kettles are only of value if you use them.

More importantly, no single kind of cookware is best for every kind of cooking (the different types are described next). So if you buy a 10-piece set but need a separate braising pan because the type of cookware you chose doesn't brown foods well, you will spend more money supplementing.

And what about space? Do you have room for the set plus the extra items? Before you buy a set, make sure you know what you're getting.

The Virtues and Vices of Different Types of Cookware

Experienced cooks don't mind having pots and pans that don't match. They want to use the pot that does the best job for a particular purpose. Which type is best for what? Here's a brief rundown that will help you buy and use cookware properly.

Copper Cookware

Copper cookware is the most responsive to heat. It heats quickly and evenly and loses heat just as quickly (which is good when cooling off is critical for a recipe). It is ideal for sautéing and sauce making, and it often is the choice of expert cooks. But copper is difficult to keep clean-looking and tin linings wear out and have to be replaced. Besides, copper is extremely expensive, and the precision heat and timing qualities of copper cookware are not necessary for most recipes.

Aluminum Cookware

Aluminum also is exceptionally responsive to heat and is outstanding for browning foods, so it is a good choice for frying, sautéing, and braising. The problem is that it "reacts" with acidic ingredients: that is, it corrodes if you put wine, tomatoes, lemon juice, vinegar, or other acidic ingredients in it. Aluminum also discolors and gives a metallic taste to foods made with these ingredients. You can't make pot roast with wine or tomato sauce in an aluminum pan.

Copper can be toxic. If you own copper cookware, and the lining wears off to the point that you can see the copper under it, do not use the pan until you can have it re-lined.

Because aluminum is simply too good to pass up as a cooking medium, manufacturers have solved its problems in several ways. Enameled aluminum is non-corrosive. It is a fine choice when you are cooking sauces, vegetables, pasta, and soups. However, the enamel cuts down considerably on the heat response, so it is not as good for foods that need to brown.

Anodized aluminum is aluminum that has been changed chemically during manufacture. It browns foods exceptionally well, and it doesn't react with acid, which makes it extremely versatile. However, anodized aluminum will darken certain delicate foods such as artichokes. Some anodized aluminum cookware comes with a lining of stainless steel. That solves all cooking problems; you can cook any type of foods in these pans. Anodized aluminum cookware is "stick-resistant," which makes it easy to clean, and some brands have non-stick coatings inside the pan, making cleanup even more of a cinch. However, you can't put most anodized aluminum cookware in the dishwasher.

Pressure Cast Aluminum is aluminum whose surfaces are coated with "non-stick" materials. The coating makes the surface safe for use with all ingredients. It is easy to clean and browns food fairly well, but it doesn't get as hot as other aluminum cookware.

Cast Iron Cookware

Many good cooks own a cast iron skillet for frying and "blackening" foods (creating a dark, almost burned surface). Cast iron heats up slowly but retains heat exceptionally well, making it ideal when you want ingredients to come out crispy and well browned. It isn't good for delicate dishes or sauces though, and the metal reacts with acidic foods. However, enameled cast iron will not corrode, and since it also heats slowly and holds heat well, it is perfect for long-simmering sauces, stews, pot roasts, casseroles, and soups. It isn't as effective for browning ingredients.

Some cast iron cookware comes with a protective surface coating that prevents corroding or pitting of the metal. Otherwise, you must season cast iron cookware periodically (heat it and rub it with a thin layer of vegetable oil).

Cast iron cookware handles get HOT! Be careful.

Stainless Steel

There are so many benefits to stainless steel it almost seems like a cook's dream come true. Stainless steel doesn't react with any ingredient. It is durable and easy to clean, and you can even put it in the dishwasher. Unfortunately, it doesn't conduct heat very well. In order for stainless steel to have any value for cooking, it must be combined in some way with better heat-conducting metals such as aluminum or copper.

Manufacturers combine stainless steel with better heat-conducting metals in several ways. Less expensive cookware has "cladding" on the bottom of the pan. The problem here is that with some brands the cladding is too thin to make a real difference. Higher quality pans have a thick metal disk attached to the bottom of the pan. In the best stainless steel cookware, the entire core of the pan (not simply the bottom) is made of aluminum but the surfaces are completely coated with stainless steel. If you buy good stainless steel pots and pans, you can use them for just about any type of cooking.

Ceramic Glass and Porcelain Cookware

You can cook almost any kind of food in glass or porcelain cookware because the surfaces don't "react" with acidic ingredients. It doesn't rust, and it is easy to clean. It retains heat well so it is particularly useful for casseroles. The best features are that you can pop this kind of cookware into a microwave oven for reheating, and you can serve the food straight from the pan. However, glass and porcelain don't conduct heat well, so you can't brown foods adequately in these pots and pans. They also are extremely fragile and need to be replaced more often than other kinds of cookware.

What About Non-Stick Cookware?

More and more people are buying non-stick cookware because it is easy to clean and it allows food to "release" from the surface with the use of little or no fat. Cheap non-stick pans have surfaces that wear off and scratch quickly. Better brands have long-lasting non-stick capabilities, and some are guaranteed for a lifetime.

Some non-stick surfaces are slicker than others, meaning you can use very little fat. They are perfect for steaming vegetables, simmering sauces, and cooking soups, rice, beans, and pasta. However, these surfaces don't get very hot, and they aren't as useful for browning foods.

Kitchen Clue
Be sure you read the manufacturer's instructions on whether you can or cannot use metal utensils with the non-stick cookware you choose.

Some brands of non-stick cookware don't have the same slick surfaces, that is, they don't "release" foods as easily (some fat is needed). However, because they get much hotter, you can use them for sautéing as well. Most manufacturers recommend that you don't use metal utensils with non-stick cookware. However, with the highest quality non-stick cookware, you are not limited; metal utensils will not damage the surface.

What Else to Look for When Buying Pots and Pans

Whether you buy sets or individual pots and pans for specific purposes, it's important to look for cookware that is well-designed, safe to use, and long-lasting. Here are some things to consider before you buy:

➤ Look for cookware that is well-balanced and heavy enough to resist wobbling or warping. Make sure the pot sits flat so the bottom will heat evenly.

➤ The handle must be comfortable for you and allow you to lift a large pan. Pick one up in the store before you buy.

➤ Handles that are riveted last longer than handles that are screwed or welded on.

➤ Wooden and plastic handles stay cooler than metal ones. You can't put wooden-handled pots in the dishwasher or oven. Some plastic-handled pots are safe in the oven (see manufacturer's instructions for temperature recommendations). Metal handles made of a material different from the pot stay cooler than handles made of the same metal. You can put metal-handled pots in the oven at any temperature.

➤ Make sure the lids fit snugly. That way they won't rattle around as food cooks inside.

➤ Look for lids that have handles or knobs made of plastic, wood, or a metal different from the pan; these stay the coolest. Be sure the handle or knob is easy to grip and large enough that your fingers don't touch the hot lid.

The Least You Need to Know

➤ You can save money by buying cookware in sets, but you may prefer to pick individual pots for individual purposes.

➤ Pot handles should be securely attached. Lids should fit snugly and have handles or knobs that stay cool and are easy to reach.

➤ Copper cookware is the most responsive to heat and is best for precision cooking.

➤ Aluminum cookware is outstanding for browning foods.

➤ Cast iron cookware is terrific for frying and "blackening" foods.

➤ Enamel cookware is super for sauces, soups, pasta, and casseroles.

➤ Stainless-steel is all-purpose cookware, suitable for (though not the best at) all kinds of cooking.

➤ Ceramic/porcelain cookware is best for casseroles.

➤ Non-stick cookware helps you cut down on dietary fat.

Chapter 21

A Primer on Small Electric Appliances

When you first start to cook, you may not own even one electric kitchen appliance. Don't despair, you *can* get along without them. However, even the best, most experienced cooks find that certain appliances save work, time, and frustration.

There are appliances for numerous kitchen tasks. Some are trendy, others are silly. Many are invaluable timesaving tools that make cooking easier and more fun. This chapter discusses the more important small electric appliances and what you should look for when buying.

Appliance Buying Basics

Forget about what's fashionable; only buy an appliance that you need. The most current "must-haves" may be a waste of space and money for you. But once you decide you need an item, compare brands. You can see for yourself which look and feel more durable. If an appliance is so lightweight you think you could throw it for a touchdown pass, it probably won't last long in your kitchen. Ask salespeople which brands are returned most often and for what reason. Ask in several stores because salespeople are apt to promote the brands they sell. You might want to ask in your local fix-it place too; which appliances do the repair people see the most?

Buying well-known brands has several advantages. Certain manufacturers have great track records for producing outstanding products. However, bear this in mind: one particular manufacturer doesn't always make the best of everything. The one who produces the best toaster oven may not manufacture the best coffee maker. So look for brands of a particular product.

While it is important to be price-sensitive when you buy an appliance, price isn't everything. If the product is poorly made, it isn't worth any money. Look for UL symbols and good warranties; these are signs of safety and manufacturer confidence. Sometimes stores sell discontinued items at terrific prices. That's good if the item was discontinued because of style or because more updated versions have more bells and whistles, but it's not good if it was discontinued because there were problems with it. It's a good idea to ask a salesperson if a sale item has been discontinued, and if so, why.

You also might be tempted to buy a "multifunction" appliance, such as a coffee maker with a built-in grinder attachment. Although they often are cheaper than the two separate appliances and take up less space, there are some disadvantages. If you already own one of the appliances, the multifunction model is a waste. And suppose one of the parts breaks? Then you are left without both until you can get the broken component repaired.

The upcoming sections describe some of the more useful kitchen appliances and tell you about some of their advantages and disadvantages.

Are Food Processors for Everyone?

Food processors are the workhorses of the kitchen. These machines chop, shred, and slice foods quickly and efficiently. The more powerful ones also knead dough. They are all similar, having a work bowl, a cover, and several types of cutting blades.

You can buy food processors in several sizes. Some small ones have a "continuous feed" chute through which you can process lots of food continuously. The processed food passes out of the work bowl into a waiting bowl.

Kitchen Clue

If any kitchen appliance can help you make the leap from a know-nothing to a world-class cook, it's a food processor. It eliminates some of the drudgery and the boredom of getting through non-creative tasks like chopping onions and slicing mushrooms.

When you buy a food processor, look for one that's heavy enough to stay in place when it's in use. The work bowl and blades should be thick and durable-looking. It isn't necessary to buy a model that has lots of parts. The primary job of a food processor is to grind, grate, shred, chop, slice, and perhaps knead.

While some fine food processors offer several speeds, you really don't need more than "high" and "low." However, a "pulse" option that lets you stop and start so you can see the ingredients before you continue processing is a good feature to look for. In addition, a wide feed-tube makes processing tasks easier, so look for one with this feature. A food processor is not the best tool for beating egg whites or whipping cream because you don't get great volume, even with special attachments for these purposes. Don't pay extra for this.

Tips on Toaster Ovens

Toast connoisseurs say toast from a toaster oven isn't as evenly browned as toast from a toaster. Although that may be true, there are other advantages to having a toaster oven. First, you can use a toaster oven to toast thick breads, including bagels. You also can use it as a mini-oven when you want to bake a couple of potatoes or reheat a small casserole. A toaster oven uses less electricity than a regular oven and keeps the kitchen cooler, too. In addition, the self-cleaning and non-stick interior models are much easier to clean than the others and usually are worth the extra price.

Toaster ovens come in 4-slice and 6-slice models, but the slice capacity doesn't tell the whole story. In some you have to squeeze the pieces together, and in others, there's lots of room inside. Look at the model in the store and see for yourself. The smaller ones take up less counter space, but the roomier ones are more versatile as extra mini-ovens. Whatever size you buy, look for a toaster oven that has a heavy, solidly built rack and broiler tray. Models with removable crumb trays are much less messy to clean than the ones in which you have to lift the toaster, lift down the tray, and shake the crumbs out.

You shouldn't use a toaster oven to broil foods such as a steak unless you bought a *toaster-broiler oven*. Be sure to check. Some toaster ovens are specifically limited to toasting.

How to Choose a Handmixer

A handmixer is useful even if you only bake occasionally. It doesn't take up much space and doesn't cost as much as a heavy duty standmixer, but performs some of the same functions, handling jobs like mixing cake batter and whipping egg whites and cream. There are many cheap handmixers around, most of which are pretty dreadful. The ones that have beaters with flat edges and center posts just don't do a great job.

Better handmixers have beaters that are wiry or curvy looking and don't have center posts. These whip ingredients extremely well, and they are easier to clean. (Some manufacturers call them self-cleaning beaters.) The curvy-beater models are more expensive, but they're always worth the difference in price because of the results they give.

Some handmixers have lots of speeds, some have only a few; more than five is overkill. Some handmixers are so strong you can mix cookie dough with them. Once you select the right type of handmixer, think more carefully about how the appliance feels. Choose the one that's comfortable and isn't so heavy it will tire out your tennis arm.

Being Savvy About Standmixers

People who love to bake will eventually want a standmixer because the best ones have powerful motors. That means they can outperform even the best handmixers for whipping egg whites and cream and mixing cake and cookie doughs—all without your having to hold the appliance. (Some standmixers are even sturdy enough to knead dough and come with dough hooks.) A standmixer is definitely a labor-saver for those who bake often and regularly.

Better standmixers have whisk-type attachments for egg whites and whipped cream. Some have a flat beater for other mixing jobs; some have handmixer-type beaters. Of those, the ones with the wiry-looking beaters that have no center posts do a better job than the old-fashioned flat-edged beaters with a center post.

One of the most important features to look for in a standmixer is its weight. If you are going to put the machine to the task of heavy duty kneading or mixing, you want it to stay still when it's in use, not creep along the counter until it falls off. That's why the ones that are said to be "all-metal construction" are better; they're heavier than the lightweight plastic machines. The other thing to look at is the way in which the beaters and bowl work together. Some models feature what the manufacturers call *planetary action*. That means the beater spins around a stationary bowl—a much more effective way to get at the ingredients than the old-fashioned models in which the bowl moves, but not the beaters. Oscillating beaters (which move back and forth in the bowl) also do a fairly decent job.

Blender Basics

Blenders are terrific for making beverages and processing liquid ingredients like soups and sauce. Although you could use a food processor for these jobs, blenders are better because the jar is so tall that you don't have to worry about the liquid leaking out.

There are several types of blenders available. Some have pushbutton controls, others have levers, switches, or touch-pad controls. Two blender speeds are enough for most purposes (and more than eight seems useless), but a pulse feature gives you more control. Glass jars are more costly than plastic ones, but they are sturdier and don't get as scratched and cloudy. Some blenders crush ice without using water, some need water, and some don't crush ice at all. If this is important to you, read the instructions before you buy a particular model.

The two most important considerations when you buy a blender are:

➤ Be sure the jar fits securely onto the motor base so it won't fall off when the machine is working.

➤ Be sure the lid fits snugly into the jar so it won't pop off during blending.

The Case For and Against Can Openers

Almost everybody buys an electric can opener. What most people don't realize is that this appliance is a potential source of trouble. If the cutting device doesn't cut the lid cleanly and sever it completely from the can, there's potential for injury when you pull at sharp edges to get the lid off. Second, because the blade touches the food inside the can, bacteria can build up. Therefore, it's important to find one with a blade that comes off completely for cleaning or with a blade that cuts the outside of the can and does not touch the food. There are a few models that cut well (without leaving sharp edges) and have cleanable blades. Look for these—a good can opener comes in handy.

Knife sharpener attachments aren't important because they don't do a good job sharpening knives and often ruin the blades. Don't pay extra for this feature.

What to Think About When Buying a Coffee Maker

Most people in this country make coffee in an electric automatic drip coffee maker. There are so many brands and models that you could go nuts in the housewares department picking the right one. There are lots of excellent models from competing manufacturers. Most of the differences among the machines from the same manufacturer have to do with extra features. That is, the basic coffee making unit is the same but one has a timer that lets you program wake-up coffee, another has a gold-mesh filter, and so on. You have to decide whether those extra features are important to you and whether they are worth more money.

Coffee makers come in several sizes, though most make either 10 or 12 cups. It is almost impossible to brew a small quantity of full-bodied coffee in the large machines. If you prepare only 2–4 cups of coffee most of the time, buy a small machine that makes up to 4 cups or buy a larger unit that has a special switch for brewing small quantities. This switch slows down the brewing process so that small amounts of coffee will have flavor and body. It is a very valuable feature that gives the large machine terrific versatility.

Espresso coffee is coffee made with water heated to such high temperatures and put under such high pressure that steam goes rapidly ("espresso") through finely ground Italian roast beans to create a strong, rich brew. *Cappuccino* is espresso coffee mixed with steamed milk and capped with a thick layer of frothed milk.

Coffee makers with "swing-out" baskets are easier to fill and clean than other types. A "pause-to-serve" feature lets you pour some coffee before all of it has brewed—a worthwhile feature when you can't wait to sip some coffee.

What About Espresso/Cappuccino Machines?

It seems everyone is drinking espresso coffee and cappuccino these days. The trend is so big that sales of special equipment for preparing these types of coffee are booming. While you can buy stove-top espresso coffee pots, most people want the newer electric machines because these appliances make both espresso and cappuccino.

There are two types of the electric appliances available: a "steam" machine and the higher powered "pump" models. Steam machines have smaller capacities but are much cheaper, and there are some excellent models on the market. Pump machines allow you to prepare more coffee quickly, but they can be costly. Many people find these appliances difficult to use. It takes practice until you get it right, but the results are worth it if you like espresso and cappuccino. Whichever type you buy, be sure to look for models that are made of metal or heavy, durable-looking plastic and that don't have unnecessary knobs and removable parts that make the coffee-making process even more confusing.

When You Want to Grind Your Own Coffee Beans

Great coffee begins with fresh beans you grind just before you brew the beverage. Because people are becoming more particular about coffee these days, sales of coffee grinders are soaring. There are two types. The smaller canister-shape models are inexpensive and easy to use: you add the beans and press down on the cap or a button until you see that the grinds are the consistency you need. However, there's some guesswork with these since you determine both the quantity of beans and when to stop processing. With the larger coffee mills, you can preset the quantity of beans you need for the amount of coffee you want, and you can also preset the type of grind you need. There's no guesswork here. However, coffee mills are much more expensive. Either type is useful and will help you make a better cup of coffee.

The Least You Need to Know

➤ Buy appliances from reputable brand-name manufacturers that have a good track record.

➤ Look at an appliance in the store to see if it looks and feels durable, and ask questions of salespeople about which appliances are returned most often.

➤ Food processors are probably the most valuable worksaving, timesaving kitchen appliances you can own.

➤ The best handmixers have wiry-looking beaters that have no center posts.

➤ Only buy a can opener that has a cutting blade you can remove completely for cleaning or that has a cutting blade that never touches the food.

➤ The most versatile coffee makers are the large ones with a separate switch that slows down coffee brewing when preparing small quantities.

Part 7
Recipes

Once you know how to cook, you face the dilemma of what to cook. This is something we all think about. What you decide has to do with several things: your mood ("Do I feel like eating pasta? Meat?"), your schedule ("Do I have time to prepare roast chicken?"), your energy level ("Do I feel like fussing or will I just make something quick and simple?"), your confidence level ("Should I be adventurous and try something new?"), and, of course, your diet ("Is there something delicious that's low-fat I can make today?").

The following recipe sections offer you a broad enough choice for you to find something to make for a meal no matter what your mood, schedule, and so on. However, I wanted to gear this book for modern eating, so this part includes dishes that call for more up-to-date or unusual ingredients.

The recipes marked "Easy" speak for themselves; even beginners are capable of cooking these. The "Intermediate" recipes entail an extra step or so, or include a technique that a beginner may worry about. The "Challenging" recipes either have several steps or include techniques that require more attention (techniques where people can make mistakes if they're not careful).

Hors d'oeuvre and First Courses

Hors d'oeuvre

The literal translation of hors d'oeuvre is "outside the work" and comes from old-time restaurant notions about the pecking order among the kitchen help. Chefs and their staff were considered too important to make hors d'oeuvre; their "work" was the main meal. It was up to the serving people to prepare the little pre-dinner morsels for diners who awaited the real food. Today, hors d'oeuvre are still outside the work. That is, you serve them before dinner. But they are by no means unimportant. Everyone looks forward to them.

Chutney Cheese Dip

Although this is first and foremost a tangy dip suitable as a spread for crackers or bread, you also can use it to stuff vegetables such as endive leaves, mushroom caps, or celery stalks.

Level: Easy
Preparation time: 4–5 minutes
Cooking time: none
Yield: about $^3/_4$ cup

Can be done completely ahead

$^1/_2$ cup grated sharp cheddar cheese
3 oz. cream cheese at room temperature
$^1/_4$ cup crumbled roquefort
  or other blue-veined cheese (about one oz.)

$^1/_4$ cup chopped bottled mango chutney
$^1/_4$ cup coarsely ground almonds or other nuts
$^1/_2$ tsp. curry powder
$^1/_8$ tsp. cayenne pepper (optional)

Place all the ingredients in a bowl and mix them together thoroughly. The cayenne pepper will make the dish hot and spicy. Serve this in a crock or other small serving bowl accompanied by crackers or cut-up bread.

Radish Dip

This is an exceptionally refreshing, lightweight dip perfect for crudites (raw vegetables) or crackers.

Level: Easy
Preparation time: 6–7 minutes by hand, 2–3 minutes in a food processor
  (plus 20–30 minutes refrigeration time)
Cooking time: none
Yield: about 2 cups

Can be done completely ahead

1 medium-size cucumber	pinch of salt
1 dozen small radishes	pinch of freshly cracked black pepper
1 TB. minced fresh parsley	2 cups plain yogurt
1 TB. minced fresh mint	

Peel the cucumber, slice it lengthwise, and scoop out the seeds. Wash the radishes. Mince the cucumber, radishes, parsley, and mint by hand or in a food processor. Place ingredients in a medium-sized bowl and add the salt, pepper, and yogurt. Mix the ingredients well and refrigerate the dip 20–30 minutes or until it is well chilled. Taste for seasoning and add salt and pepper as desired.

Roasted Garlic

Did you ever think you could eat garlic straight? Believe it or not, when you cook garlic, it becomes pretty tame. Try this ultra-easy hors d'oeuvre and see for yourself.

Level: Easy
Preparation time: 2–3 minutes
Cooking time: $1\frac{1}{2}$ to 2 hours
Yield: serves 4–6

Can be done completely ahead

1 large whole head of garlic	$\frac{1}{8}$ tsp. freshly ground black pepper
1 TB. olive oil	2 tsp. freshly minced herbs of any kind
$\frac{1}{4}$ tsp. salt	or $\frac{1}{2}$ tsp. dried (optional)

Preheat the oven to 350 degrees. Remove the loose paper from the outside of the garlic head. Put the garlic on a small sheet of aluminum foil and drizzle the olive oil over it. Sprinkle the garlic with salt, pepper, and herbs. Wrap the garlic completely in the foil. Bake $1\frac{1}{2}$ to 2 hours or until the garlic is soft when pierced with the tip of a sharp knife. Remove the garlic from the foil. Slice a piece of the top to expose the garlic flesh. To serve, let the garlic cool and have guests scoop some from the head or take a clove of the cooled garlic off with fingers and squeeze it onto a cracker or cut-up vegetable.

Kitchen Clue
You can make this on a special "garlic baker" if you've got one.

Smoked Trout Spread

This is a very versatile dish since you can use it as a spread (put it in a pretty serving bowl) or on top of canapé rounds when you really want to bother. You can buy smoked trout at fish stores and in many supermarkets.

Level: Easy
Preparation time: about 10 minutes
Cooking time: none
Yield: enough for 4 dozen canapés (about 2¹/₂ cups of spread)

Can be done ahead up to the * in the instructions

2 whole boneless smoked trout (4 fillets, or about 1 lb.)
6 oz. cream cheese
3 TB. plain yogurt
2 TB. lemon juice
24 slices firm, homestyle white bread for canapés

4 tsp. prepared white horseradish
1 tsp. Dijon mustard (optional)
1 TB. snipped fresh chives (or the green part of scallions)
fresh dillweed or lemon slices for garnish

Break the fish into small pieces by hand or in a food processor. Blend the trout with the cream cheese, yogurt, lemon juice, horseradish, mustard (if used), and chives by hand or in a food processor or blender. The mixture can be a smooth puree or be slightly chunky to suit your tastes. Place the mixture in a serving bowl to use as a spread. Place a leaf of dill on top to serve as garnish or surround the spread with ¹/₂" slices of lemon (put the flat part down so the lemon border looks like a scallop design). To make canapés, cut small rounds about 1¹/₂" in diameter out of the bread slices with a cookie cutter. Canapés can become soggy if you spread them too far ahead of serving time. About an hour ahead is right. If you don't have a small cookie cutter, use the top of a bottle (such as the one that comes with green olives) instead. Or, you can trim the bread and cut it into triangles or squares instead of cutting out circles.

* About an hour before serving time, spread the fish mixture on the bread rounds and garnish the top of each with a tiny leaf of dill.

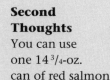

Second Thoughts
You can use one 14³/₄-oz. can of red salmon instead of smoked trout. Drain the salmon and proceed with the recipe as written.

Guacamole

This is one of America's favorite dips—hot and spicy with the velvety-creamy texture that fresh avocados provide. If you've got any guacamole left, you can use it as a sauce on grilled chicken breasts for dinner.

Level: Intermediate
Preparation time: 15 minutes
Cooking time: none
Yield: about 2 cups

Can be done completely ahead

1 large tomato
1 jalapeño chili pepper (or use 1-2 TB. chopped bottled jalapeño peppers)
2 medium avocados
3 TB. lemon or lime juice
¹/₄ cup finely chopped onion

1 medium clove garlic, minced
2 tsp. finely chopped fresh cilantro (coriander) (optional)
³/₄ tsp. salt (or salt to taste)
corn chips

Cut the tomato in half crosswise, squeeze out the seeds, and chop the pulp into small pieces. Remove the stem, fleshy white part (membrane), and seeds from inside the jalapeño pepper and chop it into small pieces. Peel the avocado, slice the flesh all the way down to and around the pit, and put the flesh in a medium-sized bowl. Add the lemon or lime juice and mash the ingredients. Stir in the chopped tomato and pepper, chopped onion, minced garlic, cilantro (if used), and salt. Mix well. You can use a food processor or blender if desired. Serve with corn chips.

Warning Jalapeño and other chili peppers can be harmful to skin and eyes. Wear disposable rubber gloves and wash your hands afterward. Do not touch your eyes or reinsert contact lenses after working with chili peppers.

Goat Cheese and Sun-Dried Tomato Tidbits

Anyone who likes tangy, intensely flavored food will appreciate these—and they're a cinch to prepare.

Level: Easy
Preparation time: 8–10 minutes
Cooking time: none
Yield: 36–40 hors d'oeuvre

*Can be done ahead up to the * in the instructions*

1 cup soft goat cheese (chevre)
6 TB. cream, any kind
36–40 toast rounds (packaged is fine)

12 sun-dried tomatoes in oil, minced
freshly cracked black pepper

Combine the cheese and cream in a bowl and mix them together until they are smooth.

* Spread the cheese on top of the toast rounds. Top each tidbit with an equal portion of the sun-dried tomatoes and just a hint of the oil they were packed in. Grind fresh pepper over the hors d'oeuvre and serve.

Second Thoughts
Instead of using toast rounds, you could substitute endive leaves. If you do this, place the cheese and tomato at the narrow end so you can pick up the hors d'oeuvre by the wide end. You can make these up completely ahead of time.

Tomato and Basil Bruschetta

This is one of the more popular hors d'oeuvre and a favorite at Italian restaurants. It is especially refreshing in the summer. You could also serve it as a first course.

Level: Easy
Preparation time: 25 minutes
Cooking time: 3–4 minutes for the toast
Yield: makes about 18

*Can be done ahead up to the * in the instructions*

1 lb. plum tomatoes (about 7–8)
1 large clove garlic, minced
$^1/_3$ cup olive oil
$^1/_3$ cup coarsely chopped fresh basil or 1 tsp. dried

a pinch of cayenne pepper
a pinch of salt or to taste
1 loaf of French bread

Preheat the oven to 400 degrees. Cut the tomatoes in half crosswise and squeeze the seeds out. Chop the tomatoes and place them in a bowl. Add the garlic, 2 TB. of the olive oil, basil, cayenne pepper, and salt to the tomatoes.

Slice the bread into $^1/_2$" thick slices. Brush both sides lightly with the remaining 3 TB. of oil. Place the bread on a cookie sheet and bake the slices 3–4 minutes or until they are slightly crispy but not browned.

* Spread equal amounts of tomato mixture on top of bread pieces.

Second Thoughts
If you can't find fresh basil, substitute $1^1/_2$ tsp. fresh thyme, oregano, or marjoram leaves (or a pinch or two of these dried). If you can't find any of these, substitute 4 slices of crumbled crispy bacon.

Ham and Asparagus Roll-ups

This is a simple but stunning hors d'oeuvre that people seem to gobble up no matter how often you serve it. Set the pieces on doilies for even greater visual effect.

Level: Easy
Preparation time: 20 minutes (plus 30 minutes refrigeration time)
Cooking time: about 3 minutes
Yield: about 2¹/₂ dozen hors d'oeuvre

Can be done completely ahead

4 medium-to-large-thickness asparagus, cooked
   (or you can use packaged frozen asparagus spears)
4 slices boiled ham
6 oz. softened cream cheese, or herb-flavored cream
   cheese

half a lemon
2 TB. fresh snipped chives
   (or the green part of scallion)
freshly ground black pepper

Cut the woody, purplish bottoms off the asparagus. Peel the asparagus if desired (this is not essential). Place the asparagus spears in a skillet, cover them with water, and cover the pan. Bring the water to a simmer over high heat. After the water begins to steam, cook the asparagus about 3 minutes or until they are fork tender. Drain the asparagus under cold water and wipe them dry with paper towels. (If you use frozen asparagus, cook them until they are tender.)

Wipe the ham slices dry and spread each slice with equal quantities of the cream cheese. Place a cooked asparagus in the center, down the length of the slice of ham. Squeeze the lemon so that drops fall on each asparagus. Sprinkle the ham and asparagus with the chives, and grind some fresh pepper over these ingredients. Roll the ham jelly-roll style to make one long roll. Place the roll seam side down on a plate in the refrigerator (cover the plate with plastic wrap). Chill for at least 30 minutes. Slice each roll into 8 sections.

Stuffed Mushrooms

Everyone loves stuffed mushrooms. You can even freeze these for about a month.

Level: Easy
Preparation time: 12–15 minutes
Cooking time: 4–6 minutes to cook the filling, 15 minutes to bake the mushrooms
Yield: 16

Can be done completely ahead

16 large mushrooms
1¹/₂ TB. melted butter
4 oz. sweet Italian-style sausage, not in casing
1 clove garlic, minced

¹/₄ cup grated mozzarella cheese
2 TB. plain bread crumbs
1 TB. grated parmesan cheese
1¹/₂ tsp. chopped fresh oregano or ¹/₂ tsp. dried

Preheat the oven to 350 degrees. Rinse and dry the mushrooms. Remove the stems and chop them; then set them aside. Brush the caps with the melted butter (if you don't have a pastry brush, use your fingers). Cook the sausage in a skillet over moderate heat for 2–3 minutes, breaking up the pieces into smaller ones as you cook them. Add the garlic and the chopped mushroom stems and continue to cook the mixture until the meat is well browned (about another 2–3 minutes). Remove the pan from the heat and drain off any excess fat (you can put the contents of the pan in a strainer). Combine the meat mixture in a bowl with the mozzarella cheese, bread crumbs, parmesan cheese, and oregano. Mix ingredients well and use the mixture to stuff each mushroom cap. Place the filled caps on a cookie sheet. Bake the mushrooms 15 minutes or until they are hot and the cheese is bubbly.

Kitchen Clue
Link-type sausage is enclosed in a thin skin or casing. If you cannot find bulk sausage meat, use the links, but remove the meat from the skin or casing.

Kielbasa En Croute

Kielbasa is a lightly cured, garlic-seasoned sausage. A glamorous sort of frank-in-blanket, this is another hors d'oeuvre that always is a best-seller at a party.

Level: Easy
Preparation time: 5–8 minutes (plus 15 minutes thawing time for puff pastry)
Cooking time: about 25 minutes
Yield: one roll, serves 8–10 people

*Can be done ahead up to the * in the instructions*

one sheet packaged frozen puff pastry	1 TB. Dijon mustard
1 piece of kielbasa (about ¹/₂ lb.)	1 large egg, beaten

Preheat the oven to 400 degrees. Let the sheet of frozen puff pastry thaw for fifteen minutes, and then roll it slightly thinner on a floured surface. Spread the mustard down the center of the pastry sheet. On top of the mustard, lay a piece of kielbasa long enough to leave a margin of one inch at each end. Wrap the pastry around the kielbasa and seal the edges of dough by pinching it together. (The edge should have an overlap no wider than ¹/₂", and you should cut away any excess dough.) If you do not cook the roll now, place it in the refrigerator.

* Place the kielbasa roll seam side down on a cookie sheet. Brush the entire surface of the pastry with the beaten egg. Bake the roll 25 minutes or until it is lightly browned. To serve, slice the roll into bite-size pieces with a serrated knife. (If you prefer, serve the roll with the knife next to it to let guests cut their own slices.)

Second Thoughts
If you want to make this hors d'oeuvre more visually appealing, cut out fancy shapes with any scraps of dough you have left from the original sheet (that is, the leftovers after you've rolled the kielbasa up in the dough). Place the shapes on top of the roll and brush them with more of the beaten egg before you bake the roll.

Wrapped Shrimp

These are glamorous and beautiful with the pink shrimp sticking out of the end of the crispy bacon. Use fancy toothpicks to skewer them.

Level: Easy
Preparation time: 12–15 minutes
Cooking time: 4–6 minutes
Yield: 12 hors d'oeuvre

*Can be done ahead up to the * in the instructions*

12 extra large raw shrimp	1 TB. minced fresh dillweed or 1 tsp. dried
2 TB. olive oil	6 slices of thin-sliced bacon
2 TB. lemon juice	

Preheat the broiler or grill. Shell and devein the shrimp as described in Chapter 13 (or buy them shelled and deveined). Rinse the shrimp and dry them with paper towels. Mix the olive oil, lemon juice, and dillweed in a non-reactive dish. Add the shrimp and make sure they are well coated with the liquid. Cut each piece of bacon in half to make two shorter strips, and wrap each shrimp with a piece of bacon.

* Grill or broil the shrimp about 6" from the heat source for 2–3 minutes per side, or until the bacon is crispy and the shrimp are pink.

Kitchen Clue
Most fish markets will shell and devein shrimp for you if you call ahead. That saves lots of time.

Royal and Not So Royal Potatoes

This is an elegant and lavish dish that you can serve to your most important company.

Level: Intermediate
Preparation time: 6–7 minutes (plus 10–15 minutes for the potatoes to cool)
Cooking time: about 15 minutes
Yield: makes 12 hors d'oeuvre

Can be done completely ahead

12 "new" yellow or small red bliss potatoes
¼ cup dairy sour cream
3 ounces of any type of caviar

Wash the potatoes, and then steam them for 15–20 minutes or until they are tender. Drain the potatoes under cold water, and then let them cool. Peel the potatoes and cut a thin slice from the bottom of each one so it can stand up straight. With the tip of a spoon, scoop a small amount of potato from each potato top to make a crater. Fill each crater with sour cream and top the sour cream with a small amount of caviar.

For Not So Royal Potatoes, substitute 2 TB. chives or 3 slices crumbled crispy bacon for the caviar. For variety, serve all three kinds of potatoes.

Second Thoughts
You may substitute low-fat or nonfat sour cream or plain yogurt for the sour cream. It's less rich, but has less fat. You could also use creme fraiche.

First Courses

Most of the time you won't serve a first course for dinner. We are all too busy to prepare multicourse meals on a regular basis, and many of us do not appreciate the extra calories another course provides. An entree and side dishes are usually sufficient. On the other hand, a special first course is appropriate occasionally when you feel more up to cooking or want a little something extra at your meal. It is particularly suitable for company. Not only does a first course set a slower pace for your meal so you and your guests can relax and chat at the table, but it also allows you to show off your culinary skills so you can hear their praise and applause.

Asparagus with Shallot-Mustard Dressing

This is a lovely first course, especially in the springtime when asparagus are tastiest.

Level: Easy
Preparation time: 15–20 minutes
Cooking time: 3–4 minutes
Yield: serves 4

Can be done completely ahead

1 lb. medium-thickness asparagus
lightly salted water
⅓ cup olive oil
3 TB. vegetable oil
4 TB. fresh lemon juice

1 shallot, finely chopped
1 TB. Dijon mustard
1 TB. freshly minced parsley
¼ tsp. salt (or salt to taste)
¼ tsp. freshly ground black pepper

Cut the woody, purplish bottoms off the asparagus. Peel the asparagus if desired. (A vegetable peeler makes this easy; peel from the bottom toward the top.) Place the asparagus spears in a skillet, cover them with the lightly salted water, and cover the pan. Bring the water to a simmer over high heat. After the water begins to steam, cook the asparagus about 3 minutes or until they are fork tender. Drain the asparagus under cold water and wipe them dry. Place the asparagus in a serving dish.

Combine the remaining ingredients in a bowl. Whisk them 30–60 seconds or until the ingredients are well blended. Pour the dressing over the asparagus. Refrigerate the dish, but remove the asparagus from the refrigerator 35–45 minutes before serving time.

Shrimp Cocktail

This is one of the easiest first courses in the world, especially if you have the fish merchant shell and devein the shrimp for you. While it's simple, it's still impressive.

Level: Easy
Preparation time: 20 minutes (plus 30 minutes refrigeration time)
Cooking time: about 6 minutes
Yield: serves 4

Can be done completely ahead

24 extra large shrimp (about 1 lb.)
water
1 slice lemon, $^1/_4$" thick

bottled cocktail sauce or lemon-dill-flavored mayonnaise

Shell and devein the shrimp as described in Chapter 13 (or buy them shelled and deveined). Rinse the shrimp under cold water. Bring a 3-quart saucepan of water to boil. Add the lemon slice and let it cook 30 seconds. Remove the pan from the heat. Immerse the shrimp in the water. Cover the pan. Let the shrimp stand in the hot water for 5 minutes or until they are pink and firm. Drain the shrimp under cold water. Refrigerate them approximately 30 minutes or until they are cold. Arrange the shrimp on a plate or around the edges of a "cocktail cup" (you can use a dessert bowl). Garnish the dish with a dollop of sauce (or place the sauce in the cocktail cup) and some lemon slices.

Second Thoughts
To make an easy lemon-dill-flavored mayonnaise for the shrimp, mix $^3/_4$ cup mayonnaise with 2 TB. of lemon juice and 2 TB. freshly minced dill.

Lemon-Scented Angel Hair Pasta with Prosciutto Ham and Thyme

This unusual dish comes from taste memories of a similar pasta dish served at a restaurant called Alouette in Philadelphia. It is the kind of first course that wows company because the flavor combinations are so interesting.

Level: Intermediate
Preparation time: 12–15 minutes
Cooking time: about 15 minutes
Yield: 4 as a first course (can be doubled to serve 4 for dinner)

Can be cooked ahead up to the * in the instructions

$^1/_2$ lb. angel hair pasta or thin spaghetti
4 TB. olive oil
2–3 oz. prosciutto ham (or any other flavorful cured ham)
1 stalk lemongrass
  (or use 1$^1/_2$ tsp. freshly minced lemon peel)
1 shallot, chopped

1 clove garlic, minced
$^3/_4$ tsp. fresh thyme leaves or $^1/_4$ tsp. dried
$^1/_4$ tsp. salt (or salt to taste)
$^1/_4$ tsp. freshly ground black pepper (or pepper to taste)

Cook the pasta until it is *al dente*. Drain the pasta under cool water. Toss the pasta with 1 TB. of the olive oil and set it aside. Chop the ham into tiny pieces and set it aside. Remove and discard the tough outer husk of the lemongrass and the tough bottom portion. Mince the remaining inside core of the lemongrass and set it aside. Place 1 TB. of the olive oil in a skillet large enough to hold the pasta. Add the shallot and garlic, and cook them over low-moderate heat 1–2 minutes or until the vegetables have wilted. Add the lemongrass, ham, and thyme leaves, and cook another 2 minutes.

* Add the pasta, salt, pepper, and remaining 2 TB. olive oil. Toss ingredients and continue cooking another 3–4 minutes or until pasta is hot and ingredients are evenly distributed.

Kitchen Clue
You can buy prosciutto ham in Italian specialty markets and at the deli counter of many supermarkets.

Stuffed Shrimp

This first course is luxurious, especially when served with a dry white wine.

Level: Challenging
Preparation time: 25 minutes
Cooking time: about 20 minutes
Yield: serves 4

*Can be done ahead up to the * in the instructions*

1 dozen jumbo shrimp
2 TB. olive oil
1 large shallot, finely chopped
1 large clove garlic, minced
$1/4$ cup finely chopped mushrooms
6 oz. scallops, finely chopped
$1/3$ cup soft fresh bread crumbs
  (or $1/4$ cup dried bread crumbs)

$1/3$ cup freshly grated parmesan cheese
2–3 TB. white wine or dry sherry
$1/4$ tsp. salt (or salt to taste)
$1/4$ tsp. black pepper
paprika for dusting

Preheat the oven to 350 degrees. Shell and devein the shrimp as described in Chapter 13 (or buy them shelled and deveined). Rinse the shrimp under cold water, dry them with paper towels, and cut into the deveined area of each one deep enough so you can flatten or "butterfly" the shrimp. (Do not cut through completely.) To butterfly them, gently press down the curvy deveined side with the palm of your hand. Place the shrimp cut-side-up in a lightly greased baking dish.

Heat the olive oil in a skillet and add the shallot, garlic, and mushrooms. Cook over moderate heat 2–3 minutes or until all the pan juices have evaporated. Add the scallops and cook another 2 minutes, stirring frequently. Remove the pan from the heat. Stir in the bread crumbs and cheese, and mix the ingredients thoroughly. Add 2 TB. wine or just enough to moisten the mixture (add more only if the mixture looks dry). Sprinkle the mixture with salt and pepper. Place equal amounts of the stuffing on the cut portions of each shrimp. Dust each lightly with paprika.

* Bake 15 minutes or until the stuffing is golden brown.

Soups and Salads

Soups

Did you know that the first restaurant in history (opened in 1765) only served soup? The owner of the place (in Paris), a man by the name of Boulanger, understood that a good hearty soup had the power to "restore" a person's energy. In fact the word "restore" influenced the new word for a public eating place: "restaurant." There are many different kinds of soup: light ones that you use as a first course and more rib-sticking ones that you can serve for supper. Soup is one course that's so versatile you can make a different one every day and not run out of recipes for years.

Old-Fashioned Chicken Soup

You guessed it! It's the familiar old "penicillin," but this version is fragrant with dill for extra flavor.

Level: Easy
Preparation time: about 12 minutes
Cooking time: $2^1/_2$ to 3 hours
Yield: serves 8

Can be done completely ahead

1 stewing hen or roasting chicken
water
1 large onion, peeled, left whole
4 carrots, peeled
3 stalks celery, peeled

1 parsnip or small turnip, peeled
small bunch of fresh dill or 1 TB. dried
1 TB. salt (or salt to taste)
6–8 whole black peppercorns

Wash the chicken inside and out and place it in a soup pot. Pour enough water in the pot to cover the chicken by one inch. Bring the liquid to a boil, lower the heat, and for the next several minutes, remove any scum that rises to the surface. Add the remaining ingredients. Cover the pan partially and simmer the soup for $2^1/_2$ hours or until the chicken meat is very soft when pierced with the tip of a sharp knife. Pour the soup through a strainer or colander into a large bowl or a second pot. Set the chicken and vegetables aside. Remove the fat from the surface of the liquid with a spoon or fat skimming tool or by patting paper towels on the surface. For best results, refrigerate the strained soup; when it is cold, the fat will rise to the surface and harden and you can scoop it off. (Refrigerate the vegetables and the chicken separately.) Serve the soup plain or with the vegetables that you cut up and pieces of chicken meat you removed from the bones (return these items to the soup when you reheat it).

Kitchen Clue
This soup is terrific when served with cooked white rice or cooked egg noodle flakes or alphabets. Although the soup freezes well, do not freeze the cooked chicken or vegetables with it. You can eat them now or make chicken salad with the chicken.

229

Old-Fashioned Carrot Soup

This is a light but satisfying soup that is superb as a first course but can also be a supper dish served with a sandwich.

Level: Easy
Preparation time: 12–15 minutes
Cooking time: about an hour
Yield: serves 8–10

Can be done completely ahead

2 TB. butter
2 TB. vegetable oil
1 medium onion, chopped (about ½ cup)
2 lbs. carrots, chopped
2 medium all-purpose potatoes, peeled and chopped
¼ cup chopped parsley
2 TB. chopped fresh dillweed or 2 tsp. dried

1½ tsp. salt (or salt to taste)
⅛ tsp. freshly ground black pepper
  (or pepper to taste)
7 cups canned or homemade chicken
  or vegetable stock
pinch of sugar
1 cup cream, any kind

Heat the butter and vegetable oil together in a soup pot. When the butter has melted and looks foamy, add the onion and cook over moderate heat 3–4 minutes or until the onion has softened. Add the carrots, potatoes, parsley, dillweed, salt, and pepper and cook 3–4 minutes, stirring occasionally. Add the stock and sugar. Bring the soup to a simmer. Cook partially covered 45 minutes. Puree the soup in a food processor or blender. Return the soup to the pan. Add the cream. Heat the soup through and serve.

Thick as Fog Pea Soup

You'll find this a great treat when the weather turns cold.

Level: Easy
Preparation time: 10 minutes
Cooking time: about 2 hours
Yield: serves 8–10

Can be done completely ahead

1 lb. dried green split peas
10 cups cold water
1 meaty ham bone or 2 ham hocks
  or a 1 lb. chunk of corned beef
3 carrots, chopped
2 stalks celery, chopped

2 medium onions, chopped (about 1 cup)
3 sprigs parsley
1 bay leaf
1½ tsp. fresh marjoram or ½ tsp. dried
¼ tsp. freshly ground black pepper

Place all the ingredients in a soup pot and bring the liquid to a boil. Reduce the heat and cover the pan. Simmer for 2 hours. Discard the bay leaf. Remove the bone. You can puree the soup in a blender if you want and then return it to the saucepan. Remove the meat from the ham bone or hocks (or chop the corned beef) and add the pieces to the soup. Heat the soup through and serve.

Second Thoughts
To make a creamier, thinner soup, you can add cream or buttermilk to taste (begin with one cup, taste the soup, and add more if desired). To give the soup some pizzazz, serve it with crunchy croutons.

Hot Leek and Potato Soup

You can serve this thick, creamy soup as dinner with a sandwich. Otherwise, it's a great first course or lunch dish.

Level: Easy
Preparation time: 20–25 minutes
Cooking time: 45–50 minutes
Yield: serves 8

Can be done completely ahead

6 medium all-purpose potatoes
2 quarts cold water
4 large leeks
2 carrots, peeled and chopped

1 TB. salt (or salt to taste)
$^1/_2$ cup cream
2 TB. chopped chives or parsley for garnish

Peel, slice, and rinse the potatoes. Place them in a soup pot and cover them with the cold water. Cut the dark green leaves off the leeks. (Only the white and pale green parts should remain.) Cut the roots off. Place the leeks under cold running water and separate the leaves to make sure any sand between them washes away. Shake the excess water from the leaves and slice the leeks. Put the leeks in the pot. Add the carrots and salt. Bring the soup to a boil, lower the heat, and cover the pan partially. Simmer the soup 45–50 minutes or until vegetables are very tender. Puree the soup in portions in a food processor or blender. (You can use a hand tool to puree the ingredients.) Return the soup to the pan. Add the cream and cook a minute or so to reheat the soup. Serve the soup garnished with the chives or parsley.

Cream of Tomato Soup with Rice

You don't have to eat this stuff from the can anymore. This version doesn't require much fuss and tastes much better. It's great as a lunch soup, but you can also use it for a first course at dinner.

Level: Easy
Preparation time: 10–12 minutes
Cooking time: about $1^1/_2$ hours
Yield: serves 6–8

Can be done completely ahead

2 TB. vegetable oil
1 medium onion, chopped (about $^1/_2$ cup)
1 carrot, chopped
1 stalk celery, chopped
3 TB all-purpose flour
3 cups canned or homemade chicken
  or vegetable stock

2 28-oz. cans of tomatoes, not drained
2 tsp. sugar
1 tsp. salt (or salt to taste)
1 tsp. fresh thyme leaves or $^1/_4$ tsp. dried
$^1/_2$ tsp. freshly ground black pepper
$^1/_3$ cup white raw rice
1 cup cream, any kind

Heat the vegetable oil in a soup pot. Add the onion, carrot, and celery, and cook the vegetables over low-moderate heat 3–4 minutes or until they have softened. Add the flour and stir it into the vegetables. Cook another 2 minutes. Add the tomatoes, sugar, salt, thyme, and pepper. Cover the pan partially and cook the soup over moderate heat 1 hour. Puree the soup in portions in a food processor or blender. (You can use a hand tool to puree the ingredients.) Return the soup to the pan. Add the rice and cover the pan. Cook 30 minutes or until rice is tender. Stir in the cream and cook the soup a minute or so to reheat it.

Andalusian Gazpacho

This is a refreshing summer soup. Make sure you buy fresh, ripe, fragrant summer tomatoes.

Level: Intermediate
Preparation time: 30 minutes
Cooking time: none
Yield: 6 servings

Can be done completely ahead

4 slices of homestyle white bread, diced
2 large cloves garlic
1 medium onion, cut into chunks
5 TB. olive oil
1 cup water
1¹/₂ tsp. salt (or salt to taste)
5 tomatoes, deseeded and cut into chunks

1 cucumber, peeled, deseeded, and cut into chunks
1 green pepper, deseeded, and cut into chunks
¹/₄ cup red wine vinegar
3 cups tomato juice
2 cups packaged croutons
optional garnishes:
    ¹/₂ cup chopped green pepper, ¹/₂ cup chopped
    cucumber, 3–4 chopped scallions

Place the bread, garlic, onion, and olive oil into the work bowl of a food processor or in a blender. Whirl ingredients until they are finely minced, scraping down the sides of the processor bowl once or twice during the process. Add the water and salt and process them briefly. Add the tomatoes, cucumber, and green pepper and process for 10–20 seconds or until it reaches the desired consistency (you may want a true puree or something chunkier). Pour the soup into a bowl and stir in the wine vinegar and tomato juice. Refrigerate for at least one hour. Taste for seasoning and add salt as needed. Serve the soup with croutons. To make the dish more authentic, serve it with the garnishes (prepare them the same way and at the same time as the other vegetables, but set them aside in separate bowls).

Beef Barley Soup

This is a hearty, rib-sticking soup.

Level: Intermediate
Preparation time: 12–15 minutes
Cooking time: about 3 hours
Yield: serves 10

Can be done completely ahead

8–10 dried mushrooms
2 lbs. meaty soup bones
12 cups water
¹/₂ cup pearled barley
2 medium onions, sliced
3 medium carrots, sliced
2 stalks celery, sliced

1 parsnip, sliced
8 sprigs of fresh dillweed, minced, or 1 tsp. dried
6 sprigs of fresh parsley, minced
2 tsp. salt (or salt to taste)
¹/₄ tsp. freshly ground black pepper
2 large peeled all-purpose potatoes
    cut into bite-size pieces

Place the mushrooms in a bowl and cover them with hot water. Let them soak until they are softened (5–10 minutes). Then rinse them off, remove the hard stems (if there are any) and discard them, chop the mushrooms, and set them aside. In a soup pot, bring the meat and water to a boil. Lower the heat and, for the next several minutes, remove any scum that rises to the surface. Simmer the soup partially covered 30–40 minutes. Add the barley and onions and simmer partially covered another 40–45 minutes. Add the mushrooms, carrots, celery, parsnip, dillweed, parsley, salt, and pepper. Simmer partially covered one hour. Add the potatoes and cook another hour. Remove the bones from the soup and cut the meat into small pieces. Discard the bones and return the meat to the pan.

Turkey Bean Soup

This hearty soup is a terrific way to use leftovers from Thanksgiving. You can make this soup as meaty as you like by adding more leftover turkey than just the scraps. You can prepare this soup with chicken as well.

Level: Intermediate
Preparation time: 15 minutes (plus 1 hour soaking time)
Cooking time: $2^3/_4$ hours
Yield: serves 8–10

Can be done completely ahead

20 oz. bag of loose mixed dried beans
  (such as pinto, navy, black, red, or kidney)
water
turkey carcass, meat scraps and bones
1 2 lb. 3-oz. can Italian style plum tomatoes,
  drained and chopped into bite-size pieces
2 stalks celery, sliced into $1/_4$" thick pieces
1 medium onion, sliced

2 cloves garlic, chopped
1 TB. Cajun blackening spices
  (or substitute chili powder)
2 tsp. salt or to taste
a sprig of fresh rosemary, thyme, or marjoram
  or $1/_2$ tsp. dried (optional)
$1/_2$ cup raw white rice
1 cup freshly grated parmesan cheese (optional)

Rinse the beans under cold water and place them in a soup pot. Cover the beans with water, bring the water to a boil over high heat, and boil the beans for 2 minutes. Remove the pan from the heat, cover the pan, and let the beans stand for one hour. Drain the beans and return them to the pot. Add 2 quarts of water, the turkey carcass, meat scraps, and bones. Bring the soup to a simmer. Add the tomatoes, celery, onion, garlic, blackening spices, salt, and fresh herb (if used). Cover the pan partially and cook at a simmer for about 2 hours. Stir in the rice and cook partially covered for about 45 minutes. Taste the soup for seasoning and add salt to taste. Remove the herb sprig. Serve soup with fresh parmesan cheese, if desired.

French Onion Soup

This soup isn't hard to make, but it involves a few extra steps. Although it tastes fine without the croutes (which involve extra work), they give this classic soup a lot of style as well as fabulously rich flavor and a delightfully chewy texture on top.

Level: Challenging (Easy if you don't make the croutes)
Preparation time: 15 minutes for soup, 10 minutes for croutes
Cooking time: $1^1/_4$ hours for soup, plus 12–15 minutes with
croutes; plus 30 minutes for croutes
Yield: serves 8

Can be done completely ahead

2 TB. butter
2 TB. olive oil
2 lbs. yellow onions, peeled and sliced
$3/_4$ tsp. salt (or salt to taste)
$1/_2$ tsp. sugar

$1^1/_2$ TB. flour
6 cups heated canned or homemade beef stock
$1/_4$ cup dry sherry
bread and cheese croutes (optional)

Melt the butter and olive oil together in a soup pot or large saucepan. When the butter has melted and looks foamy, add the onions, salt, and sugar. Cook the onions over low-moderate heat, stirring occasionally, for about 30 minutes or until onions have softened and become caramel-colored. Add the flour and mix ingredients together gently over the heat for 3 minutes. Gradually add the beef stock, stirring gently as you pour it into the soup. Cook the soup partially covered for 35 minutes. Add the sherry. Cook another 5 minutes. Serve the soup as is or topped with bread and cheese croutes.

continues

continued

Bread and Cheese Croutes:

8 1" thick slices of French bread
1 TB. olive oil
1 garlic clove, cut in half

1¼ cups freshly grated swiss cheese
2 TB. freshly grated parmesan cheese

Preheat the oven to 350 degrees. Bake the bread on a cookie sheet for 15 minutes. Brush the bread tops with the olive oil and rub the surface of the bread with the cut side of the garlic. Turn the bread slices over and bake them another 15 minutes. Just before serving the soup, place the soup in oven-proof bowls and top each with one slice of the bread. Sprinkle the cheeses evenly over the bread. Place bowls on a cookie sheet and bake the soup for 12–15 minutes or until the cheese melts and is bubbly.

Kitchen Clue
While almost any kind of good sherry will do, an Oloroso has the best flavor for this recipe. Do not use "cooking sherry."

Homemade Stock and Bouillon

It's somewhat time consuming to make your own homemade stock and bouillon, but it's worth it. Stock is the basis for many soups and sauces, and bouillon comes in handy for a multitude of recipes. When you make your own, you control the level of salt, fat, and flavor. You can freeze stock in small containers so you can use it in small portions as needed. You can also freeze bouillon.

Level: Challenging
Preparation time: 15 minutes
Cooking time: about 3 hours for stock; 4½–5 hours for bouillon
Yield: 10 cups of stock; 1½ cups concentrated bouillon

Can be done completely ahead

1 stewing hen 4–5 lbs. or 4–5 lbs. chicken necks,
  backs, or giblets
16 cups water
1 large onion, peeled and cut in half
2 carrots, peeled
2 stalks celery, rinsed
2 unpeeled cloves garlic

2 bay leaves
3 sprigs parsley
2–3 sprigs fresh thyme or 4 sprigs fresh dill,
  or 1 tsp. dried
1 tsp. salt (optional)
8 whole black peppercorns

To make the stock, place the hen in a soup pot and add 16 cups of water (or enough to cover it by about 1"). Bring the water to a boil over high heat, lower the heat, and for the next several minutes, remove any scum that rises to the surface. Add remaining ingredients. Be sure there is enough water to cover all ingredients, adding more water if necessary. Cook the ingredients partially covered for 2½ to 3 hours. Pour the stock through a strainer or colander into a large bowl or second pot. Remove the fat from the surface of the liquid with a spoon or by patting paper towels on the surface. For best results, refrigerate the strained soup; when it is cold, the fat will rise to the surface and harden and you can scoop it off. Discard the vegetables. You can use the chicken for chicken salad.

Kitchen Clue
You can make beef or veal stock and bouillon the same way, using 5 lbs. bones and meat instead of chicken.

To make the stock into bouillon, cook the degreased stock (the stock with the grease removed) over low heat for several hours or until it has reduced to 1½ cups. Pour the liquid into 16 ice cube tray sections. Refrigerate for several hours or until firm. When dissolved in one cup boiling water, each section will make one cup bouillon to which you may add salt as needed. You can freeze bouillon cubes in little plastic bags.

Salads

Salads are among the more refreshing foods you can make because you eat them when they are cool. That makes them handy too: you can prepare them ahead and not worry about reheating. There are scads of different types of salads. Green salads, potato salad, and macaroni salad are familiar to most of us. But there are also interesting salads you can make from grains and starches such as barley, beans, and rice. Here's a hint to bear in mind: salads always taste better at room temperature or slightly chilled, but not cold.

Potato Salad with Lemon-Oregano Dressing

This is a perfect picnic salad since it doesn't contain mayonnaise (which spoils quickly in hot weather), and it's terrific for a cookout, too.

Level: Easy
Preparation time: 15–20 minutes (plus 1 hour standing time)
Cooking time: 15–20 minutes
Yield: serves 4–6

Can be done completely ahead

2 lbs. small red potatoes
$^1/_4$ cup olive oil
$^1/_4$ cup fresh lemon juice
2 scallions, finely chopped
1 TB. minced fresh parsley

$1^1/_2$ TB. minced fresh oregano or $1^1/_2$ tsp. dried
$^3/_4$ tsp. salt (or salt to taste)
freshly ground black pepper (or pepper to taste)

Place the potatoes in a saucepan, cover them with lightly salted water, and bring the water to a boil. Lower the heat and cook the potatoes at a simmer 15–20 minutes or until they are fork tender. Drain the potatoes under cold water and peel them when they are cool enough to handle. Cut into bite-size pieces and place them in a large bowl. Pour in the olive oil and lemon juice, and add the scallions, parsley, oregano, salt, and pepper. Toss gently. Let stand at least one hour before serving. Serve at room temperature.

Second Thoughts For a more intense flavor, add one minced garlic clove. Leave the potatoes unpeeled if you prefer.

Potato Salad, French Style

This classic salad is suitable for your loveliest summer dinner, but you can use it at any cookout or take it to a picnic. It's versatile because there's no mayonnaise (which spoils easily in hot weather).

Second Thoughts You can substitute chicken stock for the white wine.

Level: Easy
Preparation time: 15–20 minutes (plus 1 hour standing time)
Cooking time: 15–20 minutes
Yield: serves 4–6

Can be done completely ahead

2 lbs. small red potatoes
6 TB. dry white wine
1 large shallot, chopped
$1^1/_2$ TB. minced fresh herbs such as thyme, savory, rosemary, basil, or chives, or a mixture of herbs
2 TB. minced fresh parsley

$^1/_3$ cup olive oil
3 TB. red wine vinegar
1 tsp. Dijon mustard
$^3/_4$ tsp. salt (or salt to taste)
$^1/_4$ tsp. freshly ground black pepper (or pepper to taste)

Place the potatoes in a saucepan, cover them with lightly salted water, and bring the water to a boil. Lower the heat and cook the potatoes at a simmer 15–20 minutes. Drain the potatoes under cold water and peel them. Cut into bite-size pieces and place in a large bowl. Pour in the white wine, add the shallot, herbs, and parsley, and toss gently. In a small bowl, whisk the olive oil, red wine vinegar, Dijon mustard, salt, and black pepper together, and pour over the potatoes. Toss gently. Let salad stand for about one hour before serving. Add salt and pepper as needed.

Buttermilk Herb Slaw

The tangy buttermilk makes this cole slaw superbly refreshing.

Level: Easy
Preparation time: about 20 minutes (plus 30 minutes standing time)
Cooking time: none
Yield: serves 4–6

Can be done completely ahead

$^2/_3$ cup buttermilk
2 TB. mayonnaise
1 TB. cider vinegar
1 TB. sugar
2 TB. minced fresh chives (or the green part of a scallion)
2 TB. minced fresh parsley

1 TB. minced fresh dill, tarragon, or savory or 1 tsp. dried
$^1/_2$ tsp. salt (or salt to taste)
$^1/_8$ tsp. cayenne pepper
3 cups shredded cabbage
$^1/_2$ cup shredded snow peas

Mix together the buttermilk, mayonnaise, vinegar, sugar, chives, parsley, herb, salt, and cayenne pepper. In a large bowl, combine the cabbage and snow peas and toss them to spread the pea shreds evenly throughout the cabbage shreds. Pour the dressing over the vegetables. Toss ingredients to coat the vegetables with the dressing. Let the salad stand for at least 30 minutes before serving. Serve the salad at room temperature.

Second Thoughts
If you don't have cider vinegar, use one TB. white vinegar plus one TB. apple juice.

Spicy Tomato Salad

This salad is especially terrific in the summer when you can get fabulous summer tomatoes.

Level: Intermediate
Preparation time: 10 minutes (plus 30 minutes standing time)
Cooking time: none
Yield: serves 6

Can be done completely ahead

4 large ripe tomatoes
6 Sichuan peppercorns
$^1/_2$ tsp. freshly ground black pepper
1 TB. chopped fresh hot chili pepper (such as a jalapeño)

3 TB. olive oil
$1^1/_2$ TB. red wine vinegar
1 TB. finely chopped fresh parsley
$^1/_2$ tsp. fresh thyme leaves or $^1/_4$ tsp. dried
$^1/_4$ tsp. salt (or salt to taste)

Chop the tomatoes into bite-size pieces and place them in a bowl. Crush the Sichuan peppercorns (you can put them in a plastic bag and bang them with a pan or roll them with a rolling pin) and add them to the tomatoes with the black pepper, chili pepper, olive oil, vinegar, parsley, thyme, and salt. Toss ingredients and let them stand at least 30 minutes before serving. Serve at room temperature.

Second Thoughts
For a tangier tasting salad, add 2–3 tsp. of chopped fresh coriander. For a less hot version, substitute 2 TB. canned green chili peppers for the fresh hot chili pepper.

Easy Tuna and White Bean Salad

This is a classic Tuscan dish you find at many antipasto bars in Italy. You can tote it to a picnic, serve it at a cookout, use it as a first course before dinner (especially before a grilled meat or poultry dinner), or serve it in warm weather as a main course. Serve with crusty Italian bread.

Level: Easy
Preparation time: 10 minutes (plus 10 minutes standing time)
Cooking time: none
Yield: serves 4

Can be done completely ahead

2 $6^{1}/_{8}$-oz. cans of tuna in oil
2 cans of white beans, about 1 lb. each
3 scallions, chopped
$^{1}/_{3}$ cup chopped parsley
6 TB. olive oil

2 TB. red wine vinegar
2 tsp. lemon juice
1 TB. chopped fresh oregano or 1 tsp. dried
$^{1}/_{4}$ tsp. freshly ground black pepper

Drain most of the oil from the tuna. Put the fish in a bowl. Rinse the beans under cold water and drain them in a strainer. Add the beans, scallions, and parsley to the tuna, and toss the ingredients gently. Mix the olive oil, red wine vinegar, lemon juice, oregano, and black pepper. Pour the dressing over the fish and beans. Let the salad stand at least 10 minutes before serving. Serve at room temperature.

Second Thoughts
You can substitute 12 oz. cooked shrimp for the tuna.

Rice and Pea Salad

If you're bored with deli macaroni or potato salad, look no further. This versatile salad goes with practically any grilled meat or poultry (see the sidebar), making it a great choice for a summer cookout. It also looks good on a buffet table and is a superb side dish at dinner.

Level: Easy
Preparation time: 5 minutes (plus time to cook and cool the rice)
Cooking time: 20 minutes for the rice
Yield: serves 4–6

Can be done completely ahead

3 cups cooked, cooled white rice
$^{3}/_{4}$ cup thawed frozen peas
$^{3}/_{4}$ cup diced boiled ham
$^{1}/_{3}$ cup olive oil
$1^{1}/_{2}$ TB. red wine vinegar

1 tsp. Dijon mustard
$^{3}/_{4}$ tsp. salt (or salt to taste)
$^{1}/_{4}$ tsp. freshly ground
   black pepper
3–4 TB. mayonnaise

Second Thoughts
You can leave the ham out of the salad if you want something meatless. And whether or not you do that, you can also add any number of ingredients to this salad. For example, try these:

➤ $^{1}/_{2}$ chopped red pepper

➤ 8 cooked, cut up shrimp

➤ 1 cup thawed frozen corn kernels

➤ 1 chopped, deseeded tomato

Mix the rice, peas, and ham in a bowl. Combine the olive oil, wine vinegar, Dijon mustard, salt, and pepper in a second bowl. Whisk the dressing ingredients to combine them, and pour the dressing over the rice. Toss the ingredients. Add 3 TB. of mayonnaise and stir it in. If you like a more moist salad, stir in the remaining mayonnaise.

Corn and Barley Salad

Most people have never tasted barley salad. For that reason alone, this novel salad is worth a try; besides, it's colorful and beautiful. Another super picnic salad because it doesn't contain mayonnaise.

Level: Intermediate
Preparation time: 12–15 minutes (plus 1 hour soaking time and 30 minutes standing time)
Cooking time: 30 minutes
Yield: serves 4–6

Can be done completely ahead

1 cup barley (sometimes packaged as pearled barley)
1 medium tomato
1 cup cooked or thawed frozen corn kernels
2 scallions, finely chopped
3 TB. finely chopped fresh parsley
2 tsp. minced fresh oregano
   or marjoram or $^3/_4$ tsp. dried

$^3/_4$ tsp. salt (or salt to taste)
$^1/_4$ tsp. freshly ground black pepper
   (or pepper to taste)
$^1/_2$ cup olive oil
3 TB. red wine vinegar
1 TB. Dijon mustard

Place the barley in a saucepan, cover it by 1 inch with water, and let it stand 1 hour. Drain the barley and return it to the saucepan. Pour in 2 cups of water. Bring the water to a boil, lower the heat, cover the pan, and cook the barley about 30 minutes or until all the liquid has been absorbed. While the barley is cooking, cut the tomato in half crosswise, squeeze out the seeds, and chop the pulp into small pieces. When the barley is cooked, add the tomato, corn, scallions, parsley, oregano, salt, and pepper to the barley, and mix ingredients. In a small bowl, whisk together the olive oil, red wine vinegar, and mustard. Pour this over the barley salad and toss ingredients. Let the salad stand at least 30 minutes before serving. Serve at room temperature.

Second Thoughts
You can use 1 cup thawed frozen peas in addition to or instead of the corn.

The Easiest Chicken Salad in the World

Everyone else puts celery in chicken salad. Why not be different? The apple and nuts in this recipe give the same crunchy texture but add much more flavor.

Level: Easy
Preparation time: 10 minutes (plus minimal refrigeration time)
Cooking time: none
Yield: serves 4

Can be done completely ahead

3 cups cooked chicken, cut up
1 large tart apple (such as a Granny Smith),
   peeled and diced into $^1/_4$" pieces

$^1/_2$ cup chopped almonds
$^3/_4$ cup mayonnaise

Mix all the ingredients together in a bowl. If you like a more moist salad, add slightly more mayonnaise. Chill the salad slightly, but do not serve it ice cold.

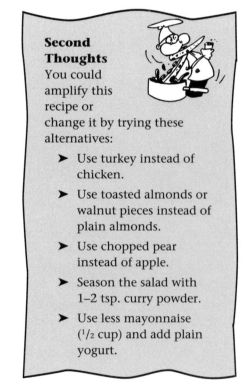

Second Thoughts
You could amplify this recipe or change it by trying these alternatives:

➤ Use turkey instead of chicken.

➤ Use toasted almonds or walnut pieces instead of plain almonds.

➤ Use chopped pear instead of apple.

➤ Season the salad with 1–2 tsp. curry powder.

➤ Use less mayonnaise ($^1/_2$ cup) and add plain yogurt.

Chicken Salad Provencale

This makes great use of leftover chicken, especially chicken from soup or stock. It looks gorgeous, too, so you can serve it as a lunch salad for company or for a light dinner during warm weather.

Level: Intermediate
Preparation time: 15 minutes (plus 15 minutes recommended standing time)
Cooking time: none
Yield: serves 4

*Can be done ahead up to the * in the instructions*

several pieces of leafy lettuce such as oak leaf lettuce
4 cups cooked diced chicken meat
1 small ripe avocado (optional)
1 large red pepper
1 small red onion, sliced
18 black olives

$^1/_2$ cup olive oil
5 TB. red wine vinegar
1 tsp. Dijon mustard
1 tsp. fresh thyme leaves or about $^1/_2$ tsp. dried
$^1/_2$ tsp. salt (or salt to taste)
$^1/_8$ tsp. freshly ground black pepper

Wash and dry the lettuce leaves and arrange them on a platter. Place the chicken in a mound in the center. Peel the avocado (if used) and cut slices from the flesh, placing them at the edge of the chicken. Remove the stem and seeds from the pepper, cut it into strips, and arrange the strips near the avocado and chicken. Place red onion slices around the platter, and put the olives here and there on the platter. Combine the remaining ingredients in a bowl and whisk or mix them to blend them well.

* Pour this dressing over the meat and vegetables. If possible, wait about 15 minutes before you serve the salad so the flavors can blend.

Salad Croutons

Use these in any green tossed salad. You can also put them on top of soup (for example, the Thick as Fog Pea Soup in the Soups section).

Level: Easy
Preparation time: 5–6 minutes
Cooking time: about 15 minutes
Yield: 2 cups

Can be done completely ahead

2 TB. olive oil
1 TB. butter
2 cloves garlic, minced

2 cups $^1/_2$" white bread cubes
$1^1/_2$ tsp. minced fresh herbs of choice
    or $^1/_2$ tsp. of dried (optional)

Preheat the oven to 325 degrees. Heat the olive oil and butter in a skillet. When the butter has melted and looks foamy, add the garlic and cook it over low heat 3–4 minutes. Add the bread cubes and herbs (if used). Toss the bread around the pan to coat the cubes with oil and butter. Place the coated cubes on a cookie sheet. Bake the cubes 12–13 minutes or until lightly browned and crispy. Store croutons in an airtight container.

Kitchen Clue
Homemade croutons are tender and absorb flavorful dressings better than firm packaged croutons. You can use whole wheat or Italian bread; trim the crusts of any bread you choose.

Main Courses

The main course is the foundation of a meal. While you can serve soup or pasta as a main course, most often you will have meat (or meat substitutes) and side dishes. In this country, we are fortunate to have a huge variety of meats, poultry, fish, and shellfish to choose from, so dinner never has to be boring. If you're not in the mood for chicken, you can cook lamb or bluefish. We're also lucky that there are scads of different cuts of main course meats, several sizes of chicken, and so on. If you don't have the time to cook a large "roast beef," you can quickly grill some chicken breasts or stir-fry some flank steak. The fact is, there are so many main courses that you'll never be stuck without an idea for dinner.

Oat Coated Trout

The oatmeal gives this dish a faintly sweet taste and a crunchy crust.

Level: Easy
Preparation time: 10 minutes (plus 25 minutes standing time)
Cooking time: 4–6 minutes
Yield: serves 4

Can be done ahead up to the * in the instructions

4 TB. olive oil
$1^1/_2$ TB. lemon juice
1 tsp. Dijon mustard
2 TB. chopped chives (or the green part of a scallion)
$^1/_2$ tsp. salt (or salt to taste)

$^1/_4$ tsp. freshly ground black pepper
4 trout fillets
1 cup uncooked quick oatmeal
vegetable oil
lemon wedges

Mix together the olive oil, lemon juice, mustard, chives, salt, and pepper in a glass, ceramic, stainless-steel, or other "non-reactive" dish large enough to hold the trout fillets. Place the fillets in the dish and coat them with the mixture. Let the fish stand 10 minutes. Crush the oats onto a flat plate. Dredge the fillets in the oats. Let the oat-coated fillets stand 15 minutes or longer.

* Heat $^1/_4$" vegetable oil in a skillet. Add the fillets and sauté them over moderate heat 2–3 minutes per side, or until the fillets are lightly browned. Serve with lemon wedges.

Kitchen Clue
If you prefer not to fry the fish, you can bake the fillets, instead. Preheat the oven to 375 degrees and bake the fish on a cookie sheet about 12 minutes, or until the surface of the fish has browned. This dish is perfect with mashed potatoes and cooked kale.

Baked Bluefish

The tomatoes and celery in this recipe flavor the fish and help keep it juicy.

Level: Easy
Preparation time: 12–15 minutes
Cooking time: 20 minutes
Yield: serves 4

*Can be done ahead up to the * in the instructions*

4 bluefish fillets
$1/4$ cup lemon juice
2 TB. olive oil
freshly ground black pepper
2 tomatoes, coarsely chopped
2 stalks celery, cut into $1/2$" slices
2 TB. minced fresh dillweed, or 2 tsp. dried dill
$1/4$ cup fine, dry plain bread crumbs

Kitchen Clue
If you peel the celery, it will be less stringy and more digestible. Use a vegetable peeler and peel starting from the thin end. Pull any strings that don't come off with the peeler. You can make this dish with mackerel, snapper, shad, pompano, or grouper.

Preheat the oven to 375 degrees. Place the bluefish fillets in a baking dish. Sprinkle the fish with the lemon juice, olive oil, and black pepper. Place the tomatoes and celery on top of the fish. Sprinkle the vegetables with the dillweed and bread crumbs.

* Bake the fish about 20 minutes, or until bread crumbs are browned and fish is cooked through.

Broiled Salmon with Mustard and Tarragon

This dish looks good and tastes as if you really fussed—and it only takes 5 minutes to prepare.

Level: Easy
Preparation time: 5–6 minutes
Cooking time: 9–10 minutes
Yield: serves 4

*Can be done ahead up to the * in the instructions*

4 salmon steaks, about $1^1/4$— thick
2 TB. olive oil
2 TB. Dijon mustard
2 TB. lime juice

2 TB. minced fresh tarragon leaves, or
  2 tsp. dried
$1/4$ tsp. freshly ground black pepper

Preheat the broiler. Place the salmon steaks in a heatproof pan suitable for use in a broiler. Mix together the olive oil, mustard, lime juice, tarragon, and black pepper. Spoon some of this mixture over the salmon. Turn the salmon over and spoon remaining sauce over the fish.

* Broil the salmon 5 minutes. Turn the steaks and broil another 4–5 minutes, basting with the pan juices once or twice, or until fish is just cooked through.

Sole Meuniere

This dish is a classic, and though it is extremely simple to make, it is one of the most elegant dishes you can serve company.

Level: Easy
Preparation time: 7–8 minutes
Cooking time: about 6–7 minutes
Yield: serves 4

Cannot be done ahead

¹/₄ cup all-purpose flour
¹/₂ tsp. salt (or salt to taste)
¹/₄ tsp. freshly ground black pepper (or pepper to taste)
4 fillets of sole

3¹/₂ TB. butter
1 TB. vegetable oil
2 TB. lemon juice
2 TB. minced fresh parsley

Preheat the oven to "warm" or 140 degrees. Combine the flour, salt, and pepper in a plate. Dredge the fish fillets in the flour and shake off the excess. Heat 2 TB. of the butter and the vegetable oil in a skillet. When the butter has melted and looks foamy, add the fish to the pan. Cook the fillets over moderate heat 4–5 minutes, turning them once with a rigid spatula, or until they are delicately browned. Transfer the fillets to a plate and keep them warm in the oven. Add the remaining 1¹/₂ TB. butter and the lemon juice to the pan and mix ingredients until the butter melts. Pour the sauce over the fish. Sprinkle the fish with the parsley and serve.

Broiled or Grilled Swordfish

Great on the grill or in the oven broiler, this is a "meaty" fish dish that's filling and satisfying.

Level: Easy
Preparation time: 5 minutes (plus 1 hour marinating time)
Cooking time: 10 minutes
Yield: serves 4

*Can be done ahead up to the * in the instructions*

4 swordfish steaks, about 1¹/₄" thick
6 TB. lemon juice
6 TB. olive oil
¹/₂ tsp. freshly ground black pepper (or pepper to taste)

1¹/₂ TB. Dijon mustard
2 TB. minced fresh basil or dillweed, or 2 tsp. dried
1 TB. minced fresh savory, oregano, marjoram, or thyme or 1 tsp. dried

Place the steaks in a glass, ceramic, stainless-steel, or other "non-reactive" dish. Combine the remaining ingredients in a small bowl and mix them thoroughly. Pour the mixture over the fish. Let the fish marinate (in the refrigerator) about one hour, turning the fish once during that time.

* Preheat the broiler or grill. Remove the fish to a rack in a broiler pan. Place the broiler pan about 6" lower than the heat source (set the grill rack about the same distance from the heat). Broil or grill the steaks 5 minutes. Turn them over and broil or grill them another 4–6 minutes, or until fish is just cooked through.

Kitchen Clue
If you wish to substitute some other fish steak, try fresh tuna, monkfish, or halibut. You also can vary this versatile dish by using lime juice instead of lemon or by adding a large minced shallot to the marinade.

Easy Shrimp Scampi

A luxurious dish for special family or company dinners, this version has a surprise ingredient.

Level: Intermediate
Preparation time: 25 minutes
Cooking time: 5–7 minutes
Yield: serves 4

*Can be done ahead up to the * in the instructions*

$1^3/_4$ lbs. large or extra-large raw shrimp
6 TB. melted, cooled butter
$^1/_3$ cup olive oil
4 TB. cream sherry

3 cloves garlic, minced
1 TB. minced shallot
2 TB. chopped, fresh parsley
$^1/_4$ tsp. salt (or salt to taste)

Preheat the broiler. Shell and devein the shrimp as described in Chapter 13 (or buy them shelled and deveined). Rinse the shrimp under cold water, dry them in paper towels, and cut into the deveined area of each one, deep enough so you can flatten or "butterfly" the shrimp. (To butterfly them, gently press down on the curvy, deveined side with the palm of your hand.) Do not cut through completely. Place the shrimp, cut side up, in a baking dish. Combine the remaining ingredients in a small bowl and pour this mixture over the shrimp.

* Place the dish in the broiler with the rack set about 6" below the heat source. Broil the shrimp without turning them, 5–7 minutes or until shrimp are pink and firm.

> **Fein on Food**
> Typically, recipes call for dry sherry. This recipe started when there was no dry sherry in the house and Harvey's Bristol Cream came to the rescue. The sweet, cream sherry has been the family's first choice for shrimp scampi and other shellfood ever since.

How to Broil or Grill Chicken

This is one of the more basic recipes in a home cook's repertoire, and you can keep changing it to create endless recipes.

Level: Easy
Preparation time: 5–8 minutes
Cooking time: about 30–35 minutes
Yield: serves 4

*Can be done ahead up to the * in the instructions*

1 broiler-fryer chicken, $2^1/_2$–4 lbs., cut into 4–8 parts
2 TB. vegetable oil or melted butter
salt, pepper, garlic powder (or garlic salt), and paprika

Preheat the broiler or grill. Wash and dry the chicken parts. Place the parts on a rack in a broiler pan. Rub the surfaces with the vegetable oil or melted butter. Sprinkle the chicken with salt, pepper, garlic powder (or salt), and paprika.

* Place the broiler pan and rack about 6" lower than the heat source. (Set the grill rack the same distance from the heat.) Broil or grill the pieces about 30–35 minutes, turning them occasionally with tongs or until the juices run clear when the thigh is pricked with the tip of a sharp knife. During this time, baste the chicken 2–3 times.

>
>
> **Second Thoughts**
> Consider these variations:
>
> ➤ Sprinkle the chicken with 2 TB. chopped, fresh rosemary or 2 tsp. dried, crushed rosemary.
>
> ➤ Coat the chicken with 2 TB. of Dijon mustard along with the other ingredients.
>
> ➤ Marinate the chicken parts in vinaigrette dressing for 30 minutes before broiling.
>
> ➤ Marinate the chicken in 1 cup plain yogurt plus 1 tsp. ground ginger, $^1/_2$ tsp. cinnamon, $^1/_2$ tsp. ground cumin, $^1/_2$ tsp. salt, and 1 minced garlic clove before broiling.

Southern Style Barbecued Chicken

This is tangy and rich: a perfect choice for a summer cookout, yet hearty in winter, too.

Level: Easy
Preparation time: 10–12 minutes
Cooking time: 30–35 minutes for the chicken; 10 minutes for the sauce
Yield: serves 4

Can be done completely ahead

1 broiler-fryer chicken, $2^1/_2$–4 lbs. cut up
2 TB. olive oil
salt and pepper
$^1/_3$ cup ketchup
$^1/_4$ cup vinegar
$^1/_4$ cup brown sugar
$1^1/_2$ TB. Worcestershire sauce

1 TB. chili powder
$1^1/_2$ tsp. powdered mustard
$^1/_2$ tsp. ground ginger
1 clove garlic, minced
1 TB. butter
1 quarter of a lemon

Wash and dry the chicken pieces, rub them with olive oil, and sprinkle them with salt and pepper. Combine the remaining ingredients in a small saucepan. Cook the sauce over moderate heat 10 minutes. Place the broiler pan and rack about 6" lower than the heat source. (Set the grill rack the same distance from the heat.) Broil or grill the pieces, turning them occasionally with tongs and basting the parts often with the barbecue sauce. Broil or grill the pieces about 30–35 minutes, or until the juices run clear when the thigh is pricked with the tip of a sharp knife.

Sautéed Chicken

This is another basic recipe every cook should know and that you can change in numerous ways. You'll be amazed at how easy and how versatile this dish is! Use the pan juices as gravy for cooked rice.

Level: Easy
Preparation time: 10 minutes
Cooking time: 35–40 minutes
Yield: serves 4

Can be done completely ahead

1 broiler-fryer chicken, $2^1/_2$–4 lbs., cut into 4–8 parts
1 TB. vegetable oil
1 TB. butter

salt, pepper, garlic powder (or garlic salt), and paprika
$^1/_2$ cup white wine or canned or homemade chicken stock

Wash and dry the chicken parts. Heat the vegetable oil and butter together in a skillet over moderate heat. When the butter is foamy, add the chicken parts. Sprinkle the chicken with salt, pepper, garlic powder (or salt), and paprika. There is no need to measure these spices, just dust the surface with them. If you use garlic salt, use slightly less salt than if you use garlic powder. Turning the pieces occasionally with tongs, cook the chicken 15 minutes or until the pieces are lightly browned. Discard excess pan fat by pouring it off or spooning it out. Pour the white wine or stock into the pan. Cover the pan and cook the chicken at a simmer about 20 minutes or until the parts are cooked through.

Like most other chicken dishes, this one is so versatile that there is an endless assortment of recipes. You may want to begin stretching your skills with these variations:

➤ After you brown the chicken, remove it from the pan temporarily and add a chopped onion and 4 peeled and cut up carrots to the pan. Cook them 2–3 minutes, return the chicken to the pan, and proceed as above.

➤ After you brown the chicken, remove it from the pan temporarily and add a chopped onion, a green pepper cut into strips, and a red pepper cut into strips. Cook them 2–3 minutes, then return the chicken to the pan and proceed as above.

➤ Add 8 oz. fresh mushrooms to the pan with the wine or stock.

How to Roast Chicken

So simple, yet so impressive. Roast chicken is always suitable for family or company meals.

Level: Easy
Preparation time: 6–8 minutes
Cooking time: depends on the weight of the chicken (plus 15 minutes standing time)
Yield: serves 6

*Can be done ahead up to the * in the instructions*

1 roasting chicken, 4$\frac{1}{2}$–7 lbs.
2 TB. vegetable oil or melted butter
salt, pepper, garlic powder (or garlic salt), and paprika

Preheat the oven to 400 degrees. Remove the plastic bag of giblets from inside the bird. Wash the giblets if you wish to roast and eat them. Put them in the roasting pan. Otherwise, freeze them for when you wish to make stock (a recipe appears in the Soups and Salads recipe section). Wash the chicken inside and out. Place the chicken on a rack in the roasting pan. Rub the surface with the vegetable oil or melted butter. Sprinkle the chicken with salt, pepper, garlic powder (or salt), and paprika. There is no need to measure these spices—just dust the surface with them. If you use garlic salt, use slightly less salt than if you use garlic powder. Place the chicken breast side down on the rack.

* Just before you put the chicken in the oven, lower the heat to 350 degrees. Roast the bird 45–60 minutes, basting once or twice during that time. Turn the chicken breast side up. Continue to roast the chicken until a meat thermometer inserted into the thickest part of the thigh registers 180 degrees, or when the juices run clear when the thigh is pricked with the tines of a fork. After you have turned the chicken breast side up, baste only during the next 15–45 minutes (depending on the size of the chicken). Do not baste for the last 25–30 minutes of roasting time. After you take the chicken out of the oven, let it stand 15 minutes before you carve it.

Lemon-Oregano Roasted Chicken

This is but one of many variations on roasted chicken.

Level: Intermediate
Preparation time: 10–15 minutes
Cooking time: depends on the weight of the chicken (plus 15 minutes standing time)
Yield: serves 6

*Can be done ahead up to the * in the instructions*

1 roasting chicken, 4$\frac{1}{2}$–7 lbs.
$\frac{1}{3}$ cup lemon juice
$\frac{1}{4}$ cup olive oil
1 large clove garlic, minced
1 TB. minced fresh oregano, or 1 tsp. dried

2 tsp. minced fresh basil, or $\frac{1}{2}$ tsp. dried
$\frac{3}{4}$ tsp. salt (or salt to taste)
$\frac{1}{4}$ tsp. freshly ground black pepper
  (or pepper to taste)

Preheat the oven to 400 degrees. Remove the plastic bag of giblets from inside the bird. Wash the giblets if you wish to roast and eat them. Put them in the roasting pan. Otherwise, freeze them for when you wish to make stock (a recipe appears in the Soups and Salads recipe section). Wash the chicken inside and out. Place the chicken breast side down on a rack in a roasting pan. Combine remaining ingredients in a small bowl and pour the mixture over the chicken.

Kitchen Clue
Generally speaking, you roast chicken 20–25 minutes per pound.

* Just before you put the chicken in the oven, lower the heat to 350 degrees. Roast the bird 45–60 minutes, basting once or twice during that time. Turn the chicken breast side up. Continue to roast the chicken until a meat thermometer inserted into the thickest part of the thigh registers 180 degrees, or when the juices run clear when the thigh is pricked with the tines of a fork. After you have turned the chicken breast side up, baste only during the next 15–45 minutes (depending on the size of the chicken). Do not baste for the last 25–30 minutes of roasting time. After you take the chicken out of the oven, let it stand 15 minutes before you carve it.

My Mother's Fried Chicken

You may think it sounds nutty to make fried chicken at home when you can buy it in all sorts of fast food places. Maybe it is nutty, but no fast-food fried chicken tastes like this. If you ever have some spare time, try it and see for yourself. This was the number #1 favorite dinner in our house. Family and friends ask for it all the time.

Level: Intermediate
Preparation time: 15 minutes plus 30 minutes standing time
Cooking time: about 20 minutes
Yield: serves 4

Can be done completely ahead

²/₃ cup all purpose flour
1 tsp. salt (or salt to taste)
¹/₂ tsp. paprika
¹/₄ tsp. garlic powder (or use ¹/₂ tsp. garlic salt
  and slightly less regular salt)

a few grindings of black pepper
1 broiler-fryer chicken, 2¹/₂–4 lbs., cut into
  8 pieces (or use 3–4 lbs. of chicken parts)
vegetable oil

Combine the flour, salt, paprika, garlic powder, and black pepper in a plastic bag. Wash the chicken parts and put them in the bag. Shake the bag to coat the chicken with the flour mixture. Remove the chicken pieces and place them on a cake rack or broiler rack (so that they can rest with air surrounding them) for 30 minutes to "air dry."

To deep fry the chicken, heat enough vegetable oil in a deep pan to cover the chicken pieces. Heat the oil to about 365 degrees (at this temperature, it should brown a tiny piece of bread fairly quickly). Add the chicken. Do not crowd the pan. If you have a small pan, fry the chicken in batches. Cover the pan. Cook the chicken 8–10 minutes. Remove the chicken pieces with a large strainer, slotted spoon, or tongs, and keep them out of the heat for one minute. Return the pieces to the pan and continue to cook them another 8–10 minutes or until the pieces are cooked through. (You can pierce the thigh or drumstick in the thickest part with the tip of a sharp knife. If the juices run clear, the chicken is done.) Drain the fried chicken on paper towels.

To pan fry the chicken, heat enough vegetable oil in a deep skillet to come halfway up the sides of the chicken. When the temperature reaches about 365 degrees, add the chicken (do not crowd the pan), cover the pan, and cook for 20–25 minutes, turning the pieces occasionally to cook all sides. Drain the fried chicken on paper towels.

Grilled Marinated Chicken Breasts

You'll love how fast this dish cooks—better have the side dishes ready first!

Level: Easy
Preparation time: 15 minutes (plus 1 hour marinating time)
Cooking time: 4–6 minutes
Yield: serves 4

*Can be done ahead up to the * in the instructions*

2 whole boneless, skinless chicken breasts
2 TB. vegetable oil
2 TB. lemon juice
2 tsp. Dijon mustard
1 shallot or scallion, minced

1 clove garlic, minced
2 tsp. fresh thyme leaves or ¹/₂ tsp. dried
¹/₄ tsp. salt (or salt to taste)
¹/₈ tsp. freshly ground black pepper (or pepper to taste)

Cut the chicken breasts in half to make 4 pieces, removing the fibrous cartilage that connects the two halves. If you wish, place the chicken breasts between two pieces of waxed paper and pound them to a thickness of about ¹/₄" using a meat mallet, the flat side of a cleaver, or pot bottom. (This step makes the cooking more even, but it isn't critical.) Place the chicken in a glass, ceramic, stainless-steel, or other "non-reactive" dish. Combine the remaining ingredients in a small bowl and whisk them together to make marinade. Pour the marinade over the chicken and let the meat marinate at least one hour. Turn the chicken once or twice during this time. Preheat the broiler. Remove the chicken from the marinade.

* Place the chicken on a broiler rack inside a broiler pan set 4–6" lower than the heat source. (Set a grill rack the same distance from the heat if you are using a grill.) Broil or grill the pieces 2–3 minutes per side, or until they are cooked through.

Chicken Breasts with Sun-Dried Tomatoes and Olives

This recipe can modernize your repertoire. It gives you the opportunity to try some popular ingredients that may be unfamiliar. And it isn't as difficult to cook as it may seem at first glance.

Level: Challenging
Preparation time: 30 minutes
Cooking time: 15 minutes
Yield: serves 4

*Can be done ahead up to the * in the instructions*

2 TB. olive oil
2 cloves garlic, minced
1 cup diced eggplant (about 1/2" pieces)
1 cup coarsely chopped mushrooms
1/2 cup sun-dried tomatoes, coarsely chopped
3 TB. chopped fresh basil, or 2 tsp. dried
2 TB. chopped fresh parsley

1/4 cup black pitted olives, preferably imported, cut up
1–2 TB. balsamic vinegar (optional)
2 whole boneless, skinless chicken breasts
olive oil for brushing
1/2 tsp. salt (or salt to taste)
1/4 tsp. freshly ground black pepper (or pepper to taste)

Heat the 2 TB. of olive oil in a skillet. Add the garlic and cook it for 30 seconds over low heat. Add the eggplant and mushrooms, raise the heat to moderate, and cook (stirring occasionally) about 4 minutes or until they are soft. Add the tomatoes, basil, parsley, and olives and cook another 3–4 minutes. Remove from heat, taste for seasoning and add balsamic vinegar, if desired, for a tangier taste.

* If you cook the sauce ahead, reheat it in the pan 3–4 minutes over moderate heat. Preheat a grill or broiler. Cut the chicken breasts in half to make 4 pieces, removing the fibrous cartilage that connects the two halves. If you wish, place the chicken breasts between two pieces of waxed paper and pound them to a thickness of about 1/4" using a meat mallet, the flat side of a cleaver, or pot bottom. (This step makes the cooking more even, but it isn't critical.) Brush or rub the chicken breasts with a small amount of olive oil and sprinkle them with salt and pepper. Grill or broil the chicken 3–4 minutes per side, or until cooked through. Remove the chicken breasts and spoon the sauce over them.

> **Second Thoughts**
> You can make this dish with 4–6 fresh plum tomatoes, deseeded and chopped, or 1 1/2 cups cut up canned tomatoes. Both give a saucier sauce.

How to Roast a Turkey

When you see how easy it is to roast a turkey, you'll be the first to volunteer for Thanksgiving dinner duty.

Level: Intermediate
Preparation time: 15 minutes
Cooking time: depends on the size of the turkey
Yield: 1 lb. of turkey per person (8 lb. turkey will feed 8 people, and so on)

*Can be done ahead up to the * in the instructions*

1 turkey
salt, freshly ground black pepper, garlic powder (or garlic salt), paprika

1/2 cup orange juice, white wine, chicken stock (optional)
2 TB. butter or olive oil (optional)

Preheat the oven to 325 degrees. Remove the plastic bag of giblets from inside the turkey. Wash the giblets and set them aside. Wash the inside of the turkey thoroughly. Wash the skin and remove any obvious hairs and pinfeathers. If the turkey legs are tied or locked with a plastic device, you may have to untie the legs or remove them from the plastic lock to wash the inside. Re-tie the legs or return them to the lock. Place turkey breast side up on a rack in a roasting pan. Sprinkle with salt, pepper, garlic powder (or garlic salt), and paprika. Turn the turkey over and sprinkle the back with the seasonings. Keep the turkey breast-side down.

* Roast the turkey 35–55 minutes, depending on the size of the bird. Baste with pan juices and orange juice (or whatever else you use). You can also place the butter or olive oil in the pan to add to the basting juices. Roast

another 35–55 minutes. Baste the turkey and turn it breast-side up. Roast the turkey until a meat thermometer inserted into the thickest part of the thigh registers 180 degrees, or when the juices run clear when the thigh is pricked. For times see the chart below. After you turn the turkey breast side up, baste it every 15–20 minutes, but stop about ¹/₂ hour before you expect the turkey to be done.

Total Cooking Time for Turkey

Weight	Stuffed	Unstuffed
8–12 lb.	3¹/₂ to 4 hours	2¹/₂ to 3¹/₂ hours
12–16 lb.	4 to 4¹/₂ hours	3¹/₂ to 4¹/₂ hours
16–20 lb.	4¹/₂ to 5¹/₂ hours	4¹/₂ to 5 hours

Many people discard the giblets, but some people like to eat them. Season them with the turkey seasonings and place them in the roasting pan to bake. You also can use the giblets for stock or gravy. (See the recipe for stock in the Soups and Salads recipe section and the recipe for gravy in the Sauces and Gravies section. The recipe is for chicken stock, but you may include your leftover turkey giblets if you wish.)

Kitchen Clue
It is better to use a fresh turkey than a frozen one. If you use a frozen turkey, thaw it in the refrigerator. This may take a couple of days. You can speed the process by putting the turkey (in its wrapper) in a sink full of cold water and changing the water occasionally.

Kitchen Clue
Stuff the turkey just before you roast it. Tie the legs together with kitchen string. Do *not* put a foil tent over the turkey—this steams the meat, rather than roasting it. Let the turkey stand 15 minutes before carving it.

Turkey Meatloaf

Like meatloaf, but not the fat? Here's a lower-fat version of the old classic. It's terrific with cranberry sauce on the side.

Level: Easy
Preparation time: 10 minutes
Cooking time: about one hour
Yield: serves 6

*Can be done ahead up to the * in the instructions*

2 cups fresh bread crumbs
²/₃ cup milk
2 lbs. ground turkey
2 large eggs
¹/₄ cup parmesan cheese
2 cloves garlic, minced
2 TB. minced shallot
1 TB. minced fresh rosemary leaves or 1 tsp. dried
1 tsp. salt (or salt to taste)
¹/₄ tsp. freshly ground black pepper (or pepper to taste)

Second Thoughts
You also can make this with ground chicken or a mixture of ground turkey or chicken and veal. If you wish, you can substitute savory or oregano for the rosemary. Or you can leave out the herb if you prefer a plainer meatloaf. If you don't have a loaf pan, you can make this free-standing: shape the meat into an oval and bake it in a jelly roll pan.

Preheat the oven to 350 degrees. Combine the bread crumbs and milk in a small bowl and let it stand for a minute or so. Place the turkey meat in a large bowl and add the soaked bread crumbs and any excess milk that has not been absorbed. Add the eggs, parmesan cheese, garlic, shallot, rosemary, salt, and pepper. Mix ingredients thoroughly and place the mixture in a 9"×5"×3" loaf pan.

* Bake the meatloaf 50–60 minutes or until the meat begins to pull away from the sides of the pan.

Turkey Cutlets with Chili Pepper and Cheese

This is spicy but not fiercely hot, and the avocado and tomatoes give it a soft, refreshing quality.

Level: Intermediate
Preparation time: 12–15 minutes
Cooking time: 15–20 minutes
Yield: serves 4

*Can be done ahead up to the * in the instructions*

1 jalapeño or other hot pepper
$1/4$ cup flour
$1/2$ tsp. salt (or salt to taste)
$1/4$ tsp. freshly ground black pepper (or pepper to taste)
$1^1/4$ lbs. turkey cutlets
3 TB. olive oil or vegetable oil
1 large tomato, sliced
1 small avocado, peeled and sliced
$1^1/2$ cups shredded monterey jack cheese
2 TB. freshly grated parmesan cheese

Second Thoughts
You can prepare this dish with veal or chicken cutlets if you wish, or substitute havarti or Muenster cheese for the monterey jack. You can save time by using bottled jalapeño pepper.

Preheat the oven to 375 degrees. Remove the stem, fleshy white part (membrane), and seeds from the jalapeño pepper and chop it into small pieces. Combine the flour, salt, and pepper and dredge the turkey cutlets in this mixture. Shake off excess flour. Heat the oil in a skillet and sauté the turkey cutlets over moderate heat, 2–3 minutes per side or until lightly browned. Place the cutlets in a baking dish. Place the tomato slices over the cutlets. Sprinkle the tomato slices with the hot pepper. Place the avocado slices on top of the tomato. Scatter the shredded monterey jack cheese and parmesan cheese on top.

* Bake the dish 10–15 minutes, or until cheese is hot and bubbly and beginning to brown lightly.

Warning
Remember to be careful when working with hot peppers. Use disposable gloves, if possible. Be sure to wash your hands carefully after you're done. Never touch your skin or eyes after working with hot peppers.

Roasted Rock Cornish Hens with Curry Stuffing

This dish takes several steps and some time. It is a stunning dish for company, though, so you might want to save this one for special occasions.

Level: Challenging
Preparation time: about 15 minutes
Cooking time: about $1^1/4$ hours (plus 30 minutes refrigeration time, plus time to cook the rice)
Yield: serves 6–8

*Can be done ahead up to the * in the instructions*

5 TB. butter
$2^1/2$ tsp. curry powder
1 medium onion, chopped
1 tart apple such as a granny smith, peeled and chopped
$1/2$ cup raisins

3 cups cooked white rice
2 tsp. lemon juice
dash of cayenne pepper
$1/2$ cup chopped almonds
6 rock Cornish hens
salt and pepper

Melt 2 TB. of the butter with $1/2$ tsp. of the curry powder and set this mixture aside. Melt the remaining butter in a sauté pan. Add the onion, apple, and raisins and cook them over moderate heat 3–4 minutes. Add the rice, lemon juice, remaining curry powder, cayenne pepper, and nuts and toss ingredients until they are well combined. Remove the pan from the heat. Let the stuffing cool in the refrigerator at least 30 minutes. Wash the hens inside and out. If giblets are packed inside the bird, remove them. Wash the giblets and roast them with the bird or freeze them for when you want to make stock (a recipe appears in the Soups and Salads recipe section).

* Preheat the oven to 400 degrees. Fill the hens with the stuffing. Truss the cavities closed (as described in Chapter 13), if desired. Brush the hens with the reserved butter-curry mixture and sprinkle them with some salt and pepper. Place the hens breast-side down on a rack in a roasting pan. Just before you put the birds in the oven, lower the heat to 350 degrees. Roast the hens 40 minutes, basting once or twice during that time. Turn the hens over and roast them another 35–40 minutes, or until the juices run clear when the thigh is pricked with the tip of a sharp knife. Let the birds stand a few minutes before you carve them.

Kitchen Clue
You can serve the hens whole. Or you can cut them in half and place them on a platter with the stuffing tucked beneath the meat.

How to Make Great Hamburgers

It's the simple dishes like hamburgers that take more thinking than more complicated dishes. Don't worry, though—the tricks of the trade are on this page.

Level: Easy
Preparation time: 10 minutes
Cooking time: 4–6 minutes
Yield: makes 4 burgers, 5-oz. each

Cannot be done ahead

1¼ lbs. ground beef round, chuck, or sirloin
  (or a mixture of all three)
½ tsp. salt (or salt to taste)
⅛ tsp. ground pepper (or pepper to taste)
1 tsp. Worcestershire sauce (optional)
4 hamburger rolls
thinly sliced Vidalia, Bermuda, or Spanish onion
thinly sliced tomato
slices of dill pickle
ketchup, mustard, or mayonnaise

Mix the meat, salt, pepper, and Worcestershire sauce, if used. Shape the meat into 4 patties. Preheat a broiler, grill, or a skillet set over moderately high heat. (If you pan fry the burgers in the skillet, brush the bottom of the pan with a film of butter or vegetable oil.) Broil (use the broiler rack), grill, or fry the patties about 2 minutes. Reduce the heat to moderate and cook the burgers, turning them once, another 2 to 3 minutes, depending on the degree of rareness you like. Serve the burgers on buns, topped with onion, tomato, and pickle. Spread the roll with the condiment of your choice.

Kitchen Clue
Here are some tips for better burgers:

➤ If you like your burgers very rare, mix 1 TB. of ice shavings into each patty.

➤ Never press down on a burger when it cooks; this releases necessary natural fluids.

➤ Turn the burgers with a rigid spatula.

Taco Meatloaf

If you're bored with meatloaf, try this version with a spicy southwest taste for a change.

Level: Easy
Preparation time: about 15 minutes
Cooking time: 50–60 minutes
Yield: serves 6

Can be done completely ahead

2 lbs. ground beef, round or chuck
2 tsp. salt
1/4 tsp. freshly ground black pepper
2 eggs, beaten
1/2 cup bread crumbs
1/2 cup plain yogurt

1/2 cup grated cheddar cheese
1 small chopped onion, about 1/4 cup
3 TB. tomato paste
2 tsp. chili powder
a dash or two of Tabasco sauce

Preheat the oven to 350 degrees. Combine all the ingredients in a large bowl. Put the mixture in a 9"×5"×3" loaf pan. Bake it about 50–60 minutes, or until the meatloaf is well-browned and begins to pull away from the sides of the pan. If you don't have a loaf pan, you can make this free-standing: shape the meat into an oval and bake it in a jelly roll pan.

Chili con Carne

Everyone's got a favorite recipe for chili. This one's thick with ground meat and comes in handy for family dinners or when you invite a crowd over for a casual get-together.

Level: Easy
Preparation time: 20 minutes
Cooking time: 50–60 minutes
Yield: serves 4

Can be done completely ahead

1 1/2 TB. vegetable oil
1 large onion, chopped
2 cloves garlic, minced
1 lb. ground sirloin or round
1 28-oz. can Italian style plum tomatoes, drained and chopped
1 6-oz. can tomato paste
1 3/4 cups canned or homemade beef broth or stock

2 TB. chili powder
2 tsp. dried oregano
1 1/2 tsp. ground cumin
1 1/2 tsp. salt (or salt to taste)
1/2 tsp. red pepper flakes
1/2 tsp. freshly ground black pepper
2 bay leaves
1 15-oz. can red kidney beans, drained

Heat the vegetable oil in a large, deep skillet. Add the onion and garlic and cook over moderate heat 3–4 minutes, or until the vegetables have wilted. Add the meat and cook it 5–6 minutes, or until the meat turns brown. Break the meat up with a wooden spoon to make sure all pieces are cooked evenly. Add the tomatoes, tomato paste, beef broth, chili powder, oregano, cumin, salt, red pepper flakes, black pepper, and bay leaves. Bring the mixture to a boil, lower the heat, and cook the mixture at a simmer 25 minutes. Add the beans and cook another 15–20 minutes, or until most of the liquid has evaporated and the meat is surrounded by sauce as thick as gravy.

Quick Three-Bean No-Meat Chili

This may come in handy on those nights when you just don't feel like eating meat but want something hearty. For extra nutrition, serve it with cooked rice.

Level: Easy
Preparation time: 20 minutes
Cooking time: about 40 minutes
Yield: serves 6

Can be done completely ahead

1/4 cup olive oil
2 onions, chopped
2 cloves garlic, chopped
2 carrots, chopped
3 cups canned tomato sauce
2 cups water
2 TB. tomato paste
1 15-oz. can garbanzo beans, drained

1 15-oz. can red kidney beans, undrained
1 cup lentils
2 all-purpose potatoes, peeled and cut into bite-sized pieces, covered with cold water
2 TB. chili powder
1 4-oz. can chopped mild green chili peppers
1 tsp. dried basil

Heat the olive oil in a large skillet. Add the onions and garlic and cook them over moderate heat 3–4 minutes, or until they have softened. Add the carrots, tomato sauce, water, tomato paste, garbanzo beans, kidney beans, and lentils. Drain the potatoes and add them to the pan with the chili powder, chili peppers, and basil. Bring the ingredients to a boil over high heat. Lower the heat to moderate and simmer 15 minutes, covered. Remove the cover and cook another 20 minutes, or until sauce surrounding the beans has thickened to a gravy-like consistency. Stir occasionally during this time.

Kitchen Clue
If you prepare this a day or two ahead (it's okay to), the beans may absorb moisture. When you reheat the chili, stir in about 1/2 cup water.

How to Make a Steak

Some people just have to have a hunk of steak every once in a while. Here's how you satisfy that whim.

Level: Easy
Preparation time: 1 minute
Cooking time: depends on thickness of steak
Yield: 8–12 oz. (serves one person)

Cannot be done ahead

steak for grilling, such as NY Strip, Sirloin, T-Bone, Porterhouse, Rib, Delmonico, Club, Shell, or Filet Mignon
salt and freshly ground black pepper

Preheat a broiler, grill, or a skillet set over moderately high heat. (If you pan fry the steaks in the skillet, brush the bottom of the pan with a film of butter or vegetable oil.) Broil (use the broiler rack), grill, or fry the steak for one minute per side, reduce the heat to moderate, and cook the steak on both sides, depending on thickness of steak and degree of doneness you like (see hints below). When you turn the steak, use a spatula or tongs, not a fork.

Second Thoughts
Most people like their steaks plain. But if you like an extra bit of pizzazz, mix 4–5 TB. of freshly minced herbs of your choice with 1 TB. lemon juice and 1/2 cup softened butter. Put a spoonful on top of each portion of finished steak.

continues

Here are some handy facts about cooking steak:

➤ Cooking times for a 1" thick steak are: 6–8 minutes for rare, 8–11 minutes for medium, 12–15 minutes for well-done.

➤ Cooking times for a 1¹/₂ " thick steak are: 9–12 minutes for rare, 12–16 minutes for medium, 17–22 minutes for well-done.

➤ Time depends on factors other than thickness: frozen steaks (yes, you can cook steaks straight from the freezer!) will take twice as long; cold steaks straight from the fridge may take a minute or so longer. Filet mignons, which can be very thick, may take a minute or so longer.

Stir-Fried Flank Steak and Broccoli

This is one of the easier stir-fries, but it has a bit of sherry to perk it up.

Level: Intermediate
Preparation time: 15 minutes (plus 10 minutes standing time)
Cooking time: 6–8 minutes
Yield: serves 4

*Can be done ahead up to the * in the instructions*

12 oz. flank steak
1¹/₂ tsp. cornstarch
1 TB. soy sauce
1 TB. Chinese rice wine or dry sherry
³/₄ tsp. sugar
1 tsp. water

3 TB. vegetable oil
2 cups cut up broccoli stems and florets (bite-sized pieces)
salt, optional
¹/₄ cup water

Cut the meat on the diagonal into strips about 2" long and 1" wide. Put the meat in a bowl and add ¹/₂ tsp. of the cornstarch, the soy sauce, and the rice wine, and ¹/₄ tsp. sugar. Mix ingredients and let them stand 10 minutes or as long as 4 hours. Mix the remaining cornstarch with the tsp. water and set it aside. This mixture will act as a thickener for the sauce.

* Heat 2 TB. of the vegetable oil in a wok or deep skillet. Add the broccoli and stir-fry over moderately high heat 1¹/₂ minutes. Add remaining ¹/₂ tsp. sugar and a pinch of salt, if desired. Add the ¹/₄ cup water, cover the pan, and cook the broccoli 1–2 minutes, or until it is tender but still firm. Dish the broccoli out and set it aside. Heat the remaining vegetable oil in the pan. Add the meat and juices and stir-fry 2 minutes. Return the broccoli to the pan and stir-fry one minute. Stir the cornstarch-water mixture and add it to the pan. Stir-fry the meat and vegetables briefly and dish them out to serve.

Kitchen Clue
If you peel the broccoli stems, the vegetable will be much more tender. To do so, cut a ¹/₂"-thick slice from the bottom of the stem and peel the stem by pulling back a thin layer of skin with a paring knife, starting at the cut end.

Lemon-Soy London Broil

This is a good choice for a summer cookout. Serve it with a big green salad.

Level: Intermediate
Preparation time: 7–8 minutes (plus 1 hour marinating time and 30 minutes cooling time)
Cooking time: about 15 minutes, plus 3–4 minutes for the sauce
Yield: serves 6

*Can be done ahead up to the * in the instructions*

1 beef for London Broil, such as shoulder,
  chuck, bottom round, rump, or flank
2 TB. vegetable oil
1 medium onion, finely chopped (about 1/2 cup)
2 cloves garlic, minced
3/4 cup ketchup
6 TB. lemon juice

1/2 tsp. freshly grated lemon peel
3 TB. sugar
3 TB. soy sauce
2 TB. prepared mustard
3/4 cup water
1/4 tsp. cayenne pepper

Wipe the meat dry and put it in a glass, ceramic, stainless steel, or other "non-reactive" dish. Heat the vegetable oil in a saucepan, add the onion and garlic, and cook over moderate heat 3–4 minutes, stirring occasionally or until the vegetables have softened. Add the remaining ingredients, stir, and cook the mixture over low heat 15 minutes. Let the mixture cool (about 30 minutes). Pour the mixture over the meat and let the meat marinate 1 hour, turning it once or twice during that time.

* Preheat the broiler or grill. Remove the meat from the marinade, broil or grill it about 6–7 minutes per side for rare, 8 minutes per side for medium-rare. For added flavor, brush the meat occasionally with some of the marinade during the broiling process.

Pearl J. Fein's Famous Standing Rib Roast

Though old-fashioned, it's still one of the most regal-looking roasts around. This version is an old family favorite.

Level: Intermediate
Preparation time: 10 minutes (10 minutes extra time if you have to tie the roast)
Cooking time: about 1 1/2 hours
Yield: serves 6–8

Cannot be done ahead

1 3-rib standing beef rib roast
kitchen string
4 tsp. paprika
2 tsp. salt

1 tsp. freshly ground black pepper
1/2 tsp. garlic powder
water

Preheat the oven to 450 degrees. If the butcher hasn't done this for you, remove the strings that tie the ribs to the bones, if there are any. Carve the meat from the bone as close to the bone as you can, so that you are left with a boneless roast and L-shaped rib bones. Tie the meat back onto the bones with kitchen string. Place the paprika, salt, pepper, and garlic powder in a small bowl and add enough water to make a mixture a bit thinner than ketchup. Brush the mixture on the surface of the roast, including the bones. Place the roast, bones down, in a roasting pan. Roast the beef 20 minutes. Lower the heat to 350 degrees and cook 15–20 minutes more per pound, depending on whether you like the meat rare, medium, or well-done. A meat thermometer inserted into the middle of the meat will read just below 120 degrees for rare, 135–140 degrees for medium, 140 plus degrees for well-done.

Let the roast beef stand 15 minutes before carving it. To carve the meat, remove the strings and place the now boneless roast on a carving board. Carve the meat into slices of equal thickness, depending on how many people you wish to serve.

Kitchen Clue
Ask the butcher to carve the meat off the bone and tie it back for you. Even if you buy meat in a supermarket and the roast is already packaged, you can ask the person in charge of the meat department. Or, you can roast the meat without carving and tying it. To carve, you can cut the meat from the bone to make it a "boneless" roast after cooking is complete.

255

Hot and Spicy Pot Roast

This isn't just any ordinary pot roast—it's hot and spicy. You can make it milder or even more fierce if you want.

Level: Intermediate
Preparation time: 10 minutes
Cooking time: about 2¼ hours
Yield: serves 6–8

Can be done completely ahead

3–4 lb. beef roast for pot roast such as
  brisket, rump, or bottom round
2 tsp. paprika
1 tsp. salt (or salt to taste)
½ tsp. freshly ground black pepper
1½ tsp. minced fresh oregano, or ½ tsp. dried
1½ tsp. minced fresh thyme, or ½ tsp. dried

½ tsp. powdered mustard
½ tsp. cayenne pepper
2 TB. vegetable oil
2 large onions, cut into large chunks
1 cup canned or homemade beef stock
1 28-oz. can Italian style plum tomatoes, drained

Wipe the meat dry with paper towels. In a small bowl, combine the paprika, salt, black pepper, oregano, thyme, mustard, cayenne pepper, and the vegetable oil and mix them thoroughly. Rub this mixture onto the meat. Preheat a Dutch oven or fireproof casserole dish over moderate heat. Add the meat and cook it 12–15 minutes, turning it occasionally, or until all sides are darkly colored. Pour off excess fat from the pan. Add the onions, stock, and tomatoes to the pan. Reduce the heat, cover the pan and cook at a bare simmer about 2 hours, or until meat is tender.

Roast Rack of Lamb

This dish can be expensive, but it's a rich and lavish-tasting treat. Besides, it's incredibly easy to make and a great idea for a company dinner. It's best when served rare or medium rare.

Level: Easy
Preparation time: 10 minutes
Cooking time: 30–50 minutes
Yield: serves 4–6

Can be done ahead up to the * in the instructions

2 racks of lamb
salt and pepper
3 large cloves of garlic, minced
3 TB. Dijon mustard

3 TB. olive oil
2 TB. minced, fresh rosemary or
  2 tsp. dried, crushed rosemary
¼ cup dry, plain bread crumbs

Preheat the oven to 450 degrees. Trim most of the excess fat from the meat. Sprinkle the meat lightly with some salt and pepper. Mix together the garlic, mustard, olive oil, and rosemary and brush this on the top surface of the meat. Sprinkle with the bread crumbs.

* Place the meat in a roasting pan. Roast 10 minutes. Reduce the heat to 350 degrees and continue to roast the meat 20–40 minutes, depending on how you like your meat. A meat thermometer will read slightly less than 120 degrees for rare and 135–140 degrees for medium. Let the roast stand about 10 minutes before you serve it.

What Is It?
A rack of lamb is a strip of uncut rib chops.

Broiled Butterflied Leg of Lamb

This is a super summer dish if you have an outdoor grill because the smoky flavor of charcoal intensifies the taste. Otherwise, use your oven broiler.

Level: Easy
Preparation time: 10 minutes (plus 15 minutes standing time)
Cooking time: 15–20 minutes
Yield: serves 6

*Can be done ahead up to the * in the instructions*

3 lb. boneless leg of lamb
1/4 cup Dijon mustard
2 TB. olive oil
2 TB. lemon juice

2 cloves garlic, minced
1/4 tsp. salt (or salt to taste)
1/4 tsp. freshly ground black pepper (or pepper to taste)
2 tsp. fresh thyme or 1/2 tsp. dried

Place the lamb in a glass, ceramic, stainless-steel, or other "non-reactive" dish. Combine the remaining ingredients in a small bowl and mix them well. Pour the mixture over the meat. Let the meat stand in the liquid 15 minutes. Preheat the broiler or grill. Place the meat on a rack in the broiler pan (or on the grill grids) set about 4"–6" away from the heat source. Cook 8–10 minutes. Turn the meat over with tongs and cook another 7–10 minutes, or until it is cooked to your liking.

Braised Lamb Shanks with Lemon

This is a good cold-weather dish that goes well with plain cooked rice and any green vegetable.

Level: Intermediate
Preparation time: 10–12 minutes
Cooking time: about 2 3/4 hours
Yield: serves 6

Can be done completely ahead

6 large lamb shanks
3 TB. flour
1/2 tsp. salt (or salt to taste)
1/4 tsp. freshly ground black pepper
  (or pepper to taste)
3 TB. olive oil
1 cup fresh lemon juice
1/2 cup canned or homemade chicken or beef stock
1 tsp. freshly grated lemon peel
3 TB. minced, fresh parsley
1 TB. minced, fresh oregano, or 1 tsp. dried
2 cloves garlic, cut in half (you don't have
  to peel them)

Kitchen Clue
If you prepare this dish a day or so ahead, you can save fat and calories. Remove the lamb from the sauce when the shanks are finished cooking. Strain the sauce and chill it in the refrigerator. When the sauce is cold, fat will rise to the surface and harden, and you can scoop it off. Return the shanks to the sauce and cook them over moderate heat until they are hot (about 10 minutes). If you prefer, you can bake this dish in a 325 degree oven for 2 1/2 hours.

Wipe the lamb shanks dry with paper towels. Mix the flour with the salt and pepper. Dredge the shanks in the seasoned flour. Heat the olive oil over moderate heat in a heatproof casserole dish or Dutch oven. Add the lamb shanks and cook about 10–15 minutes, turning them occasionally or until they are browned. Pour off any excess fat from the pan. Add the lemon juice, stock, lemon peel, parsley, oregano, and garlic. Cover the pan and cook over low-moderate heat about 2 1/2 hours, or until the shanks are tender. Remove excess fat with a spoon (the fat will rise to the top) and serve the lamb shanks with some of the pan juices.

Veal Marsala

This is an old-fashioned favorite that everyone still loves. The wine gives it a festive touch, making it appropriate for company meals.

Level: Easy
Preparation time: 5 minutes
Cooking time: 5–6 minutes
Yield: serves 4

Cannot be done ahead

4 TB. flour
1/2 tsp. salt (or salt to taste)
1/8 tsp. freshly ground black pepper (or pepper to taste)
1 1/4 lbs. veal cutlets

2 TB. butter
2 TB. olive oil
1/2 cup Marsala wine

Preheat the oven to 140 degrees. Combine the flour, salt, and pepper in a plate. Dredge the veal cutlets in the flour mixture and shake off the excess. Heat half the butter and olive oil in a large skillet over moderate heat. When the butter has melted and looks foamy, add some of the cutlets. Cook 4–6 minutes, turning the meat once, or until the cutlets are cooked through. Repeat with the remaining butter and olive oil and the remaining cutlets. As you finish cooking the cutlets, put them on a dish and keep them warm in the oven. When the cutlets are all cooked, add the wine to the skillet and stir the ingredients with a wooden spoon to release any browned bits and particles that may have stuck to the bottom of the pan. Cook a minute or so, then pour the wine sauce over the veal and serve.

Roast Rosemary Veal

This dish is terrific with mashed potatoes or egg noodles and a yellow vegetable, such as carrots or yellow squash.

Level: Intermediate
Preparation time: 7–8 minutes
Cooking time: about 2 1/4 hours
Yield: serves 6–8

Can be done one hour ahead and kept warm in 140 degree oven, covered

1 veal for roasting such as round, rump, or shoulder, about 5 lbs.
1/3 cup olive oil
3/4 tsp. salt (or salt to taste)
1/4 tsp. freshly ground black pepper (or pepper to taste)

1 large clove garlic, minced
2 TB. chopped fresh rosemary, or 2 tsp. dried, crushed rosemary
3 TB. lemon juice

Preheat the oven to 350 degrees. Wipe the meat dry with paper towels. Heat 1 1/2 TB. of the olive oil in a Dutch oven, roasting pan, or other flameproof casserole dish. Brown the meat over moderate heat about 10 minutes, or until all surfaces have browned. Combine the remaining olive oil, salt, pepper, garlic, rosemary, and lemon juice in a small bowl and pour the mixture over the meat. Cover the pan (you can use aluminum foil if you don't have a covered casserole dish) and cook over low-moderate heat 30 minutes. Remove the cover and cook, basting the meat every 15 minutes or

What Is It?
A Dutch oven is a large heatproof, short-handled casserole dish or pan.

so with the pan juices, for another 1 1/2 hours, or until juices run clear when the roast is pierced with a sharp knife. A meat thermometer inserted into the thickest part should read about 165 degrees.

Stuffed Pork Chops

The apples and raisins in this dish harmonize deliciously with the pork, which has its own faintly sweet flavor.

Level: Easy
Preparation time: 10–12 minutes (plus 15 minutes cooling time)
Cooking time: 40 minutes
Yield: serves 4

*Can be done ahead up to the * in the instructions*

1 TB. butter
1 medium tart apple, peeled and finely chopped
$^1/_4$ cup raisins
$^1/_4$ cup chopped nuts

$^1/_4$ tsp. salt
$^1/_8$ tsp. ground ginger
$^1/_8$ tsp. cinnamon
8 thick pork chops, cut with a pocket

Preheat the oven to 350 degrees. Heat the butter in a skillet. When the butter has melted and looks foamy, add the apple and raisins and cook 2–3 minutes, until the fruit has softened. Remove the pan from the heat and stir in the nuts, salt, ginger, and cinnamon. Set the mixture aside to cool (about 15 minutes). Place equal amounts of the mixture inside the pockets of the pork chops.

* Put the pork chops in a baking pan. Bake them 35 minutes, or until they are cooked through.

Roast Loin of Pork

This dish is exceptionally tasty with sautéed rosemary potatoes, mashed potatoes, or cooked rice and a leafy green such as kale or spinach.

Level: Easy
Preparation time: 8–10 minutes (plus 10–15 minutes standing time)
Cooking time: about $1^1/_4$ hours
Yield: serves 6

*Can be done ahead up to the * in the instructions*

1 boneless loin of pork, tied (about 4 lbs.)
$^3/_4$ tsp. salt (or salt to taste)
$^1/_2$ tsp. freshly ground black pepper (or pepper to taste)
1 small onion, minced

1 large clove garlic, minced
1 TB. Dijon mustard
1 TB. olive oil

Preheat the oven to 450 degrees. Wipe the meat dry with paper towels and place the meat in a roasting pan. Combine the remaining ingredients in a small bowl. Spread this mixture on the top surface and part of the sides of the meat.

* Roast the meat about 15 minutes, then lower the heat to 350 degrees. Roast another hour, or until juices run clear when the roast is pierced with a sharp knife. A meat thermometer inserted into the thickest part should read about 155 degrees. Let the meat stand 10–15 minutes before carving it.

Second Thoughts
This is a basic dish that can stand all sorts of variations. Try adding 2 tsp. caraway seeds—this gives the pork an unusual flavor and crunchy texture.

Roast Ham with Sugar and Spice Glaze

This is pink and lovely—pretty enough for holiday dinners. Use the leftover ham bone to your advantage: cook it with Thick as Fog Pea Soup (see the Soups section).

Level: Easy
Preparation time: 5–6 minutes
Cooking time: 1¹/₂ to 2 hours
Yield: serves 10–12

Can be done completely ahead

1 fully cooked half ham with bone intact, about 5–7 lbs.
18 whole cloves
²/₃ cup brown sugar
3 TB. orange or apple juice

1 TB. Dijon mustard
¹/₂ tsp. ground ginger
¹/₄ tsp. ground nutmeg

Preheat the oven to 325 degrees. Place the ham on a rack in a roasting pan. Cook it 1 to 1¹/₂ hours. Remove the ham from the oven. Increase the oven heat to 425 degrees. Remove the ham rind, if there is any, except for a small portion near the narrower end. Make diagonal slashes on the top and part of the sides and insert cloves into the corners of the slashes. Mix the brown sugar, juice, mustard, ginger, and nutmeg together and spread this on the ham surface. Return the ham to the oven and cook it another 30 minutes.

Texas Ribs with Orange-Scented Barbecue Sauce

Everyone says his or her recipe for barbecued ribs is the best. This one really is! It's tangy and sweet at the same time, and well worth the effort it takes to make.

Level: Challenging
Preparation time: 25 minutes
Cooking time: 50–55 minutes, plus 5 minutes for the sauce
Yield: serves 4

Can be done completely ahead

3¹/₂ to 4 lbs. regular pork spare ribs (you can also use country-style ribs)
¹/₂ cup molasses
¹/₂ cup ketchup
1 TB. soy sauce
¹/₃ cup orange juice
1 TB. white vinegar
¹/₂ tsp. hot pepper sauce

1 medium onion, finely chopped (about ¹/₂ cup)
grated peel of half an orange, about 1 TB.
1¹/₂ TB. butter
1 large clove garlic, minced
1 tsp. powdered mustard
¹/₂ tsp. ground ginger
¹/₄ tsp. ground cloves, or 4 whole cloves
dash of salt, if desired

Cut the ribs into sections of 3–4 ribs. Bring a soup pot half filled with water to a boil over high heat. Lower the heat. Immerse the ribs in the liquid. Cook the ribs at a simmer for 25 minutes. Remove the ribs and set them aside. Preheat the oven to 375 degrees. While the ribs are cooking, combine the remaining ingredients in a saucepan and stir to blend. Bring the mixture to a boil over high heat. Lower the heat and simmer the sauce 5 minutes. Put the ribs in a roasting pan and brush most of the sauce over them. Cook 25–30 minutes, brushing more sauce onto the ribs and turning them frequently during the cooking process. Use all of the sauce.

Second Thoughts
If you prefer, you can grill the ribs on an outdoor grill. Cook them over moderate heat 25–30 minutes, turning them often and brushing with sauce until all the sauce has been used.

Pastas, Rice, and Grains

Pasta and grain dishes have really become big favorites in the last few years. For those who want to cut down on dietary fat, they are a healthy, nutritious alternative to meat dishes. They make ideal side dishes too because they are versatile and offer several different tastes and textures. Most people are familiar with different forms of pasta—spaghetti and ziti and so on—and with white rice. But there's more, much more to consider: bulgur wheat, wild rice, beans, and so on. Anyone who wants to add a little pizzazz to everyday or company meals can learn how to use pasta and grains to make delicious food without too much fuss.

Crunchy Crusted Macaroni and Cheese

This is a treasured old family recipe that we always loved because of its unique crunchy crust. The crust looks good and keeps the macaroni beneath it moist.

Level: Easy
Preparation time: 6–8 minutes
Cooking time: about 40 minutes with the crust; 6–8 minutes without (plus time to cook the macaroni)
Yield: serves 4–6

*Can be done ahead up to the * in the instructions*

1^1/$_2$ cups elbow macaroni
2 TB. butter
2 TB. flour
2 cups milk
^{1}/$_2$ tsp. salt

^{1}/$_4$ tsp. freshly ground black pepper
^{1}/$_8$ tsp. freshly grated nutmeg
2 cups grated cheese, preferably cheddar and American
1 ^{1}/$_2$ cups rice krispies cereal (optional)
2 TB. melted butter (optional)

Preheat the oven to 350 degrees. Cook the macaroni until it is al dente. Drain the macaroni. While the macaroni is cooking, melt the butter in a saucepan. Add the flour and cook stirring constantly (preferably with a whisk) over low heat for 2–3 minutes. Add the milk gradually, mixing the ingredients to incorporate the flour mixture and make a smooth sauce. Add the salt, pepper, and nutmeg. Stirring with the whisk or a wooden spoon, add the cheese and continue to cook 4–5 minutes or until the cheese has melted and the sauce is smooth. Pour the sauce over the cooked macaroni and mix them thoroughly. You can eat the dish like this, but if you prefer it baked, place the mixture into a buttered baking dish. Combine the rice krispies and butter (if used) and sprinkle this over the cheese-coated macaroni.

Second Thoughts
Corn flakes make a good substitute for the rice krispies.

*Bake about 30 minutes or until the top is crispy.

Gillian's Ziti Casserole

This recipe was created by our teenage daughter and goes over in a big way at parties. Serve it with salad and Italian bread.

Level: Easy
Preparation time: 15 minutes
Cooking time: 25–30 minutes (plus time to cook the pasta)
Yield: serves 4

*Can be done ahead up to the * in the instructions*

5–6 large fresh shiitake mushrooms
  (or substitute 12 common white mushrooms)
1 TB. olive oil
1 lb. ziti
1 15-oz. container ricotta cheese
  (you can use nonfat ricotta)

1 cup sun-dried tomatoes, cut up
1 cup black olives, cut in half
1^1/$_2$ cups shredded mozzarella cheese
1 TB. chopped fresh basil or 1 tsp. dried
3–4 TB. freshly grated parmesan cheese

Preheat the oven to 350 degrees. Rinse and dry the mushrooms and cut them into bite-size pieces. If you use shiitake mushrooms, discard the tough inedible stems. Heat the olive oil in a small pan. Add the mushrooms and cook them over moderate heat 3–4 minutes. Set the mushrooms aside. Cook the ziti until it is al dente. Drain the ziti. Combine the ziti with the ricotta cheese, mushrooms, sun-dried tomatoes, olives, ^{1}/$_2$ cup of the mozzarella cheese, and the basil. Mix ingredients well. Place the mixture in a deep casserole dish. Top with the remaining mozzarella cheese and sprinkle it with parmesan cheese.

* Bake the casserole 20–25 minutes or until cheese is bubbly.

Meredith's Pasta with Eggplant Sauce

One of the easiest, freshest-tasting dishes you can whip up in a hurry, this recipe was created by our daughter for her college friends—but everyone loves it.

Level: Easy
Preparation time: 8–10 minutes
Cooking time: about 20 minutes
Yield: serves 4

*Can be done ahead up to the * in the instructions*

1 small eggplant
6 Italian plum tomatoes
^{1}/$_2$ cup olive oil
8–10 black olives, sliced

2 tsp. capers, drained (optional)
2 TB. chopped fresh basil or 2 tsp. dried
a pinch of salt and pepper
1 lb. pasta, preferably penne or ziti

Cut off and discard the stem of the eggplant. Cut the eggplant into bite-size pieces and set it aside. Cut the plum tomatoes into pieces (it is not necessary to peel them or discard the seeds). Heat the olive oil in a skillet. Add the eggplant, tomatoes, olives, capers (if used), basil, salt, and pepper. Stirring occasionally, cook over moderate heat about 10 minutes or until vegetables have softened.

* Either keep the sauce warm over low heat or reheat it when you make the pasta. Cook the pasta until it is al dente. Drain the pasta. Top it with the sauce and serve.

Kitchen Clue
Some people salt egg-plant because they think the vegetable is bitter. If you think so, put the cut up eggplant in a colander, sprinkle it with salt, and let it stand for 30 minutes. Then wipe the pieces off with paper towels and proceed with the recipe.

Pasta with Sun-Dried Tomatoes and Pignoli Nuts

This dish is such a favorite that people eat it hot, warm, or cold, and it can even be reheated without its losing flavor.

Level: Easy
Preparation time: 10 minutes
Cooking time: 8–10 minutes (plus time to cook the pasta)
Yield: serves 4

*Can be done ahead up to the * in the instructions*

1 lb. pasta, preferably eggbow-shaped "farfelle"
$^{1}/_{2}$ cup olive oil
$^{1}/_{3}$ cup pignoli nuts
2 cloves garlic, minced
$^{2}/_{3}$ cup coarsely chopped sun-dried tomatoes
1 TB. coarsely chopped fresh basil, or 1 tsp. dried
$^{1}/_{4}$ tsp. salt (or salt to taste)
$^{1}/_{4}$ tsp. freshly ground black pepper (or pepper to taste)

Cook the pasta until it is al dente. Drain the pasta. While the pasta is cooking, heat 2 TB. of the olive oil in a skillet. Add the pignoli nuts and cook them, stirring occasionally, 3–4 minutes or until the nuts are lightly toasted. Add the garlic, sun-dried tomatoes, and basil and cook another 1–2 minutes to heat them. Add the remaining olive oil.

* Cook another minute or until ingredients are hot. Add the pasta. Toss the ingredients to coat them completely and cook another 3–4 minutes or until the pasta is hot. Taste the dish for seasoning and add salt and pepper to taste.

What Is It?
Pignoli nuts are the same as pine nuts. You can find them in specialty stores, many produce markets, and almost all supermarkets.

Second Thoughts
This dish also is excellent if you add a cup of shredded smoked turkey or baked ham. If you decide to use these ingredients, add them with the sun-dried tomatoes. If you can't find sun-dried tomatoes, substitute 2 cups drained, chopped canned plum tomatoes.

Pasta with Bacon and Tomatoes

The bacon adds just a hint of heartiness to this otherwise simple tomato sauce.

Level: Intermediate
Preparation time: 10–12 minutes
Cooking time: 17–22 minutes (plus time to cook the pasta)
Yield: serves 4

Can be done completely ahead

6–7 slices bacon, cut into bite-size pieces
2 TB. olive oil
1 medium onion, finely chopped (about $^{1}/_{2}$ cup)
2 cloves garlic, minced
3 TB. finely chopped fresh parsley
3 cups canned crushed tomatoes
$^{1}/_{4}$ tsp. salt (or salt to taste)
$^{1}/_{4}$ tsp. freshly ground black pepper
1 lb. pasta, preferably bucatini, perciatelli, or spaghetti
freshly grated parmesan cheese (optional)

Second Thoughts
If pancetta is available, you might want to use that instead of regular bacon. You don't have to blanch pancetta (which is uncured Italian bacon) because it doesn't have the same smoky taste as American bacon. You can find pancetta in Italian specialty stores.

Blanch the bacon by putting the pieces in a saucepan half filled with simmering water and cooking it $1^{1}/_{2}$ minutes. Then drain the pieces and set them aside. Heat the olive oil in a large skillet. Add the bacon and cook it over moderate heat for 4–5 minutes or until the bacon is crispy. Add the onion, garlic, and parsley and cook 1–2 minutes or until the vegetables have wilted. Add the tomatoes, salt, and pepper. Stir the ingredients and cook over low-moderate heat for 12–15 minutes or until sauce has thickened slightly. While the sauce is cooking, cook the pasta until it is al dente. Drain the pasta. Pour the sauce over the pasta and serve it with freshly grated parmesan cheese (if desired).

Pasta with Peas and Wild Mushrooms

This is a beautiful dish that can also be used as a first course to serve 6–8 people.

Level: Intermediate
Preparation time: 15–20 minutes
Cooking time: 8–10 minutes (plus time to cook the pasta)
Yield: serves 4

Can be done completely ahead

8 oz. mixed fresh wild mushrooms,
  or use white mushrooms
1 lb. pasta, preferably penne or ziti
4 TB. olive oil
2 large cloves garlic, minced
1 large shallot, minced

3 TB. chopped fresh basil, or 2 tsp. dried
$1^1/_2$ cups thawed frozen peas, or blanched fresh peas
$1^1/_2$ cups freshly grated parmesan cheese
$^3/_4$ tsp. salt (or salt to taste)
$^1/_4$ tsp. freshly ground pepper (or pepper to taste)

Rinse the mushrooms, chop or slice them into smaller pieces, and set them aside. Cook the pasta until it is al dente. Drain the pasta. While the pasta is cooking, heat the olive oil in a skillet. Add the garlic and shallot and cook them over low-moderate heat 1–2 minutes or until the vegetables have softened slightly. Add the mushrooms and basil and cook another 3–4 minutes or until the mushrooms have softened and all the pan juices have evaporated. Add the peas and pasta to the pan and toss the ingredients to evenly distribute them. Add the cheese and cook the ingredients 3–4 minutes or until the pasta and cheese are hot. Taste the dish for seasoning and add salt and pepper to taste.

Kitchen Clue
You can make the sauce after you finish preparing the pasta if you find that less confusing. If so, run hot water through the pasta to separate the pieces, and drain it before adding it to the pan.

How to Cook Rice

This is a recipe every good cook should know. Rice goes with practically every main dish you can think of.

Preparation time: 1 minute
Cooking time: about 20 minutes (plus 10 minutes standing time)
Yield: 3 cups cooked rice; serves 4–6

Can be done completely ahead

1 cup raw long grain white rice, NOT converted
$1^3/_4$ cups water

Place the rice in a 2–3 quart saucepan and cover it with the cold water. Bring the mixture to a boil over high heat. Let the mixture boil one minute. Remove the pan from the heat, but do not turn off the heat. Lower the heat to low. Stir the rice mixture with a fork. Cover the pan and let the rice stand (off the heat) one minute. Return the rice to the heat and cook it without lifting the cover for 18 minutes or until grains are fluffy and all the liquid has been absorbed. Remove the pan from the heat and let the rice stand, covered, for about 10 minutes before serving.

Need some interesting but simple ideas to spruce up rice? Try these:

➤ Use canned or homemade chicken, beef, or vegetable stock instead of water to cook the rice.

➤ Dissolve $^1/_2$ tsp. saffron threads in 1 TB. boiling water and add it to the rice cooking water.

➤ Add the juice of one large lemon and 3–4 TB. chopped parsley to the cooked rice.

➤ Add 3–4 TB. olive oil and 1 cup cooked corn kernels and/or peas to the cooked rice.

➤ Add 4–5 TB. lightly toasted pignoli nuts to the cooked rice.

Rice Pilaf with Raisins and Curry

This dish is sensational with grilled or roasted poultry or other meat.

Level: Easy
Preparation time: 3–4 minutes
Cooking time: 24–26 minutes (plus 10 minutes standing time)
Yield: serves 4–6

Can be done completely ahead

2 TB. vegetable oil
1 small onion, finely chopped (about $^1/_4$ cup)
1 cup raw long grain white rice, NOT converted
$^1/_3$ cup dark raisins

$2^1/_2$ tsp. curry powder
$^3/_4$ tsp. salt (or salt to taste)
$1^3/_4$ cups canned or homemade chicken stock or water

Heat the oil in a deep skillet. Add the onion and cook over moderate heat 2–3 minutes or until the vegetable has wilted slightly. Add the rice, raisins, curry powder, and salt and cook, stirring frequently, for 2–3 minutes or until the rice grains are hot and uniformly coated. Pour in the stock. Bring the mixture to a boil. Let the mixture boil one minute. Remove the pan from the heat, but do not turn off the heat. Lower the heat to low. Stir the rice mixture with a fork. Cover the pan. Let the rice stand (off the heat) one minute. Return the rice to the heat. Cook the rice without lifting the cover for 18 minutes or until grains are fluffy and all the liquid has been absorbed. Remove the pan from the heat and let the rice stand, covered, about 10 minutes before serving.

Rice Pilaf with Mushrooms

This is the kind of dish that looks and tastes as if you fussed a lot—but it's not at all difficult to make.

Level: Intermediate
Preparation time: 10–12 minutes
Cooking time: 24–26 minutes (plus 10 minutes standing time)
Yield: serves 4–6

Can be done completely ahead

2 TB. vegetable oil
1 TB. butter (optional)
1 medium onion, finely chopped (about $^1/_2$ cup)
6–8 oz. mushrooms, sliced
1 cup raw long grain white rice, NOT converted
2 TB. chopped parsley
1 tsp. salt (or salt to taste)
$^1/_4$ tsp. freshly ground black pepper
$1^3/_4$ cups canned or homemade beef, chicken, or vegetable stock

Heat the oil and butter (if used) in a deep skillet. Add the onion and cook over moderate heat 2–3 minutes or until the vegetable has wilted slightly. Add the mushrooms and cook another 1–2 minutes, stirring once or twice. Add the rice, parsley, salt, and pepper, and cook stirring frequently for 2–3 minutes or until the rice grains are coated with oil and are beginning to color slightly. Pour in the stock. Bring the mixture to a boil. Let the mixture boil one minute. Remove the pan from the heat, but do not turn off the heat. Lower the heat to low. Stir the rice mixture with a fork. Cover the pan. Let the rice stand (off the heat) one minute. Return the rice to the heat. Cook the rice without lifting the cover 18 minutes or until grains are fluffy and all the liquid has been absorbed. Remove the pan from the heat and let the rice stand, covered, about 10 minutes before serving.

Second Thoughts
This is such a basic pilaf that you can change it in numerous ways. For example, try one of these options:

➤ Add a minced garlic clove with the onion.

➤ Add $^1/_2$ cup chopped sweet red pepper with the onion.

➤ Use wild mushrooms instead of common white mushrooms.

➤ Sprinkle 1 tsp. fresh thyme leaves (or about $^1/_2$ tsp. dried thyme) on the rice before you stir and cover it.

➤ Add 1 cup diced leftover chicken or turkey with the mushrooms.

Fried Rice

This dish is colorful, so it makes a delightful addition to a buffet table. It's also suitable as a brunch food or a side dish, especially with other stir-fried foods.

Level: Intermediate
Preparation time: 12–15 minutes
Cooking time: 5–7 minutes (plus time to cook and cool the white rice)
Yield: serves 4–6

Can be done completely ahead

$2^1/_2$ TB. vegetable oil
2 large eggs, beaten
3 scallions, chopped into $^1/_2$" pieces
$^2/_3$ cup $^1/_2$"-diced boiled ham or barbecued pork
$^1/_2$ cup thawed frozen peas or blanched fresh peas
6–8 canned water chestnuts, cut into small chunks (about $^1/_4$ cup)
3 cups cold cooked rice
$^3/_4$ tsp. salt (or salt to taste)

Heat $^1/_2$ TB. of the vegetable oil in a wok or skillet. Add the eggs and fry them, without stirring, over moderate heat about 1 minute. Then turn them over to cook on the reverse side. If you are using a wok, you will have to move the egg as it cooks to make sure raw egg slides to the bottom of the pan to cook. Cook the eggs on the reverse side 30–45 seconds or until they have set. Remove the cooked eggs, chop them into pieces, and set them aside. Heat the remaining vegetable oil in the wok or skillet. Add the scallions and stir-fry over high heat 30–45 seconds. Add ham, peas, water chestnuts, and rice and stir-fry 2–3 minutes. Add the salt and egg and stir-fry 1–2 minutes. Dish out the fried rice and serve.

How to Cook Wild Rice

With its chewy texture and nut-like flavor, wild rice is a perfect accompaniment to roasted or grilled meats or poultry. It also is visually interesting, and when you serve it, people will be impressed with it and with you. This version is a bit different from standard recipes that call for more liquid and longer cooking time—hence, the texture is firmer.

Level: Easy
Preparation time: 3–4 minutes
Cooking time: 35–40 minutes
Yield: 3 cups; serves 4–6

Can be done completely ahead

1 cup wild rice
water to cover the rice
$^1/_2$ tsp. salt (or salt to taste)
$^1/_8$ tsp. freshly ground black pepper (or pepper to taste)
1 cup water or canned or homemade chicken, beef, or vegetable stock
$^1/_2$ cup additional water
1 small bay leaf

Put the wild rice in a saucepan and cover it with water by at least one inch. Bring the mixture to a boil over high heat and boil the mixture for 5 minutes. Drain the rice. Return the rice to the pan and add the salt, pepper, stock, water, and bay leaf. Bring the mixture to a boil. Lower the heat, cover the pan, and cook 30–35 minutes or until the rice is tender and all the liquid has been absorbed. Discard the bay leaf.

Second Thoughts
Many people are used to fried rice that is brown. In Hong Kong and many parts of mainland China, traditional fried rice is white. However, if you prefer the brown color, add 2–3 TB. of soy sauce when you add the rice, but then do not use as much salt. You also can add numerous ingredients when you add the ham or pork to make "many precious" fried rice. Try adding $^1/_2$ cup cut up cooked shrimp, $^1/_2$ cup diced cooked lobster meat, $^1/_2$ cup diced cooked chicken, 1 cup bean sprouts, and/or $^1/_4$ cup chopped soaked and softened dried shiitake mushrooms.

Fein on Food
Wild rice isn't rice at all, nor is it related to rice. It is the seed of a type of aquatic marsh grass. Early English settlers in this country called it rice because its narrow, tapering shape bears a superficial resemblance to rice. Before the English colonized Minnesota, where wild rice has its origins, the French fur trappers who lived in the region called wild rice "crazy oats." But wild rice isn't related to oats either. Wild rice has an interesting, chewy texture, quite unlike the soft textures of cooked rice or oats.

Wild Rice Fritters

This dish is an outstanding choice of side dish to serve with the Thanksgiving turkey.

Level: Intermediate
Preparation time: 5–6 minutes
Cooking time: 4–6 minutes per batch (plus time to cook and cool the rice)
Yield: serves 6–8

Can be done completely ahead

1½ cups cooked, cooled wild rice
1½ cups cooked, cooled white rice
1 large onion, minced (about ¾ to one cup)
3 large eggs

5 TB. flour
1 tsp. salt (or salt to taste)
¼ tsp. freshly ground black pepper
vegetable oil for pan frying

Mix together the wild rice, white rice, and onion in a large bowl. Beat the eggs and add them to the rice mixture. Stir the mixture to combine the ingredients. Stir in the flour, salt, and pepper. Heat about ½" of vegetable oil in a large skillet. When the oil is hot enough to make a tiny piece of bread sizzle around the edges, drop some of the wild rice mixture into the pan to form "pancakes" about 2" to 4", depending on the size fritters you want. Fry the fritters over moderate heat about 2–3 minutes per side or until they are crispy and golden brown. Drain on paper towels.

Kitchen Clue
Remember that when you reheat fried foods, you must put them in a single layer on a cookie sheet and bake in a preheated oven at 400 degrees. Put the food on a rack if possible for even better results.

Tuscan Style White Beans with Tomato Sauce

This dish is a perfect accompaniment to grilled poultry and meats.

Level: Easy
Preparation time: 3–5 minutes
Cooking time: about 15 minutes
Yield: serves 4

Can be done completely ahead

3 TB. olive oil
1 clove garlic, minced
1 TB. fresh minced sage (or 1 tsp. dried) or 2 tsp. fresh thyme (or ½ tsp. dried)
¼ tsp. freshly ground black pepper (or pepper to taste)
2 cups canned white beans (rinsed under cold water and drained)
1 cup canned crushed tomatoes

Heat the olive oil in a saucepan. Add the garlic and cook over low heat 1–2 minutes, stirring often. Add the sage and pepper, stir briefly, and add the beans and crushed tomatoes. Cook the beans 10–12 minutes until the flavors have had a chance to blend.

Old-Fashioned New England Style Baked Beans

This recipe may spoil you. Once you taste homemade baked beans, you may never want to eat the canned kind again. This version is rich, dark, and sweet. It's perfect with grilled burgers or steaks.

Level: Intermediate
Preparation time: 10–12 minutes
Cooking time: 5–6 hours (plus 1 hour soaking time)
Yield: serves 6–8

Can be done completely ahead

1 lb. dried white beans (Navy, Great Northern, Pea)
6 cups water
1 medium onion, finely chopped (about $1/2$ cup)
6 oz. salt pork
$2/3$ cup molasses

$1/4$ cup brown sugar
1 TB. powdered mustard
$1/2$ tsp. salt
$1/4$ tsp. freshly ground black pepper
$1/8$ tsp. ground cloves or 2 whole cloves

Rinse the beans and let them drain. Place the beans in a large saucepan, cover them with water, and bring the water to a boil over high heat. Boil the mixture 2 minutes. Remove the pan from the heat, cover the pan, and set it aside one hour or more. Return the pan to the heat and bring the mixture to a simmer over moderate heat. Cook the beans 45 minutes. Preheat the oven to 300 degrees. Add the onion to the beans and stir. Remove and discard the rind from the salt pork (if it has one), cut the pork into bite-size chunks, and add it to the beans with the remaining ingredients. Stir the beans to blend ingredients. Pour the mixture into a casserole dish, cover the dish, and bake it 3–4 hours, stirring the beans occasionally, or until the beans are very tender and the sauce has thickened to a gravy-like consistency. Peek at the beans once in awhile. If the beans become too dry during cooking time, add water $1/4$ cup at a time.

> **Second Thoughts**
> For more gently flavored beans, you could substitute $3/4$ cup maple syrup for the molasses and sugar.

Bulgur Wheat and Lentil Pilaf

You may use this side dish as stuffing for chicken, turkey, or crown roast of pork. Let the mixture cool completely before you transfer it to the poultry or meat.

Level: Challenging
Preparation time: 10–12 minutes
Cooking time: about 45 minutes
Yield: serves 6

Can be done completely ahead

1 cup lentils
3 cups water
2 TB. olive oil
1 TB. butter
3 TB. pignoli nuts or coarsely chopped almonds
1 medium onion, finely chopped (about $1/2$ cup)

1 cup bulgur wheat
$1/3$ cup currants or golden raisins
2 cups canned or homemade chicken or vegetable stock
$3/4$ tsp. salt (or salt to taste)
$1/8$ tsp. freshly ground black pepper (or pepper to taste)

Place the lentils and water in a saucepan and bring them to a boil over high heat. Lower the heat and simmer the lentils 10 minutes. Drain the lentils and set them aside. Heat the olive oil and butter in a large skillet. When the butter has melted and looks foamy, add the pignoli nuts and cook them over moderate heat 2 minutes or until they begin to color lightly. Add the onion and cook 6–8 minutes or until it is lightly browned. Add the bulgur wheat and cook 3–4 minutes. Add the lentils, currants, stock, and some salt and pepper. Bring the mixture to a boil. Lower the heat to low, cover the pan, and cook 25–30 minutes or until all the liquid in the pan has been absorbed. Taste for seasoning and add salt and pepper to taste.

> **Kitchen Clue**
> You can find bulgur wheat in many supermarkets. It is also available in health food stores and specialty shops.

268

Rice and Fruit Stuffing

This simple dish is a super side dish as well as a stuffing for roasted chicken or rock cornish hens.

Level: Easy
Preparation time: 15 minutes
Cooking time: 3–4 minutes (plus time to cook the rice)
Yield: enough for 1 roasting chicken or 6 cornish hens or to serve
4–6 people as a side dish

Can be done completely ahead

$^1/_2$ cup butter or margarine
1 medium onion, chopped (about $^1/_2$ cup)
1 stalk celery, chopped
3 cups cooked white rice
2 tart apples, peeled and chopped

1 cup chopped dried fruit
$^1/_2$ cup raisins
$^1/_2$ cup broken cashew nuts or toasted chopped almonds
1 tsp. salt (or salt to taste)
1 TB. fresh thyme or 1 tsp. dried thyme

Melt the butter in a skillet. Add the onion and celery and cook over moderate heat 3–4 minutes or until the vegetables have softened. Remove the pan from the heat. Add the onion mixture plus the remaining ingredients and stir gently to distribute the solid ingredients throughout the rice. Cool completely before you use this as a stuffing.

Nana's Egg Noodle Stuffing

Nana calls this egg noodle "filling"—which it is because no one can stop eating it.

Level: Easy
Preparation time: about 20 minutes
Cooking time: 50–60 minutes
Yield: serves 6–8

Can be done completely ahead

1 lb. barley shaped egg noodle pasta
   (or use acini pepe pasta)
2 TB. vegetable oil
1 large onion, finely chopped (about $^3/_4$ to 1 cup)
3 stalks celery, coarsely chopped

12 oz. mushrooms, sliced
4 TB. melted butter
2 large eggs
1 tsp. salt (or salt to taste)
$^1/_4$ tsp. freshly ground black pepper (or pepper to taste)

Preheat the oven to 375 degrees. Cook the egg noodle pasta until it is al dente. Drain the pasta and set it aside. Heat the 2 TB. of vegetable oil in a skillet. Add the onion and celery and cook it over moderate heat 3–4 minutes or until the vegetables have wilted. Add the mushrooms and cook another 5 minutes or until the mushrooms have softened and most of the water has evaporated from the pan. Add the vegetable mixture to the egg noodle pasta. Stir in the melted butter. Beat the eggs and add them. Add the salt and pepper. Stir to blend the ingredients. Put the mixture in a baking dish. Bake the stuffing 40–50 minutes or until it is crispy and browned on top.

Kitchen Clue
Instead of baking the egg noodle mixture in a baking dish, you can use it to stuff poultry.

Chestnut and Sausage Stuffing

This is a rich stuffing suitable for the Thanksgiving table. The sherry gives it a lively flavor. The dish's many textures make it interesting enough to fuss with.

Level: Challenging
Preparation time: about 25 minutes
Cooking time: about 50–60 minutes
Yield: about 8 cups

Can be done completely ahead

1 lb. Italian style sweet sausage, not in casing
  (or casing removed)
2 TB. olive oil
1 large onion, finely chopped (about $^3/_4$ to 1 cup)
2 stalks celery, sliced into $^1/_4$" thick pieces
10–12 oz. mushrooms, coarsely chopped or sliced
1 TB. thyme leaves or 1 tsp. dried

$1^1/_2$ tsp. chopped fresh sage leaves or $^1/_2$ tsp. dried sage
2 cups coarsely cut up bottled or canned chestnuts
  (about 10 oz.)
6 cups $^1/_2$" bread cubes
$^1/_3$ cup half and half cream
4 TB. melted butter
$^1/_4$ cup sherry wine

Breaking the pieces into smaller bits, fry the sausage meat in a skillet over moderate heat for 12–15 minutes or until the meat is thoroughly browned and lightly crispy. Drain the fat from the pan, remove the meat, and set it aside. Heat the olive oil in the skillet and add the onion and celery. Stirring occasionally, cook over moderate heat 2–3 minutes or until the vegetables have wilted. Add the mushrooms and cook another 3–4 minutes or until mushrooms have softened and most of the liquid has evaporated from the pan. Add the sausage to the vegetables and sprinkle the ingredients with the thyme and sage. Break the chestnuts into pieces using your hands, and add them and the bread cubes to the mixture. Toss ingredients so they are evenly distributed in the pan. Pour in the cream, melted butter, and sherry wine and toss ingredients thoroughly. Put stuffing aside until you are ready to stuff a bird. If you will be baking the stuffing separately, put it into a large casserole dish, preheat the oven to 375 degrees, and bake the stuffing 40–50 minutes or until it is crispy and browned on top.

Kitchen Clue
You can find bottled or canned chestnuts in many supermarkets or in specialty food stores. Be sure to buy the plain ones, not those packaged in sugar syrup. Most people use dry sherry for stuffing, but if you want an unusual and delicious surprise, use sweet sherry.

Vegetables

Years ago when cookbooks recommended boiling vegetables to death, foods like spinach, cabbage, broccoli, green beans, and even the more accepted carrot developed bad reputations as foods to avoid. Mushy canned vegetables were even worse. In recent times, however, we have learned more about how to cook vegetables: keep them crunchy and keep them colorful. Not only do vegetables taste and look better that way, they're also more nutritious. In addition, we have more vegetables to choose from today. Fresh zucchini, eggplants, and sugar snap peas were barely known to most people a generation or two ago, but they now supplement the more familiar choices. As a result, more and more people appreciate vegetables today, and they don't say "ugh" as often.

Baked Acorn Squash

This is a wonderful choice for Thanksgiving dinner or other holiday dinners.

Level: Easy
Preparation time: 4–5 minutes
Cooking time: 30–35 minutes
Yield: serves 4

Can be done completely ahead

2 acorn squash
$^1/_2$ tsp. salt or to taste
$^1/_4$ cup finely chopped nuts
$^1/_4$ cup golden raisins
2 TB. brown sugar
$1^1/_2$ TB. softened butter or margarine

Preheat the oven to 425 degrees. Cut the squash in half, cutting perpendicular to the ridges so you wind up with 2 deep halves. Slice a small piece from the bottom of each half so the squash can stand up straight on a baking dish. Scoop the seeds and stringy flesh from inside the cavity and sprinkle the orange flesh with salt. Lightly grease a baking dish with vegetable oil. Place the squash halves cut side down on the baking dish. Prick the shell in 3–4 places with the tines of a fork. Bake 20–25 minutes. Combine remaining ingredients. Remove the squash from the oven and turn it cut-side up. Fill the cavities with the nut mixture. Return the squash to the oven and bake it another 10 minutes or until the flesh is tender when pierced with the tip of a sharp knife.

Second Thoughts
You can fill the cavities with cranberries if you'd like instead of the nut mixture. (See the recipe for cranberry sauce in the Sauces section.) In that case, cook the squash completely and serve it hot with the cranberries at room temperature.

Boiled Corn on the Cob

This is America's first choice of vegetable—by far. Be sure to buy the freshest corn possible with the husks still on. Don't peel the husks until just before you cook the corn.

Level: Easy
Preparation time: 2 minutes for the corn; 2–3 minutes for the flavored butter
Cooking time: 5 minutes
Yield: serves 6
The flavored butters can be done completely ahead of time; the corn cannot

6 ears fresh corn
4 quarts water
1 cup milk

Remove the husks and silk from the ears of corn. Bring a large pan of water (about 4 quarts) to a boil. Add the milk. Let the liquid return to a boil. Immerse the corn and cover the pan. Remove the pan from the heat. Let the corn stand in the milk/water 5 minutes. Remove the corn with tongs and serve with plain butter or one of the suggested flavored butters.

To make any of the flavored butters, simply blend the ingredients in a small bowl with a whisk.

Flavored Butters for Cooked Corn (Enough for 6 Ears of Corn)

Chili butter:
  4 TB. softened butter
  1 tsp. chili powder

Curry butter:
  4 TB. softened butter
  1 tsp. curry powder

Marjoram butter:
  4 TB. softened butter
  1 TB. freshly minced marjoram or ½ tsp. dried

Scallion butter:
  4 TB. softened butter
  2 TB. finely minced scallion

Zesty butter:
  4 TB. softened butter
  1 TB. Dijon mustard
  2 tsp. prepared white horseradish

Lemon herb butter:
  4 TB. softened butter
  1 TB. fresh lemon juice
  ½ tsp. freshly grated lemon peel
  2 tsp. minced chives (or the green part of a scallion)
  2 tsp. freshly minced basil or ½ tsp. dried

Broccoli with Garlic and Lemon

If you hate broccoli because it's tough and rubbery, you'll love this version. The stems are peeled, which makes the vegetable pleasantly tender.

Level: Easy
Preparation time: 10–12 minutes
Cooking time: 10–12 minutes
Yield: serves 4
*Can be done ahead up to the * in the instructions*

1 bunch broccoli (2 large or 3 medium-size stalks)
2 TB. olive oil
2 large cloves garlic, sliced in half

¼ tsp. salt (or salt to taste)
⅛ tsp. freshly ground black pepper (or pepper to taste)
juice of half a lemon (about 2 TB.)

Remove the florets of the broccoli stalks by cutting them with a paring knife. Cut the florets into bite-size pieces. Cut a ½" thick slice from the bottom of each stem. Peel the stems by pulling back a thin layer of the skin with the paring knife, starting at the cut end. (You also could peel the stems with a vegetable peeler.) Cut the broccoli stems into bite-size pieces. Steam the broccoli in a steamer insert in a saucepan or in a vegetable steamer 6–8 minutes or until barely tender. Drain the broccoli under cold running water and set it aside.

* Heat the olive oil in a skillet. Cook the garlic over moderate heat 1 minute or until it is just beginning to brown. Discard the garlic. Add the broccoli pieces to the pan, sprinkle them with salt and pepper, and cook 1–2 minutes or until they are hot, stirring occasionally. Dish the broccoli out to a serving plate, sprinkle it with the lemon juice, and serve.

Low-Fat Creamed Spinach

Even people who think they hate spinach like creamed spinach. This version doesn't have the high-fat and caloric ingredients of the classic recipe, but it's still rich, creamy, and delicious.

Level: Easy
Preparation time: 6–8 minutes
Cooking time: 6–8 minutes
Yield: serves 4

Can be done completely ahead

1 lb. fresh spinach
1 cup low-fat or nonfat ricotta cheese
1 cup low-fat or skim buttermilk

$^{1}/_{2}$ tsp. salt (or salt to taste)
pinch of freshly ground black pepper
pinch of freshly grated nutmeg

Wash the spinach carefully to remove any dirt and sand. Place the still-wet spinach in a saucepan, cover the pan, and cook the spinach over moderate heat 4–5 minutes or until spinach has wilted. Drain the spinach and squeeze out as much of its juice as possible. Strain the ricotta cheese through a sieve or whirl it in a food processor for several seconds or until it looks smooth and creamy. Blend the ricotta cheese and buttermilk together. Mince the spinach and stir it into the cheese mixture. Season the spinach mixture with the salt, pepper, and nutmeg. Return the mixture to the saucepan and cook over moderate heat (stirring often) 2–3 minutes or until it is hot. (You could also place it in a casserole dish and bake it in a preheated 350 degree oven for 4–5 minutes.)

Wilted Kale with Sesame Dressing

This dish is delicious, different, and healthy too.

Level: Easy
Preparation time: 3–4 minutes
Cooking time: about 10 minutes
Yield: serves 4

Cannot be done ahead

2 TB. sesame seeds
salt
2 lbs. fresh kale, leaves left whole
3 TB. vegetable oil

Place the sesame seeds in an ungreased frying pan and cook them over moderate heat for 3–4 minutes or until they are lightly toasted. (You could also toast them for 3–4 minutes in an oven or toaster oven preheated to 350 degrees.) Set the seeds aside. Wash the kale leaf by leaf to get rid of all the sand. Remove any extra-large stem portions. Bring a large soup pot of water to a boil. Add salt ($^{1}/_{2}$ tsp. for each quart of water). Add the kale leaves to the boiling water and cook the leaves 8–9 minutes or until they have wilted and the stems have softened. Remove and drain the kale in a strainer or colander. Press excess moisture out. Toss the kale with the vegetable oil and sprinkle it with the toasted sesame seeds.

Second Thoughts
If you don't care for the taste of sesame seeds, sprinkle the kale with 1–2 TB. lemon juice plus the vegetable oil instead. Or you can sprinkle the kale with 1–2 TB. balsamic vinegar.

Sautéed Dill-Scented Carrots

This is the most requested vegetable dish in the Fein household—by all family members and friends. We always keep carrots and dill in the fridge to ensure that we can have this dish whenever we want it.

Level: Easy
Preparation time: 6–7 minutes
Cooking time: 12–15 minutes
Yield: serves 4

Can be done completely ahead

1 lb. carrots
lightly salted water
3 TB. butter
$^1/_2$ tsp. sugar
$^1/_4$ tsp. salt (or salt to taste)
1 TB. minced fresh dillweed or 1 tsp. dried

Peel the carrots and cut them into bite-size chunks. Place the carrots in a saucepan and cover them with lightly salted cold water. Bring the water to a boil, lower the heat, and simmer the carrots 12–15 minutes or until they are fork tender. Drain the carrots. Heat the butter, sugar, salt, and dillweed, and toss the ingredients in the pan. When it's melted and looks foamy, add the carrots and serve. Alternatively, you can steam the carrots; in that case add the remaining ingredients and toss them in the serving bowl.

Second Thoughts
A second way to serve this dish is to puree the carrots by mashing them with a potato masher, putting them through a ricer, or processing them in a food processor. For this method, once you have pureed the carrots, add the remaining ingredients plus 3–4 TB. cream or evaporated milk to make the consistency a bit creamier. Taste for seasoning and add salt and pepper as necessary. You can reheat this dish in a preheated 350 degree oven for 6–7 minutes or in a saucepan over moderate heat for 3–4 minutes (stir frequently to prevent sticking).

Sautéed Sugar Snap or Snow Peas

This is an easy, well-liked dish suitable for family or company.

Level: Easy
Preparation time: 5–6 minutes
Cooking time: 2–3 minutes
Yield: serves 4

Can be done ahead up to the * in the instructions

$^1/_2$ lb. sugar snap or snow peas
1 TB. butter
1 TB. vegetable oil

$^1/_2$ tsp. sugar
pinch or two of salt

Wash the peas. Remove the top "string" by cutting a tiny piece from the curvy tip and pulling backwards. Bring about 2 quarts of lightly salted water ($^1/_4$ tsp. salt) to a boil. Add the peas and cook 45 seconds. Drain the peas. Rinse them thoroughly under cold water.

* Heat the butter and vegetable oil in a skillet. When the butter has melted and looks foamy, add the peas, sprinkle them with the sugar and salt, and sauté them 1–2 minutes over moderate heat or until they are hot.

Sautéed Zucchini, Pepper, and Corn

This dish is so colorful it looks grand next to almost any meat or poultry dish.

Level: Intermediate
Preparation time: 10–12 minutes
Cooking time: about 6 minutes
Yield: serves 4

Cannot be done ahead

1 red bell pepper
4 TB. olive oil
2 cloves garlic, minced
1 small onion, finely chopped
3 small zucchini, sliced $\frac{1}{8}$" thick

1 cup thawed frozen corn kernels
$\frac{1}{4}$ tsp. salt (or salt to taste)
$\frac{1}{8}$ tsp. freshly ground black pepper (or pepper to taste)
3 TB. freshly minced basil

Remove the stem from the pepper. Cut the pepper in half and remove the seeds and any extra white membrane that clings to the red inside. Chop the pepper into bite-size pieces. Heat the olive oil in a skillet. Add the garlic, onion, and pepper and cook over moderate heat 2–3 minutes or until they have softened slightly. Add the zucchini and corn and stir the ingredients. Sprinkle in the salt, pepper, and basil and cook 3–4 minutes or until vegetables are tender.

Second Thoughts
You can add a cup of thawed frozen peas or blanched fresh peas for extra bulk, texture, and color.

How to Make Baked Potatoes

Centuries ago when the Spanish conquistadors discovered Inca tribesmen baking potatoes in hearth fires, they knew they had found a winner and took the recipe for baked potatoes back to Europe. We still love baked potatoes today, and this winner is among the easiest foods to prepare.

Level: Easy
Preparation time: less than a minute
Cooking time: 45–55 minutes
Yield: serves 4

Cannot be done ahead

4 large russet baking potatoes

Preheat the oven to 400 degrees. Scrub the potatoes thoroughly. Do NOT wrap them in foil. Do NOT brush the skin with vegetable oil. Bake the potatoes 10 minutes. Prick the potato skin in 2 or 3 places with the tines of a fork. Continue to bake the potatoes another 35–45 minutes or until they are tender all the way through when pierced with the tip of a sharp knife.

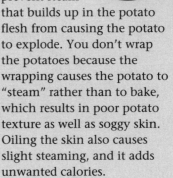

Kitchen Clue
You pierce the potato to prevent steam that builds up in the potato flesh from causing the potato to explode. You don't wrap the potatoes because the wrapping causes the potato to "steam" rather than to bake, which results in poor potato texture as well as soggy skin. Oiling the skin also causes slight steaming, and it adds unwanted calories.

Baked Stuffed Potatoes

This is the ideal company dish because you can make it a day ahead and because it tastes and looks great.

Level: Easy
Preparation time: 10 minutes
Cooking time: 1–1¼ hours
Yield: serves 4

Can be done completely ahead

4 large russet baking potatoes
2 TB. softened butter
2 TB. softened cream cheese
3 TB. freshly minced chives or parsley

½ tsp. salt (or salt to taste)
¼ tsp. freshly ground black pepper (or pepper to taste)
6–8 TB. milk
paprika

Preheat the oven to 400 degrees. Scrub the potatoes thoroughly. Do NOT wrap them in foil. Do NOT brush the skin with vegetable oil. Bake the potatoes 10 minutes. Prick the potato skin in 2 or 3 places with the tines of a fork. Continue to bake the potatoes another 35–45 minutes or until they are tender all the way through when pierced with the tip of a sharp knife. When the potatoes are cool enough to handle but still warm, split them in half lengthwise. Scoop the flesh into a bowl but reserve the skins. Add the butter, cream cheese, chives, salt, and pepper to the potato flesh and blend the ingredients with a fork or mash them with a potato masher. Do NOT use a food processor. Add 6 TB. of milk and stir the potatoes briefly until the mixture is smooth. If the mixture seems dry, add the remaining milk and stir it in. Place the potato mixture into the hollowed potato skins. Dust the top lightly with paprika. Bake the potatoes 12–15 minutes or until they are lightly crispy on top.

> **Second Thoughts**
> If you want a more low-fat version of baked stuffed potatoes, try this: substitute 1 cup low-fat cottage cheese and ½ cup skim buttermilk for the butter, cream cheese, and milk.

Mashed Potatoes, Basic and Beyond

Is there anyone who doesn't love mashed potatoes? Smooth or lumpy, this is the classic comfort food most of us crave on occasion.

Level: Easy
Preparation time: 12–15 minutes
Cooking time: 15–20 minutes
Yield: serves 6

Can be done completely ahead

2 lbs. all-purpose potatoes
Lightly salted water
4–5 TB. butter or margarine

½ cup hot milk
1 tsp. salt (or salt to taste)
¼ tsp. freshly ground black pepper (or pepper to taste)

Peel the potatoes and cut them into chunks. Place them in a saucepan and cover them with lightly salted cold water (about ½ tsp. salt for each 6 cups of water). Bring the water to a boil, lower the heat, and simmer the potatoes 15–20 minutes or until they are fork tender. Drain the potatoes. In the saucepan or a bowl, mash the potatoes with a potato masher, fork, or electric mixer or hand beater set on low speed. Do NOT use a food processor or the mixture will acquire a glue-like consistency. Add the butter in chunks and continue to mash until the mixture is free of lumps. Add the milk, salt, and pepper, and stir briefly with a wooden spoon until ingredients are smooth and thoroughly blended. Taste for seasoning and adjust salt and pepper to taste.

Mashed potatoes are so versatile you can change the recipe easily to suit your own tastes. Here are a few suggestions:

- ➤ If you like your mashed potatoes super-rich, add 3–4 TB. softened cream cheese and/or 1/2 cup dairy sour cream when you add the butter.

- ➤ If you like your mashed potatoes more low-fat, use 3 TB. diet margarine and 1/2 cup low-fat cottage cheese instead of the butter. Use skim milk.

- ➤ If you want your mashed potatoes to have a Mediterranean flair, use 1/4 cup olive oil instead of the butter and stir in 1 large clove of garlic, minced, plus 1/2 tsp. fresh thyme leaves (or a few pinches of dried thyme).

- ➤ If you prefer a dish with an Irish accent, add 1/4 cup more milk plus 2 cups of chopped cooked kale or cabbage.

Sweet Potato Casserole

This is a traditional Thanksgiving dish, but there's no need to wait for a holiday to have it.

Level: Easy
Preparation time: 15–20 minutes
Cooking time: 35–40 minutes
Yield: serves 8–10

Can be done completely ahead

6 large sweet potatoes
4 TB. butter or margarine
1/2 cup maple syrup or honey
1 1/2 tsp. salt (or salt to taste)
1/2 cup orange or apple juice
1 tsp. cinnamon
1/2 tsp. freshly grated nutmeg

Peel the sweet potatoes and cut them into chunks. Place them in a saucepan and cover them with lightly salted cold water (about 1/2 tsp. salt for each 6 cups of water). Bring the water to a boil, lower the heat, and simmer the potatoes 15–20 minutes or until they are fork tender. Drain the potatoes. In the saucepan or a bowl, mash the potatoes with a potato masher, fork, or electric mixer or hand beater set on low speed. Do NOT use a food processor. Add the butter in chunks and continue to mash until the mixture is free of lumps. Add the maple syrup, salt, orange or apple juice, cinnamon, and nutmeg, and stir ingredients 1–2 minutes or until ingredients are smooth and thoroughly blended. Taste for seasoning and adjust salt to taste. To reheat this dish, preheat the oven to 350 degrees and bake the casserole 20–30 minutes or until it is hot (slip a long spoon or fork into the mixture, lift it out, and taste it).

> **Second Thoughts**
> Lots of people like to put marshmallows on sweet potato casserole. While some people are snobby about this and say it's terribly unsophisticated, others claim it's the only way to eat the dish and would rather eat well than worry about what people think. If you like marshmallows, add them to cover the top of the casserole after you have baked the casserole 15 minutes (20 minutes if the casserole is cold). Bake the dish an additional 12–15 minutes or until the marshmallows are lightly browned.

Sautéed Rosemary Potatoes

You better make lots of these—they go like wildfire. You can reheat extras to serve with eggs for breakfast.

Level: Easy
Preparation time: 3–4 minutes
Cooking time: about 40 minutes
Yield: serves 4–6

Can be done completely ahead

16–18 "new" or small red bliss potatoes
lightly salted water
2 TB. butter
2 TB. vegetable oil

1/2 tsp. salt (or salt to taste)
1/4 tsp. freshly ground black pepper (or pepper to taste)
1 1/2 TB. minced fresh rosemary or 1 1/2 tsp. dried, crushed rosemary

continues

continued

Place the potatoes in a large saucepan and cover them with lightly salted water. Bring the water to a boil, lower the heat, and simmer the potatoes 15–20 minutes or until they are fork tender. Drain the potatoes and peel them when they are cool enough to handle (after about 5 minutes). Heat the butter and vegetable oil over moderate heat in a large skillet. When the butter has melted and looks foamy, add the potatoes to the pan. Sprinkle the potatoes with the salt, pepper, and rosemary. Shaking the pan occasionally, sauté the potatoes 15–20 minutes or until the potatoes are browned on all sides and are lightly crispy.

Kitchen Clue This dish is excellent with roast chicken or meat. It also makes a super side dish for brunch.

How to Roast a Red Pepper

If you know how to roast a pepper, your culinary repertoire will change for the better. You can use roasted pepper as an hors d'oeuvre, slice it into a salad, serve it as part of an antipasto, add it to cooked pasta, and so on. Sure you can buy these already cooked, but they don't taste like homemade.

Level: Intermediate
Preparation time: less than a minute
Cooking time: about 15 minutes (plus 10 minutes standing time)
Yield: 1 pepper serves 2–3 people

Can be done completely ahead

1 sweet red pepper
1 brown paper bag (preferred) or 1 plastic bag

Preheat the oven broiler. Be sure the rack is about 4–6" from the heat source. Put the red pepper on the rack and broil it 2–3 minutes or until the surface is lightly scorched. Turn the pepper and repeat this process until all sides are scorched (the number of times you do this usually is 4 in total, but it depends on the size of the pepper). Remove the pepper and put it in the paper bag. Let it cool at least 10 minutes. When the pepper is cool enough to handle, remove it from the bag. The skin will peel off easily. Pull out the stem, cut the pepper in half, and pull out the seeds. The pepper will seem "wet." When you have removed the stem, seeds, and skin, carve the pepper into fat or narrow strips, as desired.

Second Thoughts When you eat roasted red pepper as a side dish, as a salad, for an appetizer, or as an hors d'oeuvre, it is delicious plain with the natural juices that accumulate as it sits. Or you can sprinkle it with a few drops of olive oil and/or balsamic vinegar, or you can scatter some freshly chopped basil on top.

278

Sauces and Gravies

The art of sauce making has always had an honored place in culinary history. That's because a great sauce provides a fabulous finishing touch for a dish. Think of spaghetti with tomato sauce or grilled chicken with barbecue sauce. Some sauces, such as vinaigrette dressing, are fluid; others are quite thick, such as cranberry sauce. Some are spicy; others are sweet. Sauces are among the most diverse of recipes.

Marinara Sauce

There is no marinara sauce that's simpler or tastier. No need to fuss with more ingredients.

Level: Easy
Preparation time: 5 minutes
Cooking time: 45 minutes
Yield: 2 cups (enough for 1 lb. of pasta)

Can be done completely ahead

1 2 lb. 3-oz. can Italian plum tomatoes, drained
3 TB. olive oil
4 large cloves garlic, minced

2 TB. minced fresh basil or 1^1/$_2$ tsp. dried
^{1}/$_2$ tsp. salt (or salt to taste)
^{1}/$_4$ tsp. freshly ground black pepper (or pepper to taste)

Drain the tomatoes and chop them. Heat the olive oil in a saucepan over low-moderate heat and add the garlic. Cook 1–2 minutes or until the garlic has softened but not turned brown. Add the tomatoes, basil, salt, and pepper. Simmer 45 minutes, taste for seasoning, and add salt and pepper as necessary. You can serve the sauce chunky or puree it in a food processor or blender.

Fresh Tomato Sauce

This sauce is outstanding when you make it with fragrant summer plum tomatoes. It's quite different from more traditional tomato sauces made with canned tomatoes.

Level: Intermediate
Preparation time: 20 minutes
Cooking time: 30 minutes
Yield: 1^1/$_2$ cups (enough for 12 oz. of pasta)

Can be done completely ahead

2 lbs. fresh Italian plum tomatoes
3 TB. olive oil
1 medium onion, chopped (about ^{1}/$_2$ cup)
1 large clove garlic, minced

^{1}/$_2$ tsp. salt (or salt to taste)
^{1}/$_8$ tsp. freshly ground black pepper
  (or pepper to taste)
1 TB. minced fresh basil or 1 tsp. dried

Bring a large saucepan of water to a boil. Add the tomatoes, blanch them 20 seconds, remove them (with a slotted spoon or by discarding the pan of water), and drain them under cold water. Pierce each tomato near the stem and peel back the skin. Cut the tomatoes in half crosswise and squeeze them to discard the seeds. Remove any leftover seeds with a spoon. Chop the tomatoes coarsely. Heat the olive oil in a saucepan over moderate heat and add the onion and garlic. Cook 3 minutes or until the vegetables have softened. Add the tomatoes, salt, and pepper and cook another 20 minutes, stirring occasionally. Add the basil and cook another 7–10 minutes. Taste for seasoning and add more salt and pepper if desired. Serve the sauce as is, or puree it in a food processor or blender.

Kitchen Clue
Plum tomatoes are the best kind for tomato sauce because they're not as juicy as regular tomatoes; therefore the sauce won't be watery. If the sauce is watery, it's best to puree it. If you use dried basil, add it with the tomatoes.

Barbecue Sauce

This all-purpose barbecue sauce can be used for almost any kind of meat or poultry but is especially good with poultry or pork.

Level: Easy
Preparation time: 12–15 minutes
Cooking time: 45 minutes
Yield: about 3 cups

Can be done completely ahead

^{1}/$_3$ cup vegetable oil
1 TB. butter, optional
1 medium onion, finely chopped (about ^{1}/$_2$ cup)
2 cloves garlic, minced
1 cup ketchup
1 cup canned tomato sauce

^{1}/$_2$ cup water
^{1}/$_3$ cup honey
^{1}/$_4$ cup cider vinegar
2 tsp. Worcestershire sauce
dash of hot pepper sauce

Heat the vegetable oil and butter (if used) in a saucepan over moderate heat. Add the onion and garlic and cook 3–4 minutes or until the vegetables have softened. Add the remaining ingredients, stir, and simmer 40 minutes, stirring occasionally.

Processor Pesto Sauce

You can use this sauce over cooked pasta or potatoes.

Level: Intermediate
Preparation time: 15 minutes
Cooking time: none
Yield: about 1¹/₂ cups

Can be done completely ahead

2 cups packed fresh basil leaves
3 cloves garlic
¹/₄ tsp. salt (or salt to taste)
¹/₄ tsp. freshly ground black pepper (or pepper to taste)

¹/₃ cup pignoli nuts (pine nuts)
¹/₂ cup olive oil, preferably extra virgin
6 TB. freshly grated Pecorino Romano cheese
¹/₄ cup freshly grated parmesan cheese

Wash the basil carefully and dry the leaves. Place the basil, garlic, salt, pepper, and pignoli nuts in the work bowl of a food processor or a blender. Process by pulsing for a few seconds, until the ingredients are well blended. With the machine turned on, add the olive oil gradually through the feed tube. Turn the machine off and scrape the sides of the bowl once or twice to make sure all ingredients are thoroughly blended. Add the cheeses, and process the ingredients briefly to combine them well.

> **What Is It?**
> *Pignoli nuts* are the same as pine nuts. You can find them in specialty stores, many produce markets, and almost all supermarkets.

How to Make Gravy

Too many people have a fear of making gravy. As former President Franklin Delano Roosevelt once said, "The only thing we have to fear is fear itself." So go ahead and try. If you follow the steps one by one, you will be successful.

Level: Intermediate
Preparation time: 1 minute
Cooking time: 4–5 minutes
Yield: 2 cups

Can be done completely ahead

the roasting pan fluids from the turkey, chicken, roast beef, or whatever
2 TB. rendered pan fat, butter, or vegetable oil
2 TB. all-purpose flour

2 cups pan fluids or water, stock, wine or a mixture of these
salt and pepper if desired

Strain all the fluids from the pan in which you have just cooked the roast. Reserve the strained liquid. Fat will rise to the top. Scoop the fat with a spoon or bulb baster. If there is little fat, you can place paper towels on top of the fluids to draw out the fat. Place the roasting pan over low heat and add 2 TB. of the scooped fat, butter, or vegetable oil. When the butter has melted, sprinkle the flour evenly in the pan. Mix the ingredients with a wooden spoon, scraping up bits and pieces that have stuck to the bottom of the roasting pan. Cook 2 minutes. Gradually add the fluids, using a whisk to mix ingredients constantly. When all the fluids have been absorbed, raise the heat to moderate and cook the gravy (whisking frequently) 1–2 minutes or until it has a uniform texture and has thickened to a gravy-like consistency. Strain the gravy if desired. Taste the gravy for seasoning and add salt and pepper as necessary. Reheat the gravy in a small saucepan or by microwave.

This recipe is for plain, medium-thickness gravy. For thicker or thinner gravy or one with additional flavor, try these variations:

➤ For thicker gravy, use 3 TB. flour; for thinner gravy use 2¹/₂ cups liquid.

➤ For giblet gravy, add chopped cooked giblets after you have cooked the flour for one minute. (You can roast the giblets with the poultry or simmer them for 30 minutes in stock or water.)

continues

281

continued

➤ For Madeira gravy add 3–4 TB. Madeira wine to the finished gravy.

➤ For cream gravy, use 1 to 1¹/₂ cups fluid plus 1 cup cream.

➤ For shallot and herb gravy, add 2 chopped shallots and 1¹/₂ tsp. fresh thyme leaves (or ¹/₂ tsp. dried thyme) to the fat before you add the flour.

Classic Vinaigrette Dressing

This is one of the world's most basic sauces. You'll find you can use it on so many foods you will give thanks that you know how to make it.

Level: Easy
Preparation time: 3–4 minutes
Cooking time: none
Yield: about ²/₃ cup

Can be done completely ahead

¹/₂ cup vegetable oil
3 TB. red wine vinegar
1¹/₂ tsp. Dijon mustard or ¹/₄ tsp. powdered mustard
1 medium garlic clove, minced (optional)

¹/₂ tsp. salt (or salt to taste)
¹/₈ tsp. freshly ground black pepper (or pepper to taste)

Combine the ingredients in a bowl and whisk them together until well blended, or place them in a covered container and shake them for several seconds until they are well blended. Taste the sauce for seasoning, and add salt and pepper as desired.

You can use vinaigrette as a salad dressing or marinade. It is such a versatile recipe you can change it in numerous ways to please your palate. Here are a few possibilities:

➤ Balsamic vinaigrette: use 2 TB. balsamic vinegar instead of the 3 TB. red wine vinegar.

➤ Shallot vinaigrette: add 1 minced shallot.

➤ Herb vinaigrette: add 1 TB. minced fresh herbs such as marjoram, oregano, basil, thyme, savory, chervil, and dill, or 1 tsp. dried herbs.

➤ Mustard vinaigrette: add 1¹/₂ tsp. more Dijon mustard.

➤ "French" dressing: add 1 TB. mayonnaise and ¹/₂ tsp. paprika.

➤ Lemon vinaigrette: use lemon juice instead of vinegar.

Cranberry Sauce

You won't find a simpler cranberry sauce. But don't save it for Thanksgiving dinner; it's also super with chicken and pork.

Level: Easy
Preparation time: 3–4 minutes (plus 1 hour refrigeration time)
Cooking time: 45–50 minutes
Yield: serves 6

Can be done completely ahead

1 12-oz. package cranberries (3 cups)
1¹/₂ cups sugar
3 TB. orange flavored brandy

Preheat the oven to 350 degrees. Wash and drain the berries and place them in a single layer in a baking dish. Add the sugar and toss the berries to coat all of them with sugar. Cover the dish with tight fitting aluminum foil. Bake 45–50 minutes. Remove the dish from the oven and remove the cover. Stir the berries and let them cool. Stir in the brandy. Chill at least one hour or until cold.

Creme Fraiche

Everyone will think you are a well-informed gourmet if you serve this marvelous, modern topping for fruit. And it's so easy to do!

Level: Easy
Preparation time: 1 minute (plus 12–15 hours standing time and 24 hours refrigeration time)
Cooking time: 2–3 minutes
Yield: about 1¼ cups

Can be done completely ahead

1 cup whipping cream, not ultra-pasteurized
¼ cup stirred plain yogurt or buttermilk

Combine the ingredients and whisk them until well blended. Pour the mixture into a saucepan. Cook over moderate heat about 2 minutes or until the chill is off and the mixture feels almost lukewarm. Pour the ingredients into a jar. Cover the jar and let the mixture stand at room temperature 12–15 hours or until it has thickened to the consistency of stirred yogurt. Refrigerate the sauce at least 24 hours to allow the flavors to mellow.

Kitchen Clue
Creme Fraiche is a gently tangy, slightly thick sauce that you can use on top of berries or chocolate cake for dessert or to enrich soups, gravy, and dozens of other dishes that call for cream sauce. You can use it as is or whip it slightly to make it a bit thicker.

Quick Breads, Brunches, and Breakfasts

Breakfast
Brunch
Breads
Bites

Quick Breads

Quick breads are suitable for breakfast, lunch, brunch, or dinner, for tea time and coffee breaks, and even for dessert when you want something less sweet. While they usually taste best within a day or so after you prepare them, you can freeze quick breads for a few weeks.

One quick note about quick breads: don't mix the dry ingredients that include baking soda or baking powder with the liquid ones such as milk or buttermilk until just before you are ready to bake the bread. The gas formed by the chemical reaction between them will dissipate, and your bread won't rise in the oven.

Buttermilk Biscuits

These are terrific for tea, breakfast, Sunday brunch, or with soup for dinner.

Level: Easy
Preparation time: 12–15 minutes
Cooking time: 20 minutes
Yield: 10–12 biscuits

Can be done completely ahead

2 cups all-purpose flour
2 tsp. baking powder
$^3/_4$ tsp. salt
$^1/_2$ tsp. baking soda

$^1/_2$ cup chilled butter, regular margarine,
   or shortening or a mixture of these
$^2/_3$ cup buttermilk

Preheat the oven to 400 degrees. Lightly grease a cookie sheet. Sift the flour, baking powder, salt, and baking soda into a bowl. Cut the butter into chunks and add the chunks to the flour mixture. Work the fat into the flour mixture using your fingers, a pastry blender, or two knives until the ingredients resemble crumbs. Pour in the buttermilk and gather the ingredients with your hands or a large wooden spoon to make a soft ball of dough. Lightly flour a pastry board or a clean work surface. Knead the ball of dough on the floured surface 10–12 times to make the dough slightly smoother. Press the dough or roll it to $^1/_2$" thickness. Use more flour on the board if the dough sticks. Cut out 10–12 circles with a cooky cutter or the top of a glass. You will have to reroll the dough to get the last 2 or 3 circles. Place the circles on the cookie sheet 1" apart for crisper, darker biscuits or closer together for fluffier, lighter biscuits. Bake 20 minutes or until the biscuits have risen and are browned on top.

Irish Soda Bread

Don't wait for St. Patrick's Day to make this easy, densely textured loaf. It's wonderful with coffee or tea or as an accompaniment to soup or salad.

Level: Easy
Preparation time: 10 minutes
Cooking time: 40–45 minutes
Yield: one loaf

Can be done completely ahead

3¹/₂ cups all-purpose flour
1 TB. brown sugar
³/₄ tsp. salt
1 tsp. baking soda

1¹/₂ cups buttermilk
¹/₂ cup currants (optional)
1 tsp. caraway seeds (optional)

Preheat the oven to 350 degrees. Lightly grease a baking sheet. Mix the flour, brown sugar, salt, and baking soda in a bowl. Add the buttermilk, and mix the ingredients until a soft dough has formed. If you use the currants and caraway seeds, work them in with your hands. Lightly flour a pastry board or a clean work surface. Knead the ball of dough on the floured surface 18–20 times to make the dough smoother. Use more flour on the board if the dough sticks. Shape the dough into a ball, and then flatten it slightly. Cut a small "X" on the top with the tip of a sharp knife. Place the dough on the baking sheet and bake it 40–45 minutes or until it is golden brown.

Banana Bread

This old-fashioned bread is delicious plain but even better when spread with softened cream cheese. It's good as a snack and is suitable for brunch.

Level: Easy
Preparation time: 10–12 minutes (plus 15 minutes cooling time)
Cooking time: about 1 hour
Yield: one loaf

Can be done completely ahead

2 cups all-purpose flour
1 tsp. baking soda
¹/₂ tsp. baking powder
¹/₂ tsp. salt
1 cup sugar
¹/₂ cup vegetable oil

2 large eggs
3 medium very ripe bananas
3 TB. milk
³/₄ tsp. vanilla extract
²/₃ cup finely chopped nuts (optional)

Preheat the oven to 350 degrees. Grease a 9"×5"×3" loaf pan. Sift the flour, baking soda, baking powder, and salt into a bowl and set it aside. Beat the sugar and vegetable oil with a hand mixer or electric mixer set at moderate speed for 2–3 minutes or until the mixture is light and fluffy. Beat the eggs in one at a time. Mash the bananas until they are mushy and add them. Beat the mixture thoroughly to incorporate the bananas. Gently stir in the flour mixture, stirring only enough to moisten the dry ingredients and blend them in. Gently stir in the milk, vanilla extract, and nuts (if used). Pour the batter into the prepared pan and bake the bread one hour or until a cake tester inserted into the center comes out clean. Cool the bread in the pan 15 minutes. Remove the bread from the pan and let it cool on a cake rack.

Kitchen Clue
This bread tastes better the second day. Wrap it in plastic wrap and let the flavors mellow.

Blueberry Muffins

These muffins are dense and cakey, and because you leave the berries whole, the muffins burst with the flavor of fresh fruit. This is a great food for breakfast or brunch.

Level: Intermediate
Preparation time: 12–15 minutes
Cooking time: 20–25 minutes
Yield: 12 muffins

Can be done completely ahead

5 TB. butter
1³/₄ cups all-purpose flour
¹/₂ cup sugar
³/₄ tsp. salt
1¹/₂ tsp. baking powder
¹/₂ tsp. baking soda

1 TB. freshly grated orange peel
1 cup buttermilk
1 large egg
¹/₂ tsp. vanilla extract
1 cup blueberries

Preheat the oven to 400 degrees. Grease 12 large muffin cups. Melt the butter and set it aside to cool slightly. Sift the flour, sugar, salt, baking powder, and baking soda into a bowl. Stir in the orange peel. Combine the buttermilk, egg, vanilla extract, and melted butter in a second bowl. Beat the liquid ingredients to form a uniformly colored mixture. Pour the liquid ingredients into the dry ones. Stir only enough to moisten all the dry ingredients. Do NOT beat into a smooth batter; this makes the muffins tough. Fold in the blueberries. Fill the muffin cups ¹/₂ to ²/₃ full with the batter. Bake 20–25 minutes or until a cake tester inserted into the center comes out clean.

Second Thoughts
If you don't like the flavor of orange, substitute 2 tsp. freshly grated lemon rind for the orange rind. Or you could leave out both and use ³/₄ tsp. cinnamon instead. If you use the cinnamon, sift it with the other dry ingredients.

Chocolate Macadamia Nut Bread

You'll get wows when you serve this rich and fudgy loaf. It's a fabulous choice for brunch, tea, or even dessert.

Level: Challenging
Preparation time: 15 minutes (plus 10 minutes cooling time)
Cooking time: 45 minutes
Yield: one loaf

Can be done completely ahead

2 oz. unsweetened chocolate
1³/₄ cups all-purpose flour
1¹/₂ tsp. baking soda
1 tsp. salt
1¹/₄ cups sugar

¹/₃ cup vegetable shortening
2 large eggs
2 tsp. vanilla extract
1¹/₄ cups buttermilk
¹/₂ cup coarsely chopped macadamia nuts

Preheat the oven to 350 degrees. Grease a 9"×5"×3" loaf pan. Melt the chocolate in the top part of a double boiler set over near-simmering water. Set the melted chocolate aside to cool. Sift the flour, baking soda, and salt into a bowl and set it aside. Beat the sugar and shortening together with a handmixer or electric mixer at moderate speed about 1 minute or until the ingredients are well blended. Add the eggs and vanilla extract and beat the mixture 1–2 minutes or until smooth and fluffy. Add ¹/₃ of the dry ingredients to the butter mixture and blend it in. Add ¹/₃ of the buttermilk and blend it in. Repeat this process two more times until all the flour and buttermilk are used. Scrape the sides of the bowl once or twice to make sure all of the batter is incorporated. Stir in the chocolate and the nuts and mix the ingredients for a short time until the color is uniform. Pour the batter into the prepared pan. Bake approximately 45 minutes or until a cake tester inserted into the center comes out clean. Cool the cake in the pan 10 minutes. Remove the cake from the pan and let it cool on a cake rack.

Breakfast and Brunch Dishes

Sometimes you want something more than a quick doughnut and a swallow of coffee for breakfast. While you may not have time for much more during the week, weekends are the ideal time to begin the day or spend the late morning with something good to eat. If you have weekend guests, you'll surely want to serve them something tasty but easy.

Michelle's Eggs

This recipe was invented by a teenage friend of the family who couldn't decide which she liked better: scrambled eggs or French toast. So she combined the two and came up with this winner.

Level: Easy
Preparation time: 3–4 minutes
Cooking time: 3 minutes
Yield: serves 2

Cannot be done ahead

3 large eggs
2 slices firm, homestyle white bread

1 TB. butter
pinch of salt and pepper

Beat the eggs in a small bowl and set them aside. Tear or cut the bread into bite size pieces. Heat the butter in a skillet over moderate heat. When the butter has melted and is foamy, add the eggs and the bread. Cook over moderate heat about 3 minutes, stirring the ingredients frequently with a fork until the eggs are set and the bread is lightly browned and glossy with the butter. Sprinkle the eggs with salt and pepper and serve.

Egg-White Omelet with Herbs

Everyone's eating egg-white omelets these days. You get the taste and texture of crispy egg without the extra fat from the yolk.

Level: Easy
Preparation time: 6–7 minutes
Cooking time: 3–4 minutes
Yield: serves 2

Cannot be done ahead

6 egg whites
2 tsp. water
2 TB. minced fresh parsley
1 TB. minced fresh herbs such as basil,
   marjoram, or oregano or 1 tsp. dried herbs
1 TB. snipped chives (or the green part of scallion)

$1/2$ tsp. salt (or salt to taste)
$1/8$ tsp. freshly ground black pepper (or pepper
   to taste)
$1^1/2$–2 TB. olive oil
1 tsp. butter (optional)

Beat the egg whites and water together in a bowl. Add the parsley, herbs, chives, salt, and pepper and mix them in. Heat the olive oil over moderate heat in a skillet. If you use the butter, melt it with the olive oil. Add the egg mixture. When you see the eggs begin to set at the edges (after about a minute), stir the mixture gently with a fork, bringing hardened edges toward the center to allow uncooked egg portions to reach the heat at the bottom of the pan. When eggs have nearly set, fold the omelet in half or thirds and cook it another half minute.

Second Thoughts
For something different, add 1 small chopped tomato. If you do this, cut the tomato in half crosswise and squeeze out the seeds first. Add it to the pan before you fold the omelet.

Salmon Studded Scrambled Eggs

This recipe started as an omelet—and it's certainly great that way. But on a lazy day, we discovered you could just mix all the ingredients together like scrambled eggs, and it tastes every bit as good.

Level: Easy
Preparation time: 3–4 minutes
Cooking time: 2 minutes
Yield: serves 6

Cannot be done ahead

8 large eggs
4 oz. smoked salmon
2 TB. snipped chives (or the green part of scallion)

1$^{1}/_{2}$ TB. butter
3 TB. cream cheese, cut into small pieces
freshly ground black pepper

Beat the eggs in a bowl. Chop the salmon and add it with the chives to the beaten eggs. Stir the ingredients. Heat the butter in a large skillet over moderate heat. When the butter has melted and looks foamy, add the eggs. Let the eggs cook for 15 seconds without stirring them. Lower the heat slightly, add the cream cheese, and cook the eggs (stirring frequently) for 1 minute or more or until they are set. Sprinkle the eggs with a little pepper and serve.

Pain Perdu

This is the New Orleans' version of French Toast, and you are in for a scrumptious surprise with this recipe. Serve it for brunch, and your guests will love you.

Level: Easy
Preparation time: 10–12 minutes (plus 4–5 minutes soaking time)
Cooking time: 2–4 minutes per slice
Yield: serves 4

*Can be done ahead up to the * in the instructions*

5 large eggs
$^{1}/_{2}$ cup sugar
$^{1}/_{2}$ cup milk
2 TB. orange flavored brandy

1 tsp. finely grated lemon or orange peel (optional)
12 slices of French or Italian bread
 (approximately), $^{1}/_{2}$" thick
butter for frying

Beat the eggs, sugar, milk, brandy, and lemon peel with an electric beater or whisk for 1–2 minutes or until they are thick and foamy. Pour the mixture into a shallow dish or a pan big enough to hold the bread slices. Add the bread slices and let them soak 4–5 minutes, turning them occasionally, or until they are thoroughly soaked through.

* Preheat a griddle or large skillet over moderate heat. Lightly butter the pan (with a teaspoon or two of butter) before you make each batch of bread. When the butter has melted and looks foamy, add the soaked bread slices and cook them 1–2 minutes or until the bottoms are golden brown. Flip the bread with a rigid spatula and cook the slices another 1–2 minutes or until the bottoms are golden brown. Serve approximately three slices per person.

Kitchen Clue
The number of bread slices depends on the width of bread. The most tender Pain Perdu is made with wider French or Italian bread.

The name Pain Perdu actually is a misnomer. It means "lost bread." This dish, which is similar to French Toast, was invented in an effort to use up stale bread that might otherwise be lost but which, in fact, isn't lost at all.

Noodle Casserole

This dish is ideal for a buffet-style party or any informal get-together, whether for brunch or in the late afternoon.

Level: Intermediate
Preparation time: 12–15 minutes (plus 10 minutes soaking time)
Cooking time: about 45 minutes (plus time to cook the egg noodles)
Yield: serves 4

Can be done completely ahead

1/3 cup dried mushrooms
hot water
1 lb. smoked turkey or boiled ham
2 TB. butter or margarine
1 small onion, chopped (about 1/4 cup)
6 sun-dried tomatoes, chopped
1/2 lb. cooked egg noodles (cooked according
  to package directions)

1/4 tsp. salt (or salt to taste)
1/4 tsp. freshly ground black pepper (or pepper to taste)
2 large eggs, beaten
1 cup light cream or half and half
1/2 cup grated Swiss or Monterey Jack cheese

Preheat the oven to 350 degrees. Lightly butter a casserole dish. Place the mushrooms in a small bowl, cover them with hot water, and let them soften (about 10 minutes). Rinse and drain the mushrooms and set them aside. (If you use shiitake mushrooms, you will have to cut off and discard the tough inedible stems. If you use large mushrooms, chop or slice them.) Cut the turkey or ham into 1/2" dice. Heat the butter over moderate heat in a skillet. When the butter has melted and looks foamy, add the onion and cook it 3–4 minutes or until it has wilted. Add the mushrooms, turkey or ham, and sun-dried tomatoes and cook another minute. Remove the pan from the heat and set it aside. Place the noodles in a bowl and add the meat mixture, salt, pepper, eggs, and cream. Stir ingredients to coat all the noodles with the liquids. Pour the mixture into the prepared dish. Top with the cheese. Bake 40 minutes or until top is crusty and golden brown.

Baked Stuffed Apples with Yogurt Sauce

Some people eat baked apples for dessert, and that's fine. But they also make a super breakfast or brunch food. The yogurt sauce isn't necessary, but it sure is delicious!

Level: Easy
Preparation time: 15 minutes
Cooking time: 45 minutes
Yield: serves 4

Can be done completely ahead

4 large baking apples
half a lemon
1/2 cup raisins
2 TB. finely chopped almonds
3 TB. maple syrup
1 cup orange juice

yogurt sauce:
1 cup plain yogurt
2 TB. orange marmalade
1 TB. orange juice
2 tsp. maple syrup
cinnamon or freshly grated nutmeg

Preheat the oven to 375 degrees. Wash the apples and remove the core with an apple corer or small knife, leaving about 1/2" of the core on the bottom. Peel the apples halfway down from the top and rub the apple with the cut side of the lemon. Mix the raisins, almonds, 1 TB. maple syrup, and 5 TB. of the orange juice. Place this mixture into the apple hollows. Combine the remaining orange juice with the remaining maple syrup and pour equal amounts over each apple. Basting the apples every 10–12 minutes with the pan juices, bake 45 minutes or until the apples are tender. Serve the apples warm or at room temperature with the yogurt sauce. To make the sauce, simply mix all the ingredients together thoroughly. Keep the yogurt sauce chilled until you are ready to serve it.

Desserts

Lots of people think dessert is the best part of the meal. In fact, some people say they would rather skip dinner and go right to dessert. How come? Dessert is pure indulgence. With dessert we don't focus on nutrition or think about what's "good for us." Eating dessert means satisfying a sweet tooth, indulging in the pleasurable. And there is an enormous variety of recipes too. Your dessert can be as diverse as a homey pie or an elegant mousse. You can serve a tall and stately cake or just some simple poached fruit. Or perhaps your choice will be just a stack of cookies that you dunk into milk. Whatever. This is the course that everyone loves.

Chocolate Fudgie Brownies

These are moist, dark ultra-fudgie brownies. Better make two recipes of these because they get gobbled up quickly.

Level: Easy
Preparation time: 10 minutes (plus about 45 minutes cooling time)
Cooking time: 30 minutes
Yield: makes 16

Can be done completely ahead

4 squares unsweetened chocolate
$^1/_3$ cup butter
2 large eggs
1 cup sugar

$^1/_2$ cup all-purpose flour
$^1/_4$ tsp. salt
1 tsp. vanilla extract
$^1/_2$ cup finely chopped nuts (optional)

Preheat the oven to 350 degrees. Lightly grease an 8" square baking pan. Melt the chocolate and butter together in the top part of a double boiler set over barely simmering water. When the ingredients have melted (about 3–4 minutes), blend them thoroughly and remove the pan from the heat and separate the top part of the double boiler from the bottom. Combine the eggs and sugar in a large bowl and beat them with an electric mixer set at moderate speed 2–3 minutes, or until the mixture is as thick as stirred yogurt and as pale as cream-colored daffodils. Add the flour, salt, vanilla extract, and nuts, if used, and stir to blend them in. Add the chocolate mixture and stir the ingredients to blend them in thoroughly. Pour the batter into the prepared pan. Bake 30 minutes. Cool the brownies in the pan. Cut them into 16 squares.

One Bowl Cocoa Fudge Cake with Fudge Frosting

This rich and fudgy dessert creates quite a dilemma: you don't know whether to eat the cake part or the frosting part first or whether to eat them together. And if you get down to your last bite, which will it be: cake or frosting?

Level: Intermediate
Preparation time: about 15 minutes for the cake (plus 10 minutes cooling time); about 5 minutes for the frosting (plus 15–20 minutes cooling time)
Cooking time: about 30 minutes for cake; about 5 minutes for frosting
Yield: serves 8–10

Can be done completely ahead

Cake:

2 cups cake flour
1^1/$_2$ cups sugar
^{2}/$_3$ cup unsweetened cocoa powder
1^1/$_2$ tsp. baking soda
1 tsp. salt

1^1/$_2$ cups buttermilk (low-fat or skim)
^{1}/$_2$ cup vegetable shortening
2 large eggs
1^1/$_2$ tsp. vanilla extract

Frosting:

12 oz. semisweet chocolate
1 cup sour cream

pinch of salt
1 tsp. vanilla extract

Preheat the oven to 350 degrees. Lightly grease two 9" cake pans. Sift the cake flour, sugar, cocoa powder, baking soda, and salt into a large bowl. Add the buttermilk and shortening. Beat the mixture with an electric mixer set at moderate speed 2 minutes, scraping down the sides of the bowl occasionally with a rubber spatula. Add the eggs and vanilla extract and beat another 2 minutes, scraping down the sides of the bowl occasionally with a rubber spatula. Pour the batter into the prepared pans. Bake 30–35 minutes, or until a cake tester inserted into the middle of the cake comes out clean. Let the cake cool in the pans 10 minutes, then invert the layers onto a cake rack to cool completely. Frost the layers and outside with fudge frosting. After you cut the cake, store the uneaten portions in the refrigerator.

To make the frosting, melt the chocolate in the top part of a double boiler set over barely simmering water. When the chocolate has completely melted, remove the pan from the heat and remove the top part with the chocolate from the double boiler. Add the sour cream, salt, and vanilla extract to the chocolate. Beat the ingredients vigorously with a whisk until the mixture is smooth. Let the frosting cool 15–20 minutes or until it is of spreading consistency. Spread about a half cup of the frosting between the layers and the rest on the top and around the sides of the cake.

Old-Fashioned Chocolate Pudding

Guaranteed to taste much better than the boxed kind.

Level: Easy
Preparation time: 5 minutes
Cooking time: 8–10 minutes
Yield: serves 4–6

Can be done completely ahead

3 cups milk
^{2}/$_3$ cup sugar
^{1}/$_3$ cup cornstarch

^{1}/$_3$ cup unsweetened cocoa powder
^{1}/$_4$ tsp. salt
1^1/$_2$ tsp. vanilla extract

Heat 3 cups milk in a saucepan over moderate heat 5–6 minutes, or until small bubbles appear around the edges of the pan. Remove the pan from the heat. Sift the sugar, cornstarch, cocoa powder, and salt into a bowl. Add a half cup of the heated milk and stir the ingredients to make a smooth paste. Return the paste to the heated milk. Stir the ingredients a minute or so to blend them well. Return the pan to the heat and cook 3–4 minutes, stirring constantly, or until the pudding is thick and smooth. If the pudding starts to bubble, turn the heat lower. Pour the pudding into a serving dish or individual serving dishes and let it cool. If you want, you can prepare the pudding ingredients in the top part of a double boiler set over simmering water. It will take several minutes longer, but you're less likely to overcook the pudding.

Kitchen Clue
Some people like chocolate pudding with a "skin" on top. If you are one of those people, do not cover the pudding with plastic wrap until it is cool.

Chocolate Mousse

This rich, dark mousse is a perennial favorite.

Level: Intermediate
Preparation time: 10–15 minutes (plus 1 hour refrigeration time)
Cooking time: about 10 minutes
Yield: serves 4

Can be done completely ahead

8 oz. semisweet chocolate
2 TB. confectioner's sugar
2 egg yolks

2 TB. rum or very strong coffee
1 TB. water
1¼ cups whipping cream

Put the chocolate in the top part of a double boiler set over barely simmering water. Stir the chocolate for 3–4 minutes, or until it has melted. Stir the confectioner's sugar and egg yolks in with a whisk. Add the rum or coffee and water, and stir them in with a whisk. Remove the top part of the double boiler from the heat. Set the mixture aside. Whip the cream until it stands in soft peaks. Fold most of it into the chocolate mixture. Reserve about ½ cup of the whipped cream for garnish. Spoon the mousse into individual serving dishes. Refrigerate at least one hour. Garnish with a spoonful of the reserved whipped cream. You can make this ahead and keep it in your fridge for 3–4 days (if it doesn't tempt you to eat it all before you have to serve it).

Two Spirited Parfaits

These parfaits are perfect for adults who adore ice cream but love a spirited sauce.

Level: Easy
Preparation time: about 5 minutes (plus 5–8 minutes refrigeration time)
Cooking time: one minute for the coffee apricot parfait
Yield: each recipe serves 2 people

Cannot be done ahead

Coffee Apricot Parfait

½ cup apricot preserves
2 TB. orange flavored liqueur
2 cups coffee ice cream

¼ cup finely chopped pistachio or cashew nuts
½ cup whipped cream

To make a sauce, place the preserves and the liqueur in a small skillet and heat them over low heat about one minute, or until the preserves are warm. Stir the ingredients and set them aside. In each of two parfait glasses (or other tall glasses), make two layers of the ingredients as follows: half the ice cream, half the sauce, half the nuts, remaining ice cream, sauce, and nuts. Top with the whipped cream. Place in the freezer for 5–8 minutes.

Irish Cream Parfait

2 cups chocolate ice cream
1 cup fresh raspberries (or use frozen, drained berries)
$^1/_2$ cup Irish Cream liqueur

$^1/_4$ cup chopped almonds, preferably toasted almonds
$^1/_2$ cup whipped cream

In each of two parfait glasses, make two layers of the ingredients as follows: half the ice cream, half the berries, half the liqueur, half the nuts, remaining ice cream, berries, liqueur, and nuts. Top with the whipped cream. Place in the freezer for 5–8 minutes.

If you prefer not to use alcoholic spirits, you can substitute water or apricot juice for the sauce in the coffee parfait recipe. Instead of the Irish Cream liqueur, substitute canned chocolate sauce.

Kiwi Fruit Fool

Level: Easy
Preparation time: 15 minutes (plus 45 minutes refrigeration time)
Cooking time: 6–8 minutes
Yield: serves 8

Can be done completely ahead

6 kiwi fruit
2 TB. butter or margarine
$^1/_3$ cup sugar

2 TB. unflavored brandy
2 cups whipping cream

Peel and slice the kiwi fruit. Heat the butter over moderate heat in a skillet. When the butter melts and begins to look foamy, add the sliced kiwi fruit and the sugar. Cook 4–5 minutes, or until the kiwi fruit is soft and sugar begins to brown faintly. Add the brandy and cook one more minute. Remove the pan from the heat. Puree the ingredients in a food processor, a blender, or by forcing it through a sieve or strainer. Refrigerate the mixture until it is thoroughly chilled (about 45 minutes). Whip the cream until it stands in peaks. Fold the kiwi mixture into the whipped cream. Pour the mixture into individual dessert dishes or into a pretty serving bowl or 6-cup souffle dish.

Kitchen Clue
You can make this dessert as much as two days ahead.

Apple Brown Betty

When this cooks, your entire house will have the most wonderful perfume of apples and cinnamon.

Level: Easy
Preparation time: about 25 minutes
Cooking time: 50–60 minutes
Yield: serves 6

Can be done completely ahead

5–6 pie apples, such as Granny Smiths, Rhode Island
  Greenings, or Golden Delicious (about 5 cups of fruit)
half a lemon
4 cups $^1/_2$"-diced homestyle white bread,
  trimmed of crusts

$^3/_4$ cup brown sugar
$^1/_2$ cup melted butter
$^3/_4$ tsp. cinnamon
$^1/_4$ tsp. freshly ground nutmeg
pinch of salt

Preheat the oven to 375 degrees. Peel the apples and remove the cores. Cut the apples into bite-sized pieces. Squeeze the lemon juice over the apples. Place the apples in a baking dish. Combine the diced bread, brown sugar, melted butter, cinnamon, nutmeg, and salt in a bowl. Toss the ingredients to coat the bread completely. Put the coated bread on top of the apples. Bake the betty 50–60 minutes, or until the top is golden brown and crusty. You can make betty with just about any fruit or mixture of fruits, such as nectarines, peaches and blueberries, or pears. You need about 5 cups of bite-size fruit pieces.

How to Poach Fruit

When you learn how to poach fruit, you can make more dessert dishes than you can imagine. It is one of the most versatile recipes around. Depending on how ripe it is when you cook it, you can store the poached fruit in the fridge from one to three days in the poaching fluid.

Level: Intermediate
Preparation time: 15–20 minutes, depending on the fruit (plus cooling time)
Cooking time: 2–15 minutes, depending on the fruit
Yield: one whole fruit will serve 1–2 people

Can be done completely ahead

1¹/₂ cups sugar
6 cups water
3 strips of lemon peel

1 4" piece of vanilla bean or 1 TB. vanilla extract
fruit

Combine the sugar, water, lemon peel, and vanilla bean in a saucepan. Bring the mixture to a boil over high heat. Reduce the heat to low-moderate and cook 10 minutes. Add the fruit. The fruit must be completely immersed in the poaching liquid. Using a smaller pan helps. Or, you can cut large fruit such as pears or peaches in half (remove the seeds or pit). Cook the fruit until it is fork tender. The time depends on the fruit. Remove the pan from the heat and let the fruit cool in the poaching fluid. The best fruit choices for poaching are pears, peaches, apricots, plums, nectarines, and blueberries. You can peel the fruit before you poach it, but you don't have to. The skin of peaches and pears comes off easily after the fruit is poached. To serve the fruit, remove the fruit to serving dishes (cut the fruit first if you wish and remove seeds, pit, core, and so on). Strain the poaching liquid. You can serve the poaching liquid as is, on top of the fruit, or you can boil it down over high heat for several minutes, until it reaches a syrupy consistency. Let the liquid cool and pour it over the fruit.

You can season the poaching liquid in several delicious ways if you want to make a change now and then. Try new versions by adding the following to the liquid:

➤ 3" piece of cinnamon stick
➤ 1 cup red wine
➤ peel from half an orange
➤ a chunk of fresh ginger or several slices of crystallized ginger
➤ 4–5 cracked cardamom pods

Kitchen Clue
This amount of poaching liquid will be enough for up to 1¹/₂ lbs. of fruit. If you use vanilla extract in a recipe instead of vanilla bean, do *not* add it until you remove the pan from the heat. Heat dissipates the intensity of extract.

Peach Melba

Level: Intermediate
Preparation time: 20 minutes, plus time to poach and cool the peaches
Cooking time: none
Yield: serves 6

*Can be done ahead up to the * in the instructions*

6 poached peaches
  (see recipe for poached fruit), cooled
2 boxes of fresh raspberries
  (or 1¹/₂ cups frozen, drained berries)
2¹/₂ TB. sugar

2 TB. orange flavored liqueur
  or Kirschwasser (optional)
6 scoops vanilla ice cream
¹/₃ cup lightly toasted chopped almonds (optional)

Peel the peaches, cut them into halves, and remove the pits. Place two halves in each of 6 dessert dishes. Crush the berries and mix them with 2¹/₂ TB. of the sugar and the orange flavored liqueur (if you use it). Set this mixture aside. (If you use frozen packaged berries that are presweetened, omit the sugar.)

* Place the scoops of ice cream on top of the peaches. Pour equal amounts of the raspberry mixture over the ice cream. Sprinkle each portion with equal amounts of the toasted almonds, if you like.

Fresh Fruit with Almond-Cheese Dip

This is a light dessert when you don't feel like going heavy on cake or pastry.

Level: Easy
Preparation time: 5 minutes
Cooking time: none
Yield: serves 4

*Can be done ahead up to the * in the instructions*

8 oz. package cream cheese at room
 temperature (low-fat is fine)
1/3 cup confectioner's sugar
1/3 cup light cream or half-and-half

1 TB. lemon juice
1/2 tsp. almond extract
sliced fruit such as apples, peaches, or nectarines,
 or cut up bananas, whole strawberries, or grapes

Combine the cream cheese, confectioner's sugar, cream, lemon juice, and almond extract in a bowl and mix the ingredients until they are well blended.

* When you are ready to serve, slice the fruit and place it on a platter. Each person dips individual slices or whole pieces of fresh fruit in the dip.

Dipped Strawberries

This one is everybody's favorite!

Level: Easy
Preparation time: 20 minutes (plus time to let the chocolate harden)
Cooking time: 3–4 minutes
Yield: about 24

Can be done completely ahead

1 pint box of strawberries
6 oz. semisweet chocolate
1 TB. shortening

Rinse the berries quickly under cold water but do *not* remove the green hulls. Dry the berries thoroughly with paper towels. Melt the chocolate and shortening together in the top part of a double boiler set over barely simmering water. When the chocolate has completely melted (about 3–4 minutes), stir the mixture and remove the pan from the heat. Dip the tips of the strawberries in the hot chocolate mixture to coat about half a berry. Place the berries on waxed paper or foil to cool. The chocolate will harden as it cools. Do *not* store the berries in the refrigerator.

Second Thoughts
While this confection is stunning and delicious as is, you can fancy it up even more. Here's how: put some ground nuts (they are better if they are toasted ground nuts, but need not be) on a plate. After you dip the berries in the chocolate, roll the chocolate part in the ground nuts, and then set the berries aside to cool and harden.

How to Make Pie Crust

Don't let yourself be intimidated by pie crust. Follow the recipe step by step, and you'll see that you can do it and be successful. Try not to handle the dough too much—it makes the crust tough.

Level: Challenging
Preparation time: 20 minutes (plus 30 minutes standing time)
Cooking time: none
Yield: enough for a two-crust, 9" deep dish or regular 10" pie

Can be done completely ahead

2 1/2 cups all-purpose flour
1 tsp. sugar
3/4 tsp. salt
1 tsp. freshly grated lemon peel (optional)

1/2 cup cold butter
1/3 cup cold vegetable shortening
4–5 TB. milk, approximately

Combine the flour, sugar, salt, and lemon peel, if used, in a large bowl. Cut the butter and shortening into chunks and add the chunks to the flour mixture. Work the fat into the flour mixture using your fingers, a pastry blender, or two knives until the ingredients resemble crumbs. You also can use a food processor. In that case, add the ingredients to the work bowl and give the ingredients 24–36 quick, short pulses, enough for the mixture to resemble coarse meal. Add the milk using only enough to gather pastry into a soft ball of dough. (Start by using 4 TB. of the milk.) If you use a food processor, add 4 TB. of milk and process the ingredients for several seconds until the mixture forms itself into a ball of dough. Add the remaining milk, if necessary, to help shape the dough. Cut the dough in half and flatten each half to make a disk shape. Wrap the dough in plastic wrap and let it stand at least 30 minutes.

Here are some interesting facts about pie dough:

➤ You can refrigerate pie dough for several days, or you can freeze it for up to 2 months. Put the wrapped dough in a plastic bag for freezing.

➤ You use the minimum amount of liquid to gather the ingredients into a ball of dough because the less liquid you use, the more tender and flaky the pastry will be.

➤ The addition of lemon peel gives the dough a pleasant fragrance that is particularly nice for fruit pies. You can use $1/2$ tsp. cinnamon in addition to or instead of the lemon peel.

➤ You can use another liquid besides milk. Most recipes call for ice water. Milk is more enriching and gives a better color. Or use fruit juice, (especially for fruit pie), melted vanilla ice cream, or even plain yogurt or sour cream (if you like a really rich dough).

➤ The reason you must let the dough stand after you prepare it is to let the flour gluten relax. If you don't, the dough can be tough. This is particularly important for food processor dough.

➤ You can halve the dough (for a streusel top pie, for example), but since you can freeze the dough, why not prepare a full recipe and use the other half for a second pie?

Lily Vail's Famous Old-Fashioned Apple Pie

This is a simple, lightly seasoned, not-overly sweet pie that is a classic you'll find yourself preparing over and over. We love it warm with cold melting ice cream oozing into the crust and fruit.

Level: Challenging
Preparation time: 20–25 minutes (plus 50 minutes to make the dough; see recipe for pie crust)
Cooking time: 50–60 minutes
Yield: one 9" deep dish or 10" regular depth pie

Can be done completely ahead

3 lbs. pie apples, peeled, cored and sliced, (about 8–9 apples)	$3/4$ tsp. cinnamon
	2 TB. flour
$1/2$ cup sugar	1 recipe pie dough
2 TB. lemon juice	1 TB. butter

Preheat the oven to 375 degrees. Combine the apple slices, sugar, lemon juice, cinnamon, and flour in a large bowl. Toss the ingredients to coat all the apple slices. Lightly flour a pastry board or a clean work surface. With a rolling pin, roll one half of the dough on the floured surface into a circle about $1/8$" thick, making sure the circle is larger than the pie pan by about an inch. Use more flour on the board if the dough sticks. Place the dough in a 9" deep dish or regular 10" pie pan. Pour the apple filling into the dough-lined pan. Cut the butter into small pieces and dot the top of the filling with them. Roll out the remaining dough and place it over the filling. Gather the bottom and top crusts together, roll them gently, then press the dough onto the edge of the pie pan. Crimp or flute the edge with your fingers or press it with the flat, back part of a fork. (If the edge seems too thick, remove some of the dough.) Make air holes in the dough with the tines of a fork or the tip of a sharp knife. Bake the pie 50–60 minutes, or until pastry is golden brown.

continues

continued

Here are some interesting facts about apple pie:

➤ The best apples to use for pie are Rhode Island Greenings, Granny Smiths, Newtown Pippin, Northern Spy, Golden Delicious, Idared, and Stayman.

➤ You only need the simplest seasoning; otherwise, you may overwhelm the delicate apple flavor. If you like you can add $^1/_2$ tsp. nutmeg or 1 tsp. freshly grated lemon peel though.

➤ You can vary apple pie by adding 1 cup raisins or other cut up dried fruit or 1 cup of cranberries (in this case, increase the sugar to 1 cup).

➤ You can freeze apple pie for several months. Double wrap it in plastic wrap. Thaw the pie completely, then warm it in a preheated 375 degree oven for about 15 minutes to freshen the crust. If you make the pie in a glass pan, you can defrost it by microwave.

➤ You can top pie with a streusel crust instead of pie dough. See the recipe for Blueberry Crumb Pie.

Blueberry Crumb Pie

This is light and fresh with a lot of real blueberry flavor. The berries aren't too sweet, and keeping them whole gives this pie great texture.

Level: Intermediate
Preparation time: 15 minutes
Cooking time: 50–60 minutes
Yield: one 9" pie
Can be done completely ahead

Streusel crust:
$^3/_4$ cup flour
$^1/_3$ cup sugar
6 TB. butter

Filling:
5 cups blueberries
$^1/_2$ cup sugar
5 TB. flour
$^3/_4$ tsp. cinnamon
$^1/_4$ tsp. salt
2 TB. lemon juice
1 pie shell, unbaked (frozen, store-bought, 9" deep)

Preheat the oven to 375 degrees. To make the streusel crust, combine the flour and sugar in a mixing bowl. Work the fat into the flour mixture using your fingers, a pastry blender, or two knives until the ingredients resemble crumbs. You also can use a food processor. In that case, add the ingredients to the work bowl and give the ingredients 18–24 quick pulses, enough for the mixture to resemble coarse meal. Set the streusel aside. Mix the blueberries, sugar, flour, cinnamon, salt, and lemon juice in a large bowl. Pour the blueberry filling into the pie shell lined pan. Cover the top with the streusel. Bake the pie 50–60 minutes, or until top is golden brown.

Kitchen Clue
You can use two "pint" boxes of blueberries.
Although a liquid pint equals 2 cups, a dry pint of blueberries from most markets is about $2^1/_2$ cups. You can freeze this pie 3–4 months.

Kentucky Bourbon Pecan Pie

If you have a sweet tooth, this is for you! It's got a crunchy crust, but it's soft and sweet beneath.

Level: Easy
Preparation time: 8 minutes
Cooking time: 45–50 minutes
Yield: one 9" pie

Can be done completely ahead

3 large eggs
1 cup light brown sugar
1/2 cup corn syrup or cane syrup
1 TB. all-purpose flour
1/4 cup melted butter

2 TB. bourbon
pinch of salt
1 cup broken pecans, about 4 oz.
1 pie shell, unbaked (frozen, store-bought, 9" deep)

Preheat the oven to 350 degrees. Beat the eggs with a whisk or electric mixer set at moderate speed 1–2 minutes, or until they are well beaten and frothy looking. Add the sugar, corn syrup, and flour and beat the ingredients 2 minutes. Add the melted butter, bourbon, and salt and beat another minute. Stir in the pecans. Pour the mixture into the pie shell. Bake 45–50 minutes, or until the top is golden brown and crusty looking.

> **Second Thoughts**
> You can substitute cashew nuts for the pecans and maple syrup for the corn syrup. If you prefer to make your own pie shell, use 1/2 of the master recipe. Roll out the dough and place it into a pie pan. Crimp or flute the outer edges onto the pan.

Pumpkin Ice Cream Pie in Graham Cracker Crust

This is a refreshing dessert after Thanksgiving dinner, but it's just as suitable in the spring when you're not expecting "pumpkin" anything.

Level: Easy
Preparation time: 10 minutes
Cooking time: none
Yield: one 9" pie

Can be done completely ahead

1 1/2 cups packaged graham cracker crumbs
6 TB. melted butter
1 quart softened vanilla ice cream
1 cup plain mashed pumpkin, (canned is fine, but do NOT use "pumpkin pie mix")
1/2 cup brown sugar

1/2 tsp. ground ginger
1/2 tsp. cinnamon
1/2 tsp. freshly ground nutmeg
1/4 tsp. ground allspice or cloves
1/4 tsp. salt

Combine the graham cracker crumbs and melted butter in a bowl. Mix the ingredients well to make sure all the crumbs are coated with butter. Press the crumbs onto the bottom and sides of a 9" pie pan. Chill the crust at least 30 minutes. (Crumb crusts made from cookies must be firm before you put a filling in, otherwise they get soggy. Chilling the crust is one way to firm them, but you can also bake the crust 10 minutes in a preheated 350 degree oven. In that case, be sure the crust is cool before you add the filling.) Mix the ice cream, pumpkin, brown sugar, ginger, cinnamon, nutmeg, allspice or cloves, and salt in a bowl. Pour the filling into the chilled crust. Freeze the pie at least 30 minutes, or until it is firm.

> **Second Thoughts**
> Instead of graham cracker crumbs, you can make this crust with gingersnaps or chocolate wafers.

How to Make Whipped Cream

Once you make fresh homemade whipped cream, you can use it on practically every dessert from apple pie to chocolate cake to ice cream sundaes. It isn't difficult to make and is really quick. Then you get to lick the beaters and scrape the bowl. This version is not cloyingly sweet. You only need a bit of sugar.

Level: Easy
Preparation time: 2 minutes
Cooking time: 10 minutes refrigeration time for the bowl and beaters
Yield: 2 cups

Can be done completely ahead

1 cup heavy cream (preferably not ultra pasteurized)
  or whipping cream
1 tsp. granulated sugar

Put the bowl and the beaters you will use to beat the cream in the refrigerator for 10 minutes. It is best to use a handmixer with curvy beaters or an electric mixer with a whisk attachment. Start beating the cream at slow speed, and then increase the speed gradually, adding the sugar after the cream has thickened slightly. Beat the cream only until the mixture stands in soft peaks. Do not let the mixture curdle by beating it too long.

Second Thoughts
You can vary the flavor by adding the following ingredients to the whipped cream as you beat it:

- ➤ 1 tsp. vanilla extract
- ➤ 1 TB. flavored brandy
- ➤ 2 tsp. instant coffee powder dissolved in some of the cream

Mom's Best Peanut Butter Cookies

No one can resist these. They're the kind of cookies that disappear from the cookie jar. If you freeze these, you can eat them straight out of the freezer.

Level: Easy
Preparation time: about 30 minutes
Cooking time: 16–20 minutes per cookie sheet
Yield: about 8 dozen

Can be done completely ahead

$2^1/_2$ cups all-purpose flour
2 tsp. baking soda
1 tsp. salt
1 cup white sugar

1 cup brown sugar
1 cup peanut butter
1 cup vegetable shortening
2 large eggs

Preheat the oven to 350 degrees. Lightly grease a cookie sheet. Combine the flour, baking soda, salt, white sugar, and brown sugar in a large bowl and beat them with a handmixer or electric mixer set at moderate speed about 1 minute, or until the mixture is uniform and ingredients evenly distributed. Add the peanut butter, shortening, and eggs and beat the mixture about 2 minutes starting at low speed, then gradually switching to moderately high speed, or until a uniform dough forms. Take off pieces of dough and shape them into balls about $1^1/_2$" in diameter. Flatten the balls between your palms. Place the cookies on the prepared sheet, leaving an inch of space between them. Press the top of each cookie with the flat, bottom side of a fork, then press again to make a crisscross design on top of each cookie. Bake 16–20 minutes, or until cookies are richly browned and crispy.

Kitchen Clue
You can freeze these cookies in a tightly covered plastic container for about 6 months.

Gingersnaps

These cookies are gently spicy and are especially good when the weather turns colder. Store extra cookies in the freezer so you can crumble them to make pie shells that call for a crumb crust.

Level: Easy
Preparation time: 25–30 minutes
Cooking time: about 12 minutes per cookie sheet
Yield: about 6 dozen

Can be done completely ahead

1 cup vegetable shortening	$^1/_4$ tsp. salt
1 cup sugar	1 tsp. cinnamon
1 large egg	$^3/_4$ tsp. powdered ginger
$^1/_4$ cup molasses	$^3/_4$ tsp. ground cloves
2 cups all-purpose flour	$^1/_8$ tsp. freshly grated nutmeg
1 TB. baking soda	3 TB. additional sugar for rolling cookies

Preheat the oven to 350 degrees. Lightly grease a cookie sheet. Combine the shortening and one cup of sugar in a large bowl and beat them with a handmixer or electric mixer set at moderate speed 1–2 minutes, or until the mixture is light and fluffy. Scrape the sides of the bowl with a rubber spatula. Add the egg and molasses and beat the ingredients to blend them in. Scrape the sides of the bowl again. Add the flour, baking soda, salt, cinnamon, ginger, cloves, and nutmeg. Beat the ingredients 1–2 minutes, or until the mixture is smooth and uniform. Take off pieces of dough and shape them into balls about 1" in diameter. Roll the balls in the additional sugar. Place the balls on the prepared sheet, leaving an inch of space between them. Bake 12 minutes, or until cookies are flat and crispy looking with lines on the surface.

Kitchen Clue
You can freeze these cookies in a tightly covered plastic container for about 6 months.

Fannies

When we were growing up, we thought everyone called these kind of cookies "Fannies." Little did we know that this was one version of a recipe for classic butter cookies. However, this particular recipe came from the recipe files of one of our ancestors whose name happened to be "Fanny."

Level: Intermediate
Preparation time: about 25 minutes
Cooking time: about 25 minutes per cookie sheet
Yield: about 5 dozen

Can be done completely ahead

$^1/_2$ lb. butter, cut into 2" chunks	$^1/_2$ tsp. salt
$^1/_2$ cup sugar	1 tsp. vanilla extract
2 cups all-purpose flour	1 can or jar of apricot "lekvar," "butter,"
2 egg yolks	or "cake filling," or use jam or preserves

Preheat the oven to 350 degrees. Lightly grease a cookie sheet. Combine the butter and sugar in a large bowl and beat them with a handmixer or electric mixer set at moderate speed about 1 minute, or until the mixture is light and fluffy. Add the flour and mix at moderate speed 1–2 minutes, or until it is almost incorporated. Add the egg

continues

301

continued

yolks, salt, and vanilla extract. Mix the ingredients 2 minutes, or until a uniform dough forms. (You may have to scrape the sides of the bowl and the beater with a rubber spatula.) Take off pieces of dough and shape them into balls about 1" in diameter. Flatten the balls between your palms. Press each circle with your thumb to make an indentation in the center. Place the cookies on the prepared sheet, leaving an inch of space between them. Fill the thumb print spaces with a small amount of the apricot lekvar (you'll use about ¹/₂ cup in all). Bake about 25 minutes, or until the cookies are golden brown.

What Is It?
Lekvar is a sweet fruit spread that's thicker than jam. You can use it for cookies and between cake layers.

You can freeze these cookies in a tightly covered plastic container for about 6 months.

Lemon Bars

These are slightly tangy, slightly sweet cookies that are exceptionally tasty with tea. But you should also try dunking them in milk or eating them with cappuccino.

Level: Intermediate
Preparation time: 12–15 minutes
Cooking time: 40–45 minutes
Yield: 30 cookies

Can be done completely ahead

Dough:
1³/₄ cups all-purpose flour
¹/₂ cup confectioner's sugar
1 cup butter or margarine, cut into small chunks
  (do not use low-fat margarine)

Topping:
4 large eggs
1¹/₂ cups sugar
6 TB. lemon juice
¹/₄ cup flour
¹/₂ tsp. baking powder

Preheat the oven to 350 degrees. Combine the flour and confectioner's sugar in a bowl. Work the butter into the flour mixture using your fingers, a pastry blender, or two knives until the ingredients resemble crumbs. You can also use a food processor. In that case, add the ingredients to the work bowl and pulse the ingredients 15–20 times, or until the mixture resembles coarse meal. Press the crumbs onto the bottom of a 9"×13" baking pan. Bake about 25 minutes, or until the dough has browned lightly. Remove the dough from the oven. Combine the eggs, sugar, lemon juice, flour, and baking powder in a bowl. Beat the ingredients with a handmixer or electric mixer set at moderate speed 1–2 minutes, or until the mixture is creamy-looking and uniformly colored. Pour the mixture over the partially baked dough. Bake 20–22 minutes, or until the surface has browned lightly. Let the dessert cool in the pan. Cut the cookies into bars by cutting the baked dough with 5 cuts on the long side (making 6 strips) and 4 cuts on the short side (making 5 strips).

Kitchen Clue
You can freeze these cookies in a tightly covered plastic container for about 2 months.

Beverages

Most of us don't think of making beverages as "cooking." But there are some beverages, such as hot chocolate, that you do cook. More important though, drinks of some sort go hand and hand with food. You might serve cocktails with hors d'oeuvre before dinner, whip up some iced tea to sip with your meal, or serve coffee after dinner. The point is, preparing beverages is one of the skills you learn as you master cooking techniques. Fortunately, most beverages are quick and easy to prepare.

Spiced Apple Iced Tea

We all love iced tea. This version is a little jazzier than most.

Level: Easy
Preparation time: 10 minutes (plus 30 minutes steeping time)
Cooking time: enough time to boil water
Yield: makes 2

Can be done completely ahead

2 tea bags
1 TB. brown sugar
$^1/_2$ an apple, sliced (no need to peel it)
4 cloves

1 3" piece of cinnamon stick
1 strip lemon peel
2 slices fresh ginger root (optional)
2 cups boiling water

Place the tea bags, brown sugar, apple slices, cloves, cinnamon stick, orange peel, and ginger root, if used, in a bowl. Pour the water over them and let the mixture steep at least 30 minutes. When you want iced tea, strain the liquid and pour it into glasses filled with ice cubes.

Lemonade

If you've never tasted homemade lemonade, you're in for a treat. Fresh lemonade made from real lemon juice tastes like "liquid fruit." It's citrusy, refreshing, and absolutely delicious. Make it by the pitcherful so you always have some on hand.

Level: Intermediate
Preparation time: 15 minutes
Cooking time: 3 minutes plus one hour refrigeration time
Yield: about one quart of lemon-flavored liquid, enough for
  12–18 drinks depending on the size of the glass you use

Can be done completely ahead

1¹/₂ cups water
1¹/₂ cups sugar
the grated rind of one lemon
1¹/₂ cups freshly squeezed lemon juice,
  about 6–7 large lemons

ice cubes
cold water or club soda

Combine the water and sugar in a saucepan and bring them to a boil over high heat. Lower the heat slightly and cook the liquid for 3 minutes. Remove the pan from the heat and stir in the lemon rind and lemon juice. Refrigerate the lemon-flavored liquid for at least one hour. Strain the mixture into a storage container. When you want a glass of lemonade, fill a glass ¹/₃ full with the lemon-flavored liquid, add a few ice cubes, and add enough water or club soda to fill the glass. Stir and enjoy the drink.

Sweet Lassi

This is a light, refreshing, and exceptionally thirst-quenching beverage from India.

Level: Easy
Preparation time: 2 minutes
Cooking time: none
Yield: one

Cannot be done ahead

1 cup plain yogurt
1 TB. sugar
3 ice cubes
3 TB. ice water
2 TB. milk or cream (any kind)

Place all the ingredients in a blender jar (or the work bowl of a food processor). Blend at high speed 30 seconds, or until the drink is well blended and frothy.

Second Thoughts
You can create all sorts of flavors of lassi by adding fruit to the ingredients. Depending on the fruit and your taste buds, you may need to increase the sugar. Try these variations:

➤ Add ¹/₄ cup sliced strawberries

➤ Add ¹/₃ cup cut up mango

➤ Add ¹/₄ cup blueberries

➤ Add ¹/₂ banana

Strawberry Lemon Shake

This makes a wonderful warm weather treat you can serve at a cookout. If you want a lower fat version, use skim milk and frozen yogurt instead of the ice cream.

Level: Easy
Preparation time: 5 minutes
Cooking time: none
Yield: makes 2

Cannot be done ahead

$^3/_4$ cup sliced strawberries
1 TB. sugar
$1^1/_4$ cups strawberry ice cream

$^1/_3$ cup lemon sherbet
$^1/_2$ cup milk (skim, low-fat, or whole)

Combine the ingredients in a blender jar (or the work bowl of a food processor). Blend at high speed 30 seconds, or until the drink is well-blended and thick.

Spiced Coffee Shake

Coffee drinking has become a national pastime in recent years. This thick, cold shake combines coffee with some warm spices, which means you can enjoy it in any kind of weather.

Level: Easy
Preparation time: 15 minutes (plus 1 hour steeping time)
Cooking time: enough time to prepare coffee
Yield: makes 2–3

*Can be done up to the * in the instructions*

2 tsp. brown sugar
2 2" cinnamon sticks
4 whole cloves
4 whole allspice

2 strips orange peel
$1^1/_2$ cups extra strong hot coffee
1 cup coffee ice cream
$^1/_2$ cup milk (skim, low-fat, or whole)

Combine the brown sugar, cinnamon sticks, cloves, whole allspice, and orange peel in a bowl and pour the coffee over them. Let the ingredients stand at least one hour. Strain the liquid.

*Put the liquid into a blender jar (or the work bowl of a food processor). Add the ice cream and milk. Blend at high speed 30 seconds, or until the drink is well-blended and thick.

Kitchen Clue
You can find whole allspice in the spice section of the supermarket.

Marshmallowed Hot Chocolate

Oh, this is so good when you come in from the cold!

Level: Easy
Preparation time: 5 minutes
Cooking time: about 6 minutes
Yield: makes 2

Can be done completely ahead

2 cups milk (skim, low-fat, or whole)
6 marshmallows
3 TB. unsweetened cocoa powder
2 TB. sugar

pinch of salt
3 TB. very hot water
¾ tsp. vanilla
   extract

Heat the milk and marshmallows in a saucepan over moderate heat 5–6 minutes, or until bubbles appear around the edges of the pan and the marshmallows have almost melted. Mix the cocoa powder, sugar, and salt in a small bowl. Add the hot water and stir the mixture to form a smooth paste. Add about ¼ cup of the hot milk to the cocoa mixture, stir the mixture, and pour the mixture back into the pan. Heat the mixture until it almost comes to a boil (you will see bubbles forming more rapidly). Remove the pan from the heat. Add the vanilla extract and serve.

> **Kitchen Clue**
> This has a much better texture if you transfer the liquid to a blender and whirl it a few seconds until it becomes frothy. You can leave out the marshmallows if you don't like your hot chocolate so sweet.

Party Punch

Light and refreshing, this punch is suitable for kids when made with seltzer and for adults when prepared with white wine.

Level: Easy
Preparation time: 6–8 minutes
Cooking time: none
Yield: about 18 cups

Can be done ahead up to the * in the instructions

2 6-oz. cans frozen pineapple juice concentrate
2 6-oz. cans apple juice concentrate
2 6-oz. cans cranberry juice concentrate
6 cups cold water

2 cups ice cubes
2 quarts seltzer or club soda (or 2 750 ml bottles white wine)
1 quart strawberries, sliced

Combine the frozen juice concentrates and stir to blend them thoroughly. Gradually stir in the water.

* Just before serving, place the ingredients in a punch bowl and stir in the ice cubes and seltzer or wine. Add the strawberries.

Raspberry-Champagne Punch

This is a beautiful punch, worthy when you are celebrating.

Level: Easy
Preparation time: 3–4 minutes
Cooking time: none
Yield: serves 8–10

Cannot be done ahead

1 pint raspberry sherbet
$^1/_3$ cup frozen lemonade concentrate
1$^4/_5$-quart bottle chilled rosé wine

1$^4/_5$-quart bottled chilled champagne
1 pint fresh raspberries

Stir the sherbet, lemonade concentrate, and a cup of the rosé wine for 2–3 minutes, or until the sherbet has softened. Place the mixture in a punch bowl and stir in the remaining rosé wine and the champagne. Add the raspberries and serve.

Three Classic Cocktails

These are the most enduring cocktails; they never go out of style.

Level: Easy
Preparation time: a minute or two per cocktail
Cooking time: none
Yield: each serves one
Cannot be done ahead

Dry Martini

ice cubes
$^1/_6$ part dry vermouth
$^5/_6$ part gin or vodka
one green olive per cocktail

Put ice cubes into a cocktail glass. Add the vermouth and the gin or vodka in the proportions given. Stir. Add an olive. You may make several of these at one time in a cocktail shaker.

Second Thoughts
Some people prefer a cocktail onion to the martini olive. You can find cocktail onions in jars near the olives in a supermarket.

Bloody Mary

3 oz. tomato juice
1 jigger vodka, (1$^1/_2$ oz. or 3 TB.)
$^1/_2$ tsp. lemon juice
$^1/_2$ tsp. Worcestershire sauce

$^1/_8$ tsp. hot pepper sauce
ice cubes, optional
freshly ground black pepper
a celery stick for garnish

Combine the tomato juice, vodka, lemon juice, Worcestershire sauce, and hot pepper sauce in a glass. Add ice cubes if desired. Sprinkle the cocktail with some fresh ground pepper and garnish with the celery stick. You may make several of these at one time in a cocktail shaker.

Second Thoughts
You can give this popular drink a little more oomph if you use V-8 juice or clam-flavored tomato juice.

Margarita

1 jigger tequila (1$^1/_2$ oz. or 3 TB.)
$^1/_2$ oz. triple sec or any orange-flavored liqueur (1 TB.)
1 oz. fresh lime juice (2 TB.)

ice cubes
lime quarter
salt, preferably Kosher (coarse) salt

Combine the tequila, triple sec, and lime juice with some ice cubes in a cocktail shaker. Shake vigorously to combine the ingredients. Moisten the rim of a cocktail glass with the lime quarter, then press the rim into some salt. Pour the beverage into the salted glass.

Mulled Wine

Mulled wine is wonderful for a cold, wintry day. It smells wonderful and tastes divine. And it's very festive-looking for a party any season of the year.

Level: Intermediate
Preparation time: 15 minutes
Cooking time: 10 minutes
Yield: serves 6

Can be done completely ahead

1 750 ml bottle of red burgundy wine (about 3 cups)
$1/2$ cup water
$1/4$ cup sugar
$1/3$ cup currants or dark raisins
$1/3$ cup golden raisins
1 orange cut in half

1 lemon cut in half
2 3" pieces of cinnamon stick
8 cloves
1 tsp. whole allspice
1 sliced orange for garnish

Combine the wine, water, sugar, currants, raisins, half orange, half lemon, cinnamon stick, cloves, and allspice berries in a stainless steel, enameled, or other "non-reactive" saucepan. Cook over moderate heat 10 minutes. Strain the liquid into a chafing dish or other heated serving vessel. (Alternatively, you may combine the cinnamon stick, cloves, nutmeg, and allspice in a small muslin pouch or a piece of cheesecloth tied with kitchen string or bag ties, and immerse the bag into the liquid, removing the bag to strain the brew.) Garnish the beverage with a few orange slices.

What Is It?
You need a non-reactive saucepan because the acid in the wine could corrode metals that react with acid. Stainless-steel, glass, ceramic, and porcelain are non-reactive materials that will not corrode with acidic ingredients.

Mulled Cider

People think of mulled cider as a winter drink, but it's delicious anytime and is especially suitable for parties as a good alternative to alcoholic beverages.

Level: Intermediate
Preparation time: 15 minutes
Cooking time: about 30 minutes
Yield: serves 8–10

Can be done completely ahead

2 quarts apple cider
$1/2$ cup brown sugar
2 3" pieces of cinnamon stick
1 dozen whole allspice
1 dozen cloves
6 black peppercorns

1 TB. crystallized ginger or a small chunk
  of peeled ginger root
peel of half an orange
1 orange studded with 12 whole cloves for garnish
  (optional)

Combine the cider and sugar in a saucepan. Cook over moderate heat 3–4 minutes, stirring frequently, or until the sugar has dissolved. Combine the remaining ingredients in a small muslin pouch or a piece of cheesecloth tied with kitchen string or bag ties. Immerse the bag into the liquid and simmer the ingredients 25 minutes. Remove the bag. (Alternatively, you can add the seasonings to the liquid and strain them out when you're ready to pour the brew into the chafing dish.) Pour the cider into a chafing dish or other heated serving vessel. Garnish the beverage if you'd like by immersing the clove-studded orange into the cider.

Sources

Bear, Marina and John Bear. *How to Repair Food.* Berkeley: Ten Speed Press, 1987.

Block, Zena. *It's All on the Label: Understanding Food, Additives & Nutrition.* Boston: Little, Brown and Company, 1981.

Brody, Laura. *The Kitchen Survival Guide.* New York: William Morrow and Company, Inc., 1992.

Cunningham, Marion. *The Fannie Farmer Cookbook (Thirteenth Edition).* New York: Bantam Books, 1994.

Frandsen, Betty Rae, Kathryn J. Frandsen, and Kent P. Frandsen. *Where's Mom Now That I Need Her? Surviving Away from Home.* Sandy, UT: Aspen West, 1993.

Hill, Barbara. *The Cook's Book of Essential Information.* Kennewick, WA: Sumner House Press, 1987.

Horn, Jane, ed. *The California Culinary Academy Cooking A to Z.* Santa Rosa: The Cole Group, 1992.

Ortiz, Elisabeth Lambert. *The Encyclopedia of Herbs, Spices and Flavorings, a Cook's Compendium.* New York: Dorling Kindersley, Inc., 1992.

Rombauer, Irma S. and Marion Rombauer Becheri. *Joy of Cooking.* Indianapolis: Bobbs-Merrill Company, Inc., 1975.

Rosso, Julie and Sheila Lukens. *The New Basics Cookbook.* New York: Workman Publishing, 1989.

Index

Who Cares What *YOU* Think?

WE DO!

alpha books

We're not complete idiots. We take our readers' opinions very personally. After all, you're the reason we publish these books! Without you, we'd be pretty bored.

alpha books

So please! Drop us a note or fax us a fax! We'd love to hear what you think about this book or others. A real person—not a computer—reads every letter we get, and makes sure your comments get relayed to the appropriate people.

Not sure what to say? Here's some stuff we'd like to know:

➠ Who are you (age, occupation, hobbies, etc.)?

➠ Which book did you buy and where did you get it?

➠ Why did you pick this book instead of another one?

➠ What do you like best about this book?

➠ What could we have done better?

➠ What's your overall opinion of the book?

➠ What other topics would you like to purchase a book on?

Mail, e-mail, or fax your brilliant opinions to:

Tom Godfrey
Product Manager
Alpha Books
201 West 103rd Street
Indianapolis, IN 46290
FAX: (317) 581-4669

CompuServe: 74140.1306
Internet: 74140.1304@compuserve.com

Don't Let Everyday Life Make You Feel Like An Idiot!

Whatever the topic, there's a Complete Idiot's Guide ready and waiting to make your life easier!

The Complete Idiot's Guide to Getting into College
ISBN: 1-56761-508-2
$14.95 USA

The Complete Idiot's Guide to Buying & Selling a Home
ISBN: 1-56761-510-4
$16.95 USA

The Complete Idiot's Guide to Making Money on Wall Street
ISBN: 1-56761-509-0
$16.95 USA

Also Available!

The Complete Idiot's Guide to Managing Your Money
ISBN: 1-56761-530-9, $16.99 USA

The Complete Idiot's Guide to Starting Your Own Business
ISBN: 1-56761-529-5, $16.99 USA

The Complete Idiot's Guide to the Perfect Vacation
ISBN: 1-56761-531-7, $14.99 USA

The Complete Idiot's Guide to the Perfect Wedding
ISBN: 1-56761-532-5, $16.99 USA

The Complete Idiot's Guide to VCRs
ISBN: 1-56761-294-6, $9.95 USA

Look for these books at your favorite bookstore, or call 1-800-428-5331 for more information!

Down-to-earth answers to complex questions!